Additional Praise For Five Key Principles of Corporate Performance Management

"This book is emblematic of Bob's considerable expertise in organizing a company around the Strategy Focused Organization approach using the Balanced Scorecard Method. As founder, chairman and CEO of Crown Castle International (CCI:NYSE) I hired Bob as a consultant to lead a program to initiate CCI on the SFO method. He later joined CCI and led a successful organizational transformation to a much more efficient global platform in the telecommunications industry.

I am now chairman and majority shareholder of two international organizations; one in the multi-jurisdictional payroll arena and another in the aerospace industry and Bob is successfully transforming those companies into Strategy Focused Organizations. He is probably THE most knowledgeable and experienced individual in implementing the SFO approach to better organizational efficiency given his hands on experience and his considerable knowledge of accounting and finance as a CPA."

—Ted B. Miller, Jr., Chairman, M7 Aerospace and Chairman, Imperium International

"This book brings strategy to life through real-life application and provides the road map needed to truly unite a company in its objectives. Bob Paladino's method encourages team work, cross functional thinking and drives company success."

—Preston Atkinson, Chief Operating Officer, Whataburger, Inc.

"Bob Paladino has taken a balanced approach of taking all attributes of high performing businesses and turning them from theory to practical application. His book also discusses a step by step approach by using case studies which, if followed, will help organizations get to the maturity level in a timely manner."

—Ashok G. Vadgama, President, Center for Advanced Management Institute (CAM-I)"

"All companies today are looking for sustainable competitive advantages—which are more difficult to achieve. Consistent execution in performance and defining the right metrics are critical steps to achieving them. This book provides excellent insights to get you started!"

—Ralph Vasami, President Universal Weather & Aviation

Five Key Principles of Corporate Performance Management

Bob Paladino

1807
WILEY
2007
BICENTENNIAL

John Wiley & Sons, Inc.

For general information on our other products and services, or technical support, please contact our Customer Care Department within the United States at 800-762-2974, outside the United States at 317-572-3993, or fax 317-572-4002.

Wiley also publishes its books in a variety of electronic formats. Some content that appears in print may not be available in electronic books.

For more information about Wiley products, visit our Web site at http://www.wiley.com.

Library of Congress Cataloging-in-Publication Data

Paladino, Bob, 1959–
    Five key principles of corporate performance management / Bob Paladino.
        p. cm.
    Includes index.
    ISBN-13: 978-0-470-00991-8 (cloth)
    ISBN-10: 0-470-00991-8 (cloth)
    1. Organizational effectiveness. 2. Management. 3. Performance—Case studies. 4. Executives.
    I. Title.
    HD58.9.P35 2006
    658.4'06—dc22   2006025192

Printed in the United States of America

10 9 8 7 6 5 4 3 2 1

My Family

I offer praise to my grandfather, Alberto "Poppy" Paladino, for his courage as a teenager to migrate from Tuscany just after the turn of the twentieth century and for imparting his values of integrity, hard work, and education to his sprawling family tree. Thank you to my parents, Albert and Dorothy, for their enduring support and for being excellent role models. Special admiration to my wife, Ellen, for her positive attitude and to my children for keeping me inspired.

Our Freedom

I express gratefulness for my freedom of speech and have enormous respect for those who have preserved it. I will share book royalties to aid injured soldiers returning home and with the United Flight 93 Tower of Voices Memorial. It contains 40 wind chimes; sounds in the wind are a living memory of the 40 persons honored, many of whose last contact was through their voices.

To express your appreciation, please go to www.honorflight93.org and www.saluteheroes.org, both IRS Section 501(c)(3) nonprofit organizations.

Pathway to Success

Waste no more time talking about great souls and how they should be. Become one yourself!

—MARCUS AURELIUS ANTONINUS

Contents

Acknowledgments

This book could not have been possible without the special contributions from a number of organizations, clients, executives, and practitioners. More important than contributions to this book is the recognition they deserve for efforts to advance the field of corporate performance management, the results they helped achieve for their organizations, and their value-centric approach to performance.

American Red Cross: Rod Tolbert, Director, Reporting and Monitoring, Chapter Quality Assurance; Kevin Hans, Manager, Knowledge and Innovation, Chapter Quality Assurance; and Steve Stegeman, Senior Director, Strategic Planning and Analysis, Corporate Strategy

APQC: Carla O'Dell, President; Cindy Hubert, Executive Director; Sebastian Francis, Senior Advisor; John Eleftheriou, Vice President Professional Services; project leaders Darcy Lemons and Rachele Williams; the APQC team; and numerous member company research project participants

ASMI: Carl DeMaio, President and Founder; and the ASMI team

Balanced Scorecard Collaborative (BSCol), a Palladium Company: Robert S. Kaplan and David P. Norton, creators of the Balanced Scorecard and Strategy-Focused Organization concepts; its employees, alumni, and numerous clients and study group members

Bronson Methodist Hospital: Michele Serbenski, Executive Director, Corporate Effectiveness and Customer Satisfaction

CAM-I: Ashok G. Vadgama, President, and numerous members of research and study groups

City of Coral Springs: Kevin Knutson, Director of Communications and Marketing (formerly Budget and Strategic Planning Manager during Sterling Award period), and Chelsea Stahl, Performance Measurement Analyst

Crown Castle International: John Kelly, Chief Executive Officer; executive and leadership teams; former Global Performance (Corporate Performance Management) team members; and Crown employees

Florida Department of Health: Donna Marshall, Performance Management Director, Office of Performance Improvement; and Laura Reeves, Performance Consultant Team Leader, Office of Performance Improvement

Hearst Publications *Houston Chronicle*: Mary Ann Wendt, Director, Human Resources (former Director, Organizational Development); Anna Singletary, Director of Productivity (former Six Sigma Organizational Leader); and numerous colleagues

Intercomp Technologies LLC: George E. Reese, Global Chief Executive Officer and a founder of Crown Castle International; and leadership teams in Geneva, Switzerland, and Moscow, Russia

KeyCorp: Michele Seyranian, Executive Vice President and Senior Planning Manager of Strategic Planning

LB Foster Company: Lee B. Foster, Chairman of the Board; Stan Hasselbusch, President and Chief Executive Officer; Jeffrey Poholsky, Manager, Strategic Planning; Merry Brumbaugh, Vice President, Tubular Products; Sam Fisher, Senior Vice President, Rail Products; Don Foster, Senior Vice President, Piling Products; John Kasel, Senior Vice President, Operations and Manufacturing; Dave Russo, Senior Vice President, Chief Financial Officer and Treasurer; Jack Klimp, General Manager; and company employees

M7 Aerospace: Ted B. Miller Jr., Chairman M7 Aerospace, Chairman of Imperium International, and a founder of Crown Castle International; Ron Frederick, Chief Executive Officer; Kevin Brown, Senior Vice President of Finance and Corporate Development; executive management and senior management team members; and employees worldwide

Medrad: Rose Almon-Martin, Vice President of Performance Excellence and Marketing Services

Ricoh Corporation: Katsumi "Kirk" Yoshida, President and Chief Executive Officer, Ricoh U.S.; Kuni Minakawa, Chief Financial Officer, Ricoh U.S.; Hede Nonaka, Vice President, Marketing, Ricoh U.S.; Robert Ingoglia, Vice President, Promotion and Communications, Ricoh U.S.; Dan Piccoli, Vice President of Quality and Business Excellence, Ricoh U.S.; Marilyn Michaels, Director, Quality and Performance, Ricoh U.S.; and Edward A. Barrows, Principal, Strategic Management System and Professor of Strategy, Babson College

Serono International: Lawrence Ganti, Corporate Director, Strategy Management

Sprint Nextel: William G. Arendt, Senior Vice President and Controller; Tolga E. Yaveroglu, Director Corporate Strategy; and Jenevieve Creary, Senior Manager Corporate Strategy; Sprint Nextel employees

Tennessee Valley Authority: Bill Kolz, Senior Program Manager, Performance Management Process; and Steve Saunders, General Manager of Benchmarking and Industry Analysis

John Wiley & Sons: Sheck Cho, Executive Editor, and the Wiley publishing team

CHAPTER 1

Introduction

FIVE KEY PRINCIPLES OF CORPORATE
PERFORMANCE MANAGEMENT

Man's mind, stretched to a new idea, never goes back to its original dimensions.
—OLIVER WENDELL HOLMES

What do award-winning companies know that eludes most of today's executives? How do they organize and conduct themselves to achieve outsized results? What core processes and best practices do they leverage? Winning executives unselfishly and gladly share their best practices with you. Will you invest your time to understand these key differentiators? If so, then welcome to the pathway of change and join me in a stimulating journey.

There is an exciting new role—the corporate performance management (CPM) executive—that is emerging in companies, government agencies, and nonprofit organizations. The CPM executive is more savvy and able to execute strategy and accelerate results by leveraging and integrating CPM best practice processes. This book is an implementation guide that offers a fresh perspective based on new award-winning CPM executives' reflections, experiences, and best practices organized around Five Key Principles in CPM. My hope is that you will rapidly adapt their best practices to realize further success in your enterprise. If executing strategy effectively is of interest to you, then welcome to the winners' circle and read on.

BEST PRACTICE AWARD-WINNING ENTERPRISE CASES

This book encapsulates best practice research from globally recognized enterprises and provides guidance to enable you to rapidly implement your strategy through integrated CPM efforts. It also draws from my direct experience as vice president leading one of Kaplan and Norton's Balanced Scorecard consulting divisions; senior vice president of global performance at Crown Castle International (Crown); and client, research, study group and advisory experiences with award-winning and high-performing organizations. Case studies include winners of these awards:

- Kaplan and Norton Global Balanced Scorecard Hall of Fame Award
- U.S. President's National Malcolm Baldrige Quality Award
- Deming Quality Award
- American Quality and Productivity Center (APQC) Best Practice Partner Award
- Governor's Sterling Award (based on Baldrige Criteria)
- *Wall Street Journal* "Top 20 Most Improved Companies in Shareholder Value Creation"
- *Fortune* "100 Best Companies to Work For"
- *Forbes* Best Managed Companies

> *I'm against a homogenized society, because I want the cream to rise.*
> —ROBERT FROST

Award recipients and high performers present a rich source of strategy management best practices for your CPM program and offer a leading edge perspective. I am grateful to the Crown executive team and employees. While my team facilitated CPM processes, *Crown employees* brought them to life. They earned Kaplan and Norton's coveted Balanced Scorecard Hall of Fame Award, the globally recognized APQC Best Practice Partner Award, and contributed to Crown being ranked on *The Wall Street Journal*'s list of "Top 20 Most Improved Companies in Shareholder Value Creation" (out of over 1,000 listed companies).

Chapter 2 explores reasons why companies fail to implement their strategies, including Kaplan and Norton's "four barriers," MIT Dr. Fine's research on Clock Speed, and five project blockers learned from years in the field. Chapter 3 provides a summary of over two dozen *Five Key Principles* best practices as a handy reference tool. Chapters 4 through 8 are devoted to in-depth case studies, one chapter for each of the *Five Key Principles*, developed in collaboration with leading award-winning enterprises and their CPM leaders. Chapter 9 provides a self-scoring CPM program diagnostic and a resource section on leading edge CPM research, a lifelong pursuit.

WHY READ THIS BOOK?

> *Optimum performance will be the only option for the business managers of tomorrow. The Five Key Principles in Bob Paladino's book and his method of*

molding them into daily effort will be the blueprint for highly successful leaders to deliver the expected positive results.
—PRESTON ATKINSON, CHIEF OPERATING OFFICER,
WHATABURGER, INC.

Executives today are expected to demonstrate results faster than ever before; chief executive officer (CEO), chief financial officer (CFO), chief operating officer (COO), and chief information officer (CIO) turnover has accelerated rapidly in the past 10 years. *HR Magazine* reports CEO churn is at an all-time high. Increasingly, new CEOs enter a company, fail to deliver, and are sent packing. Sometimes, if they do produce results, other companies snatch them up. Either way, the process starts all over again. Turnover among chief executives soared 53 percent between 1995 and 2001, according to the 2002 study "Why CEOs Fall: The Causes and Consequences of Turnover at the Top," conducted by Booz Allen Hamilton of McLean, Virginia. The number of CEOs who left their jobs under pressure more than doubled during that period, and average CEO tenure plunged more than 23 percent, according to the study of 2,500 publicly traded companies. More recently, Booz Allen Hamilton reported the rate of departure for underperformers quadrupled since 1995, with European and North American CEOs topping the list of involuntary exits in 2005. Global CEO departures reached record levels for the second year in a row, and may be peaking, according to the fifth annual survey of CEO turnover at the world's 2,500 largest publicly traded corporations. The study also found that performance-related turnover set a new record in North America.[1]

A different study—"CEO Turnover and Job Security"—released by Drake Beam Morn (DBM) estimates that two-thirds of the world's companies have changed CEOs at least once in the last five years.[2] Clearly, the amount of time allotted to implementing strategies to achieve results has been compressing. This book provides reasons why companies fail to implement their strategies and offers a blueprint for change.

The measure of success is not whether you have a problem to deal with, but whether it's the same problem you had last year.
—J. F. DULLES

Fortune magazine reports, "If making the Fortune 100 Best lists is an enormous accomplishment, consider how tough it is to repeat the feat every single year. Just 22 companies have appeared on our list every year since its 1998 inception."[3] Between 1998 and 2004, the turnover of Fortune 500 companies has been staggering.

Research shows that CEOs and enterprises benefit from a CPM Office,

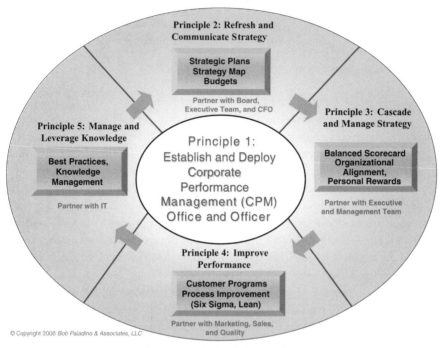

EXHIBIT 1.1 Five Key Principles of CPM

Officer, and integrated processes based on the Five Key Principles more than ever to enable higher organizational performance. High-performing enterprises practice these Five Key Principles:

Principle 1. Establish and deploy a CPM Office and Officer.
Principle 2. Refresh and communicate strategy.
Principle 3. Cascade and manage strategy.
Principle 4. Improve performance.
Principle 5. Manage and leverage knowledge.

Exhibit 1.1 shows the CPM Office at the center of the *Five Key Principles*. The Office integrates and facilitates the *Five Key Principles* concurrently throughout the enterprise; dozens of best practices and case studies are discussed throughout the book.

PRINCIPLE 1: ESTABLISH AND DEPLOY A CPM OFFICE AND OFFICER

> *By three methods we may learn wisdom. First, by reflection, which is noblest; second, by imitation, which is easiest; and third, by experience, which is bitterest.*
> —CONFUCIUS

This book short draws from all three learning methods above. *Principle 1, Establish and Deploy a* CPM Office and Officer, is at the center of the CPM efforts and is responsible for implementing strategy through a portfolio of CPM methods, processes, and frameworks collectively referred to as the *Five Key Principles.* This Office reports to the CEO or a CEO direct report to integrate a defined set of CPM processes to drive global and local performance. Basically, they aid contemporary CEOs and their teams to deliver results faster. This book devotes significant attention to better understanding and providing in-depth case studies to define the new, vital role in enterprises. As a former executive in the Office of the CEO and currently a practitioner assisting enterprises to establish and execute the duties of the CPM Executive, I provide a road map to key roles and responsibilities. Crown will serve as a reference point for each CPM principle, complemented by numerous case studies as told by the executives from award-winning enterprises and last valuable experiences from the field. Although my title at Crown was Senior Vice President Global Performance, for purposes of establishing common terminology for this book I shall refer to this role as the CPM Officer and the department as the CPM Office.

Five Key Principles provides a lean best practice case study approach to strategy management to simplify and bring together disparate methods into an integrated, simplified CPM framework. Many public and private enterprises create islands of CPM expertise but fail to provide for an integrated CPM framework to drive results. Have you heard these comments in your organization? Are there some disconnects in implementing strategy?

- "We complete our strategic plan each year but it sits on the shelf until next year."
- "The executives always roll out the initiative du jour."
- "The folks in quality know about quality, we don't, it is too complicated."
- "The sales team deals with the customer, we only focus on operations."
- "They never communicate the strategy, I am not high enough in the company."
- "We are too busy fighting fires to deal with strategic issues."
- "Our dashboard has hundreds of measures, but which ones are important?"

Five Key Principles cases are told by experienced executives. The cases have been selected to enable you to understand how to rapidly integrate and leverage proven methods and processes to manage strategy. This book is based on my direct experience as a CPM Officer, on best practices research with enterprises that have won numerous awards, and direct consulting experience to high performing enterprises.

We learn from pattern recognition, repeating steps and processes that enable us to build and achieve. Over many years, I have studied strategy management patterns of success, both as a Crown executive and as a global consultant providing professional services on behalf of Towers Perrin, PricewaterhouseCoopers, and Kaplan and Norton's firm The Balanced Scorecard Collaborative (a Palladium company). I have had the good fortune and privilege of collaborating with globally known experts and thought leaders in the CPM field who have provided validation for establishment of a dedicated CPM executive role in enterprises to drive meaningful change.

INTEGRATING PRINCIPLES 2 THROUGH 5 CPM PROCESSES AND METHODS

> *Measurement without the opportunity to improve is harassment!*
> —W. EDWARDS DEMING (FATHER OF QUALITY)

The current fragmented approach to strategy management has resulted in islands of competencies (see Exhibit 1.2) rarely optimized. Many programs fail, many companies fail.

Recall the turnover of companies in the Fortune 100 list. Further, with so many experts today marketing single tools, so-called silver bullets, how

EXHIBIT 1.2   **CPM Processes Disconnected**

do you know where to start? The "experts" would have you believe their wrench, hammer, or screwdriver is the panacea or single solution to your performance problems. However, is your organization one-dimensional? How do you simultaneously deal with global competition, accelerated outsourcing, shortened product and service life cycles, customers that are more sophisticated, fleeting intellectual property, a mobile labor force, and demanding investors? How could you expect one method to address all these challenges?

> *Only the fool learns from his own mistakes, the wise man learns from the mistakes of others.*
> —OTTO VON BISMARCK

The beauty of the hammer is that it can readily fix the problem of the nail. What about the problem of the crooked screw or loosely fitting bolt? Does your organization suffer from many tools or competencies that lack integration? Do process owners or department heads conflict at times? Nevertheless, when do you use which tool? At what speed do you introduce these tools to the organization? How will you optimize the many moving parts in your organization? By now this simple metaphor has highlighted the fact that one tool or process is not sufficient today; your organization has many interrelated issues and pressures and requires a CPM executive to facilitate an integrated toolbox and provide guidance and direction to vital CPM processes.

Five Principles provides a clear road map for executing enterprise strategy by drawing on and integrating multiple methods to optimize results. The book provides a lean, simplified approach to development and use of integrated CPM. How long will your CEO or boss remain patient? Experience in strategy implementation captured in book case studies is the best teacher and guide.

SUMMARY

The organizations selected for in-depth case studies have earned several notable awards, some multiple awards. Exhibit 1.3 displays a subset of awards, those reserved for truly distinguished performances and granted to a very limited group of recipients. For example, the U.S. President's Malcolm Baldrige National Quality Award is reserved for just five organizations annually. The *Fortune* "100 Best Companies to Work For" is a broader group, but, as thousands of companies apply, recipients are a very distinguished group. Similarly, *Fortune* magazine reports thousands of enterprises use the Balanced Scorecard but approximately a dozen annually earn the coveted and globally renowned Balanced Scorecard Hall of Fame Award.

Case study enterprises offer unique insights to their CPM processes,

EXHIBIT 1.3   Award-Winning Case Study Companies

Enterprise	Balanced Scorecard Global Hall of Fame Award (Kaplan Norton)	APQC Best Practice Award	U.S. President's Malcolm Baldrige National Quality Award	Governor's Sterling Quality (Baldrige) Award	Deming Award	Fortune 100 Best Companies to Work For Award	Forbes Award
Crown Castle International							
City of Coral Springs							
Tennessee Valley Authority							
Medrad							
Serono International							
LB Foster Company							
Florida Dept of Health				2 times			
American Red Cross							
Bronson Methodist Hospital				2 times		3 times	
Ricoh					2 times		
KeyCorp							
Hearst Publications							
Sprint Nextel							
Raytheon							

methods, approaches, roles, responsibilities, organization, and results for your research and reuse to accelerate your CPM program.

MY PROMISE

Five Key Principles provides practical executive and practitioner best practice examples on how to establish the new CPM Office to manage strategy using integrated CPM processes. I am fortunate to have experienced hundreds of improvement programs and projects at Fortune 500 companies, government agencies, and nonprofit organizations over the past 20-plus years. I am glad to report that most were successful. In this book I am not evangelizing theory but rather providing proven, real-world implementation insights from award-winning organizations.

> *An honest tale speeds best, being plainly told.*
> —WILLIAM SHAKESPEARE

NOTES

1. Chuck Lucier, Paul Kocourek, and Rolf Habbel, Strategy+Business, "CEO Succession 2005: The Crest of the Wave" Summer 2006, www.boozallen.com.

2. Robert Grossman, "Forging a Partnership Executive Turnover," *HR Magazine* (April 2003).

3. "Blue Ribbon Companies 2004," www.fortune.com Web site, November 4, 2005.

CHAPTER 2

Why Do Most Companies Fail to Implement Their Strategies?

*Planning is an unnatural process; it is much more fun to do something. And
the nicest thing about not planning is that failure comes as a complete surprise.*
—SIR JOHN HENRY-JONES

This chapter discusses the four barriers, popularized by Kaplan and Norton, that companies encounter by failing to realize their strategic objectives. This chapter expands this thinking and brings a brand new perspective on the strategic context for these failures. We turn to MIT professor Dr. Charles Fine's research on industry rate of change, or "Clock Speed," and its impacts on companies brought about by failing to understand and develop strategic and management processes to address it. In reactionary efforts to address the four barriers and Clock Speed, enterprises often commence corporate performance management (CPM) projects, many of which fail. For this reason, we will touch on the top five blockers that undermine well-intended business improvement efforts. *Five Key Principles* offers a comprehensive, lean, and proven approach for strategy implementation and management.

FOUR BARRIERS TO STRATEGY IMPLEMENTATION

One of my fondest and most enlightening professional growth experiences was leading one of Kaplan and Norton's Balanced Scorecard consulting practices. Not only did I have regular interactions with Bob and Dave, but I also had the opportunity to participate with them on research, conferences, and study projects. During these years, my practitioner and client teams designed and implemented the Balanced Scorecard in scores of enterprises. I found myself immersed in a kind of applied research firm where the founders, arguably the most prolific and successful business thinkers of our time, provided a wellspring of new ideas the consulting division innovated and deployed with clients. In turn, the consulting clients provided a rich environment for discovering new approaches to adapting the strategy-focused organization (SFO) principles of the Balanced Scorecard to drive results.

One of Norton's key findings is that "9 out 10 companies fail to implement their strategies."[1] Exhibit 2.1 provides a framework and evidence to help us understand why this is true.

The "four barriers" explains this failure rate. I will describe each barrier shortly, but in keeping with my promise for practical advice, I will also include some best practice client case examples to demonstrate how successful enterprises have overcome the four barriers. The number of failed strategies, mergers and acquisitions, and bankruptcies in Corporate America has left large groups of investors dismayed and perplexed. It has also resulted in public outcry for increased regulatory action and controls and reporting transparency to protect investors. Publicly traded companies have been faced with increased disclosure and mandatory compliance with the Sarbanes-Oxley Act (SOX), one of the most far-reaching acts of its kind in recent memory. How could so many bright and energetic executives and their teams fail to understand the key drivers of value in their business and poorly execute their company strategies? Some companies unfortunately resorted to the unsavory practice of fabricating

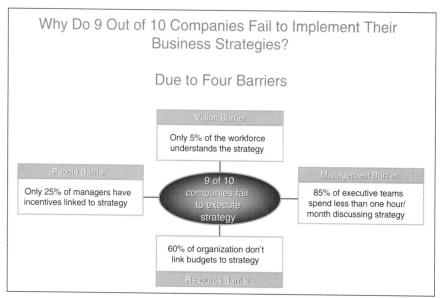

EXHIBIT 2.1   **Four Barriers to Strategy Implementation**

results rather than executing on sound business strategies supported by solid budget and performance management practices. But just what are the barriers to success? How does use of integrated CPM methods enable achievement of company strategy objectives?[2]

Barrier 1: Vision

The difference between a vision and a hallucination is the number of people that see it.
                                                                    —T. PAULSON

The "vision barrier" research shows that only 5% of company employees fully understand their company's strategy. Why is it so hard for employees to understand the company's direction? In developing Strategy Maps and Balanced Scorecards for scores of companies, I learned that the strategy is rarely communicated in terms that relate to people's everyday objectives, roles, and responsibilities. In your organization, take a survey by randomly asking 10 people to define or share their understanding of your company strategy. You will be amazed at how few can discuss it.

For example, during a trip to the field in the early days at Crown, I asked local office employees about the company strategy. Their responses ranged from "make money for shareholders" to "help customers," which are good intentions but they lack clear actionable and measurable content. These employees did not clearly see how their daily activities drove Crown's strategy. With the establishment of the CPM office and implementation of the CPM processes including the Strategy Map, Balanced Scorecard, six sigma, customer surveys, and knowledge management processes, responses to later surveys were tied more closely to company strategic objectives and measures, and strategic awareness was dramatically improved. Later, employee responses to the same questions about their role in company strategy resulted in more focused responses:

Employee Responses to How They Felt Their Role Impacted Company Strategy	
Prior to CPM Process Implementation	With Established CPM Processes (all figures are illustrative)
Make money for shareholders Help customers	Improve working capital (objective) by reducing days sales outstanding from 60 days to less than 15 days (measure) Reduce order to installation cycle time (objective) from over 80 days to under 50 days (measure) to increase customer satisfaction from 4.0 to 5.0 (measure) in our customer surveys

Responses improved from the initial "make money for shareholders" to the more mature response, "improve working capital (as the objective) by reducing days sales outstanding (DSO in accounts receivable (the related measure)." Clearly this is an improvement and one more reliably linked to results. Similarly we went from the early response of "help customers" to a more focused one of "reduce order to installation cycle time (the objective), from 80 days to 50 days (the first related measure) to increase customer satisfaction from 4.0 to 5.0 rating (the second related customer measure)." The improved employee understanding of company strategy and their role in driving specific results is obvious. Companies challenge themselves in the absence of CPM methods to harness the creativity and energy of their people, a primary resource. In summary, Crown overcame the vision barrier by observing all Five Key Principles:

Principle 1. Establish and deploy a CPM Office and Officer.
Principle 2. Refresh and communicate strategy (Strategy Maps).
Principle 3. Cascade and manage strategy (balanced scorecard).
Principle 4. Improve performance (six sigma).
Principle 5. Manage and leverage knowledge.

We will review the *five key principles* in depth in Chapters 4 through 8.

Barrier 2: Management

The brain is a wonderful organ. It starts working the moment you get up in the morning and does not stop until you get into the office.
—ROBERT FROST

The "management barrier" indicates that 85% of executive teams spend far less time discussing strategies and strategic issues than traditional operating results. Is it no wonder that strategy implementation rates are so low? Why do leaders spend so much time in company meetings but fail to grasp the message conveyed by company reports and analyses? Companies frequently have disconnects among financial, customer, and operational objectives, measures, and targets until they are defined and used in a CPM environment.

Traditional measurement and management tools do not account for intangible assets, such as customer relationships, employee skills, knowledge, innovativeness, customer relationships, employee skills, and knowledge that are increasingly the source of corporate value and competitive advantage in today's economy. The Strategy Map, however, does. For a high-technology company, the Strategy Map might show that employees need selected skills, motivation, and knowledge to develop new products, provide for merger integration, excel at employee relations, and be operationally efficient.[3] Citing a best practice example, prior to its development of Strategy Maps and Balanced Scorecards, Bob Paladino & Associates, LLC telecommunication client Sprint Nextel conducted multiday operating review meetings covering hundreds of indicators in a well-intended effort to identify key management actions. This leading company then developed a strategic plan, Strategy Map, and balanced scorecard to focus on key strategic and operational objectives. Performance-based content of these meetings changed dramatically. Current meetings are far more strategically management focused.

Meeting Content	Prior to Using the Strategy Map and Balanced Scorecard for Meetings (%)	Using the Strategy Map and Balanced Scorecard to Manage Meetings (%)
Focused on historical data and replaying history	80	10
Problem solving	10	20
Discussing strategic issues, forward looking	10	70
Totals	100%	100%

With the establishment of the CPM office and the use of integrated CPM processes and tools, executive meetings have been reduced from days monthly to about half a day. Meetings now are sharply focused on the top-underperforming objectives as indicated by balanced scorecard measure results and on specific key actions and initiatives to "move the dial" toward improved results. The integration of these CPM processes enabled a critical shift in focus from lengthy, data-driven meetings to focused issue and strategic solutions–based meetings. In this case, our best practice telecommunications company overcame the management barrier. This telecommunications giant overcame the meeting management barrier by observing three of the *Five Key Principles*:

Principle 1. Establish and deploy a CPM Office and Officer (i.e., CSO).
Principle 2. Refresh and communicate strategy (Strategy Maps).
Principle 3. Cascade and manage strategy (Balanced Scorecards)

Barrier 3: Resource

> *It is thrifty to prepare today for the wants of tomorrow.*
> —AESOP, "THE ANT AND THE GRASSHOPPER"

The "resource barrier," shows that most companies do not link budgets to strategy. In short, companies may be pursuing financial strategies that differ from or, worse, may be in conflict with their operational and customer strategies. For instance, you may have an operating unit making its financial targets at the expense of not investing in preventive maintenance, in essence deferring inevitable interruptions in performance that impact customers until next quarter or year. One of the best examples of a major improvement in this arena lies with a utility client. The utility CPM executive integrated strategic planning, Strategy Mapping, budgeting (operational and capital), and Balanced Scorecard management processes. The budgeting process provided a robust initiative scoring approach aligned with the Strategy Map clearly prioritized and funded strategic and operational projects, spanning business units and budget accounts. Through fact-based initiative scoring linked to strategy, the utility overcame the resource barrier and posted measurable improvements in results by observing three of the *Five Key Principles*:

Principle 1. Establish and deploy a CPM Office and Officer.
Principle 2. Refresh and communicate strategy. (Strategy Maps and Budgeting)
Principle 3. Cascade and manage strategy. (Balanced Scorecards)

Barrier 4: People

That some should be rich, shows that others may become rich, and, hence, is just encouragement to industry and enterprise.
—ABRAHAM LINCOLN

The "people barrier" shows us that management incentives link to the company strategy only 25% of the time. Conversely, most companies are rewarding management for activities not linked to company strategic and operational plans. M7 Aerospace offers a solution. One of M7 Aerospace's business units focused on contract logistics support (CLS) for government State Department planes established team- and individual-based Balanced Scorecards linked to the annual bonuses. Bonuses focused its entire globally distributed workforce from headquarters in Houston and San Antonio, Texas, to remote teams on U.S. military bases as far away as Kaneohe Bay, Hawaii; Ramstein Air Base in Germany; and Sigonella Base in Italy. Business unit and support services have Balanced Scorecards to focus on strategic and operational objectives, measures, targets, and initiatives. M7 Aerospace in general and the CLS program in particular overcame the people barrier in a highly competitive industry to align a globally distributed workforce by observing three of the *five key principles*:

Principle 1. Establish and deploy a CPM office and officer.
Principle 2. Refresh and communicate strategy. (Strategic Plan, Strategy Maps)
Principle 3. Cascade and manage strategy. (Balanced Scorecard, Incentives)

In summary, we learned from leading enterprises that establishment of a CPM Officer and CPM processes provided a strong countermeasure and allowed their organizations to overcome the four barriers to strategy implementation. In Chapters 4 through 8, more in-depth case studies provide you with visibility into and opportunities to leverage CPM best practices.

INDUSTRY CLOCK SPEED: A NEW CONSIDERATION TO IMPLEMENTING STRATEGY

I wasted time, and now doth time waste me.
—WILLIAM SHAKESPEARE

In addition to establishing the CPM Office and deploying CPM processes and methods to overcome the four barriers, your enterprise also is dealing with new and accelerating market forces not fully appreciated even a decade ago. The speed of information, inventions, and competitive innovation has been transforming the enterprise landscape for over 100 years but recently at an accelerating rate. The past 10 years bear witness to some of the most transformational forces in U.S. history: global competition, the emergence of China and India as trading partners, wholesale outsourcing of industries, and unbundling and rebundling of company value chains. Overcoming the "four barriers" using integrated CPM processes more rapidly takes on a new significance in light of the acceleration and greater impact of market pressures on today's enterprises. It is no longer sufficient for companies to have and to use methods; they must deploy and choreograph them rapidly and judiciously to confront strategic and operational issues for competitive advantage.

MIT Professor Charles Fine researched and published his findings on industry transformation in his book *Clock Speed, Winning Industry Control in the Age of Temporary Advantage.*[4] I was so intrigued by his findings that I completed his executive education course to gain insights directly.

Facts are stubborn things; and whatever may be our wishes, our inclinations, or the dictates of our passions, they cannot alter the state of facts and evidence.
—JOHN ADAMS

What Is Clock Speed?

Fine sets the stage for us by carefully documenting the Clock Speed, or evolution of businesses, embodied in his quote, "In the natural world, species evolve, that is, they change to meet new challenges or they die. The same genetic imperative operates in business."[5] Clock Speed provides concrete examples of how industries exhibit different rates of evolution, hence the book's name. Strategically minded CPM executives and programs must understand and integrate CPM processes not only to deal with today's challenges but also to help the enterprise for evolutionary changes. Clock Speed provides us with a template for understanding evolutionary dynamics of industries. Fine states, "The faster the industry Clock Speed, the shorter the half life of competitive advantage." As a result, the strategic management processes should identify and leverage your competitive advantages.

A wise man will make more opportunities than he finds.
　　　　　—FRANCIS BACON

The most valued contribution of Clock Speed from a strategic perspective is what Fine postulates as the "double helix" model (visualize a horizontal figure ∞), which borrows from Nobel Prize winners James D. Watson and Francis Crick, who discovered the molecular structure of DNA. The model proposes quite convincingly that strategic adjustments occur in predictable patterns; your CPM Office and CPM processes must incorporate strategic and operational methods to address these patterns.

Vertical Industry Structure (Left Side of the ∞)

A vertical market-competitive advantage comes from economies of scale in fabrication of components; control over delivery, quality, and rates of technical change; reduced vulnerability to holdup by suppliers; and a quicker information flow. Vertical markets have limited direct competition, and competitive threats do not exist. However, a trade-off does exist; the vertical nature of the market reduces the competition for complementary products and drives slower adoption.

The transition from a vertical market to a horizontal market increases the competitiveness of the market. Niche competitors provide incentives for firms to give up pieces of production, which increases entry and supplier power. Higher dimensional complexity limits the economy of scale and increases potential vulnerability to holdup, while organizational rigidities decrease the transparency of information. All this increases the pressure to disintegrate and increases both competition and adoption.

In theory there is no difference between theory and practice.
In practice there is.
　　　　　—YOGI BERRA

Horizontal Industry Structure (Right Side of the ∞)

A horizontal industry is highly competitive. Competitors enter the market freely driving down profits and competing on costs. Firms seek to use their small differentiated advantage to push other competitors out of the market. As prices drop through price wars, adoption accelerates and the market continues to expand from new entrants.

As adoption slows, firms identify technical advantages in one subsystem and gain competitive advantage over their many competitors. This market power encourages bundling with other subsystems to increase control and add more value. Further increases in market power in one subsystem encourage engineering integration with other subsystems to develop proprietary integration solutions. Competition begins to decrease as suppliers are squeezed out of the market and larger firms regain vertical control.[6]

The double helix model provides some insights into the reordering of industry leaders and contributes to the shortening of tenure in senior executives discussed earlier. We will continue to learn from this model in conjunction with a set of CPM methods including the Strategy Map when we review strategic planning in Chapter 5. The Strategy Map offers particular value to companies in fast-changing industries like telecommunications, where tactics, strategy, and market positioning may need rapid revision. It helps organizations understand performance drivers and cause-and-effect relationships across the perspectives, enabling more rapid and proactive decision making and a better understanding of the impacts of those decisions. Companies can be more focused and set realistic targets—and better communicate strategy and show accountability to all employees.[7]

Why is it that there are few seats available on airlines today but there is no room in the industry for defunct TWA or Eastern Airlines? Why are shoppers flocking to metropolitan malls, but Zayres or Hills stores have disappeared? Why are Starbucks stores sprouting up everywhere, but few local coffee shops exist? In all these cases, the incumbents failed to adjust to changing industry dynamics and deploy value-adding strategies to deal with new players.

Big Blue and Supply Chain Unbundling

> It's like déjà-vu, all over again.
> —YOGI BERRA

IBM presents an instructive case to illustrate Clock Speed and market forces at work. Observe IBM's now-famous decision to outsource its PC operating system to Microsoft Windows and its PC processors to Intel; this so-called Win-Tel supply chain in turn created billions in value for the Microsoft and Intel shareholders. These two companies have come to dominate their industries globally with the famous "Intel Inside" and "Windows" brands. IBM decided to outsource to allow it to focus on its core strengths, marketing and branding. While it is common to develop supplier rivalries, what is most telling about this example is the next scene in the play that exemplifies market forces at work: IBM in 2005 sold its PC division to China's Lenovo. Why? I believe Dell, a company not even on IBM's radar screen a decade earlier, overcame IBM's marketing supremacy by redefining its supply chain and using mass customization to the end consumer as a strategic weapon. Continuing this story, Dell recently outsourced the help desk portion of its value chain overseas. How do I know this? Well, when my new Dell PC keyboard failed while typing this manuscript, I found myself struggling to understand Dell's overseas help desk person. Dell's "on-site" premium service program entitled me to receive, by mail, "on-site" at my office a replacement keyboard and tiny screwdriver for me to complete installation. My Dell laptop now serves less proudly as a bookend. My new laptop from a competitor has true on-site service. Has the Dell value chain unbundled too far? What are your enterprise's pressure points, what market forces are at work to transform your business model? Does your CPM program incorporate and respond to these market forces?

The four barriers and Clock Speed inform us about the strategic level, but this is not the full story. There are CPM process and project-level blockers that regularly repeat themselves. That is, management reacts to the four barriers and impacts from industry Clock Speed by undertaking single or multiple CPM projects. Along the way, however, things go off the tracks.

TOP FIVE BLOCKERS TO CPM PROJECT AND PROCESS SUCCESS

The things that hurt, instruct.
—BENJAMIN FRANKLIN

This section is not be found in today's textbooks; rather it reflects many years of assisting enterprises to turn around or restart troubled programs. CPM processes such as Six Sigma problem solving generally begin as projects, demonstrate results, and become formal CPM processes. The successful evolution of the project to the process stage is essential to the establishment of an integrated set of CPM processes in your enterprise. For example, after your company's three-day strategy meeting offsite, do you have a list of action items lost in your notebook because day-to-day business has taken over? This section it identifies five pitfalls to avoid during the project or process development phase. How can we help the proverbial CPM acorn grow into the strong oak tree? Although there are dozens of reasons for failure, five blockers show up most frequently.

I hear and I forget. I see and I remember. I do and I understand.
—CONFUCIUS

Blocker 1: Executive and Management Attention Spans

Executive and management attention spans have shortened due to greatly shortened industry Clock Speeds and impacts from the four barriers noted earlier. We discussed the insidious impacts and risk of industry Clock Speed where one day you are on top of the food chain, the next you are a fallen hero looking for a niche market. Consistent with the Clock Speed doctrine, CPM best practice processes are expected to deliver results fast. You frequently hear leaders discussing their lack of bandwidth or lack of cycles. Translation? Short, high-impact projects or proofs of concept projects are more accepted. CPM processes or methods themselves should be streamlined and used in a smarter manner to demonstrate traction far sooner than when they were conceived. For example, your Six Sigma team charter and timeline should be adapted and geared for short, high-impact projects to move the Balanced Scorecard measure dashboard dial. Executive teams generally lack the appetite for sponsoring a CPM project with long lead times—for instance, with a one- to two-year project charter—unless the probabilities for demonstrable business improvements are high. Proactively manage your risk factors and minimize those project charters that promise of distant future savings. An experienced CPM Officer directing experienced personnel is of tremendous value particularly to calibrate CPM processes to the Clock Speed of your business and the focus of your leadership team. The CPM Office has the added benefit of being neutral or independent.

> *A chain is only as strong as its weakest link.*
> —PROVERB

Blocker 2: Stovepipes and Islands

Islands of competencies and processes consist of local experts who fail to integrate across the organization with their counterparts or those with complementary methods. For example, are your strategic planning and budgeting processes linked? Does your compensation system align with your scorecard? Do your management meetings discuss strategic issues, or are they financial statement or operating reviews? Do job descriptions contain clear objectives?

It is common for different teams to be pursing their own versions of a CPM best practice process competency. Lacking peripheral vision or centralized governance, they pursue projects or strategies that might be at cross-purposes. For example, I was invited to assist a client "purchasing" team focused on reducing inventory; they did not have visibility into the "sales" team strategy of using fast ship times and order fill rates as a competitive selling advantage. Oops. Well-intended leaders in purchasing embraced a CPM project but failed to understand that their purchasing project would detract from sales efforts in another part of the company. In short, stovepiped or vertical organizations are challenged to optimize overall company results. The top 10 projects pursued separately by business units A and B may not represent the top 20 consolidated-level projects that will bring about the most enterprise-level improvements. Perhaps larger opportunities for creating value exist in business unit A and it should launch and manage 15 projects, where business unit B should undertake

5 projects. An optimized business unit may not lead to an optimized company. The CPM office here would assist or facilitate project selection and scope, and assist with cross-organizational executive management oversight.

> *The only good is knowledge and the only evil is ignorance.*
> —SOCRATES

Blocker 3: Type A Personality, Expert or Apprentice?

Have you observed the A (or triple A) personality player who has been successful most of his or her career and views CPM as just another challenge or trophy for the wall? My advice is to secure help from a true CPM professional. The analogy here is the do-it-yourself homeowner who takes a two-day apprentice electrician's course and proceeds to set the house on fire. These well-intended employees may be good at reciting the process and quoting leading experts, but they may lack the insight necessary to execute the CPM method and synchronize project progress to match or beat the company's Clock Speed. They are convinced they are following the right steps to connect the red and white wires on the ceiling fan (or was it the red and blue wires?), but they lack the experience to see warning signs of impending failure or disaster. Type A personalities are well intended but accidentally spark the circuit box and start fires, though they manage to put the fire out before any real damage. Sometimes the fire just smolders as innocent bystanders are subsumed in the smoke. Such CPM project leaders often unwittingly undermine your CPM Office and CPM processes. In short, they will follow the method or textbook without true experience and often at great peril. Although there are some competent do-it-yourselfers, most achieve only a fraction of the results in comparison to an expert. An experienced CPM officer will be able to influence the right mix of personnel on a project to guide it to becoming part of the *Five Key Principles* processes.

> *Be careful about reading health books. You may die of a misprint.*
> —MARK TWAIN

Blocker 4: The Red Sports Car and Scope Creep

Have you seen this scenario? A leader has just secured the shiny new red sports car (a new method, such as Six Sigma) and is taking it out for a test drive on the first project. The project charter is ambitious and reads:

> Reduce cycle time posting checks to accounts receivables from 45 days to 30 days to increase cash flow by $15 million ($1 million for each day reduction) and carrying costs of 10% or $1,500,000 per annum in 8 weeks.

The ride is going well so, along the way, our driver revs the engine, the crowd cheers, and he now feels confident to raise the stakes. Therefore, he does what any rational but excited manager would do and *expands* the project scope or targets and sets out to rule the Indy brickyard. Have you seen this before? The new charter is a bigger challenge to our new race driver who envisions life as an action figure (note the italicized changes).

> Reduce cycle time for posting checks to accounts receivables from 45 days to *5 days* to increase cash flow by *$40 million* ($1 million for each day reduction) and carrying costs of 10% or *$4,000,000* per annum in *6 weeks*.

Our driver is aware of but unconcerned with scope creep and remains enthusiastic because now his initial team has expanded to included five sub-teams. The newfound adrenaline rush from taking the corner at top speed will clearly allow for solving world hunger, or will it? The team brainstorms and comes up with a solution: Purchase an enterprise resource planning (ERP) system for $20 million to streamline and improve all the broken processes. Our manager is way in over his head but is still running on excitement. Then the reality finally hits home. The project manager's boss or his boss's boss gets wind of this recommendation, and our driver has slammed into a dirt pile. The sports car crashes and burns. Thankfully, our racecar metaphor has run its last lap. An experienced CPM officer would have the insight and experience to advise and consult the well-intended "driver" and help him win his first race and establish Six Sigma as an enterprise CPM process competency.

> *Things do not change; we change.*
> —HENRY DAVID THOREAU

Blocker 5: Sponsoring Mr. Magoo

Misplaced sponsorship of a low-level project manager or of a leader lacking executive visibility or influence is dangerous. Here we turn to the cartoon character Mr. Magoo: We all want him to win but can only see the disasters left in his wake. Have you seen this? A well-liked or underachieving project leader many levels deep in the organization is given a chance to prove him- or herself. You scratch your head and wonder why the executive is taking care of Mr. Magoo. This story ends like a Greek tragedy; we know the outcome but we are still rooting for the underdog. This drama unfolds across enterprises almost everywhere. To maintain momentum, projects consume political, financial, and human capital for launch, care, and feeding. It is critical that project leaders are positioned appropriately in the organization. It is surprisingly common for an aspiring manager or director to kick off a project only to be derailed by his or her own ineptness or by a leader who has to save Mr.

Magoo from himself. Again, a CPM Office can advise the sponsors on the appropriate mix of personnel and can provide advice to the project leader to help this project succeed.

SUMMARY

The four barriers combined with the dynamics of Clock Speed clearly provide executives with a more comprehensive set of challenges in defining and implementing their enterprise strategies throughout both complex and simple organizations. Management often responds to pressures by initiating CPM projects or processes, but they are not always successful. Since successful CPM programs often result in adoption as ongoing CPM processes, we reviewed the top five blockers or reasons for project and hence process failure.

> *The probability that we may fail in the struggle ought not to deter us from the support of a cause we believe to be just.*
> —ABRAHAM LINCOLN

Observing Principle 1, establishing a dedicated CPM Office led by an Officer who understands and will facilitate delivery of comprehensive, integrated solutions around the *Five Key Principles*, will enable your enterprise to overcome these challenges. Organizations that deploy single tools or methods and move through different methods each year, using the "initiative du jour" approach in an ad hoc manner, do so at their own peril. However, how do you establish a dedicated CPM executive role? What processes and methods should be in this new executive's portfolio? Whom should he or she report to organizationally? What sort of department size is required for success? What competencies should this person possess? How do you integrate key processes such as strategic planning and budgeting? These are just some initial questions; we will further develop the *Five Key Principles* including over 25+ related best practices in the next chapter.

> *Failing to plan is planning to fail.*
> —PROVERB

NOTES

1. David Norton and Robert Kaplan, "Strategy Management Officer," *Harvard Business Review* (November 2005).

2. Robert E Paladino, "Strategic Balanced Scorecard-Based Budgeting and Performance Management," in *Handbook of Budgeting,* ed. W. Lalli (Hoboken, NJ: John Wiley & Sons, 2005), p. 2.

3. Robert E. Paladino, "Survival Strategies for Unmerciful Markets: The Telecom Experience," *Balanced Scorecard Report* (Boston: Harvard Business School Press, 2001), p. 3.

4. Charles H. Fine, *Clock Speed: Winning Industry Control in the Age of Temporary Advantage* (New York: Perseus Books, 1998).

5. Ibid., p. 3.

6. Charles Fine, *A Value Chain Perspective on the Economic Drivers of Competition in the Wireless Telecommunications Industry* (Boston: MIT Publishing, June 2001), p. 13.

7. Paladino, "Survival Strategies for Unmerciful Markets," p. 5.

CHAPTER 3

Research and the Five Key CPM Principles

A BEST PRACTICE MODEL

This book brings value to any person or organization that has a passion to be successful. Bob Paladino's method shows how it is possible to turn philosophical thinking into real results.

—PRESTON ATKINSON, CHIEF OPERATING OFFICER,
WHATABURGER, INC.

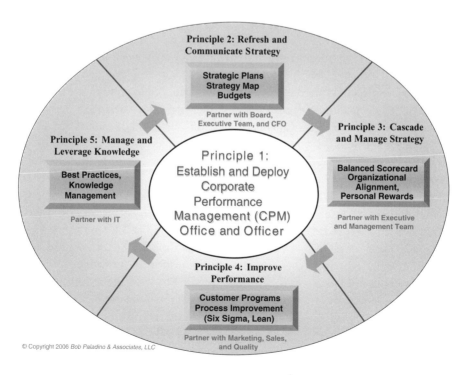

© Copyright 2006 *Bob Paladino & Associates, LLC*

This chapter provides background on the careful research used to develop the *Five Key Principles*. I share corporate performance management (CPM) Office experiences from the office of the senior vice president of global performance at Crown; research and best practices from numerous Malcolm Baldrige, Deming Quality, Sterling, APQC Best Practice, Balanced Scorecard Hall, Fortune, Forbes of Fame award winners; and best practices from notable high-performing enterprises. Organizations that won just one such prestigious awards would present a rich source of best practices for your CPM program, but we will learn from enterprise executives who have won multiple awards. In addition, this chapter condenses and groups best practices around the *Five Key Principles* to enable your enterprise to accelerate its CPM program.

PRINCIPLE 1: ESTABLISH AND DEPLOY A CPM OFFICE AND OFFICER

The first step to becoming a high-performing CPM enterprise is observing Principle 1, Establish and deploy a CPM Office and Officer for your enterprise. The CPM Office and Officer are at the center of the five CPM principles. Establishment of this office must be your enterprise's first step toward formalizing CPM competencies in your organization.

> *The beginning is the most important part of the work.*
> —PLATO

I invite you to join me and return to my journey as an executive with Crown Castle International (Crown). This condensed review will provide clear visibility into the early CPM model that evolved into the one adopted for this book. In 2001, while leading a strategy focused organization/Balanced Scorecard consulting practice for Drs. Kaplan and Norton's firm, the Balanced Scorecard Collaborative (BSCol), I received a call from the office of Crown's chief executive officer (CEO) to refine and help implement their company strategy globally. Little did I know, this call would significantly change my life. Through the efforts of a dedicated Crown executive team and workforce we created employee and shareholder wealth and enabled Crown to receive many prestigious awards. I researched Crown and candidly the more I learned, the more I became very intrigued by its strategic business model, market position, and executive team. Briefly, Crown was an early innovator in the wireless industry pioneering the cell tower industry. Crown by then had acquired, built, owned, and operated roughly 16,000 cell towers from the wireless carriers in the United States, United Kingdom, and Australia, and its customers were leading wireless service providers such as Verizon, Orange, Telstra, Sprint, and Cingular as well as being the digital television transmission provider for the BBC.

Be great in act, as you have been in thought.
—WILLIAM SHAKESPEARE

A few weeks later, I was facilitating a strategy session at Crown's strategic retreat at King Ranch in Texas, with the top 40 to 50 members of the U.S, Australia, and the U.K leadership teams. Many credit Ted B. Miller Jr., founder and CEO of Crown, and his extensive real estate experience for having pioneered the cell tower industry. This sector today is worth billions of dollars in market capitalization. Miller is a rare leader and visionary; he has also established an enviable record of accomplishment with innovative corporations in the global aviation and global human resources outsourcing sectors.

The tower business model focuses on initial or one-time setup fees to install carrier antennas and long-term leases to create financial annuities. Crown had recently gone public and was experiencing rapid growth, but the strategic message was not getting through to its employees. Crown faced both the four barriers and rapid telecommunications industry Clock Speed; the company's situation was further complicated by its geographical distribution. In response to an interview question on the biggest organizational challenge facing Crown, John Kelly, who would take over from Miller as CEO, spoke to the importance of aligning the organization.

> People get accustomed to operating a certain way; good people do things they believe are adding value to the organization. But consider the first element of our strategy: "grow revenue organically." If you are used to building towers, you might view that as organic growth opportunity. It was part of the business, and in your heart, you might be convinced that by continuing in that direction you'll also get a higher return with lower execution risks. The challenge is this, how do executives help people understand that if they kept going down that path they would not be optimizing current strategic direction?[1]

On Dr. Fine's double helix model, introduced in Chapter 2, the telecommunications industry was moving from a vertically integrated (left side of the figure ∞) to a horizontally structured industry (the right side of the figure ∞). Wireless carriers had taken on billions in debt to pay for spectrum licenses, and they were under pressure to sell assets and de-leverage their balance sheets. The pressure to sell of portions of their value chain resulted in wireless carriers outsourcing tower assets, the so-called last mile of their value chain, to the end customer. During this same period, upstart tower company, Crown emerged to gain control of many outsourced carrier assets.

Genius is one % inspiration and ninety-nine % perspiration.
—THOMAS EDISON

Retail demand for cell phone usage was exploding, resulting in dramatic increases in minutes of use (MOU), thus driving the need for more cell towers and tighter clusters of towers. Not only did Crown have to satisfy its current customer base through excellent delivery of existing services, it had to expand rapidly to meet MOU demand in a brutally competitive industry characterized by a handful of powerful wireless carriers. End retail customer subscribers changed wireless carriers, or "churned," at a mind-boggling 30% per annum. Can you imagine being in rivalry with a small number of competitors and losing on average 2.5% of your customers monthly? Two factors caused churn: (1) a downward-sloping retail pricing curve and (2) perceived or real shortcomings in network quality measured by dropped calls, poor reception, and delays. Crown's tower portfolio represented a factor of this network quality, the last mile to the end customer. In short, there were enormous industry demands to help wireless carriers establish and maintain a quality network to reduce churn.

Consequently, the CEO and CEO team who were actively involved in strategic planning understood the value offered by deployment of strategy maps and Balanced Scorecards enterprise-wide. (See Chapter 5 for an in-depth discussion on strategy maps.) These strategy management methods and processes would permit leaders to increase visibility of focused objectives and key lead and lag indicators, strongly align a distributed organization, and make well-timed decisions in the rapidly moving telecommunications sector. The Balanced Scorecard project team focused on designing and rolling out, in the first 90 days, a three-level architecture of strategy maps and BSCs consisting of level 1 corporate, level 2 country, and level 3 within a country, a very rapid deployment. Could one achieve 100 % accuracy and effectiveness in this short time frame? Not really; however, this is where many companies fall into a trap, and I borrow a phrase from a study partner: "Do not let perfection be the enemy of the good." Get started with your program and refine it as you go. CEO Kelly stated, "We moved quickly through the implementation process, though there are negatives alongside benefits. One negative was that we did not always get the measures right. And we certainly didn't always get the targets right. If you look at a stoplight report and see a lot of red, that's not necessarily a good indicator that there's a problem. It might mean that you got the target wrong."[2] To this point, Crown lacked a practiced CPM leader to focus on this global project and institute global processes. Several capable people resided in different departments throughout the organization again representing islands of competencies. Further, the use of my Kaplan and Norton outside consulting team had its innate limitations, the most prominent being our impermanent nature. Crown needed to rethink a sustainable approach toward strategy management.

CROWN CPM OFFICE AND OFFICER IS BORN

In 2001, Crown CEO Kelly invited me to join his executive team and launch a CPM department. For sake of common terminology we will use CPM Office, although our actual department title was Global Performance. When asked to define this function, I pondered how to best assist Crown in the deployment of its strategy: "What portfolio of methods would work best in this culture?" "What impacts does Clock Speed have on the CPM department personnel selection?" As I reflected on dozens of leading enterprises and their approaches to strategy management, I decided to deploy a best practice–based approach to enhance chances for success and diminish implementation risk and failure as seen in other companies.

Since I believed other organizations faced my same challenges, I decided to pursue practical application of CPM principles at Crown while at the same time researching CPM efforts of leading companies to boost effectiveness of the Crown CPM Office. It was apparent to me then that we were not only defining a new role at Crown but also breaking new ground in the CPM field. This premise was validated through several research and study projects described in the next section.

It's not enough that we do our best; sometimes we have to do what's required.
—SIR WINSTON CHURCHILL

CPM RESEARCH

This section outlines the research, study groups, and selected award-winning organizations that played a role in shaping my Crown CPM Office and this book. Research on CPM is a continuous process to evolve and adapt the *Five Key Principles* to changing conditions and innovations. The final chapter contains a self-scoring diagnostic for your CPM program and a comprehensive list of CPM research resources to support continued learning.

When your values are clear to you, making decisions becomes easier.
—ROY DISNEY

APQC Best Practice Consortia Study Projects

The CPM Office and Officer executive role and integrated CPM processes were emerging as a proven model through research with APQC and its world-renowned study projects. Between 2002 and 2004, I directed Crown CPM Office employees to participate in several APQC studies and ongoing research projects providing valuable inputs to shape our CPM Office. The Crown CPM Office adopted early the *Five Key Principles,* an expert model with senior-level employees as competency leaders in Six Sigma, knowledge management, strategy and BSC; process improvement and customer surveys/customer relationship management (CRM); and exercised a collaborative model with internal business leaders. APQC research projects included Baldrige, Sterling, Balanced Scorecard Hall of Fame, and APQC Best Practice Partner Award winners; research projects included:

- Customer Relationship Management (CRM) Consortia Best Practice Study Project
- Knowledge Management (KM) Consortia Best Practice Study Project
- Best Practice Sharing Consortia Study Project
- Performance Management Consortia Best Practice Project (discussed below)

(These study reports are available from APQC. For more information go to www.apqc.org.)

APQC Performance Management Consortia Best Practice Study Project

In 2004 APQC invited me in my position as Crown CPM Officer to participate in a Performance Management Consortia Best Practice Study; other best practice CPM enterprises studied included Bank of America, Saturn, LL Bean, and Jet Blue. These core five best practice companies were studied individually and as a group. Best practice companies were compared and contrasted with sponsor organizations shown in the next table.

Alliant Energy Corp.	Aramco Services Company	BellSouth Corp.	CenterPoint Energy Inc
Defense Finance & Accounting Service	Federal Reserve Bank of Boston	Grupo IMSA, S.A. de C.V.	Internal Revenue Service
Johnson & Johnson	Laclede Gas Company	Marsh Inc.	Serono S.A.
U.S. Food & Drug Administration	U.S. General Accounting Office	U.S. Census Bureau	U.S. Navy
University of Texas Medical Branch at Galveston	Unocal Corp.		

The primary purpose of the study was to understand and document CPM organization, process, methods, and technology best practices common to best practice CPM organizations. During the study we learned a great deal from each other and from sponsor enterprises.

Kaplan and Norton's Office of Strategic Management Study Group

Kaplan and Norton are the most prolific and influential business framework thinkers in many generations. They invented both the balanced scorecard and strategy-focused organization (SFO) concepts, central workings to the *Five Principles*. The Crown CPM Office was one of early cases studied in March 2004 by Kaplan and Norton in their groundbreaking Office of Strategic Management (OSM) project. Their firm The Balanced Scorecard Collaborative led this research. The distinguished group of study companies (see Exhibit 3.1) included eight Balanced Scorecard Hall of Fame Award winners. Remarkably, the OSM study group findings converged with the Crown CPM Office design.

In July 2004 the BSCol research team invited me to take part in a knowledge-sharing net meeting to explain Crown's OSM Office (CPM Office) processes to hundreds of companies participating globally. In May 2005 BSCol's director of research and I conducted a joint knowledge-sharing workshop at a CPM conference in Madrid, Spain, to share the OSM research and the award-winning Crown journey. The new OSM Office executive role and the practice of integrated CPM processes and methods to implement strategy was well received by delegates from dozens of countries. The OSM research project output was the subject of Kaplan and Norton's *Harvard Business Review* article.[3]

APQC Best Practice in Government Performance Management Consortia Project

In June 2005 APQC invited me, in my new position leading Bob Paladino & Associates, to serve as subject matter expert and facilitator to their performance management research project in the government and nonprofit sectors. In this

EXHIBIT 3.1   OSM Project Study Companies

Ameritrade	Bank of Tokyo Mitsubishi	Canadian Blood Services	Canon *	Chrysler Group*
CorVu	Crown*	Freddie Mac	Grupo Nacional Provincial*	Handleman*
KeyCorp*	Hilton Hotels*	Lockheed Martin	Nabi Pharmaceuticals	Oracle Latin America
U.S. Air Force	U.S. Army*			

* Recipient of Kaplan and Norton's Balanced Scorecard Hall of Fame Award

study we carefully screened dozens of enterprises and identified five best practice award-winning organizations and several sponsor organizations to study. The five finalist best practice CPM organizations included the American Red Cross, City of Coral Springs, Florida Department of Health (FDOH), State of Washington, and Tennessee Valley Authority (TVA). As noted earlier, City of Coral Springs and FDOH were recipients of the Florida Governor's Sterling Award for Organizational Excellence, the state equivalent to the National Malcolm Baldrige Quality Award. TVA was the recipient of the globally recognized Kaplan and Norton Balanced Scorecard Hall of Fame Award. The best practice organizations were studied in-depth and were compared and contrasted to several successful sponsor organizations. Sponsor organizations included:

American Association of Retired Persons (AARP)	Army Installation Management	California Public Employees' Retirement System (CalPERs)	Defense Finance and Accounting Service
U.S. Coast Guard	U.S. General Accounting Office (GAO)	U.S. Navy—Carrier Team One	World Bank

The study results converged around the BSCol OSM and APQC Best Practice studies that both agreed a CPM Office and Officer were best practices and major contributing factors to success at award-winning enterprises.

> *Men occasionally stumble over the truth, but most of them pick themselves up and hurry off as if nothing ever happened.*
> —SIR WINSTON CHURCHILL

HIGH-PERFORMING ORGANIZATIONS

While leading the CPM office at Crown I had the good fortune of collaborating with many executives from award-winning enterprises outside of the recognized research projects noted. These executives spanned many industries and continents, but many of the CPM challenges they faced were astonishingly common.

My firm, which I founded in January 2005, has been providing CPM Office and CPM best practice process services to leading executives not only to help establish and define the CPM executive role in their enterprises but also to assist them achieve meaningful strategy implementation results. This both therefore draws from my work with these clients as well as collaboration with other leading enterprises; I am grateful to high-performing client organizations Anheuser Busch, Bronson Methodist Hospital, Federal Reserve Bank, Hearst Publications, Imperium International, Intercomp Technologies, LB

Foster Company, Medrad, M7 Aerospace, Serono, Raytheon Company, Ricoh Corporation, Sprint-Nextel, Universal Weather and Aviation, Whataburger, and many others.

In summary, this book is based on research and established, real-world enterprise best practice experiences as well as dozens of Fortune 500 projects performed throughout my career in the CPM field. Again, my promise: I will provide fundamental theory but will largely focus on authentic examples to bring out proven best practices for your use.

> *The other teams could make trouble for us if they win.*
> —YOGI BERRA

Five Key Principles Best Practices summarized in Exhibits 3.2 through 3.6 provide a handy reference tool as a normative framework for detailed case studies in the following chapters; enterprises demonstrate adaptations, where some titles and terms may vary.

PRINCIPLE 1: ESTABLISH AND DEPLOY A CPM OFFICE AND OFFICER

Principle 1, Establish and Deploy a CPM Office and Officer, is the starting point and foundation for deploying the remaining four principles. This table will describe CPM Office best practices found at the center of successful commercial, nonprofit, and government sector organizations. (See Exhibit 3.2.)

PRINCIPLE 2: REFRESH AND COMMUNICATE STRATEGY

Principle 2, Refresh and Communicate Strategy, links back to the four barriers and Clock Speed of your enterprise. Most enterprises fail to effectively translate their strategies to operations, and communicate their strategies to employees. We learned earlier that most employees are neither conversant with nor comprehend their role in driving the organization's strategy. Principle 2 consists of several best practice elements shown in Exhibit 3.3.

PRINCIPLE 3: CASCADE AND MANAGE STRATEGY

Principle 3, Cascade and Manage Strategy, links back to the four barriers and Clock Speed as well. Principle 3 focuses on translating the outputs from Principle 2 into strategic objectives and measures that are actionable by employees. A key influence on development of these best practices and credit goes to Kaplan and Norton and experiences from leading one of their largest consulting divisions. Principle 3 consists of several best practices shown in Exhibit 3.4.

EXHIBIT 3.2   **Principle 1 Best Practice Summary**

Best Practice	Description
Executive sponsorship	CEO or direct report actively sponsors CPM Office and CPM projects for sustained period and with the right visibility to enable maturity to process state.
Organizational level and reporting relationship	CPM Office executive reports to the CEO or a CEO direct report.
CPM Office staff	Small senior team (three to eight people) experienced in change programs, full-time role in CPM Office.
Leadership, influence factors	Able to organize large-scale virtual teams to drive results in one or more CPM methods.
Ownership of CPM Processes and methods (Principles 2 through 5)	The office owns or substantially influences the portfolio of CPM processes enterprise-wide, with each Office CPM practitioner possessing deep expertise in at least one methodology.
CPM, industry, and company knowledge	One or more team members has deep industry and company specific knowledge to help guide resolution of project issues.
Collaborative maturity	Experienced in working horizontally and vertically through the organization.
Ability to learn	Open to new ideas, methods, and approaches; able to streamline, integrate, and adapt methods; able to think concurrently.

EXHIBIT 3.3   **Principle 2 Best Practice Summary**

Best Practice	Description
Strategic planning	Leverage the strategic planning process as either owner or partner to understand changing market conditions including competitor, supplier, rival, and potential entrants and substitutes in the marketplace.
Core and adjacent products and services	Define and determine core and adjacent products and services to focus on highest probabilities for success.
Strategic plan	Produce a comprehensive strategic plan.
Strategy mapping	Develop a strategy map containing objectives along four perspectives including financial, customer/constituent, process and people. Observe strategy map design parameters of 20 to 25 objectives.
Link strategic planning and budgeting processes	Link strategic planning to the budgeting process, partner with finance to provide for a seamless continuum. Ideally, provide a rolling forecast or a flexible, lean budget linked to strategy.
Communications plan	Communicate strategy throughout the organization using a comprehensive communications plan.

EXHIBIT 3.4   **Principle 3 Best Practice Summary**

Best Practice	Description
Partner with business owners	Partner with line and staff leadership team members to gain support and influence as partners to help them achieve results.
Develop level 1 balanced scorecard (BSC)	Translate strategy into level 1 BSC measures, and measure targets at the highest organizational level.
Leverage proven BSC of comparable methods	Observe BSC or comparable design parameters, assigning one to two measures to each strategy map objective.
Cascade BSC to lower levels	Cascade and align level 1 BSC to levels 2, 3, 4, and so on, depending on organizational and accountability structures.
Align support services	Identify and define measures for all support services that align with levels 1 and below.
Align teams and individual employees	Define personal BSCs for teams and/or individuals that align with higher-level and support services Balanced Scorecards.
Link compensation	Align rewards, recognition, and compensation programs to the Balanced Scorecard.
Manage using measures	Manage BSC meetings to address the appropriate mix of strategic and operational issues; link these issues with Principle 4: Business Improvement.
Automate measurement	Implement CPM software to manage BSC program with links to other principles.

PRINCIPLE 4: IMPROVE PERFORMANCE

Principle 4, Improve Performance, focuses on improving CRM, core business, and support processes. Key influences on this section were my training and facilitation of GE Six Sigma Black Belt teams; collaboration with Motorola University, the pioneers of Six Sigma; and plentiful quality and total quality management (TQM) projects with Meritus Consulting, a joint venture with IBM Manufacturing and Coopers & Lybrand consulting. In concert with Principle 3, if your Balance Scorecard indicates low customer satisfaction or long operations cycle time moving products from design to commercialization, then it may be fitting to launch an initiative to improve performance. Principle 4 consists of several best practices shown in Exhibit 3.5.

PRINCIPLE 5: MANAGE AND LEVERAGE KNOWLEDGE

Principle 5, Manage and Leverage Knowledge, focuses on capturing and reusing enterprise-wide intellectual property to leverage the organization's best minds, best practices, and innovations. As enterprises increasingly rely on knowledge workers, it is essential to have core knowledge management (KM) processes

EXHIBIT 3.5   **Principle 4 Best Practice Summary**

Best Practice	Description
Prioritize improvement projects	Identify and prioritize strategic and operational initiatives to improve organization's performance along financial, customer or constituent, process, and people dimensions.
Leverage customer-facing processes	Develop and exercise customer and constituent processes to understand and recalibrate processes around changing customer needs. Gather customer and competitor intelligence using regular customer surveys, focus groups, call centers, quality function deployment, and related methods and approaches.
Leverage process improvement methods	Design and maintain an ongoing process improvement and problem-solving program based on Six Sigma black belt or green belt, or Lean methods and tools to identify and eliminate root causes of issues.
Realize value from benchmarking processes	Leverage benchmarking and comparative methods to identify and regularly improve core and support processes. APQC has developed a process classification framework with standard process definitions and benchmarking (www.apqc.org).
Create a performance improvement culture	Create a virtual community of practitioners to coordinate and optimize improvement efforts enterprise wide.

embedded in the organization to capture and propagate best-in-class and world-class results. Key influences for development of this section was my Crown KM program but particularly the KM expertise shared selflessly by Carla O'Dell, president of APQC, and her talented KM team. The logic is if while benchmarking field operations your BSC (in Principle 3) informs you of a location that performs in the top quartile, then it is advantageous to understand, document, and share this location's winning formula with all locations. Principle 5 best practices are shown in Exhibit 3.6.

> *You got to be very careful if you don't know where you're going, because you might not get there.*
> —YOGI BERRA

SUMMARY

Earlier chapters reviewed the four barriers, industry Clock Speed, and the top five blockers to project success that no doubt contribute to increased rates of CEO turnover. In this chpater we identified a large group of award-winning and

EXHIBIT 3.6   Principle 5 Best Practice Summary

Best Practice	Description
Develop KM processes	Establish and leverage best practice identification, gathering and sharing processes and technology solutions. (APQC has compiled an impressive list of KM best practice case studies; www.apqc.org).
Leverage technology	Partner with the information technology (IT) function to launch and maintain KM systems.
Develop expert locater systems	Design and use expert locater systems to capture employee skills inventory within the enterprise to accelerate problem solving in Principle 4 and to optimize human capital.
Link KM with improve performance process	Link best practice or knowledge management processes with Principle 4 processes to capture solutions and innovations.
Share best practices with strategic planning	Share best practices with strategic planning processes to better understand core competencies and possible strategic advantages.
Maintain a virtual KM network	Establish and maintain virtual network of KM experts throughout the enterprise to optimize knowledge and to keep processes evergreen.

leading enterprises that have overcome these challenges. A road map to our research was provided and the *Five Key Principles* best practices were summarized.

> *The best and fastest way to learn a sport is to watch and imitate a champion.*
> —JEAN CLAUDE KILLY

Attitude and positive traits are as much a part of success as deploying best practices. As an avid reader, I enjoy *Investor Business Daily*'s "Leaders and Success" section, which contains the "10 Secrets to Success" list:

> *Investor Business Daily* has spent years analyzing leaders and successful people in all walks of life. Most have 10 traits that, when combined, can turn dreams into reality.
> 1. *How You Think Is Everything*: Always be positive. Think of success, not failure. Beware of a negative environment.
> 2. *Decide upon Your True Dreams and Goals*: Write down your specific goals and develop a plan to reach them.
> 3. *Take Action*: Goals are nothing without action. Don't be afraid to get started. Just do it.

4. *Never Stop Learning:* Go back to school or read books. Get training and acquire skills.

5. *Be Persistent and Work Hard:* Success is a marathon, not a sprint. Never give up.

6. *Learn to Analyze Details:* Get all the facts, all the input. Learn from your mistakes.

7. *Focus Your Time and Money:* Don't let other people or things distract you.

8. *Do Not Be Afraid to Innovate; Be Different:* Following the herd is a sure way to mediocrity.

9. *Deal and Communicate with People Effectively:* No person is an island. Learn to understand and motivate others.

10. *Be Honest and Dependable; Take Responsibility:* Otherwise, numbers 1–9 won't matter.[4]

My hope is that you practice the 10 traits of leaders and successful people and apply the *Five Key Principles* contained in this book to achieve your goals.

> *Perpetual optimism is a force multiplier.*
> —COLIN POWELL

■ NOTES

1. Janice Koch, "The Challenges of Strategic Alignment: Crown Castle's CEO Shares His Perspectives," *Balanced Scorecard Report,* (July–August 2004): 10.

2. Janice Koch, interview with John Kelly, CEO Crown Castle International, in ibid., p. 11.

3. Robert S. Kaplan and David P. Norton, "Office of Strategic Management," *Harvard Business Review* (October 2005).

4. *Investor's Business Daily,* May 19, 2006.

Principle 1

ESTABLISH AND DEPLOY A CPM OFFICE AND OFFICER

> *The world is full of willing people, some willing to work, the rest willing to let them.*
>
> —ROBERT FROST

In this chapter, we will explore *Principle 1, Establish and Deploy a CPM Office and Officer,* by studying numerous award-winning enterprises. The case studies

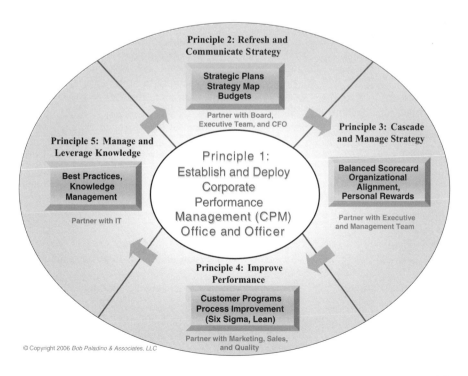

© Copyright 2006 Bob Paladino & Associates, LLC

range from public and private companies, governmental agencies, and nonprofit entities and are representative of more organizations studied but for sensible reasons were not included. These enterprises share many common behaviors, observe similar best practices, and have proven their ability to function at high levels. Nearly all case study enterprises have won one or more of these awards:

- U.S. President's National Malcolm Baldrige Quality Award
- Governor's Sterling Award for Excellence (based on Baldrige Criteria)
- Deming Quality Award
- American Quality and Productivity Center (APQC) Best Practice Partner Award
- Drs. Kaplan and Norton Global Balanced Scorecard Hall of Fame Award
- *Wall Street Journal* Ranked "Top 20 Most Improved Company in Shareholder Value Creation"
- *Fortune* "100 Best Companies to Work For"
- *Forbes* Best Managed Companies

EXHIBIT 4.1   **Principle 1: Establish and Deploy a CPM Office and Officer Best Practice Summary**

Best Practice	Description
Executive sponsorship	CEO or direct report actively sponsors CPM Office and CPM projects for sustained period and with the right visibility to enable maturity to process state.
Organizational level and reporting relationship	CPM Office executive reports to the CEO or a CEO direct report.
CPM Office staff	Small senior team (three to eight people) experienced in change programs, full-time role in CPM Office.
Leadership, influence factors	Able to organize large scale virtual teams to drive results in one more CPM methods.
Ownership of CPM processes and methods (Principles 2 through 5)	The office owns or substantially influences the portfolio of CPM processes enterprise-wide, with each Office CPM practitioner possessing deep expertise in at least one methodology.
CPM, industry and company knowledge	One or more team members has deep industry and company-specific knowledge to help guide resolution of project issues.
Collaborative maturity	Experienced in working horizontally and vertically through the organization.
Ability to learn	Open to new ideas, methods and approaches; able to streamline, integrate, and adapt methods; able to think concurrently.

Principle 1 presents normative corporate performance management (CPM) office and officer terminology for ease of understanding; however, case study organizations may use variations that have enabled them to best meet their needs and fit their cultures.

> *The difference between a successful person and others is not a lack of strength, not a lack of knowledge, but rather a lack of will.*
> —VINCENT T. LOMBARDI

For a summary of Principle 1, see Exhibit 4.1.

> *A journey of a thousand miles begins with a single step.*
> —PROVERB

CROWN CASTLE INTERNATIONAL: BEST PRACTICE CASE

The first step to establishing the CPM Office is insistent sponsorship; the rest of the best practices follow from this point. At Crown, founding company chief executive officer (CEO) Ted Miller Jr. supported establishing strategy-focused organization (SFO) principles and the Balanced Scorecard at multiple levels in the organization. Later CEO John Kelly established my Crown CPM Office (Global Performance). He also provided sustained support to enable the BSC project and related CPM processes (e.g., Six Sigma, knowledge management, customer surveying, process improvement, and Sarbanes-Oxley) to mature into CPM processes. In terms of sponsorship and change management, at times some operating unit leaders indicated they were uncomfortable with the CPM Office, for instance, when they had to administer surveys to their external customers. However, over time these same leaders made significant contributions to updating and upgrading the content and quality of customer survey content and tools to enhance results. Similarly, there was initially some employee resistance to document core and support processes for it was hard work. Over time, however, the leadership teams in the organization answered the challenge and found significant benefits from

- Recipient of Balanced Scorecard Hall of Fame Award
- Recipient of APQC Best Practice Partner Award
- Ranked "Top 20 Most Improved Company in Shareholder Value Creation" by the *Wall Street Journal* (out of 1,000 listed companies)

having online process documentation; in fact, they initiated numerous process improvements. For instance, one area conducted weekly employee trainings using the e-process documentation to become more proficient and to train new employees.

Research of award winning enterprises shows that successful CPM Office and CPM executives are sponsored at the highest levels in the organization. In providing this support, the organization signals its priority and importance and removes many obstacles. Thus, sponsorship from the CEO or CEO equivalent in the public or nonprofit sectors (e.g., commissioner, governor, general, etc.) is vital; or a CEO direct reporting relationship. In the corporate sector, CEO direct report translates into chief financial officer (CFO), chief operating officer (COO), or an influential business unit or department leader (e.g., human resources, quality). The sponsor supports the CPM Office and CPM executive and is out in front prior to launch to provide appropriate "air cover" and to alert the organization of its importance. Postlaunch, the sponsor is dynamically involved in "telling the story" as events and projects unfurl and wins are cataloged. Sponsorship must be sustained since there will be CPM missteps and the organization will go through stages of the grief cycle (i.e., anger, denial, and acceptance) during significant transformational projects. Although some people move from one phase to the next in sequence, life is rarely that straightforward. Some employees will move back to a previous phase and go through some phases more than once. Employees also will pass through this cycle at different speeds, whether it is 10 seconds, 10 days, or 10 months.

> *My motto was always to keep swinging. Whether I was in a slump or feeling badly or having trouble off the field, the only thing to do was keep swinging.*
> —HANK AARON

Organizational Level and Reporting Relationship

At Crown, I reported to the CEO. I attended board of director meetings, including strategy subcommittee meetings. Why is this important? CPM executive positioning enabled the Crown Strategy Map (described in Chapter 5) to be regularly refreshed for noteworthy and subtle changes in company strategy and strategic intent. For example, in a strategic shift, company leadership modified "optimize revenue" into its component parts placing an even greater emphasis on motivating consistent "recurring revenue" from long-term leasing and less emphasis on current term, "one-time" antenna installation revenue. This redefinition resulted in sharpening the published Crown Strategy Map objective from "optimize revenue" to "increase recurring revenue," thus clearly directing company personnel to focus on long-term revenue agreements and less on current-quarter, one-time installation fees that contributed to lumpier, sawtooth revenue profiles. The "strategy map" and BSC are both organizing tools and communications devices, so this change was speedily reflected on over dozens of BSCs globally.

> *Even if you are on the right track, you'll get run over if you just sit there.*
> —WILL ROGERS

Further and more important, the BSC targets for each type of revenue, recurring and one-time, updated with the new importance to motivate new employee behaviors. That is, by expanding or relaxing targets for each type of revenue, the company communicated desired employee behaviors. By forming a high level CPM Office in this fast-moving organization, the strategic shift was rapidly communicated using the Strategy Map and BSC targets for all employees to be aware of and implement.

The CPM executive Office must also report to either the CEO or a CEO direct report in the organization or public and nonprofit equivalent. For example, the CPM Office at the Royal Canadian Mounted Police (RCMP), a Balanced Scorecard Hall of Fame winner, reported to the Commissioner Giuliano Zaccardelli, the highest-ranking official in RCMP. This configuration and proximity to the seniormost executives enabled a practical link to enterprise strategy and for the translation of strategy into and through CPM methods. At AT&T Canada, another Balanced Scorecard Hall of Fame company, then CEO Bill Catucci undertook employment of the BSC and drove extraordinary results during his tenure.

> *The way a team plays as a whole determines its success. You may have the greatest bunch of individual stars in the world, but if they don't play together, the club won't be worth a dime.*
> —BABE RUTH

CMP Office Staff Size

The Crown CPM Office consisted of five direct reports including a vice president, three directors, and a manager. However, they served as CPM process competency leaders multiplying their talents across many more employees.

Research has shown CPM Office executives surround themselves with a small number, between three to eight senior, mature, and experienced individuals. This size did not deviate significantly across enterprises that had a wide variation in employee bases ranging from 500 to 80,000 employees. What appears to be a common characteristic is not the size of the CPM Office staff but their ability to influence and integrate across the organization with virtual team members, discussed in the next section.

> *The will to win is important, but the will to prepare is vital.*
> —JOE PATERNO

Leadership: Ability to Influence

CPM Office staffs are lean in terms of direct reports but very effective in their ability to influence at times large numbers of employees, mobilizing them as the program calls for shifts in strategy and tactics. It is not the CPM Office team size but rather its ability to influence and multiply its talents. For example, at one point, the Crown CPM Office team of five was facilitating over 15 CPM project teams with membership rosters totaling over 400 personnel in three countries. Project team leaders, members of the country senior leadership teams (SLTs), were responsible for improvement targets totaling well over $100 million in free cash flow.

Ownership of CPM Processes

Research has shown that CPM Offices entirely own, provide substantial governance and standards to, or heavily facilitate CPM processes (e.g., strategic planning, knowledge management). As discussed earlier, uncoordinated and distributed CPM process ownership invariably leads to inconsistencies in CPM process application, different versions, and, worse yet, silos or islands of projects lacking overall company optimization. At Crown, Balance Scorecard competency was centralized in the CPM Office, where, among other things, the Balance Scorecard competency leader:

- Contributed substantially to the design of the Strategy Map, objectives, measures, and preliminary targets
- Owned the software infrastructure including report suite design and access and read and write permissions
- Designed and facilitated enterprise-wide Balance Scorecard training classes on a range of CPM topics
- Facilitated a central Balance Scorecard council with wide organization representation responsible for regular refinements of Balance Scorecard measures
- Collaborated with human resources on the enterprise-wide rewards and recognition program

To deliver on targeted results, it is important that organizational leaders, from the most senior executive to the supervisor in the field, are accountable for Balance Scorecard results and performance.

CPM, Industry, and Company Competency Levels

Research shows CPM Office employees possess deep expertise in one or more competencies. Note that employees are not CPM generalists who lack depth in any one competency. It is important for team members to possess deep organizational knowledge to understand the political topography and have the ability to read changes in the organization and shifts in the agendas of key executives and influencers. In addition, these employees leverage industry-specific knowledge during the course of improvement projects, so it is also important to have CPM Office employees with deep industry experience.

The Crown CPM team of five direct reports possessed over 20 years of Crown organizational experience and 100 years of industry and consulting experience. The mix of deep company and industry expertise, both wire line and wireless, was invaluable. Although many CPM-related projects covered generic support processes (e.g., collect accounts receivables, pay vendors) that could be addressed by a generalist, several higher-value-added CPM projects and processes required expertise specific to the telecommunications industry (e.g., cell tower signal strength, technical maintenance) to drive strategic change. CPM Office team members specialized in CPM competencies including strategy, Balance Scorecard, customer surveys and CRM, process improvement, and Sarbanes-Oxley and Six Sigma.

Collaborative Maturity

CPM Office personnel are willing and interested in traveling throughout the enterprise and facilitating and leading key CPM process initiatives.

> *Ask not what your teammates can do for you. Ask what you can do for your teammates.*
>
> —MAGIC JOHNSON

CPM Office team members possess the ability to work horizontally and vertically through their active networks in the organization. That is, they are politically mature enough to navigate the formal and informal communications and influence channels. The combination of effective teaming skills and CPM subject matter expertise creates a powerful new edge necessary for rapidly implementing change and creating a sustainable difference. These mature and seasoned employees have been through numerous change or transformational programs and have developed an organizational awareness for rapid change. CPM Office employees have experienced successful and some less successful initiatives during their careers.

Ability to Learn

CPM Office team members enjoy an ability to learn and remain open to new ideas and self-development opportunities. As CPM employees become more accepted and leveraged by the organization, they are regularly invited to key meetings and operating reviews and are treated as trusted business advisors. Doing this requires CPM employees to be able to learn new skills to facilitate and aid key decision making. Further, advanced internal customers assist with the integration of CPM process competencies. For example, a Crown area president noticed a Balance Scorecard dashboard indicating underperformance in a process measure (cycle time) and subsequently worked with the CPM Office Six Sigma leader to deploy a Six Sigma team to improve this process. Thus, the area president was calling on the two CPM experts for assistance.

At Crown, while each CPM Office team member owned a competency and possessed deep skills, they were also sufficiently cross-trained to provide for a flexible CPM team able to adjust to changing company needs. For instance, in addition to the Six Sigma competency leader, three other CPM Office personnel were certified Six Sigma green belts and could facilitate Six Sigma teams as needed. This was particularly valuable given the regular ebbs and flows of projects in the Six Sigma pipeline. To understand the dynamic

---

BEST PRACTICE HIGHLIGHTS

Principle 1: Establish and Deploy a CPM Office and Officer

- *Executive Sponsorship.* The CEO actively sponsored the CPM Office and CPM projects for a sustained period and with the right visibility to enable maturity to processes state.
- *Organizational Level and Reporting Relationship.* The CPM Officer reported directly to the CEO.
- *CPM Office Staff.* The staff consisted of a small senior team experienced in change programs who played a full-time role in the CPM Office.
- *Leadership and Ability to Influence.* CPM employees were able to organize large-scale virtual teams to drive results in one or more CPM methods.
- *Ownership of CPM Methods.* The office owns or substantially influences the portfolio of CPM processes enterprise-wide, with each Office CPM practitioner possessing deep expertise in at least one methodology.
- *CPM, Industry, and Company Knowledge.* Many team members had deep industry and company-specific knowledge to help guide resolution of project issues.
- *Collaborative Maturity.* CPM team members were very experienced in working horizontally and vertically through the organization.
- *Ability to Learn.* CPM Office team members were open to new ideas, methods, and approaches; they were able to streamline, integrate, and adapt methods, and to think concurrently.

nature of the CPM Office team, weekly meetings resulted in real-time cali-
brations in projects, which continuously assisted Crown leaders operating in a
fast Clock Speed industry.

> *The principle is competing against yourself. It's about self-improvement, about*
> *being better than you were the day before.*
> —STEVE YOUNG

Unlike most employees, CPM Office team members have the ability to
work sequentially *and* concurrently. That is, they understand that integrated
CPM processes and methods are choreographed and used in combination as
the situation calls for their use. Many unsuccessful CPM efforts result from
employees who lock into a track with a method and fail to adjust to changing
conditions.

CITY OF CORAL SPRINGS:
BEST PRACTICE CASE*

The City of Coral Springs, Florida, is a high-performing municipal corporation—a city government following a corporate management model. Since 1994
that model has been driven by the Sterling Criteria. Coral Springs is a centrally
planned community, incorporated in July 1963. The city is 23 square miles and
has 132,611 residents. It is one of only two centrally planned communities in the
nation that has achieved residential build-out. There are a wide range of housing types, as well as retail and commercial properties, and a corporate park.
Unlike most South Florida cities, Coral Springs is a city of young families; 48%
of the households have children under the age of 18. The principal reasons
families move to Coral Springs are the reputation of the public schools, the low
crime rate, and the diverse recreational facilities and opportunities.

The city has 789 full-time and part-time employees and a net budget for fis-

- Recipient of Florida Governor Sterling Award for Organizational
  Excellence (based on Malcolm Baldrige Criteria)
- Recipient of APQC Best Practice Partner Award

* Portions of this case are adapted from "Performance Measurement in the Public Sector,"
APQC (November 2005), Governors Sterling Application 2003, and internal documents. The
author would like to thank Kevin Knutson, Director of Communications and Marketing (formerly Budget and Strategic Planning Manager during Sterling Award period), and Chelsea
Stahl, Performance Measurement Analyst, for their contributions to this case.

BEST PRACTICE HIGHLIGHTS

Principle 1 Establish and Deploy a CPM Office and Officer

- *Executive Sponsorship.* Established CPM central oversight by the Management and Budget Office for CPM efforts.
- *Organizational Level and Reporting Relationship.* The process was also supported by the Senior Assistant City Manager and Organizational Development Manager, who works in Human Resources. It would be fair to say that it is a permanent cross-functional task team that implements CPM, of which the Budget and Strategic Planning Manager was the team leader.
- *CPM Office Staff.* Department staffed with experienced personnel with deep understanding of government and community.
- *Collaborative Maturity.* Department displayed a mature, collaborative approach and partnered across the organization.
- *Ability to Learn.* CPM employees demonstrated a willingness and ability to learn continuously.

cal year 2006 of $122 million. The city's core services include public safety, streets and utilities, building safety, parks, aesthetics, support services, charter schools, and a center for the arts.

CPM Office and Executive Oversight

Four city commissioners and a mayor, elected at large by the residents, establish city priorities and policies. They are the city's "board of directors." The city manager, with the senior management team, directs staff in the implementation of commission policies and manages city operations. The city manager functions as the CEO of the city. The directors of 13 city departments form the senior management team. Twenty-six citizen advisory committees are highly involved in city government, providing input on customer priorities and requirements and playing a significant role in decision making and operations. The city delivers direct services through seven departments and two "wholly owned" subsidiaries. Another six departments provide specialized support. All Coral Springs service delivery systems have three distinguishing characteristics.

1. Departments are very flat; there is a short chain of command. This promotes short cycle times and employee empowerment.
2. The focus is on the customer, which means accessible services, provided by pleasant, helpful staff.
3. Customers are part of delivery systems, as partners, as volunteers, on advisory committees, even running sports leagues and special events.

The APQC project was hosted by the management and budget office. This office functions as the city's CPM Office by facilitating the annual strategic planning processes and ongoing performance management (which are discussed in depth in later chapters).

> *If a job is worth doing it is worth doing well.*
> —PROVERB

TENNESSEE VALLEY AUTHORITY: BEST PRACTICE CASE*

Tennessee Valley Authority (TVA) is the nation's largest public power producer. Wholly owned by the U.S. government, TVA was established by Congress in 1933 primarily to provide navigation, flood control, and agricultural and industrial development and to promote the use of electric power in the seven-state Tennessee Valley region.

Through 158 public power utilities, TVA supplies electricity to 8.6 million people in its seven-state service territory. Along with affordable, reliable power, TVA delivers value to the regional economy by supporting a thriving river system and promoting economic growth.

The original purpose of TVA was to prevent flooding on the Tennessee River, and it built a system of multipurpose dams to control flooding, generate electricity for economic development, and provide for navigation. While the organization did not begin as strictly a utility company, the utility component of its services now predominates. For the past 72 years, TVA has been governed by a three-member full-time board of directors appointed by the President of the United States and confirmed by Congress. During their nine-year terms, the directors fulfill the role of a chief executive officer.

In 2004 the TVA Act was reopened and the governance structure changed to better prepare the organization for the competitive environment of deregulation.

- Recipient of APQC Best Practice Partner Award
- Recipient of the Balanced Scorecard Hall of Fame Award

* We acknowledge the fine contributions made by these dedicated TVA employees to this case study: Bill Kolz, Senior Program Manager, Performance Management Process, and Steve Saunders, General Manager of Benchmarking and Industry Analysis. Portions of this case are adapted from "Performance Measurement in the Public Sector," *APQC* (November 2005) and internal company documents.

TVA is now transitioning to governance by a nine-member board, of which one of the members will be selected as chairperson. Seven of the board members must come from the states in the Tennessee Valley region. Members of the board continue to be appointed by the President and confirmed by Congress; they serve a five-year term. Under the new governance structure, the board will hire a chief executive officer. TVA currently has a full-time president/chief operating officer.

TVA receives no federal funding but generates income through the sale of electricity. Its electrical rates are significantly below the national average, so it should be well prepared for a deregulated environment. TVA has a net dependable capacity of 33,189 megawatts and uses an array of fuel sources, including fossil, nuclear, hydro, combustion turbine, solar wind, and methane. The organization generates more than $7.5 billion in annual revenue; it serves 158 local utilities, 62 large industries, and federal installations through a network of 17,000 miles of transmission lines.

TVA performs in its area like the federal government performs in other areas. It maintains 800 miles of commercially navigable waterways and 49 dams for integrated river management. TVA is responsible for avoiding $211 million in flood damage annually; however, in flood-prone years, such as 2004, the amount of avoided costs skyrockets. TVA manages 11,000 miles of public shoreline, a large part of which is set aside for recreation. TVA does not pay federal taxes, but it does pay the states that it serves $338 million annually in tax-equivalent payments, and it pays $1.3 billion in total annual employee compensation. It provides about $20 million annually for economic development loan commitments to valley businesses and invests seed money into valley companies so that the investment is multiplied as the new companies succeed and grow.

CPM Office and Executive Oversight

TVA's performance management process is named "Winning Performance." The initiative began with the organization asking "Can we improve the overall performance of the company if we improve the quality of decision making?" The answer is "yes" if each employee (1) understands the direction in which TVA is moving, (2) shares the same sets of priorities, and (3) understands how he or she aligns to those priorities. Bill Kolz, the senior program manager for the Winning Performance program, believes that, although the three concepts are simple to express, they are difficult to implement, especially in a workforce spread across seven states.

Winning Performance is designed to create the context and content of the business environment, articulate a compelling case for action, and motivate the workforce to make the necessary decisions and take the appropriate actions to drive TVA forward. A TVA-wide team incentive compensation plan is a key component of the Winning Performance process.

The Winning Performance concept originated from a corporate-wide reengineering initiative that was centered primarily around five broad areas: (1) operational excellence, (2) support processes, (3) customer relationship management, (4) workforce management, and (5) performance management (the area in which Winning Performance would ultimately reside).

A "Performance Management, Phase I" final report was issued. TVA's executive committee reviewed and approved the report and its recommendation that the performance management redesign team develop a "scorecard" approach to performance management. Although the charter strongly recommended a scorecard, the redesign team thought the scorecard concept was too prescriptive. After it spent time and resources exploring other methods of measurement, it returned to the idea of the Balance Scorecard. The scorecard became a feature of the performance management system, and (although it began as a small part of the vast effort) it evolved into a key aspect of the program.

TVA is a process-oriented organization. In the early 1990s it adopted the total quality management (TQM) approach, so the redesign team knew it had to outline an end-to-end process for performance management—and it focused on that goal above all others. The team developed a four-step methodology for the process.

Step 1. Articulate the strategic direction of the company.
Step 2. Establish a common set of priorities that manifest this direction.
Step 3. Identify the means to accomplish these priorities.
Step 4. Demonstrate how all employees align and contribute to overall company success.

BEST PRACTICE HIGHLIGHTS

Principle 1: Establish and Deploy CPM Office and Officer

- *Executive Sponsorship.* TVA provided executive sponsorship for the BSC/CPM Office.
- *Organizational Level and Reporting Relationship.* The Balance Scorecard program office reported one level below the COO. CPM established centralized CPM oversight with senior employees.
- *CPM Office Staff.* The department was staffed with experienced personnel with deep understanding of TVA organization.
- *Leadership and Ability to Influence.* The CPM team demonstrated leadership and the ability to influence program design as the Balance Scorecard was cascaded through the organization.
- *Collaborative Maturity.* Department displayed a mature, collaborative approach and partnered across the organization.
- *Ability to Learn.* CPM Office employees demonstrated a willingness and ability to learn continuously.

EXHIBIT 4.2   Winning Performance Management Structure

Accountable Office	Responsibilities
Board of Directors	• Establish strategic direction for TVA. • Authorize overall approach to performance management and related incentives. • Approve the Winning Performance budget that funds the incentive plan. • Approve annual scorecards, performance measures, and targets.
Winning Performance Executive Sponsor The original president/COO served as the sponsor when the program began. He has recently retired, and TVA is working out details of succession and who will fill this role in the future.	• Formulate strategies to address financial and operational performance. • Set performance expectations to support strategic direction. • Engage key stakeholders to ensure active participation, commitment, and support. • Communicate with, visibly support, and motivate executive management. • Mediate strategic priorities among board, executive management, and stakeholders.
Core Team The core team was created to push the program forward. Not only was Winning Performance sponsored at the highest level, it was composed of executive management: the executive vice president of human resources, the senior vice president of strategic planning, the senior vice president of marketing, the senior vice president of economic development, the vice president controller, and the advisor to the president.	• Translate strategies into quantifiable financial/operational objectives and measures. • Initiate achievement planning to address performance gaps and opportunities. • Ensure organizational commitments are aligned to key performance objectives. • Review Balanced Scorecards for equity, alignment, and consistency. • Authorize ongoing development of performance management program.
Vice President Responsible for Program Management	• Responsible for day-to-day program management and standardized deployment. • Responsible for negotiating timetables, milestones, and resources to support program-related initiatives. • Coordinates change management, business messages, and communications activities. • Ensures cross-organizational processes are integrated and support objectives. • Reports scorecard performance results and status tracking of actions. • Serves as core team chair.

The "key areas" identified in Step 3 are the components of the BSC. The redesign team realized that the performance management system (Winning Performance) required an "inclusionary" management infrastructure that promotes buy-in and teamwork across all organizations. Employees should be able to demonstrate a line of sight between company goals and their team/ individual activities. The team concentrated on developing a performance management system that emphasized ownership and accountability. Finally, the team determined how it would articulate a compelling case for change that would motivate the workforce to take the necessary actions. Many of TVA's business units operate in an autonomous environment, which makes the implementation of company-wide programs affecting all organizations even more challenging.

After the redesign team finished its work, the development of Winning Performance entered Phase II. During Phase II, the system continued to be supported by the highest level of TVA executives. (Exhibit 4.2 describes the Winning Performance management structure.)

> *Hard work never did anyone any harm.*
> —PROVERB

MEDRAD: BEST PRACTICE CASE*

Medrad's headquarters in Indianola, Pennsylvania, a small town near Pittsburgh, includes a facility housing administrative functions and the sterile disposables enterprise production unit. The electromechanical assembly enterprise and service operations reside in a nearby facility. The majority of Medrad's employees are located in these two facilities.

Medrad was a publicly traded company until October 1995, when it was purchased by and became a wholly owned subsidiary of Schering AG, a $5.6 billion German pharmaceutical company headquartered in Berlin. As

- Recipient of Malcolm Baldrige National Quality Award
- Recipient of the APQC Best Practice Award

* Special thanks to Rose Almon-Martin, Vice President of Performance Excellence and Marketing Services, for her input and insights into this case study. I would also like to thank Medrad for its unselfish sharing of customer surveying methods, techniques, and process contributions to my Crown Global Performance team to advance our program. Portions of this case were adapted from the MEDRAD Malcolm Baldrige National Quality Award Application, internal company documents, and employee input.

an independent subsidiary, Medrad provides its own business support functions. The president and chief executive officer of Medrad meet semiannually with the Medrad board of directors and annually with the board's executive committee.

Medrad develops, manufactures, markets, and services equipment and sterile disposable products that enable or enhance diagnostic and therapeutic medical imaging procedures. Medrad's products are sold to hospitals and medical imaging centers worldwide and are used in computed tomography and magnetic resonance procedures, as well as in cardiovascular imaging performed in angiography and cardiology. Medrad began in 1971 with the introduction of the first "flow-controlled" vascular injector, which improved pictures of the heart and blood vessels by precisely injecting the liquid contrast agents used for cardiovascular imaging. In 1986, and again in 1992, Medrad created new markets for vascular injection systems, first for CT applications and then for MR. In 1988, in cooperation with an original equipment manufacturer (OEM) partner, Medrad expanded into MR surface coils. Medrad's expertise in the design, manufacture, and sale of MR-compatible equipment led the company to expand into other MR accessory products in 2000.

CPM Office and Executive Oversight

Medrad's performance improvement efforts began with the formation of the President's Quality Council, now known as the Performance Excellence Team (PET), comprised of senior staff. In 1997 the senior leadership team began using a BSC featuring five corporate scorecard goals. The specific targets are reviewed each year at the beginning of portfolio planning. Medrad maintains an organizational focus on performance improvement by aligning the activities

---

BEST PRACTICE HIGHLIGHTS

Principle 1: Establish and Deploy a CPM Office and Officer
- *Executive Sponsorship.* Medrad sponsored CPM Office at a high level.
- *Organizational Level and Reporting Relationship.* Established centralized CPM oversight with senior employees
- *CPM Office Staff.* Department staffed with experienced personnel with deep understanding of strategic planning and Balance Scorecard
- *Collaborative Maturity.* Department displayed a mature, collaborative approach and partnered across the organization
- *Ability to Learn.* CPM Office employees demonstrated a willingness and ability to learn continuously

of functions, teams, and individuals with these corporate goals and the top 12 objectives.

The director of performance excellence (referred to as a CPM leader) reports directly to the CEO, is a member of the senior staff, and chairs the Performance Excellence committee.

A corporate Performance Excellence Center and productivity centers in selected departments provide resources for improvement initiatives and also look for opportunities to share best practices with other parts of the company. At the organizational level, Medrad has been using the Baldrige Criteria to assess and improve its management system, and has received three site visits. Medrad's senior management uses the Baldrige Criteria feedback report in the PET meetings where improvement initiatives are reviewed and selected.

> *A good beginning makes a good ending.*
> —PROVERB

SERONO: BEST PRACTICE CASE*

Serono is a 100-year-old biotechnology company based in Geneva, Switzerland. It is the largest biotechnology company in Europe and the third largest worldwide. Serono develops and markets specialized medicines in four therapeutic areas: (1) multiple sclerosis, (2) women's reproductive health, (3) growth hormone, and (4) psoriasis. Serono is one of the world's only fully integrated biotechnology companies, which means it covers the entire value chain from drug discovery and product development to manufacturing and sales to physicians. Serono has seven recombinant biotechnology products on the market and revenues of $2.5 billion. With a workforce of 4,900 employees spanning 45 countries, the company has a truly global presence.

In 1995 Ernesto Bertarelli, then deputy CEO, began to take over the reins of the company. Having recently graduated from Harvard Business School, he understood the need to formalize the company's strategy in order to take the company to the next level, which had been run as a family business since the early 1900s. The current CEO, Fabio Bertarelli, had more than 30 direct

• Recipient of the Balanced Scorecard Hall of Fame Award

---

* Special thanks is given to contributing author Lawrence Ganti, Corporate Director, Strategy Management, for his time and generous contributions to this case study.

reports and immersed himself in all aspects of the business. As the CEO and owner of the company, he held himself and himself only accountable for the company's success and failures. Ernesto knew that this leadership and management style would have to change in order to grow the company. He would need to hold others accountable and to delegate the management of the various aspects of the business to experts. It was his belief that in order to go from a $500 million company to a $1 billion company, he would have to make some significant changes. The organizational changes would take time, but the structure was clear in his mind. However, how would he change a culture that has been developed over decades?

Ernesto formalized a comprehensive company strategy for the first time in 1996. He began to reorganize the management structure by creating an executive management board, thereby slimming down the number of direct reports to 10. He held each of the members of the board accountable for their part of the business. In 1997 he introduced BSC to translate the company strategy into actionable objectives and to align the entire organization toward achieving a common vision and strategy. It was the BSC's ability as a tool to align the masses that really drew Ernesto to support it. His initial support was so strong that he advocated and spearheaded the implementation throughout the entire company, not just in a single business unit.

In 1998, to further strengthen the BSC as a management tool for performance management and alignment, it was linked to global compensation schemes. Soon after realizing the link to compensation, Serono began to connect the BSC to its budgeting and planning processes. Today the BSC continues to be a key management tool that links all aspects of planning, objective setting, and strategy formulation. Most important, the BSC enables Serono to ensure that everyone in its 45 regional offices across all functions are aligned toward going after the same objectives and goals.

The strong support of the CEO and executive management board has allowed Serono to continue to improve the BSC program year after year and continue to look for new ways to improve. Over the last six years, Serono has seen double-digit growth in total revenues and net income. The company launched a number of fully recombinant products; its flagship drug for multiple sclerosis, Rebif, reached blockbuster status; and it doubled revenues to $2.5 billion in five years.

CPM Office and CPM Officer

Serono's CEO has advocated additional responsibilities to strategic planning over the years to help achieve and manage the change and to ensure focus on strategic priorities. The head of strategic planning, who reports directly to the

CEO and serves on the executive management board, is also in charge of: internal audit, corporate quality assurance, risk management, compliance, the CEO office, strategic projects, performance management, and business reviews. These functions facilitate not only CPM change activities but also the monitoring of such activities and ensure tight focus on the strategic priorities and objectives. The office is led by Roland Baumann, Senior Executive Vice President, Head of Corporate Administration and Group Compliance Officer, who is responsible for these CPM office responsibilities:

- *Strategic planning.* Custodian of the process to formulate and update the strategy; ensure that strategy is at the center of the process.
- *Performance management.* Design and report on the BSC measures that describe and monitor the strategy.
- *Governance.* Custodian of the governance process that puts strategy at the center of the organization.
- *Compliance.* Manage and ensure the company is compliant with the necessary authorities and regulations in a value-adding manner.
- *Risk management.* Oversee and manage the enterprise risk management program.
- *Initiatives.* Identify and oversee management of strategic initiatives required to execute the strategy.
- *Alignment.* Ensure alignment with the strategy at all levels of the organization and with all core business processes (financial, commercial, human resources, research and development).
- *Reviews.* Work with senior management to continually shape the agenda for strategic review and learning.
- *Best practices.* Facilitate processes to identify and share best practice.
- *Awareness.* Create a comprehensive communication and education process focused on the strategy.

Lawrence Ganti, Corporate Director, Strategy Management, has been leading Serono's strategic Balanced Scorecard program and functions as the CPM officer. Ganti comments, "We have a very strong performance oriented culture. We use the Balanced Scorecard as the management tool which helps us to align global objectives and harness the power of the collective efforts across all functions." He participated in the APQC performance measurement project, Serono was a sponsoring organization.

Ganti offers this commentary: "We first implemented the balanced scorecard in 1997. Over the years, we have linked our BSC to compensation, then planning, and then budgeting. The entire organization is aligned to the BSC and people consider the BSC to be their marching orders from the CEO. As the communication of 'What the BSC is' has been some time ago, the CEO

Principle 1: Establish and Deploy a CPM Office and Officer
- *Executive Sponsorship.* Serono sponsored a CPM office at a high level.
- Serono established centralized CPM oversight with senior employees.
- *CPM Office Staff.* The department is staffed with experienced personnel with deep understanding of strategic planning and BSC.
- *Collaborative Maturity.* The department displayed a mature, collaborative approach and partnered across the organization.
- Serono established a virtual BSC community of over 20 champions.
- *Ability to Learn.* CPM office employees demonstrated a willingness and ability to learn continuously.

and executive board commissioned a benchmark of our Balanced Scorecard in early 2004 to better understand the internal perceptions and to see how we compare to our peers and best practitioners. Our benchmark uncovered some areas that we could further develop. The next two years entailed a comprehensive implementation program that included: enhanced communication, additional alignment, tie-ins to risk management, and a further development of our OSM (office of strategy management)."

Never put off until tomorrow what you can do today.
—PROVERB

LB FOSTER COMPANY: BEST PRACTICE CASE*

At LB Foster Company we have made great strides in our implementation of our Strategic Planning process. I have seen improved focus and results in the Company's performance since the inception of the program. Our challenge going forward is to drive the execution of the Strategic Plan through the Balanced Scorecard methodology. As our employees learn more about the integration and strong relationships between the two phases, I am convinced our benefits will only increase.

—President and CEO Stan Hasselbusch

* Special thanks is given to these employees who generously contributed their time and, more important, their ideas and helped author the LB Foster case study: John Kasel, Senior Vice President Operations and Manufacturing; Merry Brumbaugh, Vice President Tubular Products; Jeff Poholsky, CPM program leader; and Jack Klimp, General Manager, Georgetown, MA, Plant.

LB Foster has a very interesting history and realized early success by establishing the CPM office and deploying the BSC in concert with Lean manufacturing techniques. However, let us set the stage with a brief review of LB Foster's history. Lee B. Foster was just 20 years old when he founded the company that bears his name. Financed in 1902 with only a $2,500 loan from his father (which was repaid within six months), LB Foster Company grew over the next century to become a national leader in the manufacture, fabrication, and distribution of products related to surface transportation infrastructure.

Foster founded the company to fulfill a transportation need he first observed while growing up around his father's oil business in Titusville, Pennsylvania. Many inquiries came to his father's company from mines, logging camps, and quarries regarding the availability of relay (used) rail. Because no truck transportation existed at that time, rail spurs, both permanent and temporary, represented the only means for transporting heavy materials to and from the job site. New rails were cost prohibitive, so Foster initiated the practice of selling relay rail—taken from abandoned and replaced railroads and urban transportation systems—to meet this need.

What set LB Foster Company apart from others in those early years and contributed greatly to the firm's success was the Foster Guarantee: "If the material is not up to the standard represented, ship it back and we will pay the freight both ways." This dedication to customer satisfaction is a core company value, and the Foster Guarantee is still in force today. Lee Foster's success attracted the notice of his three brothers, Reuben, Sydney, and Byron, who all joined the company upon completion of their education and military service. The four brothers worked well together (Lee changed his sole proprietorship into a four-way partnership in 1918) and expanded the company into new markets and regions, opening offices in New York City in 1922 and Chicago in 1926.

The company, which became publicly traded in 1981 (Nasdaq: FSTR), continues to supply products for rail markets, offering a full line of new and relay rail, track work, and accessories to railroads, mines, and industry. Today LB Foster's core business shares focus with other products used in the construction of the nation's infrastructure including piling, fabricated products for bridges and highways precast concrete modules, and pipe-related products.

Lee B. Foster II, the founder's grandson, became president and chief executive officer of the company in 1990, providing a vital link between the company's past and present, expanding the firm's core competency, and developing new niche markets. Today, as chairman of the board, he remains a vital part of the team shaping the company's future. In 1999, the firm acquired CXT Inc., a leading manufacturer of engineered concrete products for the railroad and transit industries. The acquisition better positioned LB Foster Company to serve rail and transit customers with a sophisticated mix of products and services, delivering comprehensive project capabilities on even the largest undertakings.

The company's products have been incorporated into many well-known national projects, such as rail serving the Port of Los Angeles, materials for the Brooklyn Bridge rehabilitation, and transit fasteners installed on the transit system rebuilt under New York's World Trade Center. As the United States has grown, LB Foster Company has grown as well, providing the products necessary to build the nation's infrastructure. And as that infrastructure continues to expand and require maintenance, LB Foster will be there with the products and services to keep it strong and vital.

LB Foster and the CPM Office and CPM Executive

In 2004 Lee B. Foster II and Stan L. Hasselbusch learned about the CPM-related successes of Crown Castle International, J.D. Irving, and several other companies through their adoption and use of the BSC.

The executive management team (EMT) consisted of:

Lee Foster	Chairman of the Board
Stan Hasselbusch	President and CEO
Merry Brumbaugh	Vice President, Tubular Products
Sam Fisher	Senior Vice President, Rail Products
Don Foster	Senior Vice President, Piling Products
John Kasel	Senior Vice President, Operations and Manufacturing (O&M)
Dave Russo	Senior Vice President, CFO, and Treasurer

Hasselbusch turned to a trusted senior employee, Jeff Poholsky, who had been leading the strategic planning process, to establish a CPM function to launch the company's BSC program. Poholsky possessed significant company knowledge and an extensive personal company network based on his successful 18 years of experience with LB Foster. Poholsky partnered with fellow executive John Kasel, considered a leading expert in Six Sigma and Lean manufacturing techniques, previously from Toyota. Poholsky also facilitated the first company customer survey and identified many opportunities for improvement. The integration of the BSC, customer surveys, and Lean process improvement will be covered in Chapter 7. Corporate CFO David Russo played a vital role in the development of the finance perspective of the Strategy Map and BSC. The rest of the EMT included the four product leaders of concrete, tubular, rail, and piling. These four leaders presiding over eight product lines drove company financial results.

CEO Hasselbusch directed the CPM Office (partnered with the Senior

Principle 1: Establish and Deploy a CPM Office and Officer

- *Executive Sponsorship.* CEO or direct report actively sponsors the CPM Office and CPM projects for a sustained period and with the right visibility to enable maturity to processes state.
- *Organizational Level and Reporting Relationship.* The CPM Office executive reports to the CEO.
- *The CPM Office,* consisting of Jeff Poholsky, partners closely with the senior VP Operations and Manufacturing, the director of marketing, and a virtual team of BSC champions in the four product groups.
- *CPM Office.* Jeff Poholsky and John Kasel are able to organize large-scale virtual teams to drive results in one of more CPM methods.
- *Leadership, Influence Factors.* Jeff Poholsky, responsible for the BSC program, and John Kasel, senior VP responsible for the Lean program, substantially influence a portfolio of CPM processes enterprise-wide, with each practitioner possessing deep expertise in his respective methodologies.
- *CPM, Industry, and Company Knowledge.* Poholsky has deep industry and company-specific knowledge including a large personal network to help guide resolution of project issues.
- *Collaborative Maturity.* Poholskyis experienced in working horizontally and vertically through the organization.
- *Ability to Learn.* The team is open to new ideas, methods, and approaches; they are able to streamline, integrate, and adapt methods, and to think concurrently.

Vice President O&M) to deploy a strategic planning process, rapidly develop and cascade the BSC three to four levels deep in the organization, establish a customer survey process, and deploy Lean improvement programs in company plants across the United States. These core CPM processes are discussed in depth in Chapter 7.

> *How you look at a situation is very important, for how you think about a problem may defeat you before you ever do anything about it. When you get discouraged or depressed, try changing your attitude from negative to positive and see how life can change for you. Remember, your attitude toward a situation can help you to change it—you create the very atmosphere for defeat or victory.*
> —FRANCO HARRIS, IMMACULATE RECEPTION STEELER LEGEND

FLORIDA DEPARTMENT OF HEALTH: BEST PRACTICE CASE*

Florida Department of Health (FDOH) is a large state public health agency that operates under the leadership of the secretary, who is also Florida's chief health officer. The FDOH can be characterized by responsiveness to a rapidly changing health and societal landscape, demands for increased accountability for public agencies, rapid technological and medical advances, escalating healthcare costs, managed care, privatization, and terrorism threats. The department maintains a readiness to address new and resurfacing health problems, diseases, and disaster management issues. FDOH is publicly funded and operates in a highly regulatory environment. While the department is accountable to citizens and taxpayers of Florida, its representation is formally heard through the voice of the legislature. The department employs approximately 16,700 people throughout the state, and its 2004–05 budget was approximately $2.2 billion.

The FDOH mission is "to promote and protect the health and safety of all people in Florida through the delivery of quality public health services and the promotion of health care standards." Its vision: "By providing quality services and promoting healthy communities, we are valued by those we serve and our partners as the leading public health organization in the nation." The FDOH is chiefly concerned with prevention through population-based community medicine. Some of the major responsibilities of the FDOH are:

- Prevent and treat infectious diseases of public health significance
- Provide a coordinated system of care for children with special healthcare needs though our children's medical services
- Monitor and regulate activities to prevent diseases of environmental origin
- Improve access to basic preventive, acute, and chronic disease healthcare for children and adults who have difficulty obtaining this care
- Evaluate, license, and discipline healthcare practitioners

- Miami-Dade County Health Department Recipient of Governors Sterling (Baldrige) Award 2002 and 2006
- Department of Health Recipient of APQC Best Practice Partner Award

* Special thanks is given to the Florida Department of Health: Donna Marshall, Performance Management Director, Office of Performance Improvement; and Laura Reeves, Performance Consultant Team Leader, Office of Performance Improvement, for their case study input. Portions of this case are derived from "Performance Measurement in the Public Sector," *APQC* (November 2005), Governors Sterling Applications 2002 and 2006, and internal documents.

- Prevent and reduce tobacco use within communities
- Ensure emergency medical service providers, personnel, and trauma centers meet standards of care
- Place healthcare providers in medically underserved areas
- Provide accurate, timely, and cost effective medical disability and medically needy determinations

CPM Office and Executive Oversight

FDOH visionary leaders have promoted organizational performance and quality improvement as a top priority. The FDOH has developed systems that help focus on improvement of organizational performance and of key processes, and evaluation. The FDOH CPM Office consists of two offices with clear roles and these responsibilities.

The Office of Planning, Evaluation, and Data Analysis is essential for assuring that FDOH is a data-driven organization and does so through these responsibilities:

- Collects, reports, and analyzes core health statistical information
- Registers, compiles, stores, and preserves all vital records within the state
- Coordinates local community health assessment and health improvement planning initiatives using standardized methods such as MAPP (mobilizing for action through planning and partnerships, a strategic approach to continuous improvement) and various tools
- Coordinates the collection, reporting, and analysis of local county health department client and activity information
- Coordinates health data reporting systems to assure optimum program integration and compliance with state, federal, and local reporting requirements
- Develops and implements FDOH's performance measurement system
- Coordinates strategic planning and long-range program plan

The Office of Performance Improvement is essential for ensuring that data and information is utilized on a continuous basis to drive performance improvement and does so through these responsibilities:

- Initiates and implements a department-wide performance management system
- Provides consultation and linkages to performance management resources for both individual and organizational improvement
- Supports design, development, deployment, and evaluation of statewide education and training opportunities
- Provides the department with marketing and graphic services including graphic design and production

Principle 1: Establish and Deploy a CPM Office and Officer

- *Executive Sponsorship.* Established CPM function at senior level in the organization.
- *Leadership and Ability to Influence.* CPM function provided governance and direction to the rest of the organization.
- *CPM Office Staff.* Department staffed with experienced personnel with deep understanding of performance improvement.
- *Collaborative Maturity.* Department displayed a mature, collaborative approach and partnered across the organization.
- *Ability to Learn.* CPM employees demonstrated a willingness and ability to learn continuously.

Staff members in both offices provide consultation to staff throughout the organization to help ensure the department is providing quality public health services.

> *The only correct actions are those that demand no explanation and no apology.*
> —RED AUERBACH

AMERICAN RED CROSS: BEST PRACTICE CASE*

The American Red Cross was founded in 1881 by Clara Barton based on concepts espoused by Henry Dunant, a Swiss national instrumental in the creation of the International Red Cross movement. The American Red Cross was chartered by the U.S. Congress to serve the American people in war and

- Recipient of APQC Best Practice Partner Award

* Special thanks goes to these dedicated American Red Cross management team members for their gracious support and knowledge: Rod Tolbert, Director, reporting and monitoring, chapter quality assurance; Kevin Hans, Manager, knowledge and innovation, chapter quality assurance; and Steve Stegeman, Senior Director, strategic planning and analysis, corporate strategy. Portions of this case were adapted from the APQC Best Practice in Government Performance Management Consortia Project, "Performance Measurement in the Public Sector," *APQC* (November 2005), and internal documents.

peace (during times of disaster and national calamity). While it is not a governmental agency, the American Red Cross works closely in partnership with the local, state, and federal branches of government. It is a 501(c)3 charitable organization that has its headquarters in Washington, D.C., and service locations throughout the world. The American Red Cross is governed by a 50-member volunteer board of governors. Some members of the board are appointed by the President of the United States; others are nominated at-large and from within Red Cross chapters.

The American Red Cross is the largest humanitarian aid organization in the nation and assists millions of people each year. Eleven million people learn Red Cross safety-preparedness and life-saving skills annually. In addition, the organization collects, processes, and distributes nearly half the nation's blood supply. The American Red Cross has an annual operating budget of $3.4 billion.

The mission statement of the organization reads: "The American Red Cross, a humanitarian organization led by volunteers and guided by its Congressional Charter and the Fundamental Principles of the International Red Cross Movement, has the mission of providing relief to victims of disasters and helping people prevent, prepare for, and respond to emergencies." This mission statement was confirmed in 2003 during an organizational strategic planning process. The strategic planning process has also resulted in the articulation of the American Red Cross strategic direction:

- Be America's partner and a leader in mobilizing communities to help people prevent, prepare for, and respond to disasters and other life-threatening emergencies.
- Inspire a new generation of volunteers and supporters to enrich our traditional base of support.
- Strengthen our financial base, infrastructure, and support systems to continuously improve our service delivery system.

CPM Office and Executive Oversight

The American Red Cross's CPM program was sponsored by the highest-level executive, the executive vice president, and approved by the board of governors. The CPM program was initiated and positioned at headquarters' location to provide centralized governance to a distributed design team including vital field organization input. The core CPM team consisted of highly trained and experienced personnel including Steve Stegeman, Senior Director, Strategic Planning and Analysis and Corporate Strategy; Rod Tolbert, Director, Reporting and Monitoring, Chapter Quality Assurance; and Kevin Hans, Manager, Knowledge and Innovation, Chapter Quality Assurance. Both top management and chapter support was essential. According to Stegeman, "This was drastic enough change for our organization that we needed that [high] level of governance sponsorship and field support."

The organization's chapter network, consisting of more than 850 chapters located across the nation and in territories and protectorates, forms the foundation for the performance management system. Chapters vary from small, all-volunteer units to large, complex operations such as the Greater New York chapter. A key challenge was to develop a performance management system that is equally effective in both small and large chapters. The network of chapters employs approximately 13,000 paid staff who support the work of more than 875,000 volunteers.

Chapters are managed by an executive director/CEO who is accountable to a local board of directors and to a service area executive. The executive director is responsible for operations, fundraising, and service delivery in his or her chapter. The nation has been segmented into eight service areas; service area personnel provide guidance, support, and oversight to their chapters and have a direct reporting relationship to the national headquarters.

In July 2004, the American Red Cross launched the Chapter Performance Standards system to meet several needs that were converging at that time. The case for change resulted from the desire to:

- Integrate and improve on performance management activities using a single consistent system.
- Align performance activities with the newly launched strategic plan so that the actions of headquarters, chapters, and individual contributors would be aligned and appropriate to the mission of the organization.
- Achieve buy-in from stakeholders that measurement and organizational attention was properly focused.

Earlier July 2003 was a particularly appropriate time for designing, developing, and implementing the Chapter Performance Standards system because the second five-year cycle of rechartering had come to an end in June 2003. Both the national board of governors and management recommended a performance management system review before the next cycle was launched. Management believed that the new system could not be fully successful unless employees and volunteers were engaged at all stages of the development process. "Engagement" not only supported the design of the best performance management system possible; it also ensured greater acceptance of the system when ultimately launched. The design team included respected individuals from both the staff and the volunteer workforce representing both the chapters and national headquarters.

The 13-member design team met during the summer and fall of 2003 to define the system's standards and processes. Additional staff resources at the

BEST PRACTICE HIGHLIGHTS

Principle 1: Establish and Deploy CPM Office and Officer
- *Executive Sponsorship.* Established CPM central oversight with senior employees.
- *CPM Office Staff.* Department staffed with experienced personnel with deep understanding of quality and American Red Cross organization.
- *Collaborative Maturity.* Department displayed a mature, collaborative approach and partnered across the organization.
- *Ability to Learn.* CPM employees demonstrated a willingness and ability to learn continuously.

national headquarters worked to support the team. To make the decisions, team members studied internal research, input from the field, and the evaluation of performance management in other organizations. The team constantly solicited employee input in order to enhance the design and build constituent buy-in.

Management sponsorship came from the executive vice president of programs and services, then the highest-ranking official in the chapter organization. The effort became one of the organization's strategic projects, which afforded the effort greater access to resources and also heightened management oversight. National headquarters units manage and support the overall performance evaluation system by:

- Compiling overall performance data
- Conducting organization-wide analyses of performance
- Developing and refining the policies, procedures, tools, training, and communications
- Providing guidance on the development of performance plans
- Ensuring strategic alignment
- Ensuring annual evaluation of the system.

The national headquarters is institutionalizing the belief that the 47 standards can be replaced or eliminated if they are no longer relevant to the strategy or if the chapters are doing so well in the area that the standard no longer needs to be measured. Chapters 4 and 5 will describe a sample of these 47 standards. The Chapter Performance Standards system was approved by the board of governors in February 2004.

A bird doesn't sing because it has an answer, it sings because it has a song.
—LOU HOLTZ

BRONSON METHODIST HOSPITAL: BEST PRACTICE CASE*

Bronson Methodist Hospital is a nonprofit medical center, providing in-patient and outpatient care from a 28-acre urban campus in downtown Kalamazoo, Michigan. Established in 1900, Bronson is a 343-bed state-of-the-art, all–private room facility designed as a peaceful, healing environment. The hospital is the flagship organization in the Bronson Healthcare Group. Bronson's 3,200 employees and 780 medical staff manage more than 77,000 emergency visits and 21,000 admitted patients each year while generating $751 million in gross patient revenues.

Bronson provides care in virtually every specialty to approximately 1 million residents in a nine-county region of southwest Michigan: cardiology (Heart Hospital at Bronson), general surgical services, orthopedics, neurosciences, obstetrics (The Bronson Birthplace), pediatrics (The Children's Hospital at Bronson), and adult critical care services. As a tertiary care center, Bronson includes a Level I trauma center, a high-risk pregnancy center, a pediatric intensive care unit (PICU), a Level III neonatal intensive care unit (NICU), the region's only accredited Chest Pain Center, and a primary stroke center certified by the Joint Commission on Accreditation for Healthcare Organizations.

The Bronson culture is built on a focus and passion for excellence. The hospital's purpose and reason for existence is stated in its mission to "provide

- Malcolm Baldrige National Quality Award
- Michigan Quality Leadership Award (2001, 2005)
- 100 Top Hospitals Award
- Governor's Award of Excellence for Improving Care in the Hospital Setting (2004, 2005
- Governor's Award of Excellence for Improving Preventive Care in the Ambulatory Care Setting
- *Fortune* magazine's "100 Best Companies to Work For" (2004, 2005, 2006)
- *Working Mother's* "100 Best Companies for Working Mothers" (2003, 2004, 2005)
- VHA Leadership Award for Operational Excellence (2005, 2006)

* We acknowledge the fine content and editorial contributions made by Michele Serbenski, Executive Director, Corporate Effectiveness and Customer Satisfaction Bronson, Healthcare Group and contributing author to this case study.

excellent healthcare services." This statement reflects what Bronson does and why it exists. The mission, values, commitment to patient care excellence, and philosophy of nursing excellence provide the foundation that supports the organizational strategy, which is illustrated in the vision to "be a national leader in healthcare quality" and the three Cs of corporate strategies (see Exhibit 4.3):

1. Clinical Excellence (CE)
2. Customer and Service Excellence (CASE)
3. Corporate Effectiveness (CORE)

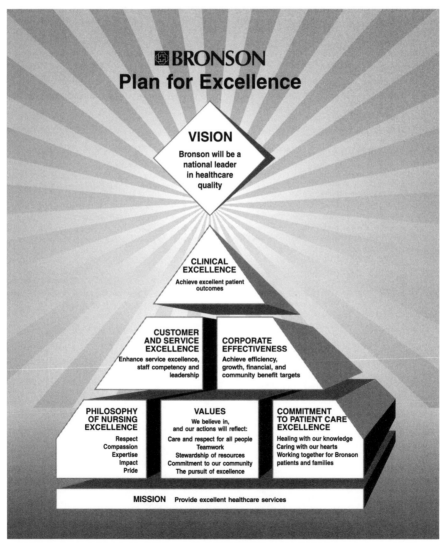

EXHIBIT 4.3   Plan for Excellence

Excellence is the thread that ties together the vision, mission, values, commitment to patient care excellence, philosophy of nursing excellence, and overall strategies. These elements, which comprise the Plan for Excellence (see Exhibit 4.4), form the culture and guide decision making.

All employees are trained and held accountable to follow the Customer Service Standards and Expectations. This statement, a supportive element in the

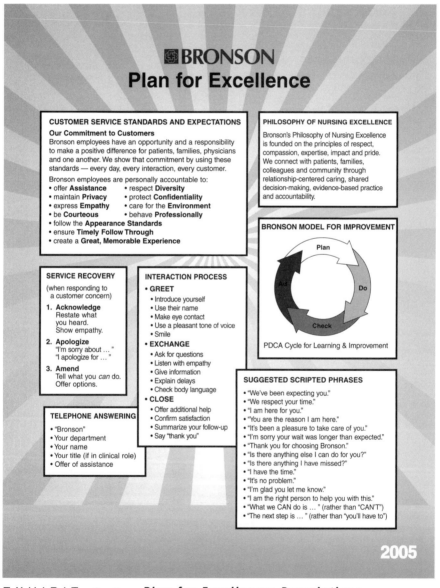

EXHIBIT 4.4   Plan for Excellence: Descriptions

Plan for Excellence, outlines the personal accountability that every staff member has every day, with every interaction, with every customer. The Customer Service Standards and Expectations, along with service recovery, the interaction process, and scripting, give staff the tools they need to meet patient requirements and expectations. Since the mid-1990s, the hospital has been on a journey in pursuit of workplace excellence, aiming to be the employer of choice in the region. As a top employer, Bronson is able to attract the best and brightest employees to care for its patients. With a primarily female workforce, Bronson has developed creative strategies to address the unique needs of working women. This commitment to workplace excellence, and providing work/life balance, has resulted in being named to the list of "100 Best Companies for Working Mothers" by *Working Mother* magazine and *Fortune*'s "100 Best Companies to Work For" for the past three consecutive years. There are no employees represented by labor organizations. Bronson values the over 400 community members who served as volunteers in 2005, providing more than 48,000 hours in 32 different service areas as helping hands to the workforce and patients.

CPM Office and Executive Oversight

Bronson's commitment to excellence begins with the visionary leadership provided by President and CEO Frank J. Sardone. "Continuously raise the bar" is Sardone's leadership mantra and a concept that has moved Bronson steadily forward in achievement of its vision to be a national leader in healthcare quality. In 1999, Sardone and his executive team adopted the Baldrige criteria as a framework for effectively running the Bronson business. As Executive Director, Corporate Effectiveness and Customer Satisfaction and a trained Baldrige examiner, Michele Serbenski assists the executive team to follow the principles of the Baldrige criteria in all of their leadership processes. This position functions as the CPM Officer within Bronson.

Serbenski is a member of the Bronson executive team reporting to the executive vice president/chief operating officer, a direct report to the CEO. She works collaboratively with the entire executive team to implement the necessary change programs throughout the organization. Bronson's organizational structure includes three strategic oversight teams, each chaired by a member of the executive team. Serbenski chairs the Customer and Service Excellence team. These teams are responsible for oversight and achievement of the organization's strategic plan and specifically the annual goals of the corporate strategies or three Cs. Bronson's focus for improvement is driven by the areas identified through the continuous planning process in the Strategic Management Model. To assist the organization in the use of its improvement model, Plan-Do-Check-Act (PDCA), Bronson has five dedicated project coordinators who lead and facilitate team-based improvements.

BEST PRACTICE HIGHLIGHTS

Principle 1: Establish and Deploy CPM Office and Officer

- *Executive Sponsorship.* BMH sponsored the CPM Officer at a high level.
- *Organizational Level and Reporting Relationship.* CPM Office executive reports to a CEO direct report.
- *CPM Office Staff.* Small senior team (three to eight personnel) experienced in change programs, full time roles.
- *Leadership, Influence Factors.* Able to organize large-scale virtual teams to drive results in one of more CPM methods (PDCA).
- *Leadership, Influence Factors.* Established centralized CPM oversight with senior executives.
- *Collaborative Maturity.* Executive team owns the Strategic Management Model (SMM) process enterprise-wide.
- *Collaborative Maturity.* Project coordinators display a mature, collaborative approach and partnered across the organization.
- Experienced in working horizontally and vertically through the organization.
- *Ability to Learn.* Project coordinators demonstrate a willingness and ability to learn continuously.
- *Ability to Learn.* Open to new ideas, methods, and approaches; ability to streamline, integrate, and adapt methods; think concurrently.

Setting a goal is not the main thing. It is deciding how you will go about achieving it and staying with that plan.

—TOM LANDRY

RICOH BEST PRACTICE: BEST PRACTICE CASE*

When an organization has a clear vision and strategy, employees are more likely to understand the rationale behind decisions and be able to link their work to broader organizational goals. People want to know what's expected of them in their jobs—the results they need to achieve and the knowledge, skills and abilities they must have to succeed.

—From Ricoh Balanced Scorecard Hall of Fame Application, 2005

* Special thanks goes to Edward A. Barrows, Jr., author of this case study. Acknowledgment is also given to the significant efforts of these Ricoh executives who aided in the development of this case: Katsumi "Kirk" Yoshida, President and Chief Executive Officer, Ricoh U.S.; Kuni Minakawa, Chief Financial Officer, Ricoh U.S.; Hede Nonaka, Vice President, Marketing, Ricoh U.S.; Robert Ingoglia, Vice President, Promotion and Communications, Ricoh U.S.; Dan Piccoli, Vice President of Quality and Business Excellence, Ricoh U.S.; and Marilyn Michaels, Director, Quality and Performance, Ricoh U.S.

- Recipient of Balanced Scorecard Hall of Fame Award
- Recipient of Deming Quality Award

Ricoh Corporation (Ricoh) is a company that has mastered the principles of high performance and the results tell the story. Over a three-year period (2001–04), as the company was starting to focus on adopting the best practice principles, Ricoh overall experienced a revenue increase of 8.7%. While this may seem modest, in the hypercompetitive document imaging market it is significant. During the same time frame, Ricoh's composite market share expanded from 17 to 25%, enabling the company to achieve market leadership with both black-and-white as well as color multifunctional products for all channels except the retail channel, where they do not compete. But perhaps the most significant statistic—certainly to anyone who measures success by the bottom line—came in the form of increased profitability. During the period under review the company's profit increased a whopping 175%. For a $3 billion sales organization, this performance is nothing short of outstanding. So how did they do it? How did they achieve the type of breakthrough performance that landed them in the Balanced Scorecard Hall of Fame? Quite simply by dedicating the entire organization to the implementation of the five CPM principles.

Founded in 1936, Japan-based Ricoh Company Limited has become one of the world's leading suppliers of office automation and electronic equipment. Revenues of Ricoh Corporation—the name for the responsible North and South American company—were approximately $3 billion (USD) at the end of 2005. Its integrated hardware and software products are designed to help businesses manage and share information more efficiently. Ricoh's products include black-and-white as well as color imaging systems, facsimile machines, printers, scanners, wide format, and digital duplicators.

Since the late 1990s, Ricoh has been working diligently to grow its presence in the United States. In 1995, Ricoh acquired two competitors within its industry: Savin Corporation and Gestetner, U.S.A. Both of these organizations, while under the direction of Ricoh, operated independently. In 2000, Ricoh acquired Lanier Worldwide, a global office automation product distribution organization. The U.S. operations of Lanier were also allowed to operate as a wholly owned subsidiary while the offices outside the U.S. were subsumed by the Ricoh Company Limited parent in the local country.

By 2001, Ricoh executives realized that in order to achieve the full benefit of the acquisitions, they would have to integrate all of the divisions with the corporate organization, thus creating one completely integrated organization. This would be no small undertaking, but they had little choice but to proceed with the project. They were finding it difficult to present one face to the market and were having challenges effectively managing customers. No doubt related, they were experiencing flattening profitability and were battling a host of internal coordination issues. One of the most pressing issues was effective communication of a consistent strategy across the domestic organization. The situation is perhaps best articulated by the Ricoh Corporation CFO, Kuni Minakawa. "Immediately following the acquisitions we were trying to communicate a consistent strategy across very different organizations. Some were global companies such as Lanier Worldwide while others were small, entrepreneurial firms like our dealers. Adding to the complexity was the mixture of the Japanese and American cultures. As you can imagine, this made our goal of establishing one strategy very, very difficult."

CPM Office and Executive, Ricoh embarked on a bold effort to consolidate the company while executing a growth strategy. This effort was called the "One Company/One System" initiative, and in many respects leaders were hoping to establish the springboard for future growth through this critically important project. While they did not realize it at the time, what Ricoh executives were doing was laying the foundation for the Strategy and Planning Office (SPO), their version of the Corporate Performance Management Office. Kuni Minakawa, CFO and member of the executive committee, tapped his team of business performance experts to begin the drive to develop and implement the BSC and associated improvement activities. Dan Piccoli—a 20-year veteran within the organization—was in the role of vice president of quality and business excellence and would be responsible for the overall One Company/One System program office. Working with him was Marilyn Michaels, Director, Performance Excellence, a seasoned veteran who had recently been hired from AT&T. Michaels brought not only deep business knowledge to her position, but she had also implemented a number of highly effective quality programs in her former corporate life. She would leverage this quality background to develop the BSC. Perhaps serendipitously, Ricoh assembled all of the elements of successful performance improvement under one roof: strategic planning, strategy execution, quality programs, customer evaluation, and process improvement. Each of these dimensions would be present on the journey toward improved performance. Today the SPO (see Exhibit 4.5) stands as an ongoing testament to the success of the company.

Michaels realized early on that implementing the different components of performance improvement would be easy in some respects but difficult in others. Ricoh, like many Japanese companies, had a long-standing history and commitment to quality and performance. As far back as 1971, the Japanese company instituted an organization-wide program to instill the principles of total quality control throughout the business. Shortly thereafter, in 1975, Ricoh was awarded the prestigious Deming prize not only on the basis of its

EXHIBIT 4.5   Strategic Planning Office (SPO) Activities

identification and application of successful quality methods but also for how well the entire company had embraced an overall commitment to quality production. The company went on to win the award again and in so doing became the only company to have won the coveted prize twice. Its quality performance continued to be recognized as recently as 1999, when Ricoh won the Japanese Quality Award. Today at Ricoh U.S., Baldrige criteria are used extensively throughout the enterprise as a way to identify opportunities for improvement. In terms of changing management practices, it seemed driving the measurement principles throughout the company would be relatively straightforward. More difficult would be the strategic management portion, the BSC development, and regional cascading of the strategy in particular. Michaels started her work by mobilizing key change agents throughout the enterprise. She knew that to be successful she had to start at the top.

After gaining support from the CEO, Katsumi "Kirk" Yoshida, she communicated personally with and then enlisted assistance from each of the key business unit leaders and their staff. Martin Brodigan, president and CEO of Ricoh Canada, joined the team as did Tom Salierno, president and CEO of Ricoh U.S. at the time. Yoshi Niimura, president and CEO of Ricoh Latin America, was added as was Nori Goto, president and CEO of Lanier Worldwide. In the words of Brodigan, "We see the Balanced Scorecard as providing a common language for our organization regarding priorities and as a means of making a culture shift to one that integrates excellence into every aspect of our business." Each leader then nominated respected managers from inside their geographic organizations to drive the effort's particulars.

Michaels had run enough performance improvement efforts to know that one of the factors that would contribute to success was adequate training and education for both the project team and key executives. Shortly after executive commitment was secured and the project team staffed, she brought in strategic management expert Ed Barrows to assist in both training their teams and helping translate their strategy from internal planning documents into the framework of the Strategy Map/BSC. Over the course of several weeks, initial training sessions were held with the corporate team as well as with representative project team members from each of the regional organizations. Teams were taught the basics of strategic management in conjunction with in-depth education regarding development, deployment, and management with Strategy Maps and BSCs. "You had the recipe for success from the start," Barrows noted. "Top managers and opinion leaders within their respective organizations committed many late nights and in no uncertain terms were dedicated to the success of the project."

By the end of 2001, the stage had been set for improvement in the organization with teams identified, mobilized, educated, and oriented on their task

BEST PRACTICE HIGHLIGHTS

Principle 1: Establish and Deploy CPM Office and Officer
- *Executive Sponsorship.* CEO actively sponsors CPM Office (called SPO) and CPM projects for sustained period and with the right visibility to enable maturity to processes state.
- *Organizational Level and Reporting Relationship.* CPM Office executive reports to a CEO direct report.
- *CPM Office Staff.* Small senior team experienced in change programs, full-time role in the CPM Office.
- *Leadership, Influence Factors.* Able to organize large-scale virtual teams to drive results in one of more CPM methods.
- *Ownership of CPM Processes and Methods.* The office owns or substantially influences the portfolio of CPM processes enterprise-wide, with each office CPM practitioner possessing deep expertise in several methods, in this case strategic planning, strategy execution, quality programs, customer evaluation, and process improvement.
- *CPM, Industry, and Company Knowledge.* One or more team members has deep industry and company-specific knowledge to help guide resolution of project issues.
- *Collaborative Maturity.* Experienced in working horizontally and vertically through the organization.
- *Ability to Learn.* Open to new ideas, methods, and approaches; ability to streamline, integrate, and adapt methods; think concurrently.

at hand. But they needed to know specifically what their charter would be. What would the strategy look like that would put them into the top spot domestically in the competitive world of document imaging?

> *A coach's greatest asset is his sense of responsibility—the reliance placed on him by his players.*
> —KNUTE ROCKNE

KEYCORP: BEST PRACTICE CASE*

Cleveland-based KeyCorp, whose roots date back to 1825, is one of the nation's largest bank-based financial services companies with assets of more than $93 billion. Today Key has two major lines of business: Key Community Bank (KCB) and Key National Banking (KNB). Key companies provide investment management, retail and commercial banking, consumer finance, and investment banking products and services to individuals and companies throughout the United States and, for certain businesses, internationally. Key has nearly 19,500 employees with more than 940 full-service branches in 13 states and maintains one of the largest ATM networks in the country.

Just five years ago, battered by stiffening competition, a weakening economy that exerted pressure on margins and its large loan portfolios, industry consolidation, along with a stringent regulatory environment, Key's performance placed it at the bottom of the 20-bank Standard & Poor's Regional Bank Index. Some people questioned the ability of the company to remain independent. Clients thought Key was just another bank—at best. Employees were disheartened by continual rumors of imminent takeover, and many had a bunker mentality resulting from a series of necessary but painful cost-reduction efforts. Investors saw Key as the company that routinely overpromised and underdelivered. Key's stock price had sunk in March 2000 to a low of $15.69.

Establishing CPM Officer Role

In February 2001, Henry Meyer took the reins as the new CEO. He was committed to not only turn the company around, but to transform it into "one of the nation's most admired financial institutions in the markets we serve." He

- Recipient of the Global Balanced Scorecard Hall of Fame Award

---

* We acknowledge the fine contributions made by Michele Seyranian, Executive Vice President & Senior Planning Manager, Strategic Planning Group.

defined Key's strategy to focus on customer intimacy to better understand and meet client needs, tailor offerings to meet those needs, and deliver distinctive service. He then charged his executive team with selecting a performance management system that could help KeyCorp execute its new strategy and focus employees on organizational goals. Having evaluated a number of performance management systems and philosophies, the management team determined that the BSC provided the most comprehensive and insightful tool for evaluating strategy execution.

By year-end, the executive team had adopted the BSC. During the first quarter of 2002, a small scorecard implementation team, sponsored by the CFO, worked with Key's executive team to design the corporate Strategy Map and scorecard. The team consisted of BSC champion and Senior Planning Manager Michele Seyranian, two business analysts, and an administrative assistant who acted as champions for the BSC across Key. The team was given the support and authority by Key's senior management to create champions in each of Key's lines of business and support areas to oversee the development and implementation of the BSC throughout the organization.

In a subtle but important transition, Key formally assigned Seyranian to facilitate and drive BSC implementation enterprise-wide. The shift from her being an initial project leader for the "corporate" map and scorecard project, to now being the executive accountable for the success of the BSC "enterprise-wide," is further evidence of Key's commitment to the BSC program's success. Her team consisted of a lean group of employees who were fast learners and possessed a deep understanding of the bank's inner workings, through both the formal and informal networks.

Seyranian undertook this new role and its largely expanded scope in stride. She fully understood it would require leveraging her internal network and launching a train-the-trainer model to multiply her team's talents. The value of her relationship-based network was realized in the cooperation secured from Key business leaders and in their readiness to adopt the BSC. How many major initiatives fail due to the failure to address change management considerations? Similarly, these same business leaders provided BSC champions to Seyranian's team to enable a successful train-the-trainer approach to gain traction for concurrent deployment (discussed more later).

Later that year, the BSC team cascaded the corporate Strategy Map and BSC to (at the time) Key's three group-level business units—first to Key Corporate and Investment Banking (KCIB; now Key National Banking), and then to Key Consumer Banking (KCB) and Key Investment Management Services (KIMS). The map and BSC were then cascaded throughout Key's 14 sub-business lines and support functions, including marketing, IT, risk management, and public affairs. Ultimately, 23 BSCs were created for business lines and staff groups. Over time, all salaried employees developed individual scorecards that aligned their daily activities to the perspectives on Key's corporate BSC.

The cascading process presented several challenges. According to Seyranian, managers initially disagreed over how to best define objectives, set targets, and collect measurement data. Moreover, many of them viewed the BSC as a "flavor of the month" initiative that would lack staying power. To gain managers' consensus and all employees' buy-in, it was important that the commitment to the BSC remain visible across the organization and that Henry Meyer and his executive management team did not waiver in their use of the BSC as a strategic management tool.

Thus Seyranian was able to mobilize this large-scale effort and continue the momentum her team started at the corporate level.

The BSC has become a strategic management tool to:

- Diagnose why Key's performance lagged its peers and determine how to improve it.
- Focus every employee's attention on shared goals.
- Unite a loose confederation of independent business lines into a "1Key" team.
- Align the work of staff areas with the needs of Key's lines of business.

BEST PRACTICE HIGHLIGHTS

Principle 1: Establish and Deploy a CPM Office and Officer

- *Executive Sponsorship.* CEO sponsors the CPM Office and CPM projects for a sustained period and with the right visibility to enable maturity to processes state.
- *Organizational Level and Reporting Relationship.* The CPM Office executive reports to the CEO direct report.
- *CPM Office Staff.* Small senior team experienced in change programs, full-time role in the CPM Office.
- *CPM, Industry, Company Knowledge.* Department staffed with experienced personnel with deep understanding of banking and the company.
- *Leadership, Influence Factors.* Able to organize large scale virtual team and drive results.
- *Collaborative Maturity.* The CPM team was experienced in working horizontally and vertically through the organization.
- *Collaborative Maturity.* Department displayed a mature, collaborative approach and partnered across the organization.
- *Ability to Learn.* CPM employees demonstrated a willingness and ability to learn continuously.

- Hold people accountable—both for what they accomplish and how they accomplish it.

The superior man blames himself. The inferior man blames others.
—DON SHULA

SPRINT NEXTEL: BEST PRACTICE CASE*

The Corporate SmartCard Management Office at Sprint Nextel would like to thank the scores of dedicated Sprint Nextel employees for their relentless drive for performance management and results. They also especially thank William G. Arendt, Senior Vice President and Controller; Atish Gude, Senior Vice President, Corporate Strategy; and Richard T.C. LeFave, Chief Information Officer, for their vision, encouragement, and support in continuously improving the company-wide Balanced Scorecard program.

Sprint Nextel Corp (NYSE: S) offers a comprehensive range of communications services bringing mobility to consumer, business, and government customers. Sprint Nextel is widely recognized for developing, engineering, and deploying innovative technologies, including two robust wireless networks offering industry-leading mobile data services; instant national and international walkie-talkie capabilities; and an award-winning and global Tier 1 Internet backbone.

Formed by the merger of Sprint and Nextel in August 2005, Sprint Nextel is a communications company that offers a broad choice of products and services, empowering its customers to conduct personal and professional business better, faster, simpler. The company's vision is to converge its unique wireless and wireline assets to create an entirely new suite of mobility products and services for customers, allowing them access to data and information how they want, when they want, and wherever they want. An overview of the company follows.

Annual Revenue (Pro Forma)	$44.1 billion (2005)
Sprint Nextel Wireless Service	47.6M wireless subscribers (2005)
Points of Distribution	20,000 stores and kiosks
Total Employees	Approximately 80,000 (2005)
Corporate Headquarters	Reston, VA
Operational Headquarters	Overland Park, KS

---

* The author would like to thank these individuals for their contributions to this case study and sharing their experiences at Sprint Nextel: William G. Arendt, Senior Vice President and Controller; Tolga E. Yaveroglu, Director, Corporate Strategy; Jenevieve Creary, Senior Manager, Corporate Strategy; and Chad Elliott, SmartCard Project Manager.

- *Forbes* magazine rated Sprint as as America's Best Managed Company in the Telecommunications Services category

Sprint Nextel met or exceeded key financial goals in 2005. In its first quarter of operations as a merged entity, the company led the industry in wireless subscriber growth, adding 2 million customers. Wireless data revenue increased 70% as the company remained the industry leader in wireless data. The company continues down the path to product and service leadership through innovative new services like the Sprint Music Store, which achieved 1 million downloads in less than four months in 2005, and formed a joint venture with four of the country's largest cable companies—with the potential to serve approximately 75 million homes with converged services including wireless and wireline communications, broadband Internet access, and video and entertainment.

CPM Office Description

The functions performed by a typical CPM Office were performed by the corporate strategy organizations (CSO) of both premerger Sprint and Nextel. Both had embraced and implemented the BSC as their CPM tool of choice. Within the premerger Nextel organization, for example, the BSC was sponsored by a cross-functional executive team in 2003 and embraced by the senior leaders as the tool to monitor the performance of the company against its strategic objectives. In fact, the BSC program was identified by the COO as one of the top-five company-wide strategic programs for 2004. The corporate balanced scorecard report was reviewed in a monthly executive strategic review meeting, and the corporate strategy was cascaded throughout several levels of the organization. Varying levels of success were achieved in the implementation of the CPM office activities as both organizations struggled with change management hurdles associated with implementing a performance management process.

Sprint and Nextel Merger

The merger of Sprint and Nextel was a merger of equals. This meant that the new company had to evaluate "where the work gets done" for each major function in both premerger companies; identify and agree on internal and external best practices; and be ready to start on August 2005 with a "clean slate" to implement those best practices. The CSO, for example, was modeled after the Kaplan/Norton Office of Strategic Management (OSM) strategic management roles. The organization owns strategic planning and development, the BSC program (known as the SmartCard), and overall strategy execution management. It does not own the financial planning and budgeting process but works closely with finance and business unit planning teams to execute that.

The CSO is comprised of a team of seasoned senior managers, directors, and a vice president, co-located in both the corporate headquarters in Reston and the operational headquarters in Overland Park. The CSO plays the role of the CPM Office. (See Exhibit 4.6.)

The CSO team members possess skill sets well aligned with the defined role of the CSO. They have deep industry and company-specific knowledge along with strong analytical backgrounds, useful in the formulation and refresh of strategy. In this newly merged organization, it was critical that team members from both premerger teams possess deep knowledge of their respective organizations to help the new team drive change. The expected challenges associated with the blending of two different cultures did surface, so team members had to be adaptable, open to new ideas, methods, and approaches, to enable the successful integration of both premerger organizations into one unified corporate strategy team. These were critical success factors in realizing the team's charter to define and present one cohesive, consistent voice on the strategic direction, the BSC methodology and terminology, and the new strategic plan to the new company.

Team members also possess strong project management skills to support managing planning deliverables and multiple stakeholders. They possess the unique ability to influence and manage vertically and horizontally in order to achieve the desired outcome in various efforts that reside outside of the CSO.

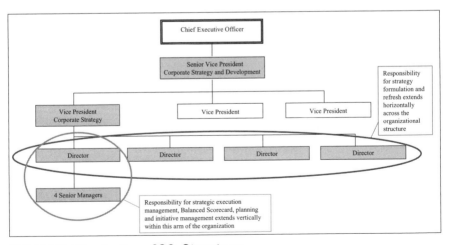

EXHIBIT 4.6   CSO Structure

Team members spend much of their time working with their peers across various organizations as well as with the senior executive team.

The team established relationships with various organizations to influence alignment with the new strategy and to foster its successful execution. For example, a virtual team—the Planning Council—with director-level representation from the planning organizations of the major functions across the new company, had a charter to ensure alignment with the corporate strategy, the strategic planning activities, and the implementation of the SmartCard framework. Beyond the Planning Council, other partnerships were also established with human resources to influence human capital and compensation alignment, with corporate communications to execute effective strategy communications, and with finance to ensure the alignment of the financial plan and budgets.

Much of the success of the CSO to date is attributable to the effective organization of these large-scale virtual teams to drive results. The Planning Council, for example, had the challenge of influencing and driving change in a postmerger organization comprised of 80,000 employees. Mergers are about change and come with a significant degree of uncertainty about the future. This associated uncertainty creates an environment where internal organizations and employees crave strategic direction, and it fosters a strong desire for

BEST PRACTICE HIGHLIGHTS

Principle 1: Establish and Deploy CPM Office and Officer

- *Executive Sponsorship.* The CPM office role is performed by the corporate strategy organization (CSO).
- *Organizational Level and Reporting Relationship.* The CSO is modeled after the Kaplan/Norton OSM strategic management roles. The CSO owns strategic planning and development, the BSC program, and overall strategy execution management.
- *Leadership, Influence Factors;* and *CPM, Industry, and Company Knowledge.* The CSO team members possess skill sets well aligned with supporting the role of the CPM Office. Key skills include: the ability manage vertically and horizontally; the ability to establish relationships across various organizations to influence strategic alignment; deep industry and company-specific knowledge; strong project management skills; and adaptability and flexibility.
- *Collaborative Maturity.* Much of the CSO's success to date is attributable to the work of virtual teams established to influence change. One success story revolves around the Planning Council—a virtual team comprised of planning directors from all of the major functions.

performance reporting against established milestones. These characteristics of the postmerger environment, along with the partnership approach (versus top-down approach) adopted by the CSO team, led to a very positive reception from the Planning Council. As the strategy was developed and socialized and the SmartCard methodology and terminology consistently defined, the Planning Council was encouraged to provide their input throughout. As a result, final decisions were embraced as the collective input of the team and resulting changes were therefore easier to implement.

> *I don't know if I practiced more than anybody, but I sure practiced enough. I still wonder if somebody—somewhere—was practicing more than me.*
> —LARRY BIRD

CHAPTER 5

Principle 2

REFRESH AND COMMUNICATE STRATEGY

> *Don't measure yourself by what you have accomplished, but by what you should have accomplished with your ability.*
> —JOHN WOODEN

This chapter covers several case studies focused on Principle 2, Refresh and Communicate Strategy best practices. Award-winning enterprises have refined and developed this core process and leveraged it as competitive advantage.

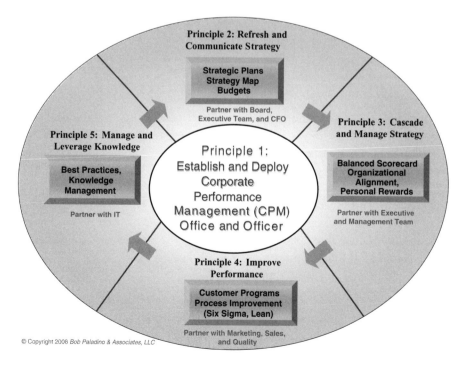

© Copyright 2006 Bob Paladino & Associates, LLC

EXHIBIT 5.1	Principle 2: Refresh and Communicate Strategy Best Practice Summary

Best Practice	Description
Strategic planning	Leverage the strategic planning process as either owner or partner to understand changing market conditions including competitor, supplier, rival, and potential entrants and substitutes in the marketplace.
Core and adjacent products and services	Define and determine core and adjacent products and services to focus on highest probabilities for success.
Strategic plan	Produce a comprehensive strategic plan.
Strategy mapping	Develop a strategy map containing objectives along four perspectives including financial, customer/constituent, process, and people. Observe strategy map design parameters of 20 to 25 objectives.
Link strategic planning and budgeting processes	Link strategic planning to the budgeting process, partner with finance to provide for a seamless continuum. Ideally, provide a rolling forecast or a flexible, lean budget linked to strategy.
Communications plan	Communicate strategy throughout the organization using a comprehensive communications plan.

The Crown case study will provide both the Crown-specific best practices and expand discussion on normative Principle 2 best practices learned from the collective companies researched. See Exhibit 5.1 for a summary of Principle 2 best practices.

Case study companies in this chapter also include recipients of these awards:

- U.S. President's National Malcolm Baldrige Quality Award
- Governor's Sterling Award for Excellence (based on Baldrige Criteria)
- Deming Quality Award
- American Quality and Productivity Center (APQC) Best Practice Partner Award
- Kaplan and Norton Global Balanced Scorecard Hall of Fame Award
- *Wall Street Journal* Ranked "Top 20 Most Improved Company in Shareholder Value Creation"
- *Fortune* "100 Best Companies to Work For"
- *Forbes* Best Managed Companies

Since a key aspect of the CPM methodology is the design and use of Kaplan and Norton's Strategy Map, we will review a case study previously published to provide foundational understanding of this effective tool. For those already familiar with Strategy Maps, feel free to move ahead to the Crown case study in this chapter.

> *You can observe a lot by just watching.*
> —YOGI BERRA

PARETO INC.: FOUNDATIONAL STRATEGY MAP CASE STUDY

The Strategy Map and balanced scorecard (BSC) focus on objectives and measures vital to executing company strategy. Central to the Strategy Map and BSC is a focus on selected key objectives and measures. Now we shall explore Pareto's Law, often referred to as the 80–20 law, named after the Italian economist Vilfredo Pareto as it relates to the BSC. Born in 1848, the son of a Genoese father, Pareto studied engineering at the University of Turin, Italy. The five-year course in civil engineering, the first two years of which were devoted to mathematics, deeply influenced Pareto's future intellectual outlook. His first work, *Cours d'economie politique* (1896–97), included his famous "law" of income distribution, a complicated mathematical formulation in which he attempted to prove that the distribution of incomes and wealth in society is not random and that a consistent pattern appears throughout history, in all parts of the world and in all societies, where 80% of the income is controlled by 20% of the population. This principle has found application across many business situations; you may have noticed in your company that 80% of the revenue is derived from 20% of the customers or that 80% of operating results come from 20% of the plants, and so on. One does not slavishly follow this principle, but business leaders and managers recognize the power of understanding the concentration of drivers and values. The BSC leverages Pareto's law by focusing on the vital few objectives that drive value.

Strategy Map and Objectives

This section begins with an in-depth review of the Strategy Map and strategic and operational objectives to set the foundation. The Strategy Map is a one-page graphical representation of your company's strategy. To put this in context, if you wanted an investor to review your financial results, you would provide him or her with your financial reports, consisting of an income statement and a balance sheet. Similarly, if you want the investor to see how well your company is achieving its vision and implementing its strategy, you would share your corporate Strategy Map and BSC. We will focus on the Strategy Map for Pareto Inc. (honorary name for our "focused" company). A more in-depth discussion of its design follows.

The Strategy Map in Exhibit 5.2 shows Pareto Inc.'s vision and business strategy. It shows how the executive team believes the organization will achieve Pareto Inc.'s strategic objectives. It also functions as a communications tool so you will be able to explain your company Strategy Map to your people inside of 30 minutes. Keep in mind that no single employee will be responsible for achieving all of these objectives; rather each employee would be responsible for a select subset of two to four objectives that will later be linked to compensation. The executive team followed the Kaplan and Norton methodology and developed a Strategy Map with four perspectives (listed down the left side of the map):

1. *Financial perspective.* What do shareholders value from Pareto Inc.? What do they expect the company to deliver to them?
2. *Customer perspective.* What are our intermediary and end customer segments and what have they told us they expect from us? What is our value proposition?
3. *Internal processes perspective.* What are the key business processes we must excel at to be able to deliver the value to customers, which translates into value for the shareholders?
4. *Learning and growth perspective.* What are the foundational factors—the people, skills, culture, and information technology (IT) infrastructure—we have to have in place to enable the achievement of the strategy?

This Strategy Map is also referred to as a cause-and-effect or linkage diagram. When read from the bottom to the top, the map is intended to capture key drivers that affect successive perspectives moving upward. For instance, if we excel at becoming a motivated and prepared workforce in the learning and growth perspective, then we can excel at our performance in the internal processes that drive customer satisfaction in the customer perspective. If the company has satisfied customers realizing the benefits from its network solutions and services, then the company will be successful at its revenue and profitability strategies. In summary, Pareto Inc. has a balanced, integrated strategy across four perspectives that can be measured to help fulfill its vision. The next section provides an in-depth discussion of the Strategy Map to help advance your understanding of this valuable tool and the linkages between and among objectives. It also provides a litmus test—the "new employee test." Imagine you have been hired as the new sales trainer at Pareto Inc. and the vice president of sales (your new boss) is walking you through the company's Strategy Map. You should have a solid understanding of your new company's strategy in about 30 minutes and be able to see where your position contributes to driving Pareto Inc.'s strategy.

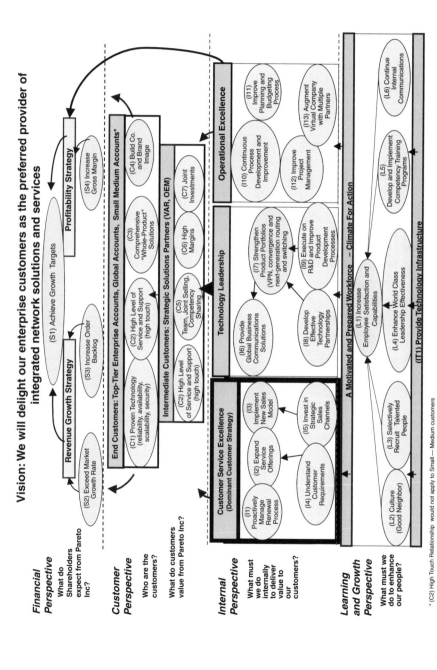

Vision: We will delight our enterprise customers as the preferred provider of integrated network solutions and services

Financial Perspective
What do Shareholders expect from Pareto Inc?

(S1) Achieve Growth Targets

Revenue Growth Strategy

Profitability Strategy

(S2) Exceed Market Growth Rate

(S3) Increase Order Backlog

(S4) Increase Gross Margin

Customer Perspective
Who are the customers?

What do customers value from Pareto Inc?

End Customers: Top-Tier Enterprise Accounts, Global Accounts, Small Medium Accounts*

(C1) Proven Technology (reliability, availability, security)

(C2) High Level of Service and Support (high touch)

(C3) Comprehensive "Whole-Product" Solutions

(C4) Build Co. and Brand Image

Intermediate Customers: Strategic Solutions Partners (VAR, OEM)

(C2) High Level of Service and Support (high touch)

(C5) Team, Joint Selling, Competency Sharing

(C6) High Margins

(C7) Joint Investments

Internal Perspective
What must we do internally to deliver value to our customers?

Customer Service Excellence (Dominant Customer Strategy)

(I1) Proactively Manage Renewal Process

(I2) Expand Service Offerings

(I3) Implement New Sales Model

(I4) Understand Customer Requirements

(I5) Invest in Strategic Sales Channels

Technology Leadership

(I6) Provide Global Business Communications Solutions

(I7) Strengthen Product Portfolios (VPN, convergence and next-generation routing and switching

(I8) Develop Effective Technology Partnerships

(I9) Execute on R&D and Improve Product Development Processes

Operational Excellence

(I10) Continuous Process Development and Improvement

(I11) Improve Planning and Budgeting Process

(I12) Improve Project Management

(I13) Augment Virtual Company with Multiple Partners

Learning and Growth Perspective
What must we do to enhance our people?

A Motivated and Prepared Workforce — Climate For Action

(L1) Increase Employee Satisfaction and Capabilities

(L2) Culture (Good Neighbor)

(L3) Selectively Recruit Talented People

(L4) Enhance World Class Leadership Effectiveness

(L5) Develop and Implement Competency Training Programs

(L6) Continue Internal Communications

(IT1) Provide Technology Infrastructure

* (C2) High Touch Relationship would not apply to Small — Medium customers

E X H I B I T   5 . 2   Pareto Inc. Strategy Map

89

Four Perspectives

Financial Perspective: What do shareholders expect from Pareto Inc.?

From the shareholders' perspective, they will expect us to (S1) Achieve Growth Targets, as depicted in the first ellipse on the map. The investment climate today has shown that Wall Street rewards growth companies that also demonstrate free cash flow. Consequently, to deliver on its growth targets, Pareto Inc.'s financial strategy will be driven primarily by a Revenue Growth Strategy (on the left side of the map) balanced with a Profitability Strategy (on the right side of the map). That is, the Revenue Strategy is defined by two strategic objectives:

1. (S2) Exceed Market Growth Rate
2. (S3) Increase Order Backlog.

The Profitability Strategy, (S4) Increase Gross Margin, recognizes that we must meet a gross margin threshold to attract and retain investors.

Customer Perspective: What do our end customers and channel partners value from Pareto Inc.?

Pareto Inc. has identified and targeted three end-customer segments as depicted in the top box: Top-Tier Enterprise Accounts, Global Accounts, and Small to Medium Accounts. These customers primarily value four things:

1. (C1) Proven Technology
2. (C2) High Level of Service and Support
3. (C3) Comprehensive Whole Product Solutions
4. (C4) Build Company and Brand Image

To achieve its aggressive financial growth objectives, Pareto Inc. will pursue what is called a "high-touch" channel strategy to leverage the sales forces of various partners (intermediate customers) as shown in the Strategic Solutions Box consisting of Value Added Resellers (VARs) and Original Equipment Manufacturers (OEMs). Using this model, Pareto Inc. will not only derive the benefit from its hundreds of salespeople, but also the selling power of several thousand intermediate direct partner salespeople to touch end customers. The Solution Partners' value proposition differs from the end customers described earlier; they value four things:

1. (C2) High Levels of Service and Support
2. (C5) Team, Joint Selling, Competency Sharing
3. (C6) High Margins
4. (C7) Joint Investments

Pareto Inc.'s goal is to shift and increase sales through the Strategic Solutions Partners shown. Pareto Inc. will embark on a program to train the indirect sales force and their supporting staff on our products to help achieve this goal. This is the clearest linkage to your new sales training position.

Internal Process Perspective: A Closer Look at Three Operations Strategies

Business research has identified and defined three types of customer strategies, and studies have shown that high-performing organizations major in *one strategy* and minor in the remaining two. Many companies have failed by losing focus and have attempted to pursue all three strategies. This singular focus also later ties into BSC-based budgeting.

The three strategies include (1) Technology Leadership, which has a product focus, (2) Customer Service Excellence/Customer Intimacy, which has a relationship focus, and (3) Operational Effectiveness, which has a low-cost-provider focus. Pareto Inc. is pursuing strategy (2) Customer Intimacy as its dominant customer strategy; this is shown in the middle box. This should help clarify the sales organization's focus and help you develop your sales training materials.

Customer Service Excellence Theme

The future of Pareto Inc. is centered on leveraging the talents of solutions partners to enhance sales volume, maintain high-quality relationships with end customers, and accelerate growth. The Customer Service Excellence strategic theme consists of three substrategies:

1. (I1) Proactively Manage Renewal Process to improve our customer relationship and encourage greater renewal rates.
2. (I2) Expand Service Offerings, which will be driven by (I4), Understand Customer Requirements.
3. (I3) Implement new "high-touch" Sales Model, which will require (I5), Invest in Strategic Sales Channels.

Pareto Inc. also recognizes its strengths in two other strategic themes: Technology Leadership to develop and/or acquire new solutions, and Operational Excellence to deliver solutions on time.

Technology Leadership Theme

Pareto Inc. will focus on providing solutions consisting of products developed in-house, through partners, and from acquisitions. This strategy consists of achieving one key objective:

- (I6) Provide Global Business Communications Solutions; this in turn is supported directly by (I7), Strengthen Product Portfolios, to include VPN, convergence, and next-generation routing and switching.
- (I7) is driven by two other objectives, (I8), Develop Effective Technology

Partnerships, and (I9), Execute on Research and Development and Improve the Product Development Processes.

Operational Excellence Theme

Pareto Inc. will achieve better operational efficiencies in its processes to support better margins.

- (I10) Continuous Process Development and Improvement focuses on four "customer-facing" processes to make it easier for customers to do business with it. These include:
  1. Integrated Planning, essentially matching demand and supply of products
  2. Integrated Order Management linked with all solutions partners
  3. Problem Resolution to solve customer problems in a timely manner
  4. Invoicing to increase the speed and accuracy of invoices to drive cash flow
- (I11) Improve Planning and Budgeting is internally focused on allocation of scarce capital to key strategic projects to achieve the strategic objectives.
- (I12) Improve Project Management is focused on the discipline of managing projects to completion, on-time, and on-budget.
- (I13) Augment Virtual Company with Partners is focused on linking suppliers and customers to internal systems and processes to speed up cycle times, improve information flows, and reduce errors.

Learning and Growth Perspective Motivated and Prepared Workforce Theme

Pareto Inc.'s success is dependent on realizing the full potential of its human capital. This is manifested in (L1), Increase Employee Satisfaction and Capabilities. Five objectives contribute to achieving L1:

1. (L2) Culture. Given the influx of many new people, the company will maintain a culture of contribution to the United Way and executive positions on local nonprofit boards, for example.
2. (L3) Selectively Recruit Talented People. This objective is focused on assessing skills needs as an enterprise and deploying a focused approach to recruiting resources to close gaps.
3. (L4) Enhance World-Class Leadership Effectiveness. The executive team recognizes its responsibility to excel at skills such as communications and motivation.
4. (L5) Develop and Implement Competency Programs. This objective focuses on leaders receiving 360-degree feedback, employees implementing career development plans, and Pareto Inc. providing top-notch training to all its employees to enhance our human capital.

5. (L6) Continue Internal Communications. This objective recognizes that a lot has been done to improve communications but rapid growth and increasingly complex business requires the company continue to aggressively communicate to ensure employees are all focused on achieving our vision through our strategic objectives.

Lastly (IT1) , Provide Technology Infrastructure, recognizes increased reliance on technology, whether voice or data for communications or enterprise resource planning (ERP), to manage a global multifaceted supply chain.

How have we done with the new employee test? Do you have a better understanding of Pareto Inc.'s strategy? Could you train the next new employee? What could be more important to Pareto Inc.'s employees understanding and executing its strategy? This clarity will help overcome the four barriers (vision, management, resource, and people) to companies successfully implementing their strategies. The executive team challenged itself to regularly communicate Pareto Inc.'s Strategy Map and objectives to their employees—think of the power of several thousand people understanding the company direction including the creativity and motivation that would unleash.[1]

> The winners in life think constantly in terms of I can, I will, and I am. Losers, on the other hand, concentrate their waking thoughts on what they should have or would have done, or what they can't do.
> —DENNIS WAITLEY

CROWN CASTLE INTERNATIONAL: BEST PRACTICE CASE

Crown adopted the use of a Strategy Map consistent with Drs Kaplan & Norton's method as described in the prior case study.

Kaplan and Norton's subsequent book *Strategy Maps* outlines a range of different Strategy Maps used in corporate, nonprofit, and government agencies.[2] This book also includes the Crown Strategy Map focused on operational excellence as a case study company; the updated map also shared at performance management conferences is shown later in Exhibit 5.3. In the Crown 10-k and in an interview with Harvard Business School Press, the Crown chief executive officer (CEO) provided clarity on the definition of the four strategies shown at the top of the Strategy Map. In 2001, Crown

- Recipient of APQC Best Practice Partner Award
- Recipient of Balanced Scorecard Hall of Fame Award
- *Wall Street Journal* Ranked "Top 20 Most Improved Company in Shareholder Value Creation"

Castle committed to a dramatic shift in strategy, from one of aggressive acquisitions to operational excellence. Senior executives formulated four elements
of the new strategy, elements that remain the cornerstones of the company's
activities.

1. *Grow revenue organically.* This involves squeezing the most out of the
   existing services and offering more to existing customers, in such ways
   as adding antennas and leasing additional tower or ground space to
   wireless customers.
2. *Expand recurring margins by driving efficiencies in existing business.* With
   high fixed costs and low variable costs, driving efficiencies has yielded
   significant operating leverage.
3. *Allocate capital to projects that achieve higher returns with lower execution risks.*
   This ultimately allows the company to invest in value-creating activities
   that maximize shareholder value.
4. *Expand revenue around existing assets.* With efficiencies realized and
   existing services leveraged, the company can enjoy growth from new
   offerings.[3]

The Crown Strategy Map contains 20 to 25 objectives that span four classic BSC perspectives: financial, customer, internal process, and people. Each
objective supported by one to two BSC measures, is discussed in more depth
in Chapter 6.

> *The price of success is hard work, dedication to the job at hand, and the deter-*
> *mination that whether we win or lose, we have applied the best of ourselves to*
> *the task at hand.*
> —VINCE LOMBARDI

Strategic Objectives and Balanced Scorecard Based Budgeting

Strong linkages between strategic planning and planning and budgeting were
a differentiating factor in award-winning enterprises and sponsor companies in
several research projects. Crown evolved its planning and budgeting process
into a BSC-based budget with a rolling forecast. The evolution of the BSC
follows a predictable path, which is shown through three stages through anecdotal quotes:

1. In the early stage, manager comments ranged from "Is this BSC the initiative du jour?" to "What does the measure called EBITDA stand for?"
   and from "The measure definition does not reflect my performance" to
   "My data is different from yours; which is right?"
2. In the interim stage, once the measure definitions were refined and
   accepted more broadly, comments reflecting greater employee understanding could be heard: "The BSC benchmark reports indicate we are

in the middle of the pack. What do we have to do to improve? Maybe we should contact the top performing office and ask what new ideas they have implemented to reduce their cycle time."

3. In the mature stage as managers embraced the BSC as a strategic management framework, improvements came and new user comments started to emerge: "I understand the value of the new measures, but can the BSC be produced faster after month-end for more timely use?" and "What I really need is a greater mix of customer and operational measures to monitor performance." As the BSC development and adoption progressed, the Crown Great Lakes Area (GLA) was at the forefront of innovation. We will explore their contributions in the next section which were the focus of an article in a leading accounting journal.

Balanced Scorecard Rolling Forecasts

All areas prepare monthly budgets for every BSC measure, enabling stoplight (red, yellow, green) color coding. The area president conducts monthly area and district BSC reviews with district managers and functional teams, which consist of reviewing exceptions to stoplight BSC reports with particular emphasis on understanding "the story" or linkages among, for instance, the four objectives noted earlier—the causal links among operations, customer, and financial results including relevant leading and lagging impacts from changes. However, the GLA president was not content to wait until month-end for his team's results, so he devised a forecasting approach whereby *weekly* his area could predict its results for current and next quarter-end using the two-quarter forecasting approach. In short, he applied a forecasting approach to understanding and driving operational, customer, and financial results. The GLA president and his team append month-end BSC reports to include actual results since the previous month-end, but, more important, they forecast results for the upcoming two quarters. His weekly senior management team roundtable meetings focus heavily on understanding key trends, reforecasts of results, and devising countermeasures to improve performance gaps; example is shown in exhibit 5.3.

To understand these dynamics, recall the interplay and causality among Strategy Map objectives described earlier for Pareto Inc. That is, a given objective is reinforced or driven by the one below it. For example, F1, Maximize Shareholder Value is driven by F3, Increase Pipeline, which is driven by C2, Meet Time Requirements. C2 in turn is driven by O5, Accelerate Application to Rent Cycle Time

How does this rolling forecast actually work? If GLA experienced yellow (actual results within 10% of target) or red (more than 10% less than target) stoplight results against budget in objective F3, Increase Pipeline, then the team could adjust their activities and focus on removing any obstacles in O5, Accelerate Application to Rent Cycle Time. They understood that the

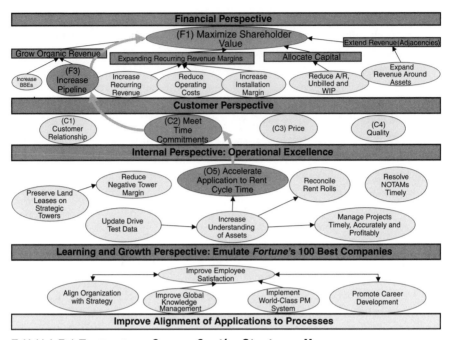

EXHIBIT 5.3   Crown Castle Strategy Map:
Four Major Themes

improvement in F3 would show up in F1 within the current or next quarterly forecast. Conversely, if the F1 results were green against budget (meeting or exceeding target) for a district in the current quarter, then the team would discuss causal factors or best practices in F3, C2, or O5 with an eye toward adoption by other districts and in repeating the performance in the next quarter.

There are several immediate benefits from using the two-quarter BSC rolling forecast:

- Predicting results with a mature understanding of intra- and inter-quarter fluctuations
- Improving resource allocation across and within different districts
- Increasing visibility and improving the timing of key initiatives
- Focusing resources on specific objectives based on current and forecasted trends
- Scheduling employee enrichment activities such as vacations, off-site retreats for planning, and training classes (such as the Six Sigma Green Belt program)[4]

Strategic Communications

The CEO regularly used the Strategy Map as a communications vehicle to share the company strategy with employees. As noted in an interview with

Principle 2: Refresh and Communicate Strategy

- *Strategic Planning.* CPM personnel conducted strategic planning including internal and external analyses, strategic scenarios, and strategic options.
- *Core Services.* The Strategy Map clearly articulated Crown's core products and services.
- *Link Strategic Planning and Budgeting Processes.* BSC links strategic, operational, and people plans.
- *Communications Plan.* The CEO communicated the BSC program throughout the enterprise for it translates the organization's vision into goals, objectives, critical success factors, and finally plans that employees can act on.

Harvard Business School Press, he stated, "For a BSC to be truly useful to this organization, it must be evergreen. On annual basis, we evaluate what we are measuring; we look at the ellipses (or Strategy Map objectives) and we fine-tune the Strategy Map. We don't want to confuse people by saying one thing and having a Strategy Map that looks different. We always want to be consistent in our message to employees; we want to be sure they can see the higher priority items depicted in the Strategy Map."[5] Crown's far-flung workforce of independent-minded managers operated autonomously in disparate markets. To spread strategic awareness among employees, the company developed a multipronged communications program. It covered the BSC extensively in the monthly newsletter, presenting the BSC as a new way of working and thinking—not just another initiative. Messages "from John" (CEO Kelly) describing the scorecard's virtues complemented articles explaining "cascading" and other challenges.[6]

CITY OF CORAL SPRINGS: BEST PRACTICE CASE[*]

The City of Coral Springs has robust integrated CPM processes. This section reviews the strategic planning process as depicted in Exhibit 5.4, which maintains the city's focus on performance improvement.

At the strategic level, an environmental scan is the data and information base

---

[*] The City of Coral Springs case team adapted portions of this case from "Performance Measurement in the Public Sector," *APQC* (November 2005), Governors Sterling Application 2003, and internal documents.

- Recipient of Florida Governor Sterling Award for Organizational Excellence (based on Baldrige Criteria)
- Recipient of APQC Best Practice Partner Award

for the planning process. The scan compares Coral Springs' performance against other cities. It includes survey data on customer satisfaction and requirements and an analysis of changing demographics and emerging technologies. With this background, the strategic plan and business plan are developed. The business plan lists specific new services and service improvements that will be affected by teams in the fiscal year. This planning process also produces key intended outcomes (KIO), measures of citywide progress vis-à-vis the strategic plan. (Since 2004, they have added a category of broad goals between the strategic priorities and KIOs: "directional statements" that provide specific direction to staff on what successful implementation of a priority would be to the commission. KIOs are frequently selected based on these directional statements.) Negative variation in these measures initiates an assessment of whether a process improvement is needed. At the operations level, in-process measures, complaint-tracking data, ideas from empowered employees, information on innovations in other communities, and new developments in a field trigger department-level improvement initiatives. However, if significant resources are needed for the project, the data becomes part of the environmental scan and the improvement idea may become a business plan initiative. Other processes that focus operations on performance improvement are training, reward and recognition, and leadership

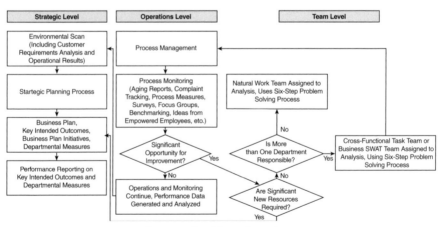

EXHIBIT 5.4   Strategic Planning Process

communications. The process of developing the business plan establishes priorities for major process improvement projects. The strategic priorities and consistency with city values are the basis for the decision to implement a process improvement project. Unit and department improvement initiatives are selected based on unit and department objectives. These projects support business and strategic objectives because objectives at all levels are aligned.

The city commission began a process of strategic planning designed to identify the issues to be addressed to achieve the city's mission and that will persist over the lifetime of the strategic plan. Reviewed and updated biennially, the strategic plan creates a shared vision for the future of the community. These long-range policy issues, or "strategic priorities," developed by the city commission and reaffirmed during the strategic planning process, emphasize the values of the community:

- Customer-involved government
- Neighborhood and environmental vitality
- Excellence in education
- Family, youth, and community values
- Financial health and economic development
- Ethnic and religious diversity

For each priority, an action plan is developed for implementing policy and operating measures. Through this process, the *business plan* is developed:

- *Commission priority.* Identify the vital issues.
- *Key intended outcomes.* Identify desired results.
- *Initiatives.* Allocate activities, resources, personnel, investment, and time planned for the year to achieve each KIO.
- *Performance measures.* Specific and measurable data indicating the effectiveness of processes designed to support the KIOs.

With the priorities and indicators set, the operations of the city are reviewed and redirected to bring the strategic vision to life. Specific actions, programs, capital purchases, staffing requirements, and funding levels are developed in response to the needs identified in the strategic plan. Known as the business plan, the resulting document is an outgrowth of the strategic priorities, capturing the city's vision in a quantifiable form, improving decision making and resource allocation. A benefit of using a business plan is the direct link between strategic priorities and costs and activities. This model is used to monitor performance through:

- Variance analysis of goal to actual
- Linking budget line items to measurable activities
- Identifying value-added and non–value-added activities

The business plan is an "organic" document, in that it is continually revisited throughout the year and may be amended by a majority vote of the commission. Changes in the environment may require realignment of resources to continue to keep city staff on target to meet the KIOs and strategic priorities. In developing the annual operating budget, departments analyze existing and potential services in light of the strategic priorities. The business plan adds and removes services, which are then quantified in the line item budget. They reflect not only strategic priorities as set by the city commission, but also incorporate feedback from customer surveys and policy initiatives that contribute to the long-term financial health of the city. Departments set goals to meet the needs identified by the strategic priorities. To meet these goals, programs within the departments have specific objectives that are measured through performance measures.

Individual staff member's objectives and performance measures are then linked to the program objectives. Each employee knows what the end result should be and how it contributes to the strategic plan. In this way, the budget becomes a tool for monitoring and controlling operating performance. The performance measure tables included with each department's summary in the annual budget document are designed to show how the program objectives support the strategic priorities. Performance measures are explicitly related to the KIO that they support and the strategic priorities that they fulfill. The policy deployment model follows this path:

- Mission statement
- Strategic priorities
- Key intended outcomes
- Performance measures
- Incentive pay system objectives

It is significant that the city executes the process in this fashion, minimizing the impact of special interest lobbying in the decision-making process. The principal participants in the process are the city commission and the senior management team. Staff and customers participate through input to the planning that provides data for the process.

Strategic Planning Process Calendar and Detailed Content

The strategic planning process begins in January of even-numbered years, when staff begins collecting data for the environmental scan, which includes input from various customer feedback sources as well as management and policy analysis of emerging issues, demographic trends, and financial conditions. A strategic planning workshop is convened in the spring where staff and the commission discuss issues in a workbook that consists of these sections:

- *Financial health.* A description of the current financial condition of the city with information on the financial trend monitoring system (analysis of current data) and five-year forecast (long-term financial planning tool).
- *Environmental scan.* Demographic trends, an economic analysis, land development trends, service demand generators, technology changes and issues, legislative challenges, and emerging issues are presented that will have an impact on the city over the next three to five years.
- *Customer requirements analysis.* Summaries of customer feedback from surveys and neighborhood meetings.
- *SWOT (strengths/weaknesses/opportunities/threats) results.* Public visioning exercises are included to identify trends and affinities.
- *Performance analysis.* A summary of the quarterly performance review (previously called Service Efforts and Accomplishments), the current status of KIOs, and a projection of the composite index are included to describe the current performance of the organization.
- *Mission, core values, and strategic priorities.* Current versions are included to provide a basis for discussing future needs.
- *Benchmarking.* Comparative data on key areas with discussions of possible improvement projects.
- *Current initiative update.* A review of the current-year business plan initiatives.
- *Other presentations.* Made on some of the emerging issues, important initiatives, or cross-functional process improvement team results as warranted.

Over the two-day workshop, the commission informs staff of the direction the strategic plan should take and makes specific changes as they respond to the data presented (as well as their own research and interaction with constituents). Staff then develops proposed changes to the slate of KIOs designed to take into account requested changes, which are discussed and approved during later business plan workshops. An emphasis is placed on selecting leading indicators, rather than lagging, to facilitate the evaluation of progress during the year. Even in odd-numbered years, a strategic planning workshop is held to review the plan and performance measures and make proactive midcourse corrections as necessary and appropriate. With the strategic priorities and KIOs in hand, staff begins to develop the business plan for the following year. While proposing new business plan initiatives, staff develops performance targets for existing programs and identifies resources necessary for both existing and new services. A senior management team staff retreat is held in May to discuss proposed business plan initiatives. Each initiative is discussed, analyzed, and weighed against the others until a slate of initiatives is reached through consensus.

Immediately following this retreat, the city manager meets with each department director to go over performance agreements and resource needs to negotiate and lock in specific budget requests. A business planning workshop is held in June with the city commission to present the proposed business plan initiatives, including major capital projects and new programs, to solicit feedback and input. A second workshop is held in July to present the refined plan, with associated budget projections, to the commission. Both workshops are televised and open to the public. Once the business plan is approved, departments use it as their action plan for the next year. Supervisors further deploy the business plan by linking individual work plans and employee's incentive pay system review objectives to it during the October review period.

The bulk of the strategic deployment planning is done at this point, so staff spends the rest of July and August preparing the proposed budget for public hearings in September. Because the city has assiduously sought input all along, there is very little discussion at budget hearings, which typically last less than an hour. Resolutions and ordinances are voted into place and the new fiscal year begins October 1. Budget staff prepares the adopted budget and planning documents and the cycle starts over again.

This system has been steadily improved and refined year after year and is now widely considered to be a best-in-class benchmark by many organizations. The system has been featured as a best practice in the National Performance Review, Government Finance Officers Association publications, the Florida Institute of Government programs, and Fitch's recommended practices for cities seeking bond-rating upgrades, and is presented in numerous universities' graduate programs in public administration as a case study. To ensure continuous improvement and test the soundness of the system, an annual review of the system is made in January. Management and budget office staff gather feedback from departments, the commission, and other end users on the ease of use and outcomes of the system. A standing business SWOT team for business planning analysis meets to discuss recommendations and results of the process review, as well as feedback from senior management team retreats and individual staff efforts in evaluating the strategic planning process.

Key intended outcomes are listed with the goal for each. Due to the nature of the planning process, the timetable is two years for each of the goals, although many of the KIOs will be used over many years, with appropriate adjustments to the goals made on an annual basis. Then the organization can deploy responsibility for achieving policy goals through the business plan, departmental work plans, and individual incentive pay system objectives. For example, the challenges concerning changing demographics were recognized through community feedback and analysis of data from the Census and American Communities Survey. The commission has responded to this issue by making customer-involved government, neighborhood and environmental vitality, and respect for religious and ethnic diversity priorities in strategy development. Staff developed measures such as "Minority residents who feel the City is a great place to live" (goal of 83%) to measure our success in

BEST PRACTICE HIGHLIGHTS

Principle 2: Refresh and Communicate Strategy

- *Strategic Planning.* CPM personnel conducted strategic planning including internal and external analyses, SWOT analyses, strategic scenarios, and strategic options.
- *Core Services.* The process focused on providing core services.
- *Strategic Plan.* The city produces a comprehensive strategic plan that provides direction to and cascades into business plans and team and individual goals.
- *Link Strategic Planning and Budgeting Processes.* The city provides a clear line of sight between strategic objectives and its planning and budgeting process outcomes.
- *Communications Plan.* The strategic direction and supporting plans are effectively communicated throughout the city departments and to the citizenry.

reaching a diverse citizenry. Departments then proposed business plan initiatives such as a "Community Pride Program" ($30,000 in resources required), "International Partnerships II" ($5,000 in resources required), and "Voter Turnout Campaign" to meet these goals. Obviously there are many more priorities, intended outcomes, initiatives, and measures used to address this challenge, but these are a few examples of how the system works.

> *I am a firm believer in the people. If given the truth, they can be depended upon to meet any national crises. The great point is to bring them the real facts.*
> —ABRAHAM LINCOLN

TENNESSEE VALLEY AUTHORITY: BEST PRACTICE CASE*

The Tennessee Valley Authority (TVA) has developed a three-part process linking strategic, operational and people plans as shown in Exhibit 5.5.

As the exhibit indicates, Winning Performance has three foci: (1) a strategic focus, (2) an operational focus, and (3) a people focus. Performance improvement begins with an expression of strategic intent to provide the context within which all internal processes and business objectives are defined and prioritized. Strategic intent must then be translated into operational terms so that the actions of management and employees may be supportive and aligned.

---

* The TVA case team adapted portions of this case from "Performance Measurement in the Public Sector," *APQC* (November 2005), and internal company documents.

- Winner of the APQC Best Practice Partner Award
- Winner of the Balanced Scorecard Hall of Fame Award

Results must be reviewed and assessed routinely. Core competencies needed to achieve the strategic and operational objectives must be identified to support sustainable performance improvement over time.

To support each focus, the core team engaged in additional activities. For example, the executive vice president of human resources participated on the core team and concentrated on implementing the people focus. As Winning Performance was implemented, he launched a number of teams: compensation, culture, retention and diversity, industrial safety, labor relations, and learning (training). He helped each team write achievement plans.

The board of directors, in conjunction with the senior vice president of strategic planning, is currently responsible for conducting work at the strategic focus level. The Winning Performance process is an umbrella that covers many functions and organizations. The process is managed primarily through influence. Kolz says, "I don't want to give the impression that anyone reports to the Winning Performance team or anyone in the performance management arena." Winning Performance contains the processes, mechanisms, infrastructure, and frameworks in which performance management is actualized.

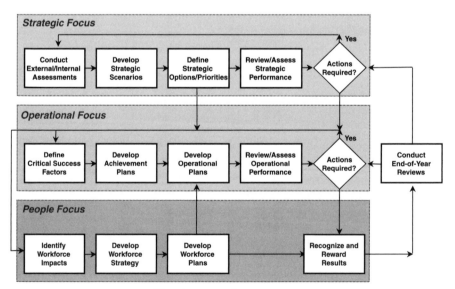

EXHIBIT   5.5   Winning Performance

TVA's Vision

Generating Prosperity in the Valley

TVA's Goals

- Supplying Low-Cost Reliable Power
- Supporting a Thriving River System
- Stimulating Economic Growth

Strategic Objectives
(Those things that MUST be accomplished)

- Improve life in the Tennessee Valley through integrated management of the river system and environmental stewardship
- Meet customers' needs with affordable, reliable electric power
- Demonstrate leadership in sustainable economic development in the Valley
- Continue the trend of debt reduction
- Reduce TVA's delivered cost of power relative to the market
- Strengthen working relationships with all of TVA's stakeholders

Critical Success Factors
(What is needed in order to achieve the Strategic Objectives)

FINANCIAL
What must we do financially?
- Generate more for less
- Invest prudently

CUSTOMER-STAKEHOLDER
What do our customers and stakeholders want from us?
- Improve power reliability to meet customer requirements
- Provide flexible contracts and competitive pricing of products and services
- Balance competing demands and optimize the river system
- Promote development through targeted growth initiatives
- Manage the environmental and safety impacts TVA's operations have on employees and the region

OPERATIONS PROCESS
What must we do to improve operational/business process effectiveness?
- Achieve excellence in the customer value and relationship processes
- Achieve excellence in the asset optimization and production processes
- Achieve excellence in stakeholder relations and communications processes

PEOPLE
How must we improve the capabilities of our workforce to support our objectives?
- Shape the culture to model TVA's values
- Develop work force capabilities required to be the supplier and employer of choice

EXHIBIT 5.6 TVA's Leadership Standard

TVA creates performance plans that are linked to its strategy. Each TVA organization has its own business manager and performance plan. All capital investments documented in the performance plans are reviewed and screened by a company-wide project review committee to ensure that the major expenditures align with the strategic direction.

TVA developed achievement plans around each of its critical success factors; achievement plans are attempts to do enterprise-wide planning. The term "Leadership Standard" was created by TVA. Exhibit 5.6 illustrates the flow of Winning Performance and how it translates the organization's vision into goals, objectives, critical success factors, and finally plans that employees can act on. The core team required approximately six weeks of work to develop the Leadership Standard because it accepted and consolidated input from many areas of the company.

These goals in turn link to the TVA BSC (see Exhibit 5.7). Note the six icons represent TVA's six strategic objectives.[7]

Difficulties are just things to overcome, after all.
—ERNEST SHACKLETON

Winning Performance

FY 04 TVA Balanced Scorecard

September 2004

	Weight	Status	Actual FYTD	Plan FYTD	Year end Actual	GOALS Target *	GOALS Mid	GOALS Stretch
Financial								
• Total O&M Costs (millions of $)	15%	↑	3,581	3,644	3,581	3,644	3,608	3,535
• Financial Strength (Net reduction in Total Financing Obligations)	15%	↑	278	225	278	225	275	375
• Productivity (MW/$)	10%	↑	156.1	147.8	156.1	147.8	150.8	152.4
Customer								
• Customer Satisfaction (Percent)	10%	↑	126.2	100.0	126.2	100.0	117.0	130.0
• Economic Development (Percent of Target)	10%	↑	120	100	120	100	110	120
Operations								
• Asset Availability (Ratio)	20%	↑	101	98	101	98	100	102
• Environmental Impact (Index of Environmental Factors) **	10%	↑	81	98	81	98	91	85
People								
• Safe Workplace (Per 100 Employees) ***	10%	↑	2.33	2.41	2.33	2.41	2.36	2.31

Notes:
* Target equals Performance Plan Target
** Reported quarterly
*** Payout at any performance level is contingent upon no TVA employee fatalities.

Status
↑ Forecast at or better than Target
◊ Forecast worse than Target, recovery is possible
↓ Forecast worse than Target, recovery is unlikely

EXHIBIT 5.7   TVA Balanced Scorecard

BEST PRACTICE HIGHLIGHTS

Principle 2: Refresh and Communicate Strategy

- *Strategic Planning.* CPM personnel conducted strategic planning including internal and external analyses, strategic scenarios, and strategic options.
- *Core Services.* Winning Performance's icons clearly articulated TVA's core products and services.
- *Link Strategic Planning and Budgeting Processes.* TVA links strategic, operational, and people plans. Capital expenditure approval process is aligned with strategic objectives.
- *Communications Plan.* TVA communicated "Winning Performance" throughout the enterprise for it translates the organization's vision into goals, objectives, critical success factors, and finally plans that employees can act on.

MEDRAD: BEST PRACTICE CASE*

Medrad understands and links its philosophy, mission, strategies, and annual plan with its BSC goals and measures, which are cascaded throughout the company. These links are depicted in Exhibit 5.8, and each element is described more fully.

Philosophy—Why Medrad Exists:

- To improve the quality of healthcare
- To ensure continued growth and profit
- To provide an enjoyable and rewarding place to work

Nine basic principles in which Medrad believes:

1. Treat all employees with dignity and fairness.
2. Produce the highest-quality products possible.
3. Assure our company's future through new products.

- Recipient of Malcolm Baldrige National Quality Award
- Recipient of the APQC Best Practice Award

---

* Portions of this case are adapted from MEDRAD Malcolm Baldrige National Quality Award Application, internal company documents, and employee input.

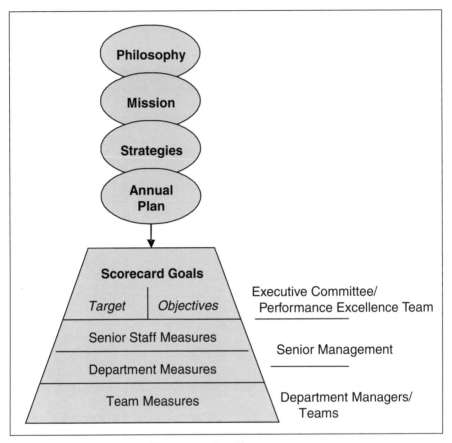

EXHIBIT 5.8   Strategy Continuum

4. Maintain our company's leadership position through customer respon-
    siveness.
5. Manage ourselves through sound planning and decision making.
6. Preserve our ability to respond quickly to opportunities.
7. Deliver on commitments we have made to ourselves.
8. Help fellow employees achieve their goals through teamwork.
9. Never lose our sense of pride in our company.

Medrad's mission continues to be a guiding principle for how it operates and
how it will grow. The mission was revised in 2001 to reflect Medrad's diversi-
fication strategy.

Medrad Mission

It is our mission to be a worldwide market leader of medical devices
and services that enable or enhance diagnostic and therapeutic imaging

procedures. We will accomplish this mission by achieving performance excellence across our five corporate goals.

Corporate Scorecard Goals

Medrad's five corporate scorecard goals arose from the enduring belief that continued growth and prosperity derive from balancing the interests of all stakeholders. These evergreen goals guide decision making at all levels, providing focus for operations and growth beyond financial cycles:

- *Exceed the financials.* (Profit) growth greater than revenue growth
- *Grow the company.* Revenue growth greater than 15 % per year
- *Improve quality and productivity.* Grow CMB per employee greater than 10 % per year
- *Increase customer satisfaction.* Continuous improvement in Top Box customer satisfaction ratings
- *Increase employee growth and satisfaction.* Continuous improvement in employee satisfaction above best-in-class benchmark

Strategic Planning

The executive committee owns the strategic planning process, which produces: (1) a five-year vision of Medrad's markets and revenues; (2) an action plan for the coming year that includes short- and long-term initiatives required to achieve the five-year vision; and (3) organizational alignment of the vision and action plan. Medrad's strategic planning process is shown in Exhibit 5.9 and consists of four subprocesses:

1. Portfolio planning
2. Improvement planning
3. Action plan budgeting
4. Objectives waterfall (cascading)

The process begins each January when the executive committee (EC) sets one- and five-year targets based on the five corporate scorecard goals, industry growth rates, and parent company Schering's financial goals for those time frames. The financial goals become targets for the first two corporate scorecard goals: achieve financials and grow the company. The portfolio planning process depicted in the next section addresses the short- and long-term achievement of these scorecard goals. Through the process, Medrad identifies business development and product development initiatives to capitalize on significant business opportunities, prioritizes the initiatives, and creates alignment throughout the company to achieve them.

EXHIBIT 5.9   **Strategic Planning Process**

Strategic Planning

Portfolio Planning Subprocess

Business development looks outside at acquisitions or alliances that strengthen Medrad's competitive position or diversify the product portfolio. Product development focuses on new platforms and products that will help grow the company. The portfolio planning process (Exhibit 5.10) consists of two phases: product line planning and product portfolio selection. Medrad's product line platform (PLP) teams drive product line planning: Computed Tomography (CT) and Magnetic Resonance (MR) procedures Cardiovascular and Multi-Vendor Service, plus an incubation team that targets long term or new market development opportunities. A marketing "champion" leads each PLP team, which is supported by business development, PIAD (Product Innovation and Advanced Design). The performance improvement advisory board chairs the improvement planning and action plan budgeting processes.

An EC sponsor assigned to each platform provides oversight and guidance. The product line planning phase of the portfolio planning process begins in January, when the EC and the marketing process manager create a kick-off package that includes the post mortem from last year's process, targets for the current planning cycle, and confirmation of the planning categories. PLP teams review the targets, action plans, and results from the previous year, analyze the current business environment, and create a platform strategy. The analysis of the

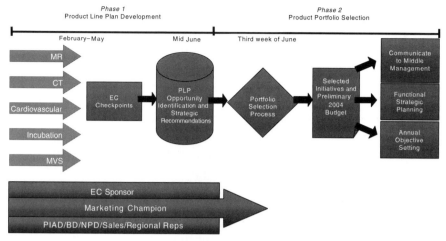

EXHIBIT 5.10   Portfolio Planning Process

business environment is guided by Medrad's product line planning assessment guidelines and other factors. The PLP teams identify opportunities, specific initiatives that will take advantage of them, and estimated resource requirements. In late May or early June, each team presents its findings and recommendations to the EC. In the product portfolio selection phase, each EC member scores each suggested initiative on: commercial risk, technical risk, return on investment, impact to sales revenue (short- and long-term growth opportunity), market share distribution and stability, short- and long-term contribution to CMB, rate of technological change, basis of product competition, and overall value proposition to customer. Open debate during a series of meetings between the EC and the PLP champions resolves scoring gaps or differences, with the marketing champions clarifying opportunities and risks as needed.

During the product line planning phase of the portfolio planning process, PLP teams analyze the current business environment in order to develop platform strategies and specific initiatives. The product line planning assessment guidelines provide a structure for gathering information by product and business about market and customer needs and opportunities, the competitive landscape (by product/business and geographic region), organizational strengths and weaknesses through the opportunities and issue analysis, and financial and other risks through issue analysis, financial justification, and resource requirements. Each area within the Business Environment category considers technological and other expected and potential changes. Supplier strengths and weaknesses are addressed during operations' functional strategic planning phase of the strategic planning process. Operations and the new product development departments use the strategic integration transformation (SIT) methodology to select and integrate material and design suppliers and partners that will support the corporate goals and initiatives. A critical factor in product line planning is timely knowledge of existing and potential customers. PLP teams acquire this knowledge through the listening posts and use it to complete a formal competitive update that presents information on current competitors and market shares, potential competition, and, for each competitor, its overall marketing strategies, SWOT analysis, and how Medrad currently competes and plans to compete moving forward. A centralized source of online competitive information, will also provide competitive information to the PLP teams.

From this process, the resulting prioritized list of initiatives feeds the remaining steps in the strategic planning process, including defining target markets as an input to the business development process.

Corporate Improvement Planning Subprocess

Corporate improvement planning uses inputs from portfolio planning, function planning, and advisory board and function reviews to identify needed improvements in key processes as shown in Exhibit 5.11. Function planning is a subset of strategic planning that may be conducted by a function or subfunction any time during the year to assess capability and plan improvements using planning tools such as Hoshin planning, Baldrige assessment review, and traditional strategic planning tools.

The Performance Excellence Team Advisory Board (PETAB) requests proposals for cross-functional initiatives, which are screened using criteria established by senior staff at a PET meeting. One of the criteria is impact on corporate scorecard goals. Senior staff selects the final list at the June PET meeting. The first two steps in the strategic planning process conclude with the assignment of a senior staff sponsor and a leader to each top 12 corporate

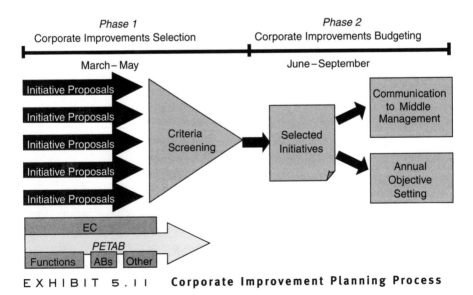

E X H I B I T   5 . 1 1   Corporate Improvement Planning Process

objective (see Exhibit 5.12), and their prioritization. Top 12 objectives include the product and business development initiatives from portfolio planning and the cross-functional initiatives from corporate improvement planning. The goals, targets, and objectives are listed in Exhibit 5.12.

Action Plan Budgeting Subprocess

During the action plan budgeting step, project managers of initiatives and programs supporting the 12 objectives develop budgets and schedules with their project teams, which include representatives from all stakeholder departments. Each functional manager (who is also an EC member) works with his or her staff and a financial representative to prepare a budget that is rolled up into an EC-level function budget and, ultimately, to a corporate profit and loss statement. Cross-functional teams plan budgets for their initiatives with individual expense lines addressed in the relevant function budget. The EC reviews overall budget roll-ups twice before the final budget is approved and forwarded to Schering for approval.

Waterfalling Subprocess

"Waterfalling" is Medrad's term for cascading corporate objectives from the corporate level to the functional and team levels to the individual employee level. Strategic planning ends with the completion of the objectives waterfalling. The entire organization is now aligned to corporate goals, corporate objectives, and individual function objectives. The resulting action plan is executed using the iterative process and performance is assessed.

At the completion of the portfolio strategic planning processes, process owners, using input from process stakeholders, evaluate effectiveness, efficiency, and cycle time. Throughout the year, they also evaluate the effectiveness of the entire process by comparing actual progress on the top 12 objectives to the strategic direction and plans. The process owners use this evaluation, self-assessments, Baldrige feedback, and external best practices to identify and implement planning process improvements. The strategic planning process has undergone eight cycles of improvement.

As part of the cycle of improving the strategic planning process introduced an approach to assessing the probability of success and translating that into a hurdle rate for financial projections that are part of portfolio planning. The approach, taken from an Institute of Electrical and Electronics Engineers IEEE journal article, begins when a product planner and team assess technical and commercial success risk factors using a weighted scale, then discuss the results to produce an overall risk factor, which is translated into a hurdle rate in the financial model. The risk factors considered include technical, proprietary position, organizational competencies and skills, complexity, access to external technology, commercial risk, manufacturing capability, customer/market need, market/brand recognition, distribution channels, raw materials

EXHIBIT 5.12 Top 12 Corporate Objectives

Mission	Corporate Goal	Scorecard Measure	Target	Benchmark	Frequency
	Exceed the financials	CMB (profit measure)	Grow CMB faster than sales – specific target set via strategic planning	Individual product line growth rates	Monthly
Ensure continued growth and profit	Grow the company	% sales growth	15%/year	Schering Parent, Medical industry	Monthly
	Improve quality and productivity	CMB/EE growth	10%/year	Supports growth CMB faster than sales	Monthly
Improve the quality of healthcare	Improve customer satisfaction	Survey Results-top box ratings	Continuous improvement year-to-year	Competitors & others surveyed	Monthly
Provide an enjoyable and rewarding workplace	Improve employee growth and satisfaction	Survey Results-very satisfied ratings	Continuous improvement above best-in-class	Hay best-in-class companies	Twice each year

BEST PRACTICE HIGHLIGHTS

Principle 2: Refresh and Communicate Strategy

- *Strategic Planning.* Medrad has effectively linked its philosophy, mission, strategies, and annual plan with its BSC goals and measures, which are cascaded throughout the company.
- *Strategic Planning.* CPM personnel conducted strategic planning including internal and external analyses, strategic scenarios, and strategic options.
- *Core and Adjacent Products and Services.* Medrad focuses intently and comprehensively on product portfolio planning during the strategic planning process.
- *Link Strategic Planning and Budgeting Processes.* Medrad links strategic, operational, and people plans. Action budgeting is aligned with strategic initiatives.
- *Communications Plan.* Medrad uses the action planning process and the waterfalling technique described to effectively communicate its strategic plans down through the enterprise.

supply, and environment, health, and safety. The acquisition and use of critical data and information continues throughout the planning cycle. As action plans are executed, senior staff, advisory boards, and functional managers assess the external and internal environments and initiate corrective actions.

> *It is the greatest shot of adrenaline to be doing what you have wanted to do so badly. You almost feel like you could fly without the plane.*
> —CHARLES LINDBERGH

SERONO: BEST PRACTICE CASE

Strategic Context

Serono's CEO has placed a high level of priority on the implementation of improvements and has mandated a company-wide communication campaign to ensure "proper" alignment. Lawrence Ganti adds, "Serono has one vision and one group strategy that is formulated and revised each year by the executive

- Winner of the Balanced Scorecard Hall of Fame Award

EXHIBIT 5.13   **Group Strategy Pyramid**

management board. The direction of the company is then shared throughout the organization through key messages, strategic themes, and the corporate Strategy Map." The strategy and the alignment of its themes are shown in Exhibit 5.13. At the highest level is the Serono mission and vision, followed by company people, culture, and values. The strategy consists of four unifying enterprise-wide themes:

1. "Manage our current business" consists of franchise plans for existing products on the market.
2. "Bring our products to markets" consists of research and development and new therapies.
3. "Invest in new opportunities" focuses on strategies for licensing products and acquisitions.
4. "Sustain corporate integrity and people development" focuses on strategies for human resources; company communications; risk, control and compliance; and quality.

Strategy Map

The Serono Strategy Map (Exhibit 5.14) follows the Kaplan and Norton methodology including four perspectives:

1. Financial perspective communicating "we are committed to creating shareholder value" consisting of four primary objectives focused on revenue, market share, free cash flow, and earnings per share.
2. Customer perspective communicating "we will provide superior innovative products and services for our customers" consisting of five primary

Financial:
We are committed to creating shareholder value

| F1: We will double Revenues in 5 years - $5.0 Billion in 2010 | F2: We will reach market leadership in each of our key brands | F3: We will grow Free Cash Flow | F4: We will Increase Earnings Per Share |

Customer:
We will provide superior innovative products and services for our customers

Patients and Physicians

Regulators and Payers

| C1: Develop a number of molecules that demonstrate our understanding of mode of action in disease | C2: Increase the number of products in the pipeline that address unmet needs for patients | C3: Achieve customer satisfaction | C4: Rapidly develop safe and efficacious products that meet regulatory standards | C5: Ensure market access by demonstrating superior value to the payers |

Business Process:
We will excel at creating best in class business processes to support customer satisfaction

Supply

Process Improvement and Efficiency

B1: Supply timely, quality, and compliant products

B2: Support the business through operational efficiency

B3: Optimize resources allocated to drive business operations

People and Organization:
We will create the world's best biotech company

| P1: Provide for an environment in which people can grow and contribute to the development of our company | P2: Manage risk and ensure compliance | P3: Increase Serono's visibility and stakeholders' confidence | P4: Provide for competitive compensation schemes and recognition programs |

EXHIBIT 5.14   Serono Corporate Strategy Map

Principle 2: Refresh and Communicate Strategy
- *Strategic Planning.* Serono has integrated strategic planning, long-range planning, Strategy Maps, and BSC implementation.
- *Strategy Maps.* Serono has developed Strategy Maps for the commercial business and support services using the Kaplan and Norton methodology containing four perspectives: financial, customer, business process, and people and organization.
- *Communications Plan.* The strategic plan is well communicated throughout the enterprise.

objectives focused on two customer segments (1) patients and physicians and (2) regulators and payors.

3. Business process perspective communicating "we will excel at creating best in class business processes to support customer satisfaction consisting of four objectives focused components of the supply chain.

4. People and organization perspective communicating "we will create the world's best biotech company" through four objectives focused on the environment, people, risk, and shareholders.

Serono cascades and replicates the four Strategy Map perspectives across and down through the organization. Strategy Map objectives contain measures and targets that are discussed more fully in the next chapter.

Rules are made for people who aren't willing to make up their own.
—CHUCK YEAGER

LB FOSTER COMPANY: BEST PRACTICE CASE

LB Foster engages in an annual strategic planning process using a disciplined approach that formed the basis for designing and refreshing company and business/product unit Strategy Maps and BSCs. Jeff Poholsky, CPM Officer, facilitates the strategic planning process annually. In many cases product leaders will update their plans every six months, depending on changing market conditions. Strategic plans are developed using a comprehensive outline and several leading tools as shown in the representative divisional Strategic Plan Table of Contents in Exhibit 5.15.

The comprehensive nature of this strategic plan outline affords us a unique opportunity to review a completed plan for best practices; plan sections follow.

EXHIBIT 5.15   Strategic Plan (Example)

LB Foster Threaded Products Division
Divisional Strategies to Build a Better Company

2004–08 Strategic Plan
Five Year Strategic Plan
Table of Contents

---

1. Business Overview
   a. History
   b. Markets and Customers
   c. Products and Processes
   d. Facilities and Technologies
2. Market Assessment and Outlook (by product)
   a. Overall Market
   b. Current Market Share
3. Competitive Assessment (by product)
   a. Competitor Profiles
   b. Key Products
   c. Market Share
4. SWOT Analysis (by product)
   a. Strengths
   b. Weaknesses
   c. Opportunities
   d. Threats
5. Strategies—Top Five
   • Links to SWOT analysis
6. Five-Year Financial Plan
   • Income Statement
   • Balance Sheet
   • Cash Flow Statement

Strategy Plan

Divisional Overview

The LB Foster Threaded Products Division is one of the nation's largest and most reliable manufacturers of pump columns used for the vertical turbine pump market. Vertical turbine pumps are normally used in agricultural, municipal, and industrial markets. These applications are primarily used to extract water at depths of over 250 feet. Pump column, a type of pipe, is the pipe used to attach the discharge head to the bowl assembly for a short setting (5 to 20 feet) or a deep well setting (20 to 250 feet) to a vertical pump. Pump column is also used on a submersible pump between a submerged motor/bowl assembly (20 to 350 feet) to the discharge elbow above the surface. Vertical pump column also protects the centering devices and line shaft that drive the impellers in the water.

Our facility is currently located in Texas occupying 60 plus acres. Our current capabilities for threading range from 2 inches to 14 inches Outer Diameter (OD) due to equipment constraints. The average pump column size range is 4 inches to 12 inches and is manufactured to specific customer requirements. We manufacture our column from carbon steel, stainless steel, and other alloy piping materials. Material is generally cut to 5-, 10-, or 20-foot sections, threaded and coupled, painted, stenciled, and palletized. In addition, we OD coat and ID line column when requested.

Pipe supplied for our industry is generally foreign ASTM A53 prime pipe or secondary pipe. Either way it is normally manufactured in the electric resistance welding process (ERW). Because price plays such a significant role in the market, grade of material is not as important as the necessity for the pipe to be round, sound, and threadable. Domestic pipe is cost prohibitive. The pipe we purchase for threading is normally foreign, and we historically buy volume quantities quarterly keeping our costs below primary competition.

Each piece of threaded pipe generally has a coupling attached. We purchase approximately $K annually from XYZ Manufacturing to convert our raw castings and in finished steel couplings.

Other products that we manufacture and/or subcontract are flush joint threads, water well couplings, tube and shaft assemblies, flange column, Victaulic style cut grooving, and API style threads.

Market Assessment and Outlook
Water Well

Our target market is customers located in the southeast, southwest, and central United States who purchase all items necessary for new installation or well rehabilitation for the industrial, agricultural, and municipal water well market. These items generally include:

- Inner column (line shaft/tube and shaft assemblies)
- Flange column
- Pump column
- Water well couplings
- ID/OD epoxy coatings for all pump columns
- Pumps
- Discharge heads
- Well casings

While we compete on a national basis, freight costs to the Northeast or West Coast often make it impossible to be competitive. Our target market segments are: inner column, flange column, and pump column with pump column being our primary target market segment. Product groups conduct extensive national and regional competitor share analyses as shown in the following tables (data is confidential however).

Market drivers include relationships and expertise followed by quality, price, customer service, consistency of product, and consistency of service. National 2004 industry sales for industrial and agricultural wells were $xxx million including all items necessary for new installation or well rehabilitation. Annual industry sales for inner column, flange column, and pump column were $xxx million broken down in this way:

2004 National Sales		
(millions) Sales	LBF Sales	Percent
Inner Column	Company Confidential	
Flange Column		
Pump Column		
Total		

For our target region, southeastern, southwestern, and central United States:

Target 2004 Regional Sales		
(millions) Sales	LBF Sales	Percent
Inner Column	Company Confidential	
Flange Column		
Pump Column		
Total		

Note that inner column and flange column is manufactured from much more expensive alloy materials. So, while their sales may be more than pump column, the quantity sold is not.

The agricultural portion of our market uses 85% of all pump column pipe due to the deeper wells settings needed to be maintained for specific output in comparison with industrial wells. However, the agricultural market is shrinking because of government regulations impacting the groundwater industry. As water tables diminish, more government regulations are being implemented to stop this from occurring. Drought conditions are positive to the market; however, this is occurring more in the West than in our Southeast target market.

In the industrial and municipal water well market, there were 146,468 municipal groundwater wells supplying public drinking water systems in 2003 serving 102,443,355 persons, down from 155,792 systems serving 111,536,345 in 1998. However, industrial wells are on the rise. Schools, hospitals, and industry are reducing their dependence on public wells and installing their own.

Micropile

Micropile in the United States has applications in: urban development and redevelopment, existing industrial facilities, seismic retrofit, emergency applications

(Mandalay Bay, Las Vegas, Leaning Tower of Pisa, Italy), and slope stabilization (new and existing highway construction).

The micropile market uses secondary, surplus, or used oil country casing pipe in sizes ranging from 2 3/8 inch to 133/8 inch heavy wall pipe (.500 wall plus) which is commonly cut into 5-, 10-, and 20-foot sections and then threaded with an ID/OD flush joint thread. The two types of flush joint threads used are 8 Round or Buttress taper threads adapted from the oil country casing market. While there can be many variations of micropile threads, they all must meet the torque, tension, compression, and lateral load requirements specified in every contract. Without extensive independent laboratory testing, a micropile thread cannot be qualified.

The micropile market is on the rise. It is an expanding market that is outpacing more expensive alternatives. It is estimated that the installed micropile market is $100 million with the actual casing representing 25 to 30%, or $30 million. This market is expected to grow 15 to 20% per annum over the next five years. While the outlook is positive, we should be cautioned that the demand for secondary casing could outstrip supply causing dramatic price increases. The installed cost of micropile might be uncompetitive with alternatives such as concrete and hollow bar technology.

The target market for micropile is nationwide and the key customers for micropile are drill shaft contractors.

Competitive Assessment: Water Well Products

For each competitor, the strategic plan captures these three attributes:

1. Product lines include
2. Target distribution markets
3. They have a long standing relationship with

The competitors profiled include:

- K&K Supply, Conroe, Texas
- Custom/Kelly Pipe, Los Angeles, CA
- 101 Pipe & Casing, Los Angeles, CA
- BHM Threading, Houston, TX.
- Fleetwood Metals, Los Angeles, CA
- Irrigation Machine, Lubbock, TX
- Vertical Turbine Specialists (VTS), Lubbock, TX
- Mid-America Pump, Hastings, NE

Market Share Analysis

The tables that follow represent the national and regional target market share broken down by competition. LB Foster Threaded Products has an x% share of the national market for pump column, but a y% share of pump column for our target regional market.

National Sales	Total Sales (millions)	Market Share		
		Inner Column	Flange Column	Pump Column
LB Foster Threaded Prod		Company Confidential		
K & K				
Kelly Pipe				
101 Pipe & Casing				
BHM				
Irrigation Machine				
VTS				
Turbine Supply				
Fleetwood Metals				
Total				

Target Regional Sales	Total Sales (millions)	Market Share		
		Inner Column	Flange Column	Pump Column
LB Foster Threaded Prod		Company Confidential		
K & K				
Kelly Pipe				
101 Pipe & Casing				
BHM				
Irrigation Machine				
VTS				
Turbine Supply				
Fleetwood Metals				
Total				

SWOT Water Well

The next table shows the SWOT (strengths, weaknesses, opportunities, and threats) component of the strategic plan; confidential information is omitted.

Strengths	Weaknesses
Company Confidential	Company Confidential

Opportunities	Threats
Company Confidential	Company Confidential

Major Strategies

The foregoing analysis provides the basis for development of primary and secondary strategies; one such strategy is flowed through to the company's Strategy Map and company and division balanced scorecards.

Strategy 1 Reduce Overall Costs: Providing a quality product with lower overall costs relative to our competition is key to the future financial success of Threaded Products. Additionally, this strategy will facilitate in providing customer satisfaction, training of new and existing employees, and moving and reconfiguring our current manufacturing processes.

Strategy Mapping and Balanced Scorecard

The strategic planning process leads into development and refinement of the Strategy Map based on the Kaplan and Norton methodology. LB Foster elected to develop a corporate-level Strategy Map and BSC and cascade key themes and objectives down through the product groups and plants. The Strategy Map in Exhibit 5.16 contains key objectives across four perspectives (financial, customer, process, and people). Those objectives derived from the strategic planning process are shown with double circled objectives to show integration and connectivity.

To best communicate the Strategy Map to employees, a narrative version was developed. We will walk through a narrative version of the Strategy Map provided to LB Foster's employee base.

The Strategy Map is used to show LB Foster's vision and business strategy on one page. It shows how the executive team believes the organization will achieve LB Foster's strategic objectives. The map is a communication tool that managers can use to explain LB Foster's key objectives to employees in about 20 to 25 minutes. To put this in context, if you wanted to review our financial results, you would review our financial reports consisting of an income statement and a balance sheet. Similarly, if you want to see how well we are achieving our vision and implementing our strategy, you would ask to see our corporate Strategy Map and BSC. The objective for today is to provide you with enough information so *you* can, in turn, explain this Strategy Map to your people inside of 25 minutes. Let us keep it simple. Keep in mind that no one here will be responsible for achieving all of these objectives, but a select set will be determined by your boss. You will also be receiving many more communications on this topic in coming months and this map will be posted on the intranet.

When discussing strategy, the executive team looked at it from four perspectives (listed down the left side of the map):

1. *Financial.* What do shareholders value from LB Foster—what do they expect us to deliver to them?
2. *Customer.* What have the customers told us they expect us to deliver?
3. *Internal processes.* What are the key business processes we must excel at to be able to deliver the value to customers, which translates into value for the shareholders?

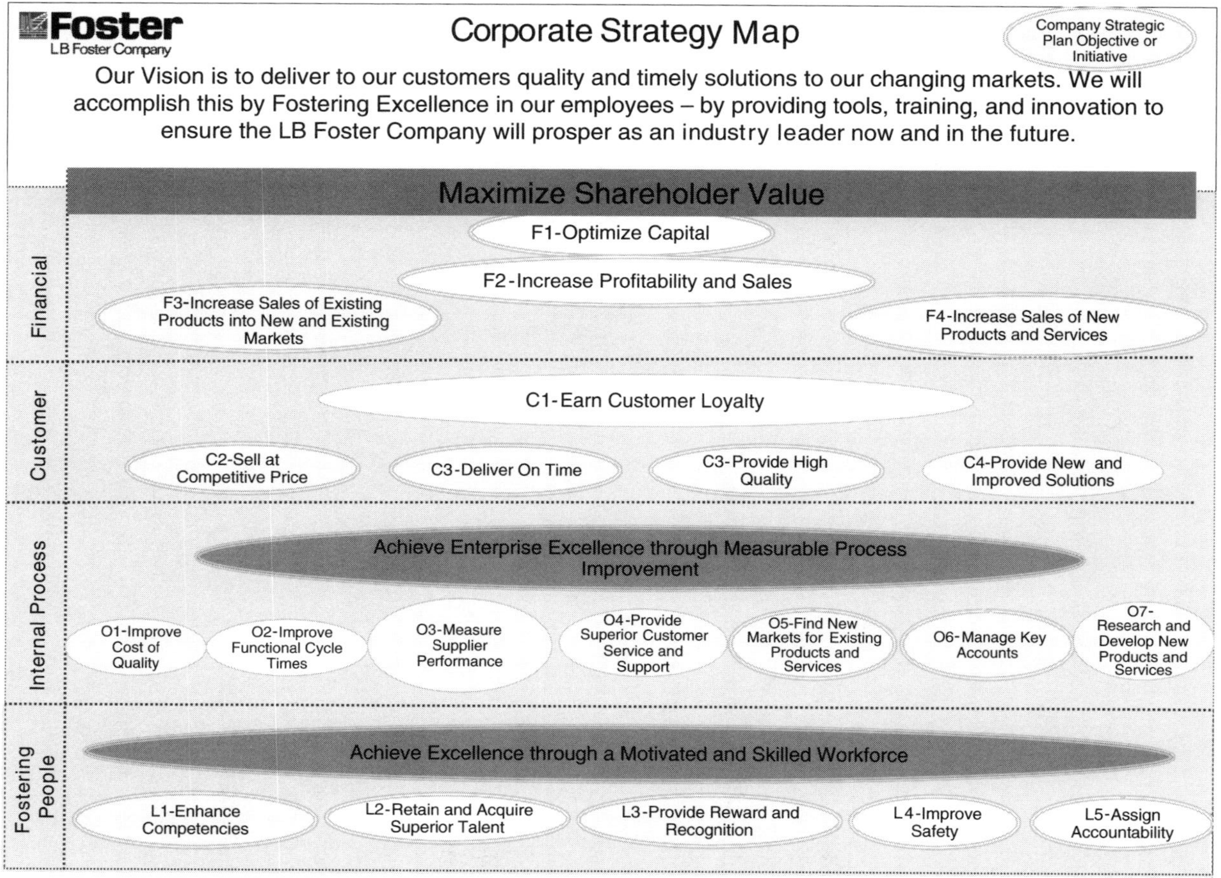

Foster
LB Foster Company

Corporate Strategy Map

Our Vision is to deliver to our customers quality and timely solutions to our changing markets. We will accomplish this by Fostering Excellence in our employees – by providing tools, training, and innovation to ensure the LB Foster Company will prosper as an industry leader now and in the future.

Company Strategic Plan Objective or Initiative

Maximize Shareholder Value

Financial
- F1-Optimize Capital
- F2-Increase Profitability and Sales
- F3-Increase Sales of Existing Products into New and Existing Markets
- F4-Increase Sales of New Products and Services

Customer
- C1-Earn Customer Loyalty
- C2-Sell at Competitive Price
- C3-Deliver On Time
- C3-Provide High Quality
- C4-Provide New and Improved Solutions

Achieve Enterprise Excellence through Measurable Process Improvement

Internal Process
- O1-Improve Cost of Quality
- O2-Improve Functional Cycle Times
- O3-Measure Supplier Performance
- O4-Provide Superior Customer Service and Support
- O5-Find New Markets for Existing Products and Services
- O6-Manage Key Accounts
- O7-Research and Develop New Products and Services

Achieve Excellence through a Motivated and Skilled Workforce

Fostering People
- L1-Enhance Competencies
- L2-Retain and Acquire Superior Talent
- L3-Provide Reward and Recognition
- L4-Improve Safety
- L5-Assign Accountability

EXHIBIT 5.16   LB Foster Corporate Strategy Map

125

4. *Fostering people.* What are the foundational factors—the people, skills, culture, and IT infrastructure—we have to have in place to enable the achievement of the strategy?

This strategy map is also referred to as a cause-and-effect or linkage diagram. When read from the bottom to the top, the map is intended to capture key drivers that effect successive perspectives. For instance, if we excel at (4) Fostering People at the foundation, then we can excel at our performance in the (3) Internal Processes that drive (2) customer satisfaction in the Customer perspective. If we have satisfied customers realizing the benefits from solutions and services, then we will be successful at our (1) Financial revenue and profitability strategies. So, in summary, we have a balanced, integrated, and measurable approach to realizing our vision.

At the top of the map is our vision: "Our vision is to deliver to our customers quality and timely solutions to our changing markets. We will accomplish this by fostering excellence in our employees—by providing tools, training, and innovation to ensure the LB Foster Company will prosper as an industry leader now and in the future."

Financial Perspective

As a public company, since shareholders have many investment alternatives such as savings passbooks, treasury bills, mutual funds, and stocks, they will expect us as a public company to deliver on objective (F1) Optimize Capital as depicted in the first ellipse on the map. The investment climate today has shown that Wall Street rewards companies that optimize investor returns. Consequently, to deliver on our growth targets, our financial strategy will be driven primarily by the objective (F2) Increase Profitability and Sales. F2 in turn, is driven by two strategic objectives: (F3) Increase Sales of Existing Products into Existing and New Markets and (F4) Increase Sales of New Products and Services. In summary, our four financial objectives F1 to F4 recognize that we must provide profitable sales to drive attractive returns for investors.

Customer Perspective

To achieve our aggressive financial growth objectives, we will pursue improving objective (C1) Earn Customer Loyalty. Research shows loyal customers are 3 to 10 times more likely to buy again from you and it costs 10 times more to acquire a customer than to retain one you have. We recently measured our customer loyalty through the customer survey and found it to be very high, 4.5 on a 5.0 point scale. But how do we continue to achieve the loyalty score? Well, (C1) Earn Customer Loyalty is driven by four other objectives: (C2) Sell at Competitive Price, (C3) Deliver on Time, (C4) Provide High Quality, and (C5) Provide New and Improved Solutions. The customer survey results are being analyzed to understand how each product group's customers prioritize these four attributes to help focus our selling efforts and to improve related internal processes. For the customers that value C3, LB Foster may kick off a Lean initiative to reduce fulfillment and delivery cycle time. Some customers may indicate (C2) Sell at Competitive Price is important, but when asked to rank C1 to C4 they indicate that (C3) Deliver on Time carries the most weight. So you might be able to hold firm on your pricing, for example. We will now turn our attention to the internal processes, the next perspective on the Strategy Map.

Internal Process Perspective

LB Foster's overarching theme is "Achieve Enterprise Excellence through Measurable Process Improvement." Business research has identified and defined three types of customer strategies, and studies have shown that high-performing organizations major in one strategy and minor in the remaining two. Many companies have failed by losing focus and have attempted to pursue all three strategies. The three strategies include (1) operational excellence—a cost and speed focus (e.g., Southwest Airlines, Wal-Mart), (2) customer service excellence/customer relationship—a relationship focus (e.g., Home Depot and IBM), and (3) technology innovation (e.g., Intel, Sony).

LB Foster is pursuing operational excellence as its dominant customer strategy but we are also recognized for our strengths in customer service excellence/customer relationship. Our third strategy, though lower on the list, is technology innovation to develop and/or acquire new solutions. But let us review our *dominant* strategy first, operational excellence. The future of our company centered on operational excellence leverages our low-cost position and ability to provide on-time delivery of purchased and manufactured products and services to our customers. This strategy will be achieved by three process objectives: (O1) Improve Cost of Quality, (O2) Improve Functional Cycle Time, and (O3) Measure Supplier Performance. These process objectives will deliver on customer objectives C1, C2, and C3 described earlier.

To deliver on customer service excellence/customer relationship strategy, three process objectives have been established: (O4) Provide Superior Customer Service and Support, (O5) Find New Markets for Existing Products and Services, and (O6) Provide Key Account Management. These three process objectives will deliver on the (C3) Provide High Quality customer objective as noted.

LB Foster's final process strategy is technology innovation, which is supported by process objective (O7) Research and Develop New Products and Services, which will deliver on customer objective (C5) Provide New and Improved Solutions. In summary, these three process strategies consisting of seven objectives will deliver on the four primary customer objectives (C2) through (C5), which in turn will improve (C1) Earn Customer Loyalty.

Learning and Growth: Fostering People

Our success is dependent on our human resources, and we have developed the theme "Achieve Excellence through a Motivated and Skilled Workforce," which will be achieved by five learning objectives L1 to L5:

- *(L1) Enhance Competencies* relates to implementing a formal training and development process to build competencies and skills of our employees to meet current and future business demands and strategic objectives.
- *(L2) Retain and Acquire Superior Talent* calls for establishing a process for recruiting qualified individuals who best match the core values, strategic objectives, and position requirements.
- *(L3) Provide Reward and Recognition* will enhance business performance by creating systems of recognition and rewards for performance (compensation and benefits).
- *(L4) Improve Safety* will strive to improve our safety program, including documentation and analysis of incidents. Research additional techniques to reduce employee accidents.
- *(L5) Assign Accountability* will provide a culture to promote accountability and pride in performance at all levels of the company

Underpinning the entire map is an information technology objective (IT1) Invest Strategically in Technology to focus on those key applications to enable people and process success.

Each Strategy Map objective relates to one to two measures that collectively make up the company's BSC (which is covered further in Chapter 6).

BEST PRACTICE HIGHLIGHTS

Principle 2: Refresh and Communicate Strategy
- *Strategic Planning.* CPM Office leverages the strategic planning process as either owner or partner to understand changing market conditions including competitor, supplier, rival, and potential entrants and substitutes in the marketplace.
- *Core and Adjacent Products and Services.* Defines and determines core and adjacent products and services to focus on highest probabilities for success.
- *Strategic Plan.* Produces a comprehensive strategic plan.
- *Strategy Mapping.* Links strategic planning to Strategy Maps and objectives.
- *Communications Plan.* Communicates strategy throughout the organization using a communications plan including a narrative Strategy Map.

In summary, the foregoing strategic planning process, strategic plan, Strategy Map objectives, and Strategy Map narrative provide for an integrated strategic planning process linking the company vision to objectives that are communicated and actionable by employees.

> *Whenever you are asked if you can do a job, tell 'em, "Certainly I can!" Then get busy and find out how to do it.*
> —THEODORE ROOSEVELT

FLORIDA DEPARTMENT OF HEALTH: BEST PRACTICE CASE*

For years, Florida Department of Health (FDOH) had a structured process for developing and updating an agency strategic plan (ASP), required by statute and submitted annually to the governor. In 2000, the legislature replaced the ASP with a long-range program plan (LRPP), a budget planning and performance measurement document. FDOH continued using its 2000–01 ASP as an adjunct to the LRPP, thus providing more detail on the nine priority areas, goals, and objectives identified in both plans. FDOH is currently implementing a revised process that includes development of an ASP, an operational business plan, and the LRPP as components of an integrated strategic planning system. The strategic and operational planning processes provide the framework for annually updating the department's LRPP and the legislative budget request. The legislative budget request is the mechanism used by state agencies to obtain new resources.

Florida's legislative session has great influence on the strategic and operational direction of the department. The secretary, deputy secretaries, division directors, and other members of the agency management team annually review the appropriations bill and relevant statutory changes to determine whether legislative or executive actions have redefined the department's mission and priorities. Substantive changes are incorporated into the strategic planning process. Concurrently, the expectations of stakeholders are considered. Once the review is complete, the strategic priorities for the upcoming five years are drafted.

Customer and stakeholder requirements are also included in the process and are obtained in a variety of ways. These requirements include the needs of clients and communities receiving direct services, legislative and executive staff, advocacy groups, professional and provider organizations, community-based organizations, and other state agencies.

Once strategic issues are identified, trends and conditions analyses are developed for each issue. These include strengths, weaknesses, opportunities, and

* The Florida Department of Health case team adapted portions of this case from "Performance Measurement in the Public Sector," *APQC* (November 2005), Governors Sterling Applications 2002 and 2006, and internal documents.

Example of Strategic Plan/Long Range Plan Goals and Objectives

Planning Evaluation and Data Analysis

Quick Section Links

Strategic Plan

Public Health Statistics

Vital Statistics

County Health Dept Mgmt Information:

Select a Report

Resource Manual

Contact Us

Goals	Indicators	Objectives
Maternal and Infant Health		
To improve birth outcomes	Total infant mortality rate per 1,000 live births.	Reduce total infant mortality per 1,000 live births from 7.06 in 1997 to 6.5 by 2003.
	Nonwhite infant mortality rate per 1,000 live births.	Reduce nonwhite infant mortality per 1,000 live births from 11.41 in 1997 to 9.0 by 2003.
	Percentage of newborns requiring intensive care services	Maintain a rate of no more than 7 percent of the infants born to high-risk pregnant women served in the High-Risk Obstetrical Satellite Clinics who will require Level III neonatal intensive care services.
Children's Health		
To increase access to care for children and adolescents	Number of children enrolled in Florida KidCare Program (Title XXI).	Ensure that 30.9 percent of the 1997-98 estimated 823,000 uninsured children receive health benefits coverage under the Florida KidCare Program by 1998-99 and through 2003-04.
	Service rates for children with special health care needs who are clients of Children's Medical Services (CMS).	Increase from 50 percent in FY 1998-99 to 96 percent the proportion of eligible children with special health care needs who are enrolled in the CMS Network by FY 2003-04.

EXHIBIT 5.17   **Strategic Plan/Long-Range Program Plan**

- Miami-Dade County Health Department Recipient of Governors Sterling (Baldrige) Award 2002 and 2006
- Department of Health Recipient of APQC Best Practice Partner Award

threats (SWOT) assessments and a review of comparable data, such as national Healthy People goals. The FDOH evaluates its internal capabilities and needs as well as societal events that impact the department's ability to fulfill its mission. The determination of strategic issues leads to the development of strategic goals and objectives for the ASP and the LRPP, which are built around measurable indicators of core functions. The operational plans are then developed and incorporate the process measures, program performance measures, and specific intervention strategies that should impact strategic goals. The operational goals, objectives, and strategies are aligned with strategic goals and objectives in the LRPP and the ASP.

Operational business plans, quarterly performance reports, and the quality improvement process are all designed to communicate and reinforce key objectives and strategies to department personnel.

An excerpt from the FDOH Strategic Plan/Long-Range Program Plan is shown in Exhibit 5.17.

> *Tomorrow morning before we depart, I intend to land and see what can be found in the neighborhood.*
> —CHRISTOPHER COLUMBUS

BEST PRACTICE HIGHLIGHTS

Principle 2: Refresh and Communicate Strategy
- *Strategic Planning.* Leverage the strategic planning process as either owner or partner to understand changing market conditions.
- *Strategic Plan.* Develops a comprehensive strategic plan.
- *Core and Adjacent Services.* Define and determine core and adjacent products and services to focus on highest probabilities for success.
- *Strategic Plan* Produce a comprehensive strategic plan.
- *Link Strategic Planning and Budgeting Processes.* Link strategic planning to the budgeting process, partner with finance to provide for a seamless continuum.
- *Communications Plan.* Communicate strategy throughout the organization using a comprehensive communications plan.

EXHIBIT 5.18 Strategic Direction and Goals

Strategic Direction	Strategic Goal		Supporting Chapter Performance Standard (CPS)
Strengthen Our Financial Base, Infrastructure, and Support Systems to Continuously Improve Our Service Delivery System	The American Red Cross has a high performance work force comprised of dedicated volunteers and employees who are committed to upholding the highest standards of conduct in the workplace.	1	The Board of Directors adopts the Standard Chapter Bylaws and governs the chapter in accordance with those bylaws (per BoG bylaws and policies).
		2	Board conducts annual performance appraisal of chapter CEO for submission to and approval by Service Area executive
		7	Board conducts a self-evaluation at least once every 24 months.
		8	Board members have completed board orientation
		9	Chapter board chair has attended Chapter Chair Institute or equivalent
		33	Chapter has documented personnel policies (which have been approved by its board) that govern the work and actions of all employees and volunteers (including policies on the evaluation process, grievance procedures and personnel development)
		34	All registered volunteers and employees have signed and comply with the American Red Cross Code of Conduct as well as Confidential Information and Intellectual Property agreement
		35	Chapter executive has completed chapter executive training
		36	Percent of volunteers indicating "Excellent" overall levels of satisfaction with their volunteer experience
	Red Cross services have a positive and demonstrable impact.	31	Percent of clients who achieve the stated outcomes of American Red Cross services
	Clients of Red Cross services are fully satisfied with the helpfulness, timeliness and convenience of our services.	32	Percent of clients who are highly satisfied with American Red Cross services
Additional Satisfaction and Trust Goals	Americans have a high level of trust in the American Red Cross.	10	Chapter produces and makes available an annual report that is complete, accurate, timely and complies with corporate guidelines
		37	Chapter is aware of and operates in accordance with all applicable local, state and federal laws
		38	All chapter solicitations and informational materials are accurate, truthful and not misleading

• Winner of the APQC Best Practice Partner Award

Principle 2: Refresh and Communicate Strategy
• *Strategic Planning.* Leverage the strategic planning process as either owner or partner to understand changing market conditions.
• *Strategic Plan.* Produce a comprehensive strategic plan.

AMERICAN RED CROSS: BEST PRACTICE CASE[*]

The alignment of standards with strategic goals is deliberate. In fact, the same personnel who developed the strategic plan were involved in developing the standards. Particular attention was paid to the relationship between chapter performance standards and the American Red Cross strategic plan. A detailed plan outlined the strategic directions, related strategic goals, and the chapter performance standards that support each. Some standards support more than one goal; most of the goals are supported by multiple standards. Exhibit 5.18 shows how the American Red Cross cascades strategic direction and goals into chapter performance standards.

> *Far and away the best prize that life offers is the chance to work hard at work worth doing.*
> —THEODORE ROOSEVELT

BRONSON METHODIST HOSPITAL: BEST PRACTICE CASE

By achieving high-quality clinical outcomes and superior service, Bronson builds customer loyalty. The hospital has experienced exponential growth in the last five years and has attained market leader status. For seven consecutive years, Bronson has been named Kalamazoo's Leading Hospital in the annual Adam's Outdoor survey. Also, Bronson has been the Consumer Choice Award winner for the past three years as the top hospital in the Kalamazoo area

[*] The American Red Cross case team adapted portions of this case from "Performance Measurement in the Public Sector," *APQC* (November 2005), and internal documents.

- Malcolm Baldrige National Quality Award
- Michigan Quality Leadership Award (2001, 2005)
- 100 Top Hospitals Award
- Governor's Award of Excellence for Improving Care in the Hospital Setting (2004, 2005)
- Governor's Award of Excellence for Improving Preventive Care in the Ambulatory Care Setting
- *Fortune* magazine's "100 Best Companies to Work For" (2004, 2005, 2006)
- *Working Mother*'s "100 Best Companies for Working Mothers" (2003, 2004, 2005)
- VHA Leadership Award for Operational Excellence (2005, 2006)

according to National Research Corporation. Although the vision challenges the organization to achieve national levels of performance for clinical quality outcomes, Bronson remains focused on serving patients in the nine-county region. Competition is defined within the local area market and includes five major competitors.

The vision and mission would be unkept promises were it not for the top-level commitment of Bronson staff, who believe in the values and demonstrate

EXHIBIT 5.19   Plan for Excellence, Key Factors

Clinical Excellence (CE)

- Achieve national best practice performance in clinical outcomes.
- Use evidence-based medicine to achieve excellent patient outcomes.
- Be recognized as a safe environment for patients.

Customer and Service Excellence (CASE)

- Distinguish BMH as an employer of choice.
- Be recognized for a culture of service excellence.
- Foster a culture of excellence that values diversity while encouraging teamwork, learning, and innovation.

Corporate Effectiveness (CORE)

- Provide strong financial performance to allow for capital reinvestment, growth, and sustainability.
- Partner with physicians, the community, and others to achieve common objectives.
- Use the Baldrige Criteria for Performance Excellence to improve processes and organizational performance.

them every day to patients. Bronson's success depends on the ability to achieve the three Cs as evidenced by key measures in the organizational scorecard. Through cycles of improvement and integration of the Baldrige criteria, Bronson identified critical success factors that have contributed to its competitive position and serve as a key element for the strategic planning process along with the Plan for Excellence. Exhibit 5.19 illustrates the principle factors critical to Bronson success.

Strategic Planning

Comprehensive, Continuous Process

Strategic planning at Bronson is a continuous process driven by the mission, values, and vision. Based on Baldrige feedback, the planning process was reevaluated and enhanced, integrating the strategic, financial, human resource, staffing, and education plans into a very robust strategic management model (SMM). The key steps of the SMM and the time frame for executing each step are shown in Exhibit 5.20.

The SMM, with its continuous planning process, allows for greater agility than a traditional, static approach to strategic planning. The SMM is the mechanism for developing organizational strategies, both short-term strategic objectives and long-term goals, and to ensure the strategic objectives cascade throughout the organization. Through the SMM, the board of directors and executive team determine the overall strategic direction for Bronson. The executive team develops and deploys annual plans to achieve it. Key participants in the process include: the board, executive team, quarterly strategic planning

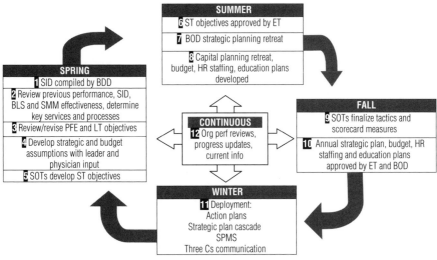

EXHIBIT 5 . 2 0   **Plan for Excellence Key Factors**

retreat attendees, and business development division leaders and physicians, who participate in several steps of the SMM process and provide input into planning through membership on organizational teams (strategic oversight teams [SOTs], Clinical Practice Council, service line teams, etc.). The following numbers link to the SMM diagram shown in Exhibit 5.20.

1. The planning cycle kicks off in the spring with the business development division preparing the strategic input document (SID). The SID contains relevant information related to all of the key factors recognized by the Baldrige criteria for performance excellence including these inputs: healthcare market needs; competitive environment; technological and innovation changes; SWOT analysis; societal, regulatory, and ethical issues; and analysis of the economic environment. Review of the SID during the spring quarter strategic planning retreat ensures that strategic planning addresses these key factors. Each key factor is presented and discussed, creating the foundation for the planning process. Source inputs are aggregated for development of the SID. Individual executives, SOTs, or the business development divison are accountable for gathering relevant information for inclusion in the SID. Revisions and updates to the source inputs are monitored and considered throughout the planning cycle.

2. A day-long quarterly strategic planning retreat, which includes the executive team and key directors, is held to review the SID along with a summary of the previous years' performance. At this time, the Bronson leadership system and SMM effectiveness are evaluated and improvements are identified for the upcoming annual cycle of planning. Key healthcare services and delivery processes are determined.

3. At the quarterly strategic planning retreat, the elements of the Plan for Excellence, including the mission, values, and vision, as well as the organization's long-term goals are reviewed and revised, if warranted.

4. Using a SWOT analysis gathered in steps 1 through 3 of the SMM, the executive team develops key strategic and budget assumptions that are tested at a series of planning meetings with leaders and physicians. The executive team assigns responsibility to the appropriate strategic oversight team. Three SOTs are aligned to support each of the corporate strategies (three Cs): Clinical Excellence (CE), Customer and Service Excellence (CASE), and Corporate Effectiveness (CORE). Each SOT is chaired by an executive team member; other team members include physicians as well as leaders from key operational and support departments.

5. The SOTs develop preliminary short-term objectives.

6. At the summer quarterly strategic planning retreat, the SOTs present short-term objectives for approval and begin tactic development.

7. During the summer, the strategic assumptions are revisited with the board of directors (BOD) at the annual strategic planning retreat. This review enables the board to validate the strategic challenges based on current information and provides the necessary foundation for the organization to prepare for strategic plan and budget approval later in the year.

8. During the capital planning retreat in the summer, human resources and finance use the SOT tactics and leader input to formulate the staffing, education, and budget plans. This day-long capital planning retreat affords the opportunity to focus on both short- and long-term capital planning needs.

9. The SOTs finalize tactics and the scorecard measures in the fall.

10. The strategies, long-term goals, short-term strategic objectives, organizational scorecard, budget, staffing, and education plans are approved by the executive team at the fall retreat and by the board at a monthly meeting in late fall.

11. Deployment begins in the winter including use of Staff Management System (SPMS).

12. In between each quarterly strategic planning retreat, the executive team meets to review organizational performance and progress in achieving the strategic objectives. Regular updates at the weekly executive team and monthly or biweekly SOT meetings support the continuous planning process and ensure that the most current information is integrated into the SMM. A systematic review of organizational performance, review of the quarterly system indicator report (QSIR), along with regular environmental scanning, mitigates the potential for blind spots caused by factors that may have changed since the initial development of strategic objectives and tactics. The business development division maintains a compilation of competitive events in the marketplace. This information assists in identifying possible market trends that could impact Bronson. The executive team establishes planning horizons based on the analysis of market dynamics. Market analysis and intelligence resources indicate that one year is currently appropriate for short-term plans to remain responsive to market forces and synchronized with the budget cycle. The long-term planning horizon, three to five years, is determined by evaluating constraints, such as the time to introduce new services, the optimum life cycle of existing services, as well as market intelligence related to competitive strategies and plans. This approach enables Bronson to be responsive to changing factors in the marketplace while maintaining stability of the long-term strategic focus. The SMM results in the development of short-term strategic objectives and long-term goals that support achievement of the vision. During the SMM, consideration is given to the necessary action plans that must be

completed to make progress in each corporate strategy. Through the integration of operational, clinical, financial, and human resource perspectives, the enhanced SMM facilitates the allocation of adequate resources to complete the action plans in support of the short-term strategic objectives and long-term goals.

At the beginning of each quarterly strategic planning session, the QSIR is reviewed. The QSIR contains the most recent information related to organizational performance and the key factors. Weekly executive team meetings include a standing agenda item to ensure discussion of any new intelligence. Necessary plan changes are deployed through the SOT action planning process. This approach allows for timely plan revisions supporting organizational agility. Through the annual review of SMM effectiveness, the executive team is able to assess its ability to execute the strategic plan and make the necessary changes to the strategic plan cascade.

Spotlight on the Alignment and Balance

Key short-term objectives and long-term goals as well as the timetable for accomplishing them are shown in Exhibit 5.21. The strategic challenges are identified during the planning process, and aligned with organizational strategies to ensure that all challenges are addressed. Once finalized by the executive team, the challenges are included in the final SID, which serves as an important reference used throughout the strategic planning process. The capability to balance short- and long-term challenges and opportunities is built into the SMM. Through the SMM, the executive team first identifies the long-term goals. Next the short-term objectives are developed; they are considered the annual milestones toward achievement of the long-term goals. A one-page planning document containing both the long-term goals and short-term strategic objectives in the three Cs format, is used to communicate plans to employees, physicians, suppliers, and the community. Balance is achieved throughout the SMM by aligning strategic objectives with the three Cs and the strategic challenges. The process draws on input from patients, employees, physician partners, suppliers, and the community to ensure needs of all stakeholders are considered and effectively balanced.

Strategic Communications

Effective communication, alignment, and deployment are essential for achievement of organizational strategy. Using the leadership communication process (see Exhibit 5.22), the executive team communicates values, plans, and expectations in the three Cs format throughout the organization and to the community.

The three Cs communication format also establishes a framework and assists

EXHIBIT 5.21   One-Page Planning Document

Strategies and Strategic Challenges	ST Objectives	LT Goals	Key Tactics and Action Plans	Changes	HR and Education Plans	Key Performance Measures
CE: Achieve excellent patient outcomes SC1 SC2	Medicare mortality at CS top 15% Recognized by Leapfrog as safe environment Exceed national standards for core indicators	Top 100 hospital 5 stars for targeted areas Third-party recognition for patient safety	Decrease VAP Optimize Medicare mortality and morbidity Optimize core indicator performance Build CPOE Optimize communication among providers	Hospitalists admitting ortho patients Medical management for adult patients w/chronic diabetes and HF	SBAR education Fill CPOE team positions	Medicare mortality VAP Patient falls Skin ulcers SIP Core measures (AMI, HF, pneumonia) Hand washing
CASE: Enhance service excellence, staff competency, and leadership SC3 SC4 SC5	Magnet status Leader in MD satisfaction Overall turnover and vacancy better than national best practice EOS diversity scores improve Patient satisfaction scores improve from benchmark	Best practice customer and MD satisfaction 100 Best Employer Maintain magnet status	Implement respiratory care development program Implement mentor program Operationalize diversity council Implement EOS and LPMS, physical surroundings, and discharge process recommendations	Gallup survey with national benchmarks Campus expansion project moves some support services off campus	Respiratory care development candidates Mentor program education Diversity education plan	Vacancy EOS diversity score MD satisfaction Patient satisfaction Patient satisfaction w/physical surroundings Patient satisfaction w/discharge Overall turnover RN turnover
CORE: Achieve efficiency, growth, financial, and community benefit targets SC6 SC7	Meet growth targets for targeted service lines, profit margin	X market share in targeted services Profit margin Baldrige recipient	Implement long-term campus expansion plan Implement short-term technology/facility plan Recruit key physician specialists	MD ambulatory surgery and outpatient diagnostics centers Expansion of adult medical unit capacity	Realign campus project leadership "Change management" training for move Hire staff for new capacity Train on new technology	SL market share SL market share SL market share SL market share Profit margin

FOCUS PDCA

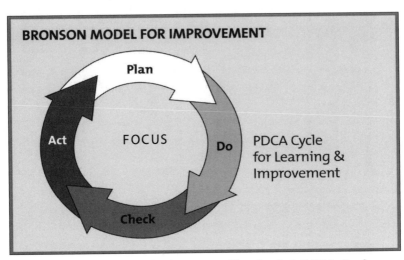

EXHIBIT 5.22. Plan, Do, Check, Act PDCA Cycle

BEST PRACTICE HIGHLIGHTS

Principle 2: Refresh and Communicate Strategy

- *Strategic Planning.* Bronson has effectively linked its philosophy, mission, strategies, and annual plan with its BSC goals and measures, which are cascaded throughout the company. Bronson links strategic, operational, and people plans.
- *Strategic Planning.* Bronson personnel conduct strategic planning to understand changing market conditions including competitor, supplier, rivals, potential entrants, and substitutes in the marketplace. SMM includes a comprehensive SWOT analysis.
- *Strategic Plan.* Bronson produces a comprehensive strategic plan that is updated continuously throughout the year.
- *Core and Adjacent Products and Services.* Bronson defines and determines core, adjacent, and new services to focus on highest probabilities for success.
- *Link Strategic Planning and Budgeting Processes.* Bronson links strategic planning to the budgeting process to provide for a seamless continuum.
- *Communications Plan.* Bronson communicates strategy throughout the organization using a comprehensive communications plan.

leaders in creating and balancing value. The executive team uses a variety of mechanisms that reinforce two-way communication and feedback. Examples include leader rounds, department meetings, CEO/chief nurse executive open office hours, shared governance, and access to e-mail for all employees. Bronson fosters a culture of employee involvement and empowerment through a commitment to workforce excellence

> *I always thought that record would stand until it was broken.*
> —YOGI BERRA

RICOH: BEST PRACTICE CASE

Ricoh has a long history of strategic planning. Every three years the parent organization, Ricoh Company, Limited, develops what is called the Mid-Term Plan (MTP). This management by objective planning process, which is driven centrally by headquarters in Japan, identifies growth opportunities and targets improvements to be made for all of the geographic operating regions. Like many corporate center planning documents, the plan covers financial targets and unit goals to be achieved by each region, leaving the details of tactical development up to each country's manager.

During the summer 2001 Ricoh Company was completing execution of its 13th MTP and ramping up to begin deploying the 14th MTP. In the Americas' organization, several important developments were occurring in the imaging market. While total document volume (TDV) was increasing, it was clear the ways in which companies would produce imaging products was rapidly changing. Whereas historically a copy of a document would be sent to a local printer and then manually reproduced, technology had reached the level of sophistication that allowed the printing and reproduction capability to be combined. For any company whose financial performance was dependent largely on copier sales, this was sobering news. Ricoh was one of these companies. It realized that a change in strategy—along with a change in internal performance—was absolutely needed. "One of the most important realization we had early on was the need to balance our product focus with more of a customer focus," said Hede Nonaka, then vice president of marketing. So while clearly not intending to abandon its core product focus, Ricoh began a shift in the types of products it sold and, equally as important, the philosophy of the market approach in

- Recipient of Balanced Scorecard Hall of Fame Award
- Recipient of Deming Quality Award

general—from one that focused on selling "boxes" to one committed to selling "solutions."

Into late 2001 and early 2002, the project team and selected senior leaders translated the specifics of the 14th MTP into a completed Strategy Map. This was a challenging process but one that yielded major insights. Creation of the Strategy Map derived from the 14th MTP was the first time executives and senior managers from across the company came together around an approach to translating the strategy into commonly understood objectives. "The process we went through was iterative and it lasted for several months. It was time consuming. But once we realized how to decompose the strategy into logical cause and effect relationships inside the Strategy Map, it all clicked. Personally this was the 'aha' moment for me. It was fascinating watching the process evolve from the outside," said Ed Barrows. "Executives were experiencing how to effectively come together to share information and make decisions. Part of this was experiential, but another major component was cultural." By the mid-2002 the Strategy Map was completed and Marilyn held a "map signing" for all of the key executives who had been involved in the process. Large-scale Strategy Maps were printed and all team members signed the map memorializing their participation in this watershed process. Pictures of the day—as well as the map itself—were framed and hung inside the corridors of the corporate headquarters. See the Strategy Map in Exhibit 5.23.

Shortly after completion of the Strategy Map, Ricoh began to create the link between budgeting and strategy execution. Most organizations have a well-established budgeting routines; Ricoh is no different. Constructed over several months each year, the budgeting process at Ricoh is designed to support primarily the operational activities of the organization. Unfortunately, also like many budgeting processes, the process was disconnected from the key strategic priorities of the organization. To change this, Ricoh established what they call a strategic investment fund. Each year a pool of funds are earmarked to resource key strategic projects within the organization. Projects are deemed to be strategic based on the extent to which they impact the objectives outlined in the Strategy Map. Each quarter the CEO and the members of the Strategy and Planning Office (SPO) meet to discuss the key investments or initiatives either under way or proposed given the investments tend to span multiple operating cycles. This activity is critical to successful management of any organization's strategy. Having a high-level group that directs investments focuses investment proposal on high-leverage activities relative to the strategy. Ricoh also instituted this process at the business unit level and found the linkage between the strategy and the resources supporting it improved significantly.

Another key success factor that Ricoh understood and executed flawlessly was the development of a company-wide communication strategy to support the strategic change. The first portion of the communication strategy occurred early on through involvement of senior leaders and capable managers from

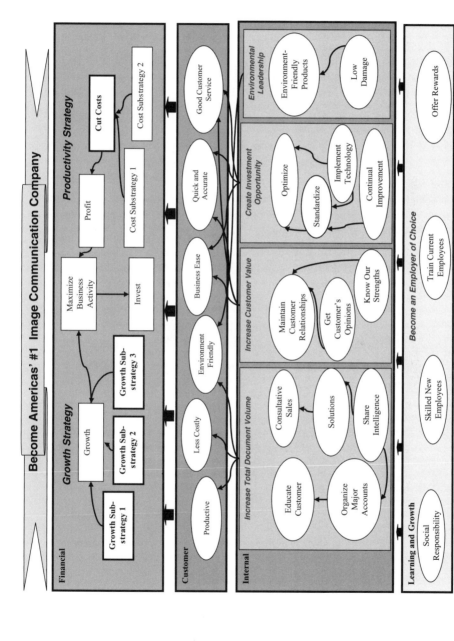

EXHIBIT 5.23   Ricoh Strategy Map

143

across the organization with the project. While informal in nature, this organized "show of support" proved a crucial initial step in establishing an effective communication strategy. Next Marilyn began to plan and execute a series of company forums designed not only to communicate the strategy but to literally excite the organization. In January 2002, with the Ricoh Strategy Map close to final, Ricoh launched the first ever Chairman's Leadership Forum in which the Strategy Map was presented, not only to hundreds of key Ricoh managers, but also to the CEO and key leaders from the Japanese parent who made the trip to Ricoh Company headquarters in New Jersey. This forum was so well received it has now become an ongoing event at the company held annually to discuss and share input regarding key elements of the strategy. "This is the main way in which top leaders from throughout the company come together to discuss strategy and to infuse the discussion with thought leadership from customers, academics, and the business community at large," notes Marilyn. The forum was also critical, not just from the standpoint of sharing ideas regarding the strategy, but because it showcased key executives—the chairman in particular—publicly communicating the importance of and the particulars within, the strategy.

But the Leadership Forums were not the only place where the strategy was communicated. Ricoh publishes and distributes internally a newsletter aptly

BEST PRACTICE HIGHLIGHTS

Principle 2: Refresh and Communicate the Strategy
- *Strategic Planning.* Leverage the strategic planning process as either owner or partner to understand changing market conditions including competitor, supplier, rival, and potential entrants and substitutes in the marketplace.
- *Core and Adjacent Products and Services.* Define and determine core and adjacent products and services to focus on highest probabilities for success.
- *Strategic Plan.* Produce a comprehensive strategic plan.
- *Strategy Mapping.* Develop a Strategy Map containing objectives along four perspectives including financial, customer/constituent, process, and people. Observe Strategy Map design parameters of 20 to 25 objectives.
- *Link Strategic Planning and Budgeting Processes.* Link strategic planning to the budgeting process to provide for a seamless continuum. Ideally, provide a rolling forecast or a flexible, lean budget linked to strategy.
- *Communications Plan.* Communicate strategy throughout the organization using a comprehensive communications plan.

named *Quality Matters*. This publication highlights ongoing performance improvement activities at the company. In April 2003 a special issue was distributed to all employees that focused specifically on the Strategy Map and BSC. The Performance Excellence Group, under the guidance of Marilyn, developed desktop training on BSC concepts for the entire 10,000-person organization. This training was translated into French to accommodate the workforce in Ricoh Canada and Spanish to reach the employees in Ricoh Latin America. For those employees who did not have access to computers on their desks, kiosks were set up at their places of business and CDs were distributed for them to take home.

While these examples represent some of the key components of the Ricoh strategy communications activities, they are by no means exhaustive. Countless discussions occurred during and after meetings to help contextualize the strategy for the organization overall.

KEYCORP: BEST PRACTICE CASE

Upon becoming CEO of KeyCorp, Henry Meyer knew that for Key to be able to meet and exceed shareholder expectations it would be critical to have a well-defined and clearly articulated strategy in place. Prior to developing Key's BSC, Meyer organized a three-day offsite of his senior leadership team to focus on and reinvigorate Key's strategy. To accomplish this, each of Key's 14 line of business leaders were asked to present a strategic overview of each of their respective businesses. A sample of the elements included in each of these presentations follows.

Business Profile	Industry, Economic and Competitive trends
Competitive Assessment	SWOT Analysis
Strategic Priorities	Financial Overview (Current and Three-Year Forecast)

The presentations made at this session were then used to formulate Key's relationship strategy and to create the blueprint of Key's transformation. This transformation entailed reorganizing many of Key's businesses, divesting from nonrelationship-based businesses, and the replacement of a number of senior managers. Six of Key's current 12 senior managers have joined the company since 2002.

The next step in the process was to define Key's vision and mission. Key's vision is to "Be the most admired financial institution in our markets" and

• Recipient of the Global Balanced Scorecard Hall of Fame Award

its mission is to "Be our clients' trusted advisor." The vision and mission coupled with Key's corporate values of teamwork, respect, accountability, integrity, and leadership became the foundational elements of Key's corporate Strategy Map and BSC.

Creating Key's Strategy Map and supporting objective statements, which provide greater detail behind each of the ovals on the map, was not an easy task. It took numerous iterations before the senior management team was comfortable with the agreed-on objectives. Prior to the development of the Strategy Map and BSC, each of Key's businesses operated in silos. A majority of Key's line of business leaders' compensation was based on how their respective units had performed versus a majority of their compensation being tied to Key's overall results.

The Strategy Map is a one-page, pictorial representation of Key's strategy containing 15 objectives expressed across four perspectives: shareholder, client, internal process, and employees. We will review Key's Strategy Map (Exhibit 5.24) starting at the base and proceeding to the top.

The employee perspective includes the theme "Proud to Be at Key" supported by the statement "Live the Key Values" and people-focused objectives:

1. Attract, develop, retain, and reward a high-performing, inclusive workforce.
2. Create a client-focused, positive, and stimulating work environment.

Key believes that by investing in these objectives, it will be better positioned to execute on core processes described next.

The internal process perspective focuses on the theme "Execute 1Key" supported by process objectives:

1. Know our clients and markets.
2. Acquire, expand, and retain profitable relationships.
3. Achieve service excellence.
4. Manage business risks (to optimize rewards and prevent loss).
5. Leverage technology (to increase revenue and deliver distinctive service).
6. Continuously improve the business.

These primary processes at the corporate level align and support the client value proposition described next.

The client perspective focuses on the theme of "Be the Trusted Advisor" and consists of objectives:

1. Deepen relationships through "Advice and Solutions."
2. Distinctive service through key service and access.

Key's strategy is based on these service value propositions, which in turn drive financial results in the stakeholder perspective.

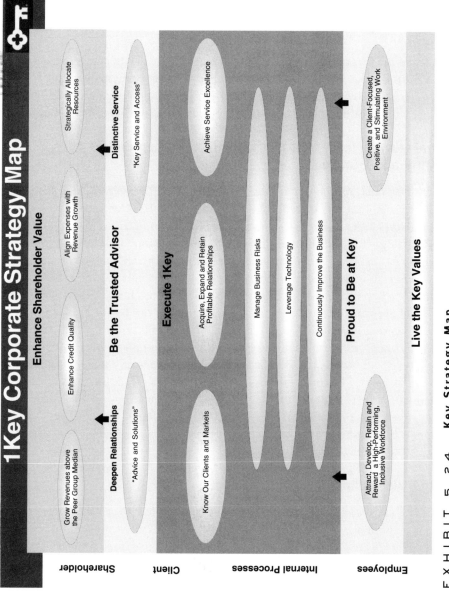

1Key Corporate Strategy Map

Enhance Shareholder Value

Shareholder

- Grow Revenues above the Peer Group Median
- Enhance Credit Quality
- Align Expenses with Revenue Growth
- Strategically Allocate Resources

Be the Trusted Advisor

Client

Deepen Relationships
"Advice and Solutions"

Distinctive Service
"Key Service and Access"

- Know Our Clients and Markets
- Acquire, Expand and Retain Profitable Relationships
- Achieve Service Excellence

Execute 1Key

Internal Processes

- Manage Business Risks
- Leverage Technology
- Continuously Improve the Business

Proud to Be at Key

Employees

- Attract, Develop, Retain and Reward a High-Performing, Inclusive Workforce
- Create a Client-Focused, Positive, and Stimulating Work Environment

Live the Key Values

EXHIBIT 5.24   Key Strategy Map

147

The stakeholder perspective focuses on the theme "Enhance Shareholder Value" composed of four financial objectives:

1. Grow revenue above the peer group median.
2. Enhance credit quality.
3. Align expenses with revenue growth.
4. Strategically allocate resources.

In summary, the Strategy Map's objectives provide the governance and direction for the rest of the organization to develop their strategic plans and objectives. Strategy Map objectives are supported by corresponding BSC measures, which are described more fully in Chapter 6.

Strategic Alignment and Integration: Origination Groups with Product Groups

A best practice example is within Key's Corporate and Investment Banking (KCIB) organization. Tom Bunn, vice chairman of KeyCorp and president of Key National Banking (KNB formerly KCIB), defined a clear vision, mission, and strategy for his organization. He began a process of integrating the Corporate and Investment Banks (previously KeyCorp's Commercial Banking businesses and McDonald Investments, Inc.'s Investment Banking Business). This approach resulted in four core origination groups being aligned with the product groups to create KCIB. The goal, to better deliver its franchise to the clients served, has enabled KCIB to more effectively penetrate existing clients, identify and target a focused list of prospects, and improve client profitability.

The line of business (LOB) Strategy Maps are regularly reviewed and discussed as part of the quarterly LOB strategy reviews with Key's senior management team to ensure that they cascade from and support the corporate Strategy Map. Further, Key's differentiating for high performance (DHP) process has resulted in personal scorecards for all exempt employees that are aligned with the corporate scorecard.

Strategic Community Banking Model

To assist in executing Key's strategic objectives, Key focuses on all aspects of the client experience. Providing a consistently great client experience is among every bank's greatest challenge. Key's strategic objectives focus on understanding client needs, tailoring offerings to meet those needs, and delivering distinctive service. This has been a challenge in the banking industry, which has traditionally not delivered products and services in an integrated manner.

To do this, the leadership team had to think outside the box, break down existing silos, and recognize what was best for its clients and for Key. It was during Key's initial Strategy Map and BSC meetings that its leaders realized that if the company was going to create significant improvements in performance and deliver enhanced shareholder value, it had to improve and deepen the quality and profitability of its new client relationships.

This strategic client relationship management focus gave rise to the announcement of Key's Community Banking model with the intent to improve the client focus at the local level and to improve profitable growth. The model places greater emphasis on how Key brings its full depth and breadth to clients within a geographic area. It breaks down the LOB silos that had existed in Key's geographic footprint. Historically, the retail banks would report low cross-sell numbers in their quarterly reviews. Today, Key has made significant improvements in client cross-sell. To assist with this process, desktop technology, better aligned incentive compensation plans, and new cross-selling programs are energizing the ways bankers deliver their ideas to customers.

The Strategy Map and BSC have provided tools to hold the executive team accountable for strategy execution across Key as an integrated team versus only the results for their respective areas of responsibility.

Communicating Strategy

Over the course of Meyer's tenure as chairman and CEO, Key's executive management team has evolved to effectively communicate and reinforce Key's strategic priorities across the organization.

Key's external communications tie to its strategy and its BSC. The scorecard tracks strategy that is reported to Wall Street, and Key is held accountable by its shareholders for these results. Key not only reports financial metrics to Wall Street but nonfinancial (process) metrics such as cross-sell and market share as well.

Key has employed numerous communication tools throughout its scorecard implementation including its intranet (KeyNet), internal publications (*Instant* and *Executive Insight*), business area newsletters, town hall and staff meetings, voice mail, and video messages. Key's communication approach was to first introduce the corporate Strategy Map and BSC at a leadership conference and in a series of corporate-wide electronic and print newsletters. Those activities were immediately followed by a meeting that every manager was required to conduct with their staff. The purpose of those meetings was to give employees an opportunity to discuss the corporate strategy and how it was relevant to their jobs. Managers were asked to respond to a survey, as well as share their employees' reactions to the strategy. Those responses helped determine the content and frequency of subsequent communications.

In its ongoing corporate and business area communications, Key consistently

EXHIBIT 5.25   Corporate Newsletter

Strategy and the Balanced Scorecard—Working Together to Ensure Success

It takes more than a vision, a defined mission, and sound strategy for a business to be successful. It also takes ongoing tracking and measuring of results.

That's why Chairman and CEO Henry Meyer is committed to linking corporate strategy more tightly with line-of-business and support-group business plans—with the objectives of every department and team—and, ultimately, with the individual performance goals of every employee. It's so every part of Key is aligned and moving in the same direction. It's to make sure good intentions turn into tangible action plans and produce outcomes that can be measured.

And it's why, this year, every Key employee can expect to be asked by his or her manager to develop personal performance objectives that align with Key's vision, mission, and strategic objectives.

BEST PRACTICE HIGHLIGHTS

Principle 2: Refresh and Communicate Strategy

- *Strategic Planning.* Leverage the strategic planning process to understand changing market conditions; establish the "community banking model" with a relationship strategy.
- *Core and Adjacent Products and Services.* Define and determine core products and services to focus on highest probabilities for success; again the new community model with a relationship strategy refocused the bank by geography to deliver products and services to key customer segments.
- *Strategic Plan.* Produce a comprehensive strategic plan.
- *Strategy Mapping.* Develop a Strategy Map containing objectives along four perspectives including financial, customer/constituent, process, and people.
- *Link Strategic Planning and Budgeting Processes.* Link strategic planning to the budgeting process; partner with finance to provide for a seamless continuum.
- *Communications Plan.* Communicate strategy throughout the organization using a comprehensive communications plan and intranet, as well as externally to analysts.

uses strategy and scorecard language to continuously reinforce those concepts. Exhibit 5.25 is an excerpt from a corporate newsletter three-part story that introduced the Strategy Map and BSC to employees. It illustrates how the Strategy Map and BSC are used together to build understanding of Key's direction and how it measures success.

Communications like this have helped create a common language and understanding of the corporate strategy and BSC across Key, providing a foundation for the 1Key Culture to take shape. Employees now focus more on Key as a whole and less on their particular line of business or support area. Employee engagement survey results have shown improvement in employees' perceptions of Key and strengthened understanding of and commitment to Key's "Teamwork" value.

> *Never fear the want of business. A man who qualifies himself well for his calling, never fails of employment.*
> —Thomas Jefferson

SPRINT NEXTEL: BEST PRACTICE CASE

To accomplish its mission, Sprint Nextel must transform and improve the business among many dimensions. Similar to an architectural plan, the strategic plan that was developed by the CSO (Corporate Strategy Organization) provides direction ("blueprint") on how to achieve the vision and strategy and keeps business functions aligned. The "mission" provides the destination and the "strategy" is the road map to get there. (See Exhibit 5.26.) Based on the assessment of Sprint Nextel's environment and working backwards from its mission, a three-year strategic road map was developed. This plan is based on six fundamental pillars that will:

- Provide a guideline to evaluate and address key strategic issues/questions.
- Help translate the strategy into an actionable set of objectives.
- Facilitate effective communication of objectives to employees.

These activities were key inputs into the development of the new SmartCard framework. The main focus areas of the six-pillar strategy became the overarching themes for the Customer and Internal perspectives within the Strategy Map framework. Exhibit 5.27 illustrates this relationship.

- *Forbes* America's Best Managed Company in the Telecommunications Services

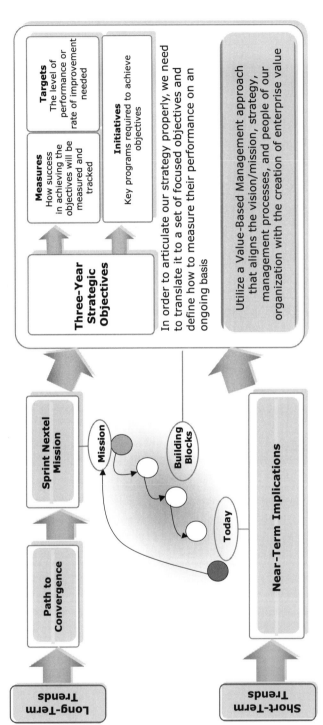

The level of performance or rate of improvement needed

Targets

Measures
How success in achieving the objectives will be measured and tracked

Initiatives
Key programs required to achieve objectives

Three-Year Strategic Objectives

In order to articulate our strategy properly, we need to translate it to a set of focused objectives and define how to measure their performance on an ongoing basis

Utilize a Value-Based Management approach that aligns the vision/mission, strategy, management processes, and people of our organization with the creation of enterprise value

Sprint Nextel Mission

Path to Convergence

Long-Term Trends

Mission

Building Blocks

Today

Near-Term Implications

Short-Term Trends

EXHIBIT 5.26 Developing the Strategic Plan: Process to Formulate and Update Strategy

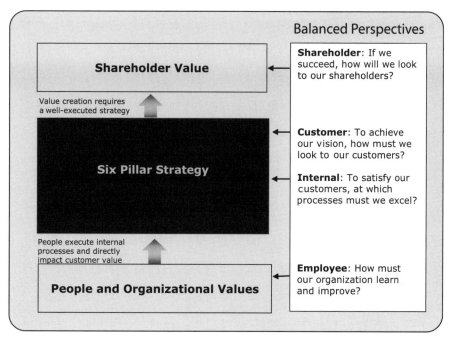

EXHIBIT 5.27   Strategy Map Framework

Linking Strategy to Value-Based Management

The next task was to define specific strategic objectives using value-based management. Value-based management is a framework and set of integrated tools for understanding, integrating, and managing customer, employee, and shareholder value. Exhibit 5.28 illustrates how that framework was used to hone in on the critical strategic objectives that would add shareholder value.

The framework identifies the shareholder value drivers and the key levers for those value drivers. To get to those levers that are relevant and strategic for Sprint Nextel, the team assessed the industry dynamics, assessed the internal capabilities of the new company, and met with the executive team to further "peel back the onion" and identify the right areas of focus. These key areas of focus became the five strategic objectives in the shareholder perspective.

A similar exercise was performed to identify the strategic objectives for the customer and employee perspectives. The strategic objectives for the internal perspective were identified primarily through interviews with the operational owners for the specific components of the six-pillar strategy and through bottoms-up input from the functions. The defined objectives aligned the core operations with the value-based drivers in the employee, customer, and shareholder perspectives and created a cohesive strategic road map (the Strategy Map) for arriving at the company mission.

Shareholder objectives are aligned with overall value drivers

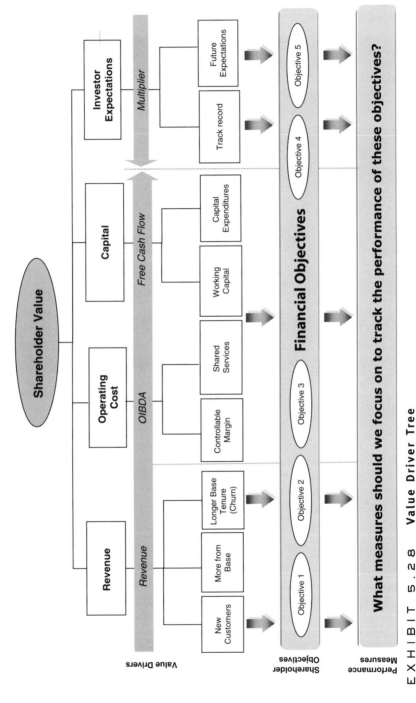

EXHIBIT 5.28   Value Driver Tree

Communications Plan (See Exhibit 5.29)

> For us to win the convergence game and accomplish our mission, we need to march in the same direction. That means we all need a clear understanding of our highly focused objectives.
> —Atish Gude, SVP Corporate Strategy and Development

Once the Strategy Map framework was complete at the corporate level, partnering with the corporate communications organization, the CSO created a deliberate communication plan to help employees understand how their activities contributed to the success of the organization, so they could support the execution of the strategy. Other goals of the communication plan included educating employees about the SmartCard as a tool to manage the company's performance against the strategic goals; educating employees about how individual and team objectives were linked to the strategy, and also making employees aware of how incentives and rewards were linked to the strategy. One key message constantly enforced was the linkage between the six-pillar strategy, the key strategic priorities for 2006, and the compensation incentive goals for 2006. This linkage helped reinforce the relevance of the strategy to all employees by tying it to a key motivator: incentive compensation.

The communication plan was deployed shortly after the strategy for the new company was finalized. Various communication tools were used including the company intranet, quarterly Web casts, senior leadership meetings, education programs, live presentations, and road shows. In addition, job aids were developed to help managers connect departmental goals to the functional strategy and a Web-tool was also released to help employees align personal goals with functional and corporate goals. Once complete, they could print the output as a poster to be displayed in their offices. These communication activities continued full force until second quarter 2006, when the focus shifted to assessing the effectiveness of the communication tools deployed. Ongoing communications are based on the results of those periodic assessments, to communicate relevant strategy refreshes and to provide quarterly updates against strategic objectives.

Another aspect of the communication strategy was to align the board of directors with the strategy and to communicate the BSC as the corporate performance management tool for assessing the new company's progress in executing the strategy.

Strategy Map, Objectives, and Balanced Scorecard

Exhibit 5.30 shows the linkage between the corporate and functional strategy and the related objectives and measures that were communicated to the board. It also shows how these components linked to the three-year financial plan and

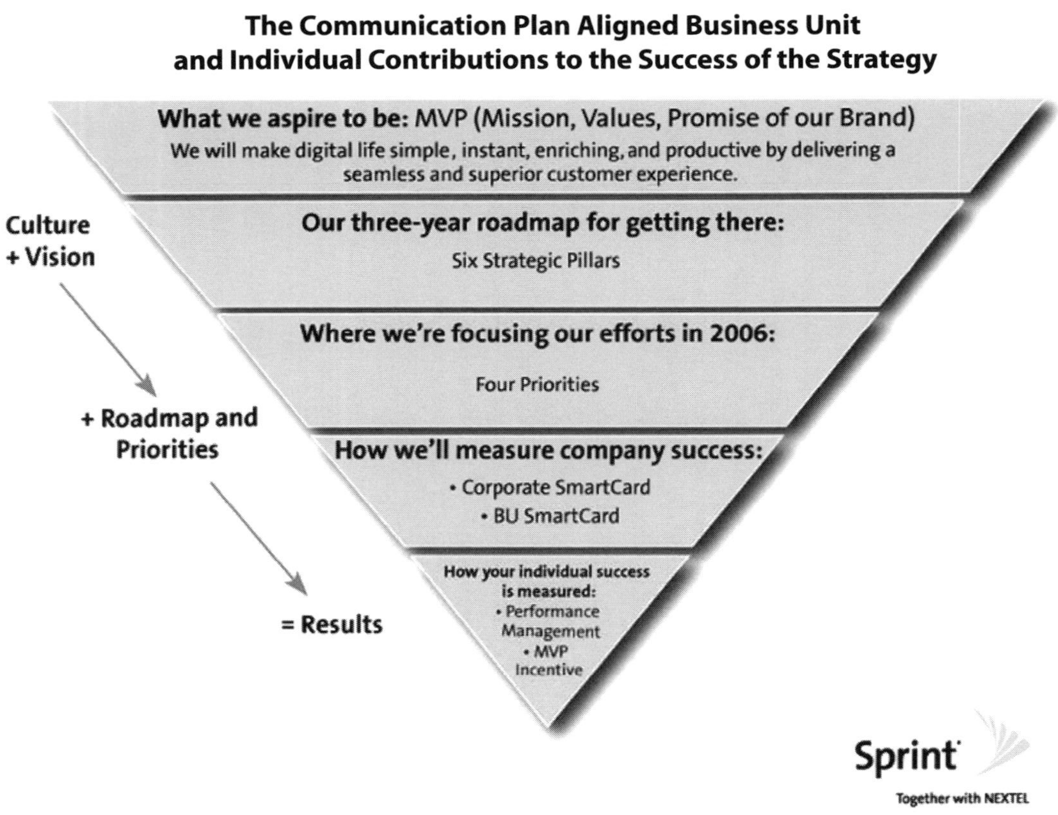

The Communication Plan Aligned Business Unit and Individual Contributions to the Success of the Strategy

What we aspire to be: MVP (Mission, Values, Promise of our Brand)
We will make digital life simple, instant, enriching, and productive by delivering a seamless and superior customer experience.

Our three-year roadmap for getting there:
Six Strategic Pillars

Where we're focusing our efforts in 2006:
Four Priorities

How we'll measure company success:
• Corporate SmartCard
• BU SmartCard

How your individual success is measured:
• Performance Management
• MVP
• Incentive

Culture
+ Vision

+ Roadmap and Priorities

= Results

Sprint®
Together with NEXTEL

EXHIBIT 5.29   Communications Plan

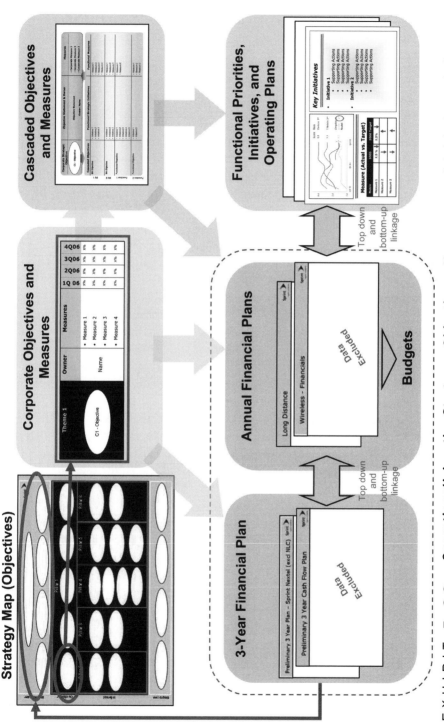

EXHIBIT 5.30 Operationalizing the Strategy: Objectives, Measures, and Initiatives Tied to a Three-Year Plan

the annual financial plans. This commitment to the board helped solidify the executive commitment to the BSC and helped firmly engrain the methodology into the strategic execution process.

Strategic Planning and Planning and Budgeting Process Links

The planning and budgeting process is owned by the finance organization. However, both finance and corporate strategy worked closely to implement an abbreviated planning cycle for 2006 in the postmerger stub year in 2005. Aligning the 2007 planning and budgeting process will be a considerably more involved effort. While the strategy refresh process will be a less significant effort than the full-blown strategy development process in 2005, a significant challenge for the corporate strategy team will be influencing a more robust planning and budgeting cycle that is tightly aligned with the strategy, where these activities are not owned by the organization.

Two significant opportunities exist for tighter alignment. The first is the introduction of one consistent planning framework for the new company. The selected framework provides both strategic and operational guidance to balance growth and profitability in a changing and competitive environment. Market-level resources such as network, distribution, and marketing are prioritized across geographies to drive long-term profitability and alignment with the strategy. Investments are then sequenced as precisely as possible in order to maximize the profit impact at the market level. Several challenges exist in the post-merger world where systems are not yet fully integrated. Data availability is one of those challenges. However, the framework has been adjusted and is becoming the basis for strategic and operational guidance for the company's 2007 planning process.

The second opportunity for tightening the alignment of the planning and budgeting process with the strategy is the successful alignment of the strategic initiative prioritization and funding process. The CSO's role in this effort is to ensure that the right set of strategic initiatives are identified to drive the achievement of the strategy and to ensure that those strategic initiatives are funded. The first step is to establish a consistent definition for strategic objectives. Strategic initiatives are defined as initiatives that close a performance gap associated with the six-pillar strategy. Next, corporate strategy provides guidance to the functions and other governing bodies involved in the strategic review process. Key inputs into that effort were the refreshed corporate strategic objectives, the identification of the performance measures for those objectives, their associated targets, current performance gaps (current performance relative to targets) as well as a summary of each business unit's expected contribution in closing those performance gaps. The various groups will use this

Principle 2: Refresh and Communicate the Strategy
- *Strategic Planning.* Sprint effectively linked its philosophy, mission, strategies, and annual plan with its BSC goals and measures, which are cascaded throughout the company. The six-pillar strategy is the road map for arriving at the company mission.
- *Strategy Mapping.* The key themes of this strategy were integrated into the themes of the corporate Strategy Map, and strategic objectives were identified using a value-based management approach.
- *Core and Adjacent Products and Services.* Sprint Nextel defines and determines core, adjacent, and new services to focus on highest probabilities for success.
- *Communications Plan.* The BSC was then integrated into the communication of the strategy to align employees to the strategy. It was also used to align the board of directors with the strategy and to align them with the plans for effective execution management. This solidified the organization's commitment to the BSC.
- *Link Strategic Planning and Budgeting Processes.* Significant strides have been made in aligning the planning and budgeting process with the strategy. However, additional opportunities exist for tighter alignment in 2007.

information to align their strategic initiatives to the strategy by identifying which measures their initiatives will impact and to prioritize those strategic initiatives by strategic pillar. Prioritized portfolios will then be submitted back to the CSO.

The CSO will play the role of global clearing house for the complete corporate portfolio of strategic initiatives. While each business unit can provide its own view on what initiatives are aligned with the six pillars of the strategy, the CSO will provide a global perspective of the strategic balance of the total portfolio and will work with the major executive initiative governance bodies to recommend funding for that portfolio.

If the CSO is able to successfully influence these processes to achieve tighter alignment through the organization, this will have a significant impact on the successful execution of the strategy.

> *With regard to excellence, it is not enough to know, but we must try to have and use it.*
> —ARISTOTLE

■ NOTES

1. Adapted from Bob Paladino, CPA, "Strategic Balanced Scorecard-Based Budgeting and Performance Management" Fifth Supplement 2005, Chapter 1A, John Wiley & Sons

2. Robert S. Kaplan and David P. Norton, *Strategy Maps: Converting Intangible Assets into Tangible Outcomes* (Boston: Harvard Business School Press, 2004), Crown Castle International case, p. 221.

3. Janice Koch, "The Challenges of Strategic Alignment: Crown Castle's CEO Shares His Perspectives," *Balanced Scorecard Report* (July–August 2004): 11.

4. Bob Paladino, "Balanced Forecasts Drive Value," *Strategic Finance Magazine* (January 2005).

5. Koch, "The Challenges of Strategic Alignment," p. 10.

6. Janice Koch, "Global Alignment: A Telecom's Tale," *Balanced Scorecard Report* (May–June 2004): p. 7.

7. "TVA Creating a Winning Performance" presentation, Cambridge, MA, June 1, 2004, p. 14.

CHAPTER 6

Principle 3

CASCADE AND MANAGE STRATEGY

> *When you can measure what you are speaking about, and express it in numbers, you know something about it; but when you cannot measure it, when you cannot express it in numbers, your knowledge is of a meager and unsatisfactory kind.*
>
> —LORD KELVIN

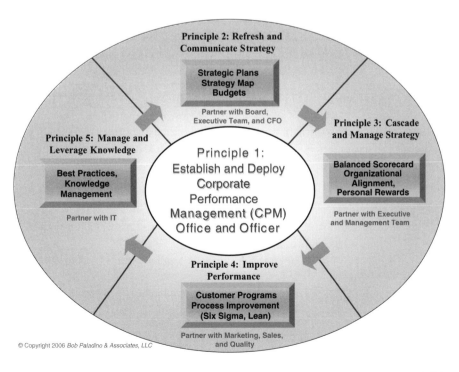

© Copyright 2006 *Bob Paladino & Associates, LLC*

EXHIBIT 6.1   **Principle 3: Cascade and Manage Strategy Best Practice Summary**

Best Practice	Description
Partner with business owners	Partner with line and staff leadership team members to gain support and influence as partners to help them achieve results.
Develop level 1 Balanced Scorecard (BSC)	Translate strategy into level 1 BSC measures and measure targets at the highest organizational level in your organization (corporate, government agency, or non-profit).
Leverage proven BSC of comparable methods	Observe BSC or comparable design parameters assigning one to two measures to each strategy map objective.
Cascade BSC to lower levels	Cascade and align level 1 BSC to levels 2, 3, 4, and so on depending on organizational and accountability structures.
Align support services	Identify and define measures for all support services that align with levels 1 and below.
Align teams and individual employees	Define personal BSCs for teams and /or individuals that align with higher-level and support services BSC.
Link Compensation	Align rewards, recognition, and compensation programs to the BSC.
Manage using measures	Manage BSC meetings to address the appropriate mix of strategic and operational issues; link these issues with Principle 4: Business Improvement.
Automate measurement	Implement corporate performance management software to manage BSC program with links to other principles.

This chapter reviews award-winning case studies focused on Principle 3, Cascade and Manage Strategy. The Crown case study will provide both the Crown specific best practices and expand discussion on the normative Principle 3 best practices (shown in Exhibit 6.1) learned from the collective companies researched.

Case study companies in this chapter also include recipients of these awards:

- U.S. President's National Malcolm Baldrige Quality Award
- Governor's Sterling Award for Excellence (based on Baldrige Criteria)
- The Deming Quality Award
- American Quality and Productivity Center (APQC) Best Practice Partner Award
- Kaplan and Norton Global Balanced Scorecard Hall of Fame Award
- *Wall Street Journal* Ranked "Top 20 Most Improved Company in Shareholder Value creation"

- *Fortune* magazine's 100 Best Companies to Work For
- *Forbes* Best Managed Companies

The next section provides an introductory understanding of Kaplan and Norton's balanced scorecard (BSC) methodology, a central organizing framework for many case studies. For this knowledge, we turn to this author's earlier publication in the *Handbook of Budgeting* and continue our case study on Pareto Inc. from Chapter 5.[1] If you already have a foundational understanding of the BSC methodology, feel free to proceed to the Crown case study in this chapter.

> *Besides pride, loyalty, discipline, heart, and mind, confidence is the key to all the locks.*
>
> —JOE PATERNO

PARETO INC.: BALANCED SCORECARD INTRODUCTION

The BSC mirrors and supports the Strategy Map described in Chapter 5. Each strategy map strategic objective links to a measure on the BSC to enable management to track implementation of the company strategy. For example, in Exhibit 6.2 we have displayed the dominant operations strategy described

	Objective	Measure	Target	Sponsor	Initiative
(I1) Proactively Manage Renewal Process / (I3) Implement New Sales Model / (I2) Expand Service Offerings	I1. Proactively Manage Renewal Process	Renewal %	80%+	VP Sales	Contract Renewal IT Project
	I2. Expand Service Offerings	$ Revenue from New Offerings	$50 million	VP Sales	
(I4) Understand Customer Requirements / (I5) Invest in Strategic Sales Channels	I3. Implement New Sales Model	% Revenue from Channel Partners	15%	VP Sales	Sales Training Project
	I4. Understand Customer Requirements	# User Group Members	20 Sessions	VP Sales	
	I5. Invest in Strategic Sales Channels	# New Partners	Grow by 20%	VP Sales	

EXHIBIT 6.2   Pareto Inc.'s Internal Perspective: Customer Service Excellence

earlier, Customer Service Excellence, including its key objectives, measures, measure target, executive sponsor, and related initiatives. This construct provides clarity or line-of-site accountability for strategy execution and supports management meetings focused on accountability and performance.

For instance, (I3) Implement New Sales Model will be measured by % Revenue from Channel Partners, which has a target of 15% for the year. The objective, measure, and target are owned by the vice president of sales, who has also kicked off the sales training project that you support to manage this transition with his team. The new employee test is where the vice president of sales would provide more granular details on sales related objectives, measures, and targets.

Categories and Types of Measures

I have seen the BSC composed of many different categories of measures or ways to express measures; some examples include:

- *Percentages.* Free cash flow percentage growth rate, repairs and maintenance percentage reduction rates, customer percentage retention rate, or process sales percentage closure rate
- *Absolute dollars.* New product revenue, payroll expenses, or ground lease expense
- *Ordinal numbers.* Sulfur dioxide (SO_2) or nitrogen dioxide (NO_2) emissions in thousands of tons
- *Survey ratings.* Customer satisfaction on a seven-point scale
- *Time.* Cycle time expressed in seconds, minutes, hours, days, weeks, and so on
- *Ratios.* Safety loss worker days per thousand hours worked
- *Indices.* System average interruption duration index (SAIDI) or customer average interruption duration index (CAIDI)
- *Rankings.* Top 10 in size, assets, market capitalization, or customer satisfaction.

Although there are many categories of measures, one can also sort and group them into complementary *types*. We will describe four types of measures consisting of two pairs that complement each other: lead and lag, and efficiency and output.

Lead and Lag Measures

Leading measures are often referred to as early-warning measures. These indicators are generally more prevalent in the operations and learning and growth perspectives of your BSC to provide a month or quarter heads-up to activities or events that will manifest themselves later in the financial results measures. On occasion you will, however, see a lead measure in the financial perspective in Pareto Inc.'s BSC front log expressed as the number and dollar value of proposals submitted to its customers for consideration. Another leading measure includes Backlog, a measure of customer contract commitments that have not yet been recognized as revenue.

Lagging measures or rearview mirror–based measures such as free cash flow record history of what took place last month, last quarter, or last year. While these measures provide a historical perspective, they are not always reliable predictors of future performance. Would you drive that eight-cylinder car in reverse? You need the visibility provided by leading indicators about the road ahead.

Efficiency (Process) and Effectiveness (Output) Measures

Efficiency (process) measures provide visibility into how well a given process or set of processes is functioning. Process measures are closely linked to quality efforts, whether we are focusing on International Organization for Standardization ISO 9000, Baldrige Award criteria, or Six Sigma. In quality terms, these are called your drivers or Xs. A complete discussion of these quality disciplines is beyond the scope of this book; the context here is understanding and appreciating how the BSC and process quality measures are reinforcing. Fundamentally, your BSC should be tracking key attributes of processes or an index of several processes. Examples of process measures include productivity measures such as process cost per unit of output (economic), turnaround time (cycle time), and process reliability and repeatability.

Effectiveness (output) measures complement efficiency measures and provide instruction on the quality of process outputs. In quality terms, these are your customer-facing deliverables or so-called Ys. Examples include percent defective items, number of errors, and invoicing accuracy. A call center example at this stage would highlight the efficiency and effectiveness measure relationship. The (X) Efficiency/Process measure of "Answer Speed" by company operators would help drive the (Y) Effectiveness/Output measure of "Call Abandon Rate." Quality programs will look at improving the Xs that drive the Y results.

To bring things together, Pareto Inc. has a new sales objective (I3), Implement New Sales Model, that will be measured by percentage revenue from channel partners. This measure fits into the percentage category and is a lagging, output Y measure. Your training program, however, is a leading X indicator, where you may adopt submeasures such as number of classes taught or number of salespeople trained. Each measure has approximately 20 attributes to ensure it is properly developed, budgeted, and managed, including, for instance, measure owner, measure reporter, data source system, measure definition and calculation. It is critical to stabilize the attributes and provide transparency so everyone is clear about the rules of the road. Your BSC program will lose creditability without healthy debate and consensus on what is being measured and how.

Measure Targets

Once a company has defined its objectives and measures, it must establish targets (we will use the terms "targets" and "budgets" synonymously) against which it can track performance. We shall discuss targets in the context of annual planning generally consisting of annual figures. Targets set and communicate the expected performance level for the organization and focus the organization on improvement. Each target should match a measure, one for one, and be quantifiable. Pareto Inc. has a new sales objective (I3), Implement New Sales Model, that will be measured by percentage revenue with a 15% target for revenue from channel partners. This should provide a clear, quantifiable target for your sales training program to help the sales team achieve.

Consider these key points when setting targets as a company:

- Define targets as a comprehensive set.
- Be sure the order of magnitude is appropriate to close any performance gaps.
- When in doubt, look back to the Strategy Map and the performance gap.
- Large performance gaps require a definitive action plan supported by appropriate resources if the stretch target is to be achieved.

> *You better cut the pizza in four pieces because I'm not hungry enough to eat six.*
> —YOGI BERRA

CROWN CASTLE INTERNATIONAL: BEST PRACTICE CASE

Crown in year 1 developed Strategy Maps and BSCs for the first three levels of the enterprise; in year 2 Crown cascaded to levels 4 and 5. The levels included:

- Level 1 for executive management team consisting of the CEO and his direct reports team
- Level 2 for the United States, United Kingdom, and Australia country-level senior management teams (SMTs)
- Level 3 for the SMT team members to manage their local operations; in the United States this included the six area presidents
- Level 4 for 40 district offices, reporting to the area presidents in the United States

- Recipient of APQC Best Practice Partner Award
- Recipient of Balanced Scorecard Hall of Fame Award
- *Wall Street Journal* Ranked "Top 20 Most Improved Company in Shareholder Value Creation"

- Level 5 covering teams and /or individuals (some would call these personal scorecards)

A key consideration in cascading measures is the degree to which you build in flexibility to address local similarities and differences without losing line of sight as you move further into the organization. At Crown five types of cascaded measures existed. These five include:

1. A corporate measure that cascades and *translates directly* into a country-level measure. This is most desired since it best supports internal benchmarking (e.g., free cash flow).
2. A corporate measure that cascades and *translates directly* with a label or title change into a related country-level measure. This is also most desirable since it best supports internal benchmarking (e.g., revenue versus turnover).
3. A corporate measure that cascades and *translates but requires modifications* to an existing country-level measure calculation to ensure alignment with corporate (e.g., tower margin).
4. A corporate measure that cascades and *translates into a brand-new* country-level measure that involves new construction (e.g., job closings).
5. A corporate measure that *does not translate* into any related country-level measure. An example may include the U.S Federal Aviation Administration, which does not have a corollary at the country level.

Given the similarities across Crown's distributed operations, we primarily used the first four types of measures; we could largely adopt what I term a "replica" model where a measure appearing at the corporate board level 1 would also replicate down to district office level 4. For example, the measures accounts receivable expressed as days sales outstanding (DSO) was used throughout the BSC levels. This approach enabled for benchmarking described in the next section. This approach to measure design also provided for alignment across a large organization.

> *The difference between the impossible and the possible lies in a man's determination.*
> —TOMMY LASORDA

An interview with Crown chief executive officer (CEO) John Kelly is most instructive. The interviewer asked, "For a company as geographically dispersed and as operationally decentralized as Crown Castle, how important has the BSC been in fostering a common understanding of the organization's strategy?" Kelly responded, "In general, the BSC has been crucial in achieving strategic alignment. This goes beyond a simple measurement question. You have to ensure that what you're measuring is linked back to strategy. Many times you'll find people doing things that are not the most important and that are not advancing the strategy. In our case, the BSC has been very important on a global basis in providing that common framework and understanding and in keeping people focused on what is important strategically."[2]

Support Function Balanced Scorecards

One centralized BSC was developed for all support services: the shared services scorecard. For example, finance has a measure related to the cycle time to close the books and provide financial statements in support of the organization. Similarly, the engineering function measured cycle time to review and provide certified engineering drawings to the field operations to support new antenna installations to towers, Crown's core business. Of the roughly 30 measures on the shared services BSC, roughly 80%, or 24, were dedicated to supporting the corporate strategy of operational excellence and were related to cycle time. Speed is a key differentiator in the industry. Some departments elected to develop more complete Strategy Maps and BSCs to run their operations. For example, the information technology department developed a more robust set of measures covering finance, internal customer, operations, and people BSC perspectives.

Measure Design and Benchmarking

Measures were explicitly designed to enable benchmarking across over 40 BSCs to identify top- and bottom-performing units. For example, the cycle time (customer order to service delivery) in office 10 was consistently faster than the cycle time in office 27. Learning this enabled us to study office 10 and transfer best practices to office 27 and across the entire system. Publishing the monthly benchmark report for the 40 U.S. district offices provided visibility into a wide range of differing business practices and in many cases created a collegially competitive environment among offices. The impact of this dynamic was to raise the overall performance across the system.

Balanced Scorecard and Total Rewards

Crown early on linked its BSC to compensation to reinforce and drive performance. CEO Kelly remarked, "In 2002, the companies tied compensation to scorecards. Now employees could see the connection between their performance and the company's. Recognition programs include Olympics-inspired monthly 'Gold,' 'Silver,' and 'Bronze' awards. The company has since integrated this program with 'Total Rewards,' the company compensation–linked rewards program."[3] The Gold, Silver, and Bronze awards relate to the top three district office performances on the benchmark report noted. This ranking also gave rise to local office adaptations and further rewards, such as American Express gift certificates, days off, or dinners. The truly interesting dimension was how creative Crown employees were in adopting and adapting the measurement framework to their operations. The unintended consequence of district office benchmarking was the creation of cross-functional, cohesive, and fun teams. In some respects, interoffice competition was similar to the environment created during college basketball's March Madness. However, this went on year round.

Meeting Management

Crown adopted an exception-based approach to using the BSC to run management meetings. While the Strategy Map contained 20 to 25 objectives, the teams would focus on the so-called yellow or red results to bring those back into desired performance ranges. The impact of this approach was to greatly shorten and improve the value of meetings. A given team moved from a line item review of financial statements to an in-depth review of four to five key strategic issues. Since objectives and measures were assigned to "owners," these responsible individuals came to the meetings prepared to discuss their action plans for remedial action. In effect, the management teams were getting out in front of issues, not reporting on rearview-mirror results as in the past. The results of these leading indicator measures provided insights into changing marketing conditions and provided leaders with an early warning system to impending issues.

Scorecard Automation

I recommend you automate using a dedicated Balanced Scorecard application early in your program development. A lesson learned is that MS Excel workbooks were used for over one year in the Crown program and it focused us too much on report preparation and allowed far less time on the higher-value-added analytics of reviewing strategic results. Once we automated and delivered Strategy Maps, scorecards, and management reports to our employees' desktops, meetings were conducted in an electronic environment and greatly accelerated the results. More time was dedicated to exception-based management instead of worrying about whether the workbook-based data were accurate or current.

Principle 3: Cascade and Manage Strategy
- *Partner with Business Owners*. Partner with line and staff leadership team members to gain support and influence as partners to help them achieve results.
- *Develop Level 1 Balanced Scorecard*. Translate strategy into level 1 BSC measures and measure targets.
- *Leverage Proven BSC or Comparable Methods*. Observe BSC or comparable design parameters, assigning one to two measures to each Strategy Map objective.
- *Cascade BSC to Lower Levels*. Cascade and align level 1 BSC to levels 2, 3, 4, and so on below, depending on organizational and accountability structures.
- *Align Support Services*. Identify and define measures for all support services that align with levels 1 and below.
- *Align Teams and Individual Employees*. Define personal BSCs for teams and/or individuals that align with higher-level and support services BSCs.
- *Link Compensation*. Align rewards, recognition, and compensation programs to the BSC.
- *Manage Using Measures*. Manage BSC meetings to address the appropriate mix of strategic and operational issues; link these issues with Principle 4, Business Improvement.
- *Automate Measurement*. Implement CPM software to manage BSC program with links to other principles.

> *I am careful not to confuse excellence with perfection. Excellence, I can reach for; perfection is God's business.*
> —MICHAEL J. FOX

CITY OF CORAL SPRINGS: BEST PRACTICE CASE*

The strategic plan and key intended outcomes are the basis for the development of the city's business plan and individual departmental work plans that constitute the action plan for meeting strategic objectives. The city manager often says that the business plan "operationalizes" the strategic plan and then, in turn, drives resource allocation through the performance-based budget. Performance measures relative to the action plans are selected by departments

---

* The City of Coral Springs case team adapted portions of this case from "Performance Measurement in the Public Sector," *APQC* (November 2005), Governors Sterling Application 2003, and internal documents.

- Recipient of Florida Governor Sterling Award for Organizational Excellence (based on Baldrige Criteria)
- Recipient of APQC Best Practice Partner Award

based on how well they support key intended outcomes (KIOs), business plan initiatives, and successful delivery of core services.

Exhibit 6.3 lists the initiatives of the fiscal year business plan. Each initiative is an example of changes in operations that are strategy driven. Any changes, including new, updated, or discontinued services, must be formulated as initiatives. All staffing and capital requests are linked to initiatives as well. One of the benefits of this is that all staffing decisions are tied to the business plan to ensure strategic alignment. Some business plan initiatives are implemented over a multiyear time frame. An example of a long-term project currently in its third year is the "Downtown Coral Springs" initiative, which will continue to be updated in each business plan for the next five years, due to the long-term nature of the project. Key human resource plans are directly linked to short- and long-term plans.

In addition to performance measures developed by the departments, the city also uses a composite index, the financial trend monitoring system, an early warning system, benchmarking, and individual performance measures to monitor performance.

- The composite index is a set of 10 key performance indicators used as an indication of the value provided to city residents. Often referred to as the "stock price," the index not only serves as a basis for relative performance evaluation, but also as a leading indicator of the city's well-being.
- The financial trend monitoring system is a set of 25 measures, balanced between objective and subjective information, that provide a snapshot of the financial condition of the city, with long-term trends identified and an analysis of the "meaning" of the measures, whether positive or negative.
- The early warning system is used to monitor and predict significant changes in core business processes throughout the organization.

Cascading Measures to Employees and Compensation

Employees are motivated to develop and utilize their full potential through the city's incentive pay system, which is discussed in more detail later. Based on the results of the end-of-year incentive pay system review, an employee will be eligible for awards ranging from 0 to 7%, depending on ratings received. Motivation is also provided through the city's instant recognition program,

EXHIBIT 6.3   Key Intended Outcomes by Strategic Priority

Key Intended Outcomes by Strategic Priority		FY2003–04 Goal	Results
Customer-Involved Government			
• Overall quality rating for City services and programs (City Survey)	↑a	91%	7.1-1
• Overall satisfaction rating of City Employees (HR Survey)	↑a	92%	7.3-12
• Percent of plan reviews completed within 15 days	↑a	90%	*
• City prime rate (primes/100,000 residents—Calendar Year)	↓a	30%	7.4-1
• Quality rating for City employees customer service (City Survey)	↑a	92%	7.1-5
• Percent of voter turnout	↑a	12%	New
Neighborhood and Environmental Vitality			
• Number of formal and informal neighborhood partnerships each year	↑c	30	7.1-25
• Number of cooperative projects and the number of different partners (public, private and intra-city depts.) focused on enhancing the environment	↑c	6 proj 4 part	7.4-24
• Percent of attendees who find Slice of the Springs meetings productive	↑a	92%	7.4-27
• Number of pounds of recycled material collected per resident each year	↑c	104	7.4-4
• Compliance with State and Federal drinking water tests	↑a	100%	
• Percent of code cases cleared on first re-inspection	↑a	75%	7.4-25
Excellence in Education			
• Student attrition at Coral Springs Charter School	↓a	20%	7.4-23
• Number of student stations added each year (contingent on completion of JJJ)	↑c	2,682	*
• Number of partnerships with institutes of higher education	↑a	???	New
• Percent of school overcrowding in public schools	↓a	117%	7.4-2
Family, Youth, and Community Values			
• Percent of repeat domestic disturbance calls	↓a	−10%	*
• Number of volunteer hours donated to the City of Coral Springs each year	↑c	25,000	7.4-7
• Number of teen volunteer hours donated to the City of Coral Springs each year	↑c	3,000	New
• Number of Middle School After-School Programs offered annually	↑c	???	
Respect for Ethnic and Religious Diversity			
• Citizen support of Community efforts to increase tolerance (City Survey)	↑a	92%	7.4-6
• Minority residents who feel that the city is a great place to live (City Survey)	↑a	83%	7.1-11
• Percentage of minority applicants per recruitment	↑a	30%	7.3-5
Financial Health and Economic Development			
• Rate of return for the City in economic development incentives	↑a	$50	7.2-15
• Residents value rating (City Survey)	↑a	77%	7.1-6
• Non-residential value as a percent of total taxable value	↑a	18.5%	7.2-1
• General Fund debt carrying costs as a percent of total expenditures	↓a	12.5	*
• Percentage increase of operating millage rate	↓a	0%	7.2-17
• Maintain City bond ratings Moody Aaa, Fitch AAA	↑a	Moody Aaa Fitch AAA	*

Key: arrows indicate positive direction, a = annual, and c = cumulative

recognition of teams at the weekly senior management team meetings, and recognition at city commission public hearings. In addition, the city provides extensive training opportunities to employees through both in-house and outside offerings. A generous tuition reimbursement program is also available to help employees meet developmental goals.

Employee performance is managed through a set of systems that were designed to specifically link the attainment of stated city goals to individual employee work plans and to reinforce the city's core values and priority areas.

The incentive pay system evaluates employees on two levels. At the beginning of each fiscal year, an employee and a supervisor agree on a work plan and measurable objectives for the year. These objectives, which may be developmental in nature, are tied to departmental objectives, which in turn link to city key intended outcomes. 50% of the rating is based on the accomplishment of these objectives. The remaining 50% of the rating is based on specific job skills, which are tied to the city's four core values. An informal session is held midyear to assess how the employee is doing relative to the goals set at the beginning of the year and adjust objectives as required. In addition to the incentive pay system, other recognition systems are in place to support high performance.

The employee excellence awards are given out to employees and teams annually in each of the four core value areas. Employees may self-submit for the award or may be nominated by a peer. Winners are recognized at the annual quality fest and receive a trip to the Sterling Conference as recognition for their accomplishments. Specific recognition systems have been established to reinforce areas of particular importance to the city: customer service (city key intended outcome) and safety (human resources department measure). In the area of customer service, "Applause Cards" are available for employees to give to coworkers who exemplify the city's customer service standards. On a quarterly basis, 10 of the cards submitted are drawn and these employees are recognized at a city commission meeting and receive a gift certificate to the local mall.

The safety rewards program provides incentives to work groups that are injury free for specific time frames and to individuals who attend safety training or identify safety concerns. Other recognition systems that reinforce the city's goals include gain-sharing and the instant employee recognition program.

The city accomplishes succession planning and development of staff through participation in several programs. In 1991 the city began a leadership development program, which was initially designed for developing employees identified as future leaders in the organization.

Scorecard Automation

In 2006, the city began the process of automating the BSC by purchasing Active Strategy software and deploying it on the city's intranet. Individualized

BEST PRACTICE HIGHLIGHTS

Principle 3: Cascade and Manage Strategy

- **Partner with Business Owners.** Partner with business owners including line and staff leadership team members to gain support and influence as partners to help them achieve results.
- **Develop Level 1 Balanced Scorecard.** Developed corporate-level BSC, the highest level in the organization.
- **Leverage Proven BSC or Comparable Methods.** The KIOs leveraged proven BSC methods but are heavily weighted toward customers/constituents, an interesting variation on the traditional four perspectives. The KIOs contain a very manageable number of measures: 25.
- **Cascade BSC to Lower Levels.** The KIO/BSC was cascaded to the lowest levels of the organization including to the individual employee level.
- **Align Support Services.** Aligned support services to the corporate BSC objectives and measures–is this true?
- **Link Compensation.** Linked compensation to the objectives and measures in the BSC.
- **Manage Using Measures.** Effectively managed the business using BSC meeting management techniques focused on exception-based management.
- **Automate Measurement.** Starting the automation process to formalize the BSC throughout the organization.

scorecards and data will be available to department directors and key staff at first, later to be rolled out to the team level. The system will also be used to manage and track business plan initiatives, using milestones. Users will be prompted to update data and initiative progress with automatic e-mail reminders.

> *The person who makes a success of living is the one who sees his goal steadily and aims for it unswervingly. That is dedication.*
> —CECIL B. DEMILLE

TENNESSEE VALLEY AUTHORITY: BEST PRACTICE CASE*

The Tennessee Valley Authority (TVA) has developed a three-part process called Winning Performance linking strategic, operational, and people plans, as shown in Exhibit 6.4.

---

* The TVA case team adapted portions of this case from "Performance Measurement in the Public Sector," *APQC* (November 2005), and internal company documents.

- Recipient of APQC Best Practice Partner Award
- Recipient of the Balanced Scorecard Hall of Fame Award

The term "leadership standard" described in Chapter 5 translates the organization's vision into goals, objectives, critical success factors, and finally plans that employees can act on. TVA's vision at the time was "generating prosperity in the Valley."

For operational planning, goals such as "supplying low-cost, reliable power" are consistent with the vision. The Winning Performance core team adopted six strategic objectives that support the goals. An example of an objective is "improve life in the Tennessee Valley through integrated management of the river system and environmental stewardship." The critical success factors were developed as responses to key questions representing the four dimensions of a Balanced Scorecard: (1) financial, (2) customer/stakeholder, (3) operations processes, and (4) people. The financial question asks, "What must we do financially (to meet the strategic objectives)?" The answers are "generate more for less" and "invest prudently." Critical success factors translate into sustainable performance consistent with the business themes reflected in the objectives.

For each critical success factor, TVA developed an achievement plan. The development of some of the achievement plans was difficult and required more than one year of work because the plans were enterprise-wide, and achieving buy-in across all business units is difficult. Various components of

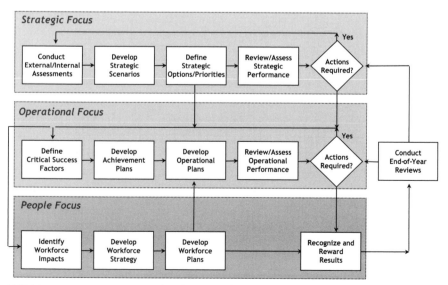

EXHIBIT 6.4   **Winning Performance Framework**

the achievement planning process fed into the overall performance management system.

Scorecard

Exhibit 6.5 provides an example of the corporate-level BSC. This scorecard format is mirrored by the strategic business units (SBU) and the business units (BUs).

Business units created their measures for the scorecards in their regular planning processes. The core team was operational as the business units were creating their measures, and it influenced the process by writing guidelines and questions that the business units could use in measurement development. One of the guidelines is a directive from top management that business units are expected to perform better each year—targets that exceed last year's performance should be set. If business units want to set targets that do not demonstrate improvement over the previous year's performance, they must make their case directly to corporate management.

The executive vice president of each of the line organizations is ultimately responsible for the performance measures. All measures are reviewed at the executive management committee level. The executive management committee was also responsible for developing the corporate-level scorecard.

The BSC has six icons at the top that represent TVA's six strategic objectives. The scorecard has four dimensions. The "people" dimension began as a learning and growth metric, but TVA had difficulty establishing a corporate-wide learning measure that was sufficiently robust that individual incentives could be tied to it. As a proxy measure, TVA adopted a safety metric a few years ago. Research shows that high safety correlates with high employee satisfaction. Although TVA continues to keep an open mind about changing the measure, safety will probably stay on the scorecard for the foreseeable future.

Measure Definitions

Behind the scorecard is the basis sheet (see Exhibit 6.6). The basis sheet has a level of detail that supports each of the indicators on the scorecard. At the beginning of the year, the basis sheet describes the basis for each of the targets. Once the targets are chosen, the basis sheets reflect progress toward the targets. The basis sheets are also called "reason for improvement" sheets because they describe the reasons why the team has decided to focus on the measure. If action is necessary, the sheet describes at a high level the action that needs to be taken so that the targets are met. The basis sheet shows past performance for the preceding three years and what management expects the future targets to be. Accountable and responsible individuals in the business

Winning Performance

FY 05

July 2005

	Weight	Status	Actual YTD	Plan YTD	Year end Forecast	Target*	GOALS Mid	Stretch

Financial
- **Total O&M Costs** *($Million)* — 15% — ◀
- **Financial Strength/Reduction of TFO** *($Million)* — 15% — ◀
- **Productivity** *(KWhs Delivered/Total Labor Cost)* — 10% — ◀

Customer
- **Customer Impact** *(Percent)* — 10% — ◀
- **Economic Development** *(Index)* — 10% — ◀

Operations
- **Asset Availability** *(Ratio)* — 20% — ◀
- **Environmental Impact** *(Index)* ** — 10% — ◀

People
- **Safe Workplace** *(recordable injuries/ hrs worked)* *** — 10% — ➡

Status
◀ Forcast at or better than Target
▲ Forcast worse than Target, recovery is possible
➡ Forcast worse than Target, recovery is unlikely

Notes:
* Target equals Performance Plan Target
** Reported quarterly
*** Any TVA Employee or staff augmentation contractor fatility will prevent payment for this indicator at the TVA level as well as the affected SBU/BU.

TVA

EXHIBIT 6.5   TVA Balanced Scorecard

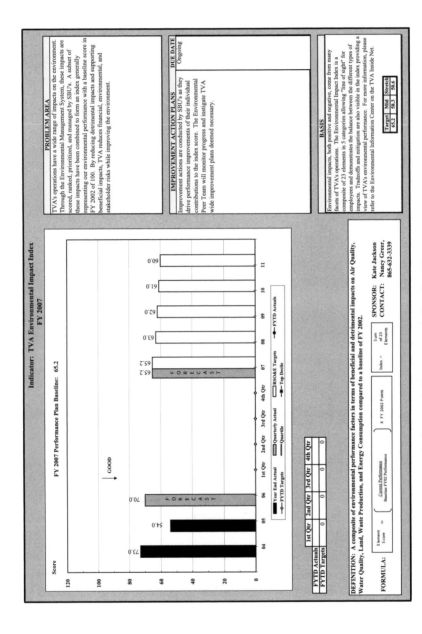

EXHIBIT 6.6 Balanced Scorecard Basis Sheet

units collect and analyze data and explain why various results are achieved or targets are missed.

TVA's Cascade to Employees

All employees are eligible for the Winning Performance payout. Team incentive is paid in addition to any monetary award received through annual performance reviews. Employees below the executive level have no pay at risk. When performance targets are achieved, employees receive their annual pay increases plus whatever incentives exist with the Winning Performance program. The payout opportunity is a lump-sum incentive award representing a percentage of base pay. There are three levels of performance on which pay is based:

1. If the company/strategic business unit/business unit reaches its target, employees receive 3.75% of base pay as an incentive. Payout is made only if the target is reached.
2. If the company/strategic business unit/business unit reaches its stretch goal (a number above the target), employees receive 6.25% of base pay as an incentive.
3. If the company/strategic business unit/business unit falls somewhere in the middle, the payout percentages are prorated for performance levels between "target" and "stretch," with an average payout of 5% of base pay as an incentive (midlevel performance).

Beginning in October 2005, managers and specialists are eligible for incentive opportunity ranges from 4.875 to 15%. TVA's ultimate goal for Winning Performance is that employees see a clear line of sight between their actions and the purpose of the organization. In summary, the line of sight is from (1) the 1933 act of Congress that created the organization, (2) the TVA strategic plan (which is currently being revised), (3) the strategic objectives and critical success factors, (4) the scorecard, (5) the strategic business unit/business unit business plans and scorecards, and (6) the performance plan of each employee. Employees are most closely aligned to their own business plan and scorecard.

TVA realizes that it cannot produce the appropriate results unless it selects the measure that drives the correct behavior. Kolz says, "Selecting the right measures is challenging. Sometimes despite our best efforts to rationally select a measure, we discover as the year progresses it drives the wrong behavior." To ensure continuous improvement, TVA sustains the Winning Performance system through:

- An annual business plan development cycle;
- Monthly reporting of measurement results;
- Online tools that allow employees to view not only their personal measures but also the company measures;

- Quarterly strategic reviews by TVA's management; and
- Dedicated corporate-level resources responsible for improving the measurement process, and benchmarking and best practices.

As Winning Performance was rolled out, TVA's 14,000 employees received extensive formal training, not only on the performance management system and the BSC, but also on related initiatives and skills. The training was led by executive and senior managers and took approximately six months to cycle all employees through. The training included breakout sessions that focused on how individual employees contribute through their strategic business unit and business unit performance plans. Employees identified the critical success factors in their own work.

TVA believes continuous communication is essential to its success. It has integrated Winning Performance messages and scorecard results into all employee communications. The organization's internal monthly publication Inside TVA includes scorecard results and related articles. Icons that represent the organization's strategic objectives are used in posters and displays. (In a few months, the organization's strategic objectives will be replaced by "Five Keys to the Future," which represents the vision of the new president and COO.)

Employees can view strategic business unit and business unit results along with other performance plan metrics on the Winning Performance Web site. The site includes monthly scorecard updates, performance measure definitions and calculations, and forecasted pay-outs. Display boards are distributed to facilities in which the employees do not have personal computer access. A reinforcement team works to standardize communications. Year-end closeout and new-year rollout is rolled out as a single, annual event covering the previous year's results and the New Year's scorecards and targets.

For several years, TVA has assessed its cultural health through a 31-question survey. Among other things, the survey asks employees how well they understand the Winning Performance program and how satisfied they are with their jobs. A high score on the cultural health index is a leading indicator of high performance on the scorecards. TVA organizations that have highly satisfied employees are more likely to receive a high incentive payout 18 months later, an indication that employee satisfaction and understanding is linked to performance results.

TVA Ongoing Management

TVA has seen positive changes since the implementation of Winning Performance. For example, forced outages have decreased, power plants are staying online longer, and the length of the outages has decreased. Employees change their behaviors based on targets set on business unit scorecards. TVA had a robust metric system in place before Winning Performance and improvements have occurred with the new scorecard and balanced approach. Bill Kolz says that it is reasonable to assume that Winning Performance is responsible for many of the targets TVA is achieving. TVA is constantly tweaking the Winning Performance weighting system to optimize employee efforts. In 2000, it began the program by weighting the overall performance of the company 50% when it determined payout to employees. In 2005, TVA applied a higher weighting to business unit results (70%) so that employees would have a greater incentive to increase their contributions to the business unit. TVA will:

- Revise the leadership standard.
- Resurrect enterprise-wide achievement planning.
- Strengthen the TVA business process model to more closely align processes and cost structure.
- Create more formal assessments of scorecard indicators and targets.

TVA will continue its guideline of having yearly targets exceeding previous year's results. However, on a case-by-case basis, it will avoid diminishing returns on investment. For example, some organizations operate at top decile performance and continuing to improve becomes increasingly challenging. Under special circumstances these organizations may be rewarded simply for maintaining their performance (if industry benchmarks verify performance attained).

TVA has recently developed a benchmarking group and intends to make greater use of benchmarking in its target setting. The organization intends to streamline and improve its performance reporting software. It currently uses a Hyperion-based application and will be seeking an enterprise-wide solution that shows not only the scorecards but also the report cards, another layer of measures that are more detailed. The new solution will improve timeliness, provide a single data source, and provide an electronic audit trail.

TVA and Balanced Scorecard Performance Management Results

The value of the BSC is captured in this quote from TVA's senior vice president of strategic planning and analysis: "In the future, increased competition could have a significant impact on how TVA carries out its mission. The BSC is one of the primary mechanisms TVA will use to measure it adapts to challenges that lie ahead."[4] TVA has realized results from its CPM Office and CPM processes including the BSC linked to strategy and business improvement including:

- Lowest three-year operating costs among 51 U.S. nuclear power generators.
- 99.999% reliability for transmission system, an organizational record.
- Annual operating budget savings of $30 million plus.
- Consumer prices 14 to 22% below the national average.
- Top industry practice award from the Nuclear Energy Institute.[5]
- Employees generated a savings of $220 million over the fiscal year 2005 budget.
- TVA paid state and local governments a record $365 million in lieu of taxes (increase of $27 million over previous year).
- TVA's generation and transmission system had its most successful year on record in fiscal year 2005, supplying more than 171 billion kilowatt-hours of electricity to customers.
- TVA met new monthly peak demand records for five consecutive months and met its highest peak demand ever of 31,924 megawatts on July 26, 2005.
- TVA's 11 fossil plants achieved the best reliability ever recorded for a fiscal year, with 6 units setting continuous run records. The coal-fired plants generated 98.4 billion kilowatt-hours of electricity, a 4% increase over 2004 generation.
- The transmission system completed its sixth consecutive year of 99.999% reliability.
- Generation at TVA dams was 13% above normal even though rainfall was 9% below normal.
- All five nuclear units operated at near full capacity during the summer months when the power system met all-time records for peak demand, and equipment reliability at the nuclear plants was the best ever with just 6.2 days offline due to equipment failure.
- In economic development, TVA and its partners helped attract or retain 57,000 jobs and leveraged investments of $3.6 billion in the region.
- TVA added two new selective catalytic reduction systems for a total of 20 in operation. These and other clean-air measures have reduced nitrogen oxide emissions that contribute to ozone during the summer by 80% since 1995.

In summary, TVA has achieved high-level sponsorship for the CPM Office from the president and chief operating officer and is supported by the direct report team. The CPM Office coordinates among leading executives including the senior vice president of strategic planning, executive vice president of human resources, the senior vice president of marketing, the senior vice president of economic development, the vice president controller, and the advisor to the president.

BEST PRACTICE HIGHLIGHTS

Principle 3: Cascade and Manage Strategy

- **Partner with Business Owners.** Partnered with business owners including line and staff leadership team members to gain support and influence as partners to help them achieve results.
- **Develop Level 1 Balanced Scorecard.** Developed corporate-level BSC, the highest level in the organization.
- **Leverage Proven BSC or Comparable Methods.** Leveraged proven BSC methods including use of the four perspectives and appropriate number of measures.
- **Cascade BSC to Lower Levels.** Cascaded the BSC to the lowest levels of the organization, including to the individual employee level.
- **Align Support Services.** Aligned support services to the corporate BSC objectives and measures. Some support organizations have scorecards (they also have SLAs), for example, procurement, IS, and facilities management. Others, such as human resources, legal, chief financial officer, and so forth are aligned to a weighted average of TVA/line organization performance: for example, 30% TVA Scorecard and 70% average SBU/BU scorecards.
- **Link Compensation.** Linked compensation to the objectives and measures in the BSC.
- **Manage Using Measures.** Effectively managed the business using BSC meeting management techniques focused on exception-based management.
- **Automate Measurement.** Automated the BSC using an off-the-shelf package but is currently developing a more robust semicustomized application to better meet needs.

You have to perform at a consistently higher level than others. That's the mark of a true professional.

—JOE PATERNO

MEDRAD: BEST PRACTICE CASE*

Medrad's key strategic objectives are the five corporate scorecard goals, which are long-term goals that rarely change from year to year (see Exhibit 6.7). The top 12 corporate objectives are short- and longer-term programs critical to achieving the corporate goals. The first 2 rarely change while the remaining 10 are product development and improvement initiatives that have milestone

---

* Portions of this case are adapted from Medrad Malcolm Baldrige National Quality Award Application, internal company documents, and employee input.

EXHIBIT 6.7   Top 12 Corporate Objectives

Corporate Goal	Target	Corporate Objective
Exceed financials	CMB (profit) growth > revenue growth	
Grow the company	Revenue growth > 15% per year	
Improve quality and productivity	Grow CMB (profit) / employee > 10% per year	
Improve customer satisfaction	Continuous improvement in Top Box ratings	Confidential
Improve employee growth and satisfaction	Continuous improvement in employee satisfaction above best-in-class Hay benchmark	

rather than numeric targets. Contribution Margin B (CMB) is the profit measure used by Medrad's parent, Schering, as a consistent measure of Schering's varied operating entities.

The top 12 objectives, which are short-term objectives with a one- to three-year time frame, support achievement of the long-term corporate scorecard goals. Medrad ensures that short- and longer-term challenges and opportunities are balanced through the long-term goals and shorter-term objectives and through the portfolio and strategic planning processes, which identify and address such challenges and opportunities. Specific goals and objectives that focus on customers, employees, and Schering's shareholders balance the needs of Medrad's key stakeholders.

Meeting Management Accountability Structure

Medrad's board of directors, which is comprised of members appointed by Schering-Berlin, Inc. and Medrad's former CEOs, is responsible for evaluating the performance of Medrad's CEO. The CEO is responsible for evaluating his staff's performance. The executive committee owns Medrad's leadership system. Based on findings from the performance review meetings, the executive committee and senior staff initiate immediate improvements in the leadership system or plan long-term changes as part of strategic planning. Inputs that shape the review findings and improvements include performance on key

- Recipient of Malcolm Baldrige National Quality Award
- Recipient of the APQC Best Practice Award

measures including the corporate scorecard and top 12 objectives, employee satisfaction surveys, customer listening posts, Schering AG expectations, the competitive environment, original equipment manufacturer (OEM) and partner discussions, ISO and Food and Drug Administration (FDA) audit results, Baldrige feedback reports, benchmarking information, professional society membership, and training events. Improvements in the leadership system through this approach include establishing senior staff meetings with specific performance excellence focus, application for the Baldrige Award, the corporate scorecard, the creation of advisory boards, and "incubator" leadership structures for multivendor services. The governance calendar is shown in Exhibit 6.8.

During the objectives "waterfalling" step in the planning process, managers and staff members at all levels create objectives and plans that support the corporate scorecard goals, top 12 objectives, and function plans. They combine these objectives, initiatives, and plans with an analysis of the function's performance based on elements that include process indicators, customer and supplier listening posts, employee listening posts, benchmark and comparative studies, ISO and FDA findings, and Baldrige feedback. They use strengths, weaknesses, opportunities, and threats (SWOT) and gap analyses, affinity diagrams, and Hoshin planning tools to identify opportunities for improvement.

Team and Individual Scorecards

Staff and team meetings and discussions refine and align these objectives, which all employees then use to create supporting individual objectives during the performance management process. Resource needs are balanced through an iterative process among functions, cross-functional teams, process teams, Product Development Teams PDT teams, and executive teams. The process involves developing objectives and plans that align with the corporate goals and objectives, sharing them with the functions and teams that must execute and/or support the plans, requesting and considering their input, and finalizing the objectives and plans after input from all affected groups. This iterative process continues through plan execution, involving the functions and teams in performance reviews and course corrections on the year's objectives and plans. Before submitting the final budget to Schering, resource conflicts are resolved at the lowest possible level. Resources are allocated to support the top 12 objectives first and then to fulfill the function plans. A fine-tuning cycle occurs in the fourth quarter after Schering approval and when the entire year's results are more visible. The executive committee and senior staff review progress and make course corrections on the top 12 objectives at the senior leadership team meetings. Function and team leaders evaluate progress on function and team objectives.

EXHIBIT 6.8   Governance Calendar

Senior Leader Performance Reviews

Group	Frequency	Topics	Measures Reviewed
Executive Committee	Monthly	Business and quality issues	• P&L results: month and YTD
Senior Staff	Monthly	Top 12 objectives; corporate performance and business issues	• P&L results: month and YTD • Top 12 objectives review • Scorecard results: month and YTD • Advisory board measures
Advisory Boards	Monthly	Surveys	• NPST: Product Tracker • CSAB: Customer Satisfaction Survey Results • HRAB: Employee Satisfaction Survey Results
Senior Staff's PET Meeting	Quarterly	Performance excellence issues	• Top 12 initiative proposals • Baldrige feedback report
Medrad Management Review	Quarterly	Quality system issues	• Action Item closure • Process indicators • Complaint and reliability trends
Field Sales and Service Meetings	Quarterly	Sales and service reviews in all global regions	• Sales to date • Outlook for quarter and year
Health and Safety Committees	Monthly	Health and safety performance	• Lost time days incidents • OSHA incidents

Employees and their managers track performance on individual objectives through the performance management process, which includes two formal one-on-one reviews each year and informal reviews as needed. The objectives water-falling process links and aligns teams and individuals across the company with the corporate goals and objectives. The process includes several methods of communicating the plan, including the employee meetings and displays of related information throughout the facilities. Medrad ensures that changes resulting from action on the top 12 objectives can be sustained by reviewing progress on them throughout the year and during the annual strategic planning process.

The top 12 objectives represent action plans that support achievement of the corporate scorecard goals. Medrad monitors progress on scorecard goals. Advisory Boards track progress on initiatives that address top 12 and functional goals. Senior Staff reviews top 12 objectives on a rotational basis. In addition, department scorecards track progress on department objectives or initiatives that address scorecard goals. Exhibit 6.9 shows the strategic planning continuum including Medrad's key performance indicators and their projections. The

EXHIBIT 6.9   Strategy Continuum

alignment of corporate goals and objectives with function and team objectives and plans and with individual development plans through the waterfalling process ensures that all functions, teams, and employees are working toward the same goals, that the strategic plan and key indicators are deployed throughout the company, and that the needs of all stakeholders are addressed.

Performance Projections and Benchmarking

Medrad compares current and projected performance with past performance on all corporate scorecard goals and measures, which have been in place for several years. The multiyear view is shown in Exhibit 6.10. Internally, departments and functions throughout Medrad benchmark against internal best-in-class performance indicators. The only available competitive benchmarks in an industry that does not share confidential information are market share, a customer satisfaction survey question asking how Medrad rates versus competitors, and the annual *Medical Imaging* magazine customer ranking.

In its Performance Excellence Team (PET) meetings, the senior staff annually confirms and prioritizes the top 12 objectives and sets targets and measures. Since these objectives support corporate scorecard goals, Medrad approves only those proposals that project substantive improvement and innovation. The top 12 objectives are reviewed regularly by the objective sponsors in depth on a rolling three-month basis by senior staff, and more frequently by exception. Executives responsible for each objective waterfall objectives and progress measures throughout the organization, working with relevant subfunctions and teams. At both the corporate and subfunction/team level, measures are selected based on their ability to predict performance or measure results, with collection and reporting established to enable course correction at appropriate time intervals. Exhibit 6.11 shows how measures align with Medrad's philosophy,

---

EXHIBIT 6.10   Multiyear Target Setting

Corporate Goal	Key Indicator	2003 Goal	2007 Goal
Exceed financials	• Grow CMB faster than sales		
Grow the company	• Sales growth > target		
Improve quality and productivity	• CMB/employee		
	• Reduce new product cycle time		
	• Reduce defects per million	Confidential	
Improve customer satisfaction	• Corporate/regional Top Box customer satisfaction score > prior year		
Improve employee growth and satisfaction	• Survey scores > Hay benchmark		

EXHIBIT 6.11   Benchmarking for Key Measures

Mission	Corporate Goal	Scorecard Measure	Target	Benchmark	Frequency
Ensure continued growth and profit	Exceed the financials	CMB (profit measure)	Grow CMB faster than sales—specific target set via strategic planning	Individual product line growth rates	Monthly
	Grow the company	% sales growth	15%/year	Schering parent, medical industry	Monthly
	Improve quality and productivity	CMB/EE growth	10%/year	Supports growth CMB faster than sales	Monthly
Improve the quality of healthcare	Improve customer satisfaction	Survey results—Top Box ratings	Continuous improvement year-to-year	Competitors and others surveyed	Monthly
Provide an enjoyable and rewarding workplace	Improve employee growth and satisfaction	Survey results—very satisfied ratings	Continuous improvement above best-in-class	Hay best-in-class companies	Twice each year

mission, strategies, and its benchmarking approach. Functions and subfunctions also identify challenging continuous improvement objectives and measures that align with the corporate goals through the waterfall objective process. Support of the top 12 objectives demands improvement and innovation in these functional level goals. The depth of measures and frequency of reporting is appropriate to the needs of the functions

Operations Scorecard

The measures and waterfalling can be extensive. For example, operations has a detailed operations scorecard through which aggregated results are reported monthly. As with the selection of measures, the selection of comparative data begins with the five corporate goals, all of which reflect benchmark data or derivatives of benchmarks. Process teams, departments, and work groups identify meaningful and cost-effective comparative data to set targets and assess performance. Senior staff promotes effective use of measures by challenging the proposed targets of the top 12 objectives and by reviewing and sharing results at monthly senior staff and PET meetings.

Supplier Scorecards

Material suppliers are Medrad's major supplier category. Since 1988, Medrad has reduced its list of material suppliers by one-third. More important, in 2002, over three-fourths of Medrad's production materials were purchased from a group of carefully selected "scorecard" suppliers. Commodity teams, organized around Medrad's critical commodity categories (injection molding, electronic components, and mechanical parts), manage the relationships with these key suppliers using a supplier scorecard. The scorecard assesses supplier performance on the basis of quality, delivery, price, and service. The list of suppliers managed using the scorecard is updated annually based on criteria such as criticality to Medrad, type of supplier, and past performance.

Scorecard Automation

Finance publishes the five corporate scorecard goal results monthly on the intranet. The scorecard displays five primary measures that support the achievement of the strategic plan. The President's Letter, e-mailed monthly to employees worldwide, also presents the latest scorecard results.

Medrad gathers, integrates, and delivers data and information from all sources through its extensive information technology network, which includes core information systems, desktop systems with e-mail, and the Medrad intranet. Approximately 85% of employees have individual computers to access the network, while the balance have access through common stations. All employees worldwide can access the network 24/7. The core system for managing daily operations is SAP, an integrated enterprise resource planning (ERP) system. Business transactions and financial data reside in the system, with information integrated from other sources including product design and field comments (Field Force Automation [FFA]). SAP is highly regarded as an outstanding trans-action processing system for data integration. Medrad has all major operations in the world working off SAP servers in Pittsburgh. To enhance reporting of mission-critical information, Medrad has developed reporting and analysis tools which extend the value of information in SAP well beyond using it for trans-actions. Since the establishment of SAP in the mid-1990s, Medrad has gone through several cycles of improvement aimed at increasing data availability and ease of analysis. Examples include converting the financial tracker from paper to Web pages on the intranet; adding ALV reporting via VAFA (value added finan-cial analysis project); and business intelligence based reporting via 3D. Medrad intentionally gives extra attention to sharing data critical to achieving the five corporate scorecard goals. For example, data on revenues and margins critical to growth and profitability have been made available in real time in the easy-to-use 3D analysis capability released in 2003. The information stored in this "data warehouse" can be sorted and totaled in numerous ways, thereby enabling finance, marketing, and sales to track and analyze performance and plan and

BEST PRACTICE HIGHLIGHTS

Principle 3: Cascade and Manage Strategy

- *Partner with Business Owners.* Partner with business owners includ-ing line and staff leadership team members to gain support and influence as partners to help them achieve results.
- *Develop Level 1 Balanced Scorecard.* Developed corporate-level BSC, the highest level in the organization.
- *Leverage Proven BSC or Comparable Methods.* Leveraged proven BSC methods, including use of the four perspectives and appropri-ate number of measures.
- *Cascade BSC to Lower Levels.* Cascaded the BSC to the lowest levels of the organization, including to the individual employee level.
- *Align Support Services.* Aligned support services to the corporate BSC objectives and measures.
- *Manage Using Measures.* Effectively managed the business using BSC meeting management techniques focused on exception-based management.
- *Automate Measurement.* Automated the BSC for broader distribu-tion and usage.

initiate effective field actions. Daily reports are published from 3D to the intranet, updating revenue and margin data globally for analysis of the very latest results. Departments such as operations, sales and service, marketing, and new product development deploy and maintain work group level systems and applications as well as support major systems such as product data management (product center), project management, and computer-aided design tools. The focus is on data that helps achieve scorecard goals, such as daily production and on-time shipments, or those critical to ensuring prompt response to out-of-bounds conditions, such as quality levels.

> *Let me tell you the secret that has led me to my goal. My strength lies solely in my tenacity.*
>
> —LOUIS PASTEUR

SERONO: BEST PRACTICE CASE

The Serono CPM Office or office of strategy management (OSM) directs the enterprises global BSC program. Serono's CEO, Ernesto Bertarelli, has placed a high level of priority on the implementation of improvements and has mandated a company-wide communication campaign to ensure "proper" alignment. Ganti further adds, "Serono has one vision and one strategy that is formulated and revised each year by the executive management board. The direction of the company is then shared throughout the organization through key messages, strategic themes, and the corporate Strategy Map. To ensure that the various functions and business units are aligned with the strategy, the corporate Strategy Map is cascaded and is then translated into operational terms." Ganti, through his work in the OSM, provides direction and governance for worldwide BSCs. The 2006 governing structure of the BSCs is depicted in Exhibit 6.12. Ganti adds, "The structure may change slightly from year to year to reflect the current organization and the business needs."

Ganti and his team conduct regular BSC alignment meetings with the BSC champions representing the organizations noted in the exhibit in the BSC program structure.

Scorecard Roles

Ganti's team provides governance and direction to dozens of BSC champions; we will now review roles, responsibilities, and reporting. A few best practice

• Balanced Scorecard Hall of Fame Award Winner

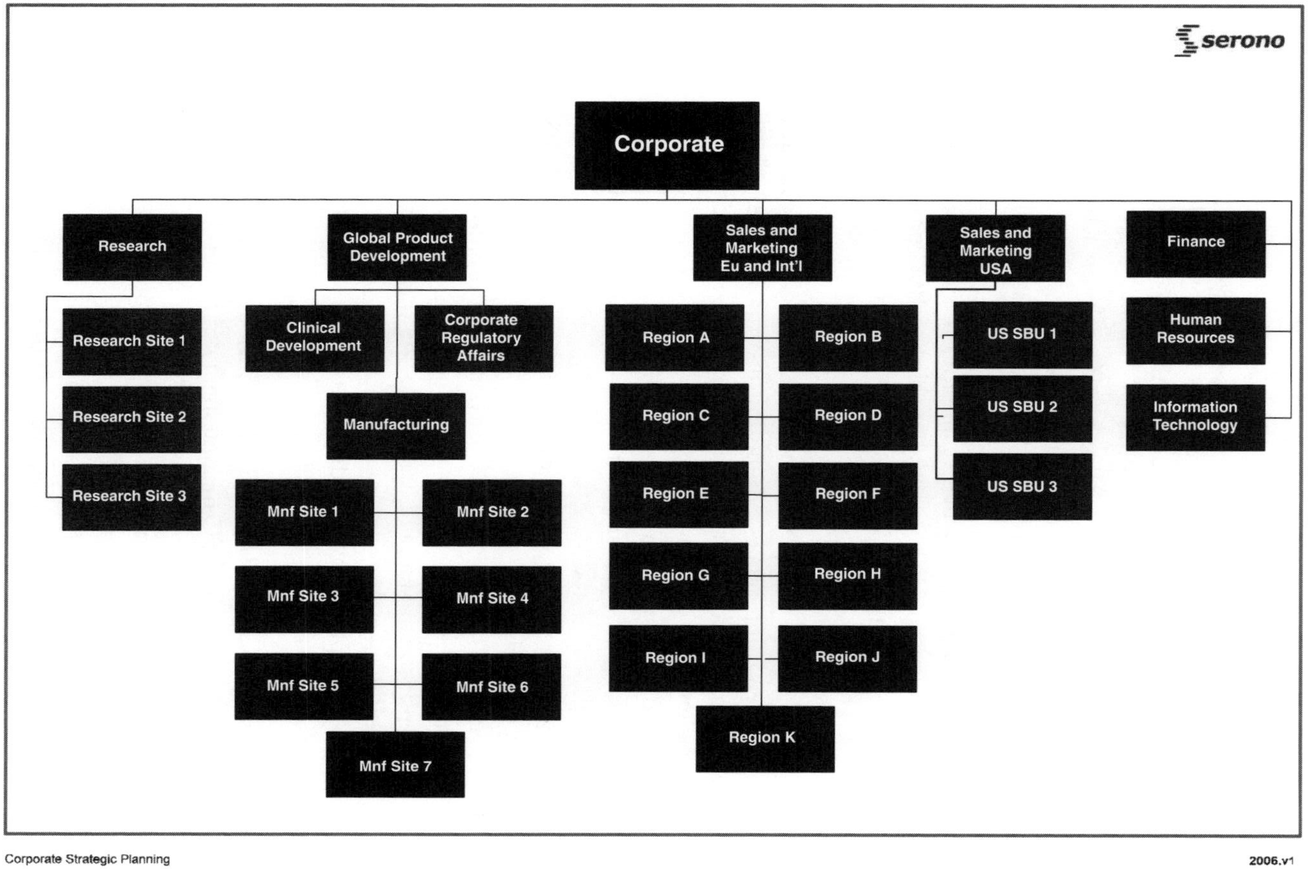

Corporate Strategic Planning

EXHIBIT 6.12   Balanced Scorecard Program Structure

193

examples include clarity in the BSC owner, representative, and measure accountable roles.

- *BSC owner.* The BSC owner is the highest-ranking entity for the function/region/site that is subject to BSC reporting. Typically that person is the function head, the site director within research and manufacturing, or the regional vice president within sales and marketing.

  The BSC Owner is responsible to:
  - Provide accurate and reliable actual results on achieved performance versus targeted objectives and measures.
  - Guarantee that reported BSC actual results reflect actual performance.
  - Appoint BSC representative and measure accountable(s).
  - Ensure compliance with the established BSC procedure in terms of timing, quality, and responsibilities.

- *BSC representative.* The BSC representative is the person authorized by the BSC owner to represent the function/region/site in the BSC operational reporting process. Typically this role is covered by the finance and administration manager, the planning manager, or a person with an equivalent level of authority.

  The BSC representative is responsible to:
  - Consolidate and validate the reported actual results for the BSC owner.
  - Coordinate the reporting of the actual results with the BSC measure accountable(s).
  - Send, on behalf of the BSC owner, the consolidated quarterly actual results.
  - Identify, maintain, and readily provide the documentation supporting BSC actual results.
  - Assist employees within the function/site/department for any issue related to BSC actual results.

- *BSC measure accountable(s).* The BSC measure accountable(s) is the person indicated in the BSC measurement definition, who, based on his or her routine job, produces deliverables/data supporting the actual results. Typically that person is the head of a lab/production unit, a product manager, or a business analyst.

  The BSC measure accountable(s) is responsible to:
  - Provide the BSC representative with the actual results for the assigned measure in line with the measure definition.
  - Provide the BSC representative with the documentation supporting the actual results.

- ○ Maintain the exhaustive documentation (including source or raw data) supporting the actual results.
- ○ Set up and document the data collection process for each measure.
- ○ Liaise with the involved staff within his or her organization.

Scorecard Documentation and Change Control

The corporate BSC results are compiled on a quarterly basis by a group responsible for all nonfinancial information reporting. The reporting group is separate from the office of strategy management to ensure independence between the target-setting process and the target-reporting process.

Therefore documentation was required to support actual results:

- Each actual result reported must include a document summarizing the achievement.
- The measurement reference number must be clearly reported on the related documentation.
- This documentation must be self-explanatory and adequately structured to allow an easy retrieval of the components leading up to the calculation of the actual results.
- Upon request, the source data maintained and archived by the BSC representative/measure accountable must be immediately available via e-mail, or if mail delivery is required, in the shortest possible time frame.

During the year, if any changes on the details of the approved metric require modification, the BSC owner/representative must submit a request in writing to the CSP, who will process the request and provide feedback using the process shown in Exhibit 6.13.

Scorecard Transparency

Upon finalization of quarterly actual results:

- The consolidated BSC quarterly actual results are published to the executive management board (EMB) by the CSP.
- The function head presents to the EMB the performance of his or her function.
- The group compliance officer and head of corporate administration present the corporate BSC to the EMB.

Upon disclosure of the official press release on the quarterly results:

- The function head can communicate the BSC actual results to his or her organization.

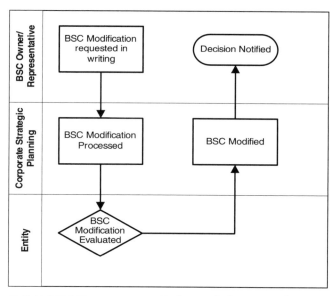

EXHIBIT 6.13   **Balanced Scorecard Modifications**

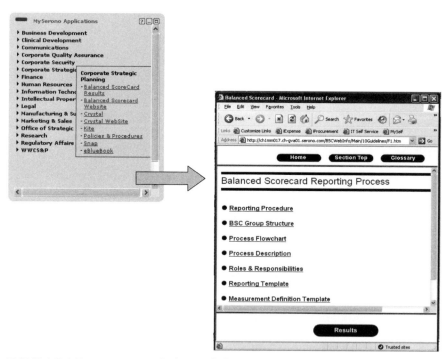

EXHIBIT 6.14   **Balanced Scorecard Web Portal**

BEST PRACTICE HIGHLIGHTS

Principle 3: Cascade and Manage Strategy

- *Partner with Business Owners.* Partnered with business owners including line and staff leadership team members to gain support and influence as partners to help them achieve results.
- *Develop Level 1 Balanced Scorecard.* Developed corporate-level BSC, the highest level in the organization.
- *Leverage Proven BSC or Comparable Methods.* Leveraged proven BSC methods including use of the four perspectives and appropriate number of measures.
- *Cascade BSC to Lower Levels.* Cascaded the BSC to the lowest levels of the organization using a BSC champion model.
- *Align Support Services.* Aligned support services to the corporate BSC objectives and measures.
- *Align Teams and Individual Employees.* Established a robust measure change control process.
- *Link Compensation.* Linked compensation to a limited set of BSC objectives and measures.
- *Manage Using Measures.* Effectively managed the business using BSC meeting management techniques focused on exception-based management.
- *Automate Measurement.* Automated the BSC and created a Web portal for users.

- Access to the relevant quarterly and full-year actual results is granted by the CSP to all the Serono employees through the company's intranet.

Scorecard Reporting

Serono has developed a robust, Web-based reporting environment to allow permission-based access to the BSC user community. The reporting process and portal are illustrated in Exhibit 6.14.

BSC Measure Terminology

Ganti's department provides direction and training to BSC champions throughout the enterprise on BSC terminology as shown in Exhibit 6.15.

> *It is no good to try to stop knowledge from going forward. Ignorance is never better than knowledge.*
> —ENRICO FERMI

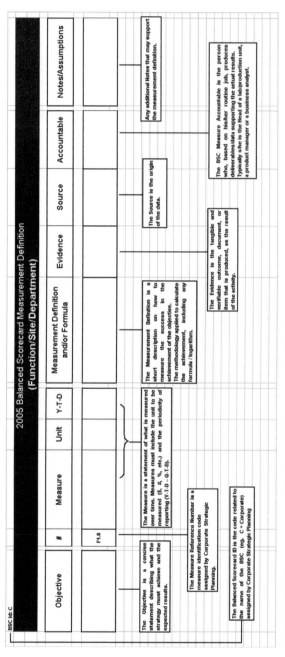

BSC Id: C

2005 Balanced Scorecard Measurement Definition
(Function/Site/Department)

Objective	#	Measure	Unit	Y-T-D	Measurement Definition and/or Formula	Evidence	Source	Accountable	Notes/Assumptions
	F1.8								

The Objective is a concise statement describing what the strategy must achieve and the expected results.

The Measure Reference Number is a measure identification code assigned by Corporate Strategic Planning.

The Balanced Scorecard ID is the code related to the name of the BSC (eg. C = Corporate) assigned by Corporate Strategic Planning.

The Measure is a statement of what is measured over time. Measures must include the unit to be measured ($, #, %, etc.) and the periodicity of reporting (Y-T-D – Q-T-D).

The Measurement Definition is a short description on how to measure the success in the achievement of the objective.
The methodology applied to calculate the achievement, including any formula / logarithm.

The Evidence is the tangible and verifiable outcome, document, or item that is produced, as the result of the activity.

The Source is the origin of the data.

The BSC Measure Accountable is the person who, based on his/her routine job, produces deliverables/data supporting the actual results. Typically s/he is the Head of a lab/production unit, a product manager or a business analyst.

Any additional Notes that may support the measurement definition.

EXHIBIT 6.15 Balanced Scorecard Dictionary

LB FOSTER: BEST PRACTICE CASE

LB Foster has adopted the Kaplan and Norton balanced Strategy Mapping (described in detail in Chapter 5) and scorecard approach based on the four classic perspectives: financial, customer, internal process, and people. Executive management team (EMT) members were engaged in and helped design the Strategy Map and BSC at the corporate level, creating the blueprint for cascading to the company's 4 product groups, 8 product lines, and 12 plants throughout its system. The development project revealed strengths in capturing and reporting financial and people measure data; however, the company had not previously conducted a customer-wide survey and was beginning to form the framework to start capturing process, more specifically cost of quality information. Customer and quality processes and methods are covered in Chapter 7. EMT recognized its BSC was going to start out somewhat unbalanced and would evolve and fill in as customer and internal processes were more fully developed.

Cascading the Balanced Scorecard

EMT recognized that to gain traction with the corporate level 1 BSC had to be cascaded thoughtfully down through the organization. But what path would optimize results? Two paths became apparent, one through the four product groups and another down to the plants through the senior vice president operations and manufacturing.

The level 1 corporate BSC contained an objective "F3 Objective Increase Profitability and Sales" as measured by "sales growth percent per year." This corporate objective and measure value was broken down and allocated to the four product leader BSCs, the concrete product group we shall call level 2 is being shown in Exhibit 6.16 This approach to cascading the BSC from level 1 to level 2 clearly defined accountability and provided line of sight to EMT for results.

The corporate BSC also cascaded directly to the operations or plant level BSC to focus and direct manufacturing departments and shopfloor work teams. In one such example, the Precise Structural Products (PSP) Georgetown, MA, location General Manager Jack Klimp enthusiastically engaged his team in the process. He said, "We were first exposed to the concepts of balanced scorecarding as we were updating our strategic plan. As a team, we found the process of moving from strategic planning directly into strategic mapping extremely engaging. Developing the map really closed the loop for us as to how best to apply the knowledge of the team to our operational processes in a way that was responsive to both the needs of our customer and our corporation and investors." Through the strategy planning and mapping process, PSP developed four operational themes:

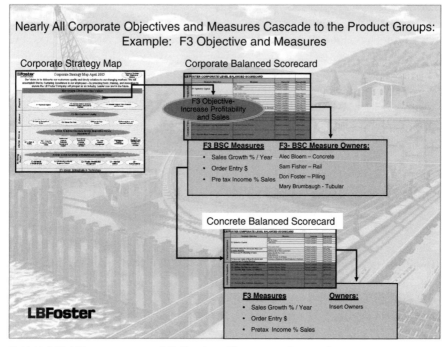

EXHIBIT 6.16   LB Foster Measure Cascade

1. Speed up the part (cycle time).
2. Eliminate the bumps (quality focus).
3. Ramp up the volume (throughput).
4. Be great to work with (teamwork).

As an example, the performance on objective "Speed up the part" is captured by three primary measures including:

1. "Batch size," with a targeted reduction of 50%
2. "Idle time," with a targeted reduction of 50%
3. "Time in, time out," with a target to reduce average production time by 75%

Klimp has focused and led his team to meet and exceed these extraordinary targets; any one of the foregoing targets would be desirable to most any general manager. Klimp stated, "As a job shop, producing unique and high-labor components for the steel bridge and building industries, we found the development of the operational level of the strategic map really gave us a whole new perspective as to how standardized metrics, reported on a scorecard, could be applied to the production of custom products. It was really an 'aha' moment for all of us and laid the groundwork for much of the gains we subsequently achieved."

Supplier Balanced Scorecard

LB Foster also extended its BSC program to include suppliers, a key factor in company performance given suppliers' potential impact on LF Foster's end customers on pricing, quality, speed of delivery, and on-time delivery. Exhibit 6.17 shows the four items and their respective weights for each supplier.

Exhibit 6.18 is a sample questionnaire form and supplier index.

Balanced Scorecard Meeting Management

EMT engaged in monthly BSC focused meetings initially covering all scorecard measures but later migrated to more efficient exception-based approach. That is, EMT focused only on measure results either trending in a negative direction over several periods or with a significant variation from target. EMT adopted this general convention for color-coding results (some permutations exist, however, to focus their attention:

- *Red color results.* Actual results 10% or more below target
- *Yellow color results.* Actual results less than but within 10% of target
- *Green color results.* Actual results either 100% or more of target

EMT is actively engaged in calibrating and resetting targets to ensure color-coding results provide relevant and timely notification of any issues. In effect,

---

EXHIBIT 6.17 **Supplier Balanced Scorecard**

Supplier Scorecard Category/Questions	Category percent	Question percent
Quality	60	
Does the supplier have a quality plan in place and is it reviewed on a regular basis?		30
Number of rejected parts/number of parts received		30
Order processing time	10	
Does the supplier react acceptably to material volume changes?		10
On-Time Delivery	20	
Percentage of on-time deliveries in the last quarter		20
Invoice Terms and Cost Accuracy	10	
Number of incorrect cost on invoice versus number of invoices received		10

EXHIBIT 6.18   Supplier Index Survey Questionnaire

Date: _____   Supplier: _____

Invoice Terms and Cost Accuracy
Number of incorrect cost on invoice versus number of invoices received: _____

On-Time Delivery
Percentage of on-time deliveries in the last quarter: _____

Order Processing Time
Does the supplier react acceptably to material volume changes?
☐ 10   Reacts to material volume changes within 1 day
☐ 9   Reacts to material volume changes within 3 days
☐ 8   Reacts to material volume changes within 1 week
☐ 7   Reacts to material volume changes within 2 weeks
☐ 6   Reacts to material volume changes within 3 weeks
☐ 5   Reacts to material volume changes within 4 weeks
☐ 4   Reacts to material volume changes within 5 weeks
☐ 3   Reacts to material volume changes within 6 weeks
☐ 2   Reacts to material volume changes in 7 or more weeks
☐ 1   Supplier maximum capacity has been reached

Quality
Does the supplier have a quality plan in place, and is it reviewed on a regular basis?
☐ 8   Has Quality Plan and Quality Certification reviewed on a quarterly basis
☐ 7   Has Quality Plan and Quality Certification reviewed on a semiannual basis
☐ 6   Has Quality Plan and Quality Certification reviewed on a annual basis
☐ 5   Has Quality Plan and is reviewed on a quarterly basis
☐ 4   Has Quality Plan and is reviewed on a semiannual basis
☐ 3   Has Quality Plan and is reviewed on a annual basis
☐ 2   Has Quality Plan and is not reviewed
☐ 1   Does not have Quality Plan

Number of rejected parts/number of parts received: _____

EMT functions as a change control council for both changes to the actual measures and measure targets.

Balanced Scorecard Software

Due to the inherent limitations of using spreadsheets and the rapidly accumulating data set and volume, LB Foster reviewed several dedicated BSC software packages and is in the process of deploying business intelligence tools to aid in decision support. LB Foster used a disciplined approach to identifying key

BEST PRACTICE HIGHLIGHTS

Principle 3: Cascade and Manage Strategy
- *Partner with Business Owners.* Partnered with business owners including line and staff leadership team members to gain support and influence to help them achieve results.
- *Develop Level 1 Balanced Scorecard.* Developed corporate-level BSC, the highest level in the organization.
- *Leverage Proven BSC or Comparable Methods.* Leveraged proven BSC methods including use of the four perspectives and appropriate number of measures.
- *Cascade BSC to Lower Levels.* Cascaded the BSC to the lowest levels of the organization using a BSC champion model.
- *Align Support Services.* Aligned selected support services to the corporate BSC objectives and measures.
- *Align Teams and Individual Employees.* The Georgetown PSP plant discussion provided clear visibility into how teams can be aligned with corporate objectives.
- *Link Compensation.* Linked compensation to a limited set of BSC measures (financial only).
- *Manage Using Measures.* Effectively managed the business using BSC meeting management techniques focused on exception-based management.
- *Automate Measurements.* Automated the BSC and created a Web portal for users.

internal functional and technical requirements and then scored leading software vendors on their ability to deliver on these requirements.

> *Knowledge is of two kinds. We know a subject ourselves, or we know where we can find information on it.*
> —SAMUEL JOHNSON

FLORIDA DEPARTMENT OF HEALTH: BEST PRACTICE CASE*

Over time, the Florida Department of Health (FDOH) leadership has been positive and provided different and diverse views. New leaders have provided new approaches to performance measurement and improvement, in the same

* The Florida Department of Health case team adapted portions of this case from "Performance Measurement in the Public Sector," *APQC* (November 2005), Governors Sterling Applications 2002 and 2006, and internal documents.

- Miami-Dade County Health Department Recipient of Governors Sterling (Baldrige) Award 2002 and 2006
- Department of Health Recipient of APQC Best Practice Partner Award

way as a diverse workforce can provide a more adept organization. The FDOH empowers staff to address the operational and immediate goals that impact strategic issues. Extensive training is provided for key operational activities related to issues.

The strategic and operational objectives are deployed in several ways. Operational business plans link strategic objectives with program objectives, strategies, and action steps. Operational business plans are developed at the central office and direct service level. The central office provides direct service personnel at the county health departments with key program objectives and strategies. Personnel then develop local operational business plans incorporating key central office objectives associated with appropriate action steps.

FDOH's quarterly performance reporting process links strategic objectives to field operations. There are two primary quarterly reports. The county health department quarterly report organizes performance data into three categories: (1) outcome indicators including the department's strategic objectives, (2) process measures that reflect how well the county health departments (CHDs) implement the activities necessary to impact strategic objectives, and (3) input measures that reflect the amount of resources devoted to activities. The department-wide secretary's quarterly performance report is built around key objectives and covers all programs and central office administrative functions.

Aligning the Organization, Cascading Objectives, and Measurement

The nature of performance measurement systems is one of ongoing change. Due to both internal and external forces, FDOH sometimes changes its emphasis on performance components. This process of adoption, adaptation, and accommodation makes alignment an ongoing process, not an end point. FDOH changes its performance measures based on public health practice trends, changes in national management culture perspectives, legislative and executive branch directives, and departmental leadership.

Examining the history of measurement in the field of population health shows the importance of population health outcome measures from the earliest days of organized public health. The use of mortality rates and birth outcome statistics has been a cornerstone of the public's health. This is evidenced by the fact that within the first few months of the creation of Florida's State Board of Health in 1889, the state health officer directed all physicians that if the state was going to measure the improvements in the public health, physicians must assure accurate and complete reporting of all births and deaths. As life expectancy increased in the early 1900s, public health began assessing morbidity rates for such common infectious diseases as tuberculosis, malaria, yellow fever, and sexually transmitted diseases.

In midcentury, organizations shifted to concerns about outputs and inputs as "managing" public health organizations took preeminence in government. For example, organizations began to look at how many people they served and the cost of service. Elected officials became more interested in what their funding was buying and less in the overall impact on the health of the population. Beginning in the 1990s, while inputs and outputs were important measures of performance, the resulting effects on the health of the population were once again the preeminent focus of public health system performance.

A return in emphasis to population health outcomes is strongly reflected with the federal government's publication of "Healthy People 2000," which set health outcome objectives for the nation. The state used the report as the basis for the 1989 Florida State Health Plan. Contemporaneously in 1991, FDOH developed its first quality improvement indicators primarily for all health departments. In 1992, the legislature and governor's office mandated that agencies develop their own strategic plan. The legislature and governor also mandated that agencies transition to performance-based program budgeting.

The initiation of performance-based program budgeting further reinforced the importance of population health status performance measures. Outcome measures such as infant mortality, HIV cases, and mortality rates became key drivers of performance management activities. In fact, FDOH reorganized components of its organization to better align programmatic organization with specific health problem domains recognized in the budget structure of performance-based program budgeting. In the 1990s, FDOH worked continuously to make strategic goals and performance measurement objectives consistent across "Healthy People 2000," the agency strategic plan, the state health plan, quality improvement indicators, and performance-based program budgeting measures. Work groups that included state and local health staff were involved in the development and review of the various plans and associated measures.

FDOH encourages cross-program dialog and builds on program office strengths, leveraging these strengths and practices throughout the organization. Although it is not always easy, leaders ensure that each program office and department has a sense of ownership in the performance measurement system.

Scorecard Report Automation

The goal of FDOH has always been to integrate the various components of measurement. The department has been successful in implementing several automation projects that have laid the groundwork for performance measurement integration. In 1980, the organization implemented the first all-county system for reporting services and clients. This system was followed by the development in 1985 of the County Health Department Contract Management System, which combined program-specific client and service data with expenditure and revenue data, thus combining key input and output measures into one system.

The collection of key population health outcome data—mortality (cause of death from death certificates), birth outcomes (birth certificates), and infectious disease mortality—is based on long-standing reporting protocols that have been enhanced, improved, and reinforced through state statute and administrative rules. Partners in the collection of these data include hospitals, medical examiners, physicians, infectious disease nurses, funeral directors, and county health departments. The state uses a system of reporting outcomes (births/deaths/morbidity) from both the county health departments and the hospitals. Births, deaths, and morbidity form the cornerstone of outcome measurement. For example, the children's medical services department uses the infant mortality measure. The organization takes "cause of death" information from death certificates.

Collecting information about all diseases is automated. The organization is hands-on in collecting data about certain diseases, and it directly contacts the hospitals, relevant healthcare professionals, and all other people involved with the reporting event. This reporting system is further reinforced by the active partnership with the Centers for Disease Control and Prevention (CDC), to which the reporting of infectious disease morbidity, death, and birth reporting is required. FDOH employees have access to high-speed Internet, and they can see information that is stored in the data warehouse through the organization's intranet (a virtual, private network).

Scorecard Meetings

Further reinforcing the integration of performance measures was the initiation of the secretary's quarterly performance report review meetings. Held quarterly at the central office, FDOH division directors and bureau chiefs report on key performance measures that are included in the agency strategic plan/long-range program plan, and the quality improvement process. (See Exhibit 6.19 for an example of the strategic plan's goals, indicators, and objectives.) Each measure has a target and managers review performance relative to these targets. Strategies for performance improvement are shared across goal areas.

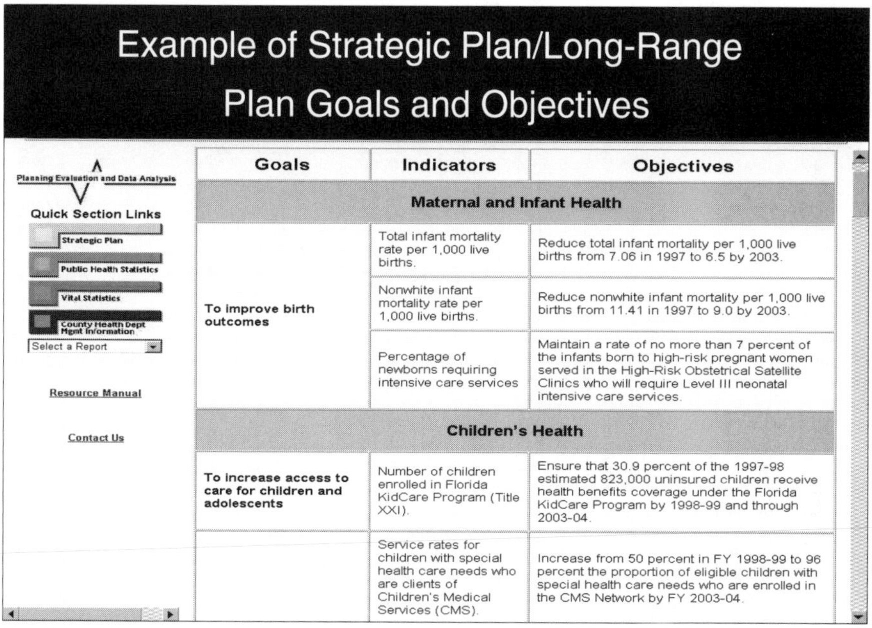

Example of Strategic Plan/Long-Range Plan Goals and Objectives

	Goals	Indicators	Objectives
Maternal and Infant Health			
	To improve birth outcomes	Total infant mortality rate per 1,000 live births.	Reduce total infant mortality per 1,000 live births from 7.06 in 1997 to 6.5 by 2003.
		Nonwhite infant mortality rate per 1,000 live births.	Reduce nonwhite infant mortality per 1,000 live births from 11.41 in 1997 to 9.0 by 2003.
		Percentage of newborns requiring intensive care services	Maintain a rate of no more than 7 percent of the infants born to high-risk pregnant women served in the High-Risk Obstetrical Satellite Clinics who will require Level III neonatal intensive care services.
Children's Health			
	To increase access to care for children and adolescents	Number of children enrolled in Florida KidCare Program (Title XXI).	Ensure that 30.9 percent of the 1997-98 estimated 823,000 uninsured children receive health benefits coverage under the Florida KidCare Program by 1998-99 and through 2003-04.
		Service rates for children with special health care needs who are clients of Children's Medical Services (CMS).	Increase from 50 percent in FY 1998-99 to 96 percent the proportion of eligible children with special health care needs who are enrolled in the CMS Network by FY 2003-04.

Left sidebar navigation:

Planning Evaluation and Data Analysis

Quick Section Links

Strategic Plan
Public Health Statistics
Vital Statistics
County Health Dept Mgnt Information
Select a Report

Resource Manual

Contact Us

EXHIBIT 6.19   **Example of Strategic Plan/Long-Range Plan Goals and Objectives**

Scorecard Cascading

The quality improvement process reinforces the importance of measures cascading down to the county health department operational level. Each county sets its own targets. Health problem analysis for each area outlines contributing factors and indirect influences (process, public health policy, and procedures) on outcome performance measures. In addition to being accountable to headquarters, each county health department is accountable to the government of the location in which it operates. Through a formal process, a contract management system, the departments report input and output performance targets to the board of county commissioners in their location. FDOH receives money from the boards and in turn promises to meet a certain level of service.

The contract between the county health department and the local board specifies planned levels of service-by-service activity; client, service, staffing, revenue, and expenditure levels by program. Exhibit 6.20 shows how the Sterling Award Winning Miami-Dade county health department's contract management system integrates client, service, staffing, revenue, and expenditure data from several data collection systems.

EXHIBIT 6.20   Balanced Scorecard Variance Report

Florida Department of Health County Health Department
Contract Management System
Variance Report
Dade County for Report Period 10/2004 to 9/2005
Run date 10/25/2005

Program Component/Title	FTES Reported	FTES Planned	FTES Percent Variance	Clients or Units Reported	Clients or Units Planned	Clients or Units Percent Variance	Services Reported	Services Planned	Services Percent Variance	Expenditures Reported	Expenditures Planned	Expenditures Percent Variance
Immunization	81.20	83.77	-3.07	39,367	31,600	24.58	202,062	160,000	26.29	$5,236,204	$5,465,101	-4.19
Sexually Trans. Dis.	67.60	72.45	-6.69	11,242	9,960	12.87	96,339	84,000	14.69	$5,011,893	$5,421,185	-7.55
AIDS	64.57	63.95	0.97	3	5	-40.00	33,497	27,289	22.75	$6,256,511	$6,188,870	-1.09
Tuberculosis	158.25	150.00	5.50	9,195	7,855	17.06	86,716	72,200	20.11	$12,337,199	$12,974,979	-4.92
Comm. Dis. Surv.	30.38	27.00	12.52	0	0		28,649	25,437	12.63	$2,355,092	$2,360,450	-0.23
Hepatitis & Liver Failure Prev.	9.93	10.00	-0.70	3,538	3,050	16.00	16,823	17,819	-5.59	$708,190	$717,418	-1.29
Public Health Preparedness and Response	16.79	16.10	4.29	0	0		2,538	2,100	20.86	$1,647,905	$1,457,352	13.08
Vital Statistics	28.34	29.43	-3.70	0	0		0	0		$1,759,502	$1,875,375	-6.66
Communicable Disease Total	457.06	452.70	0.96	63,345	52,470	20.73	466,624	388,845	20.00	$35,303,495	$36,460,730	-3.17
Chronic Disease Prevention Pro.	12.26	12.00	2.17	5,388	4,650	15.87	3,098	2,720	13.90	$891,721	$938,799	-5.01
Tobacco Program	0.00	0.00		0	0		0	0		$15,108	$0	
Home Health	0.01	0.00		0	0		0	0		$624	$0	
WIC	174.37	157.25	4.26	115,183	102,390	12.49	514,656	430,000	19.69	$9,962,110	$10,297,636	-3.26

Family Planning	53.90	55.83	-3.46	11,675	10,555	10.61	56,213	46,000	22.20	$3,885,523	$4,068,979	-4.51
Maternal Health/IPO	3.68	4.45	-17.30	300	260	15.38	4,078	3,360	21.37	$288,315	$361,719	-20.29
Healthy Start Prenatal	9.84	9.33	5.47	1,752	1,410	24.26	34,165	29,640	15.27	$563,469	$596,234	-5.50
Comprehensive Child Health	0.00	0.03	-100.00	0	0		0	0		$50,202	$56,524	-11.18
Health Start Infants	6.60	6.51	-1.38	28	6	366.67	10,643	8,960	18.78	$395,613	$436,330	-9.33
School Health	46.94	47.73	-1.66	0	0		354,067	496,130	-28.63	$4,251,651	$4,849,896	-12.34
Comprehensive Adult Health	0.00	0.00		0	0		0	0		$48	$0	
Dental Health	0.00	0.00		0	0		0	0		$11,996	$0	
Primary Care Total	307.60	303.13	1.47	134,326	119,271	12.62	976,920	1,016,810	-3.92	$20,316,380	$21,606,117	-5.97
Water and Onsite Sewage	26.02	25.65	1.44	4,724	3,922	20.45	20,314	17,278	17.57	$1,938,703	$2,074,353	-6.54
Facility Programs	41.10	41.69	-1.42	13,913	10,712	29.88	28,579	22,875	24.94	$2,599,972	$2,779,257	-6.45
Groundwater Contamination Program	0.77	0.71	8.45	141	122	15.57	343	300	14.33	$51,946	$56,196	-7.56
Community Hygiene	21.82	22.31	-2.20	713	607	17.46	27,629	23,142	19.39	$1,370,615	$1,479,180	-7.34
Environmental Health Total	89.71	90.36	-0.72	19,491	15,363	20.87	76,865	63,595	26.87	$5,961,237	$6,388,986	-6.70
Grand Total	854.37	846.19	0.97	217,162	187,104	16.06	1,520,409	1,469,250	3.48	$61,581,112	$64,455,833	-4.46

Advanced Benchmarking and Automation

FloridaCHARTS.com is a tool for the entire community; it provides useful measurement information not only to employees but also to community partners and to the public in general. Some of its extensive functionality includes:

- Columns that can be sorted
- Maps that can help the reader zoom in on specific areas and isolate information
- Information that can be exported into a Microsoft Excel file
- Mouse-over for information pop-up
- Ability to see trends in measures—statistically smoothed for the very small populations
- Interactive community maps
- Profiles of counties and census demographics
- The provision of statistical quartiles

FloridaCHARTS.com was done in conjunction with other measurement efforts and uses the same data warehouse that contains all of the performance measures. This Web site has evolved. Meade Grigg, Director of the Office of Planning, Evaluation, and Data Analysis, says of the site, "We keep adding on rooms to a big house. We revise as we go." The site was created in-house in the Office of Planning, Evaluation, and Data Analysis, not in information technology. Grigg estimates that five people spent half of their time working on the project for two years. Personnel in this office have not only analytical abilities but also Web design skills.

FDOH relies heavily on benchmarking. When the populations served by the county health departments are very different in size and demographics, direct benchmarking is difficult. To help, FDOH provides its departments with expected as well as actual results.

Relying on the correct number of measures is a challenge. FDOH reviews various programs annually and discards measures that it no longer needs. However, according to Grigg, "We seem to add more than we subtract." Health measures are collected from so many various areas and are used to meet so many needs (e.g., to meet state and federal requirements) that many will never lose their utility.

Cascading to and Aligning with Employee Training and Rewards

The overriding purpose of FDOH's training activities is continuous improvement that moves the department closer to accomplishing its mission and strategies. The training program is designed to provide education, professional development, and personal growth opportunities that improve individual and organizational performance to ensure the delivery of quality services to FDOH customers. Selection of training offerings is based on an identified and documented need generated through surveys and needs assessments. A training need may be identified when deploying new equipment or software, establishing a new policy, changing health information, identifying a gap in desired performance versus actual performance, and through reviewing incident reports or other sources of data. To educate its employees, FDOH uses several venues in order to offer employees the opportunity to reach their full potential. Examples of workforce development activities include:

- Using a distance learning network to provide educational opportunities to the public health workforce.
- Collaboration with the Public Health Leadership Institute in the University of South Florida to provide leadership training.
- Increasing individual competencies. For example, individuals from the performance management team received ASQ certification so that they can better help the organization look at data and share best practices. Self-assessments (360 degree) are available for employee use and to assist in building individual development plans.
- Contracting with the Florida Sterling Council to allow employees to attend training on topics related to the Sterling Criteria for Organizational Performance Excellence. Local agencies and program offices use the Florida Sterling framework to evaluate their organization, recognize their strengths, and address their opportunities for improvement.
- Providing orientation to new initiatives such as the 2005 CHD Pilot Performance Improvement Process. The organization oriented 20 counties participating in the redesign of the FDOH county health department performance improvement process. Six additional counties also volunteered to participate in the orientation.
- Providing routine, annual, and ad hoc performance measurement training on core data collection systems. Staff throughout the organization can access a wide variety of video tapes and online manuals.
- With encouragement from FDOH leadership and the Florida Association of County Health Department Business Administrators, FDOH funded a field trainer position. This field trainer shares knowledge and best practices while providing consistent training in public health business practices to business managers at county health departments. This field trainer also works with an advisory committee to develop standardized training materials needed by each new business manager to be thoroughly proficient in the various financial intricacies of a small, medium, or large county health department.[6]

BEST PRACTICE HIGHLIGHTS

Principle 3: Cascade and Manage Strategy
- *Partner with Business Owners.* Partner with line and staff leadership team members to gain support and influence as partners to help them achieve results.
- *Develop Level 1 Balanced Scorecard.* Translate strategy into level 1 BSC measures and measure targets at the highest organizational level in your organization.
- *Leverage Proven BSC or Comparable Methods.* Observe BSC or comparable design parameters assigning one to two measures to each Strategy Map objective.
- *Cascade BSC to Lower Levels.* Cascade and align level 1 measures to lower levels for alignment.
- *Align Support Services.* Identify and define measures for all support services that align with levels 1 and below.
- *Align Teams and Individual Employees.* Define personal BSCs for teams and/or individuals that align with higher-level and support services BSCs.
- *Link Compensation.* Align rewards and recognition to the BSC.
- *Automate Measurement.* Implement CPM software to manage BSC program with links to other principles.

As a state government organization, FDOH cannot provide a financial reward to employees unless the compensation is tied to achieving strategy or mission. However, employee recognition is plentiful, as these examples show:

- The annual quality management showcase recognizes excellence, and counties are encouraged to present at non–FDOH conferences and meetings.
- On the department's intranet, the organization recognizes its employee-authors who have published in academic or professional journals.
- FDOH nominates employees and teams for Florida's Davis Productivity Awards, an award system that provides some monetary rewards.
- Because the shortage of registered nurses affected FDOH's ability to achieve its strategy and mission, the organization recently worked with Florida's Office of Public Health Nursing to increase the base rate of pay for nurses.

There is no security on this earth, there is only opportunity.
—GENERAL DOUGLAS MACARTHUR

AMERICAN RED CROSS: BEST PRACTICE CASE*

One of the first tasks of the American Red Cross performance management design team was developing the nine key design principles on which the system would be based. As the system was implemented, the team always looked back on these principles to ensure they were upheld with every step. The nine principles are:

1. *Constituents'* expectations should be reflected in standards.
2. *Inspire and motivate* superior performance and continuous improvement.
3. Provide *consolidated, measurable, and clear* performance expectations.
4. Provide a *continuum* of performance standards and monitoring.
5. Performance targets should be *scalable* in response to significant community demographics.
6. Expectations should be *reasonable, consistent, and reflect organizational priorities.*
7. *Do not add administrative burden to chapters.*
8. Information needs to be *tailored to multiple audiences.*
9. Provide *classifications* of overall performance.

At each stage of design and implementation, these nine principles were revisited to ensure that the ultimate performance management system held true to the bases on which it was established.

The chapter performance standards are an integrated system of compliance and performance monitoring activities that not only ensures a threshold of chapter compliance but also has higher-level standards that promote excellence. Whereas the previous systems lacked the ability to reward chapters that were extraordinarily innovative and productive, this new system recognizes excellence in those chapters that go above and beyond basic expectations.

After much discussion, the design team arrived at 47 performance standards reflecting categories important to the organization and its constituents. The

- **Recipient of APQC Best Practice Partner Award**

---

* The American Red Cross case team adapted portions of this case from "Performance Measurement in the Public Sector," *APQC* (November 2005), and internal documents.

organization continues to review the standards to identify the optimum number of measures. Each standard falls into one of these categories:

- Governance (9 standards)
- Financial strength and stability (stewardship, 12 standards)
- Service delivery (11 standards)
- Human resources (4 standards)
- Business practices (6 standards)
- Organizational unity/corporate citizenship (cooperation and collaboration with partners and other chapters, 5 standards)

An example of a governance standard is "The local chapter board conducts a self-evaluation at least once every 24 months." Another example of a governance standard is "The board reviews and approves annual budget for submission to and approval by the service area executive on an annual basis." An example of a financial strength and stability standard is "Annual fundraising expenses as a percentage of related contribution (a Better Business Bureau key external watch-group requirement)." An example of a service delivery standard is "Chapters assure 24-hour public access to Red Cross emergency services." In addition, one standard deals with disaster readiness levels—chapters should have the capacity to respond to disasters based on their community makeup and geographical region.

Chapter Measurement

Chapters are measured against two data sources: (1) prior-year results and (2) the performance of other similar chapters. The organization believes that the rechartering process was inherently unfair because it compared small chapters against large ones, so it adjusted the new system to overcome the disadvantage of the small charters.

Whereas the former rechartering process had 33 equal standards, the new system prioritizes the standards through a process of applying weights and mandatory minimums (where applicable). Each standard has a weight of "1," "2," or "3" that serves as a multiplier for scoring.

Each chapter receives a score, and the scores help the service areas to triage chapters needing greater or lesser degrees of support. Service areas can learn from the successful behaviors of high-scoring chapters and potentially apply those behaviors and practices to help lower-scoring chapters. The design team selected standards based on research, field engagements, and input. Originally, it had more than 47 standards, but it reflected on the strategic plan to ensure that each standard was linked to at least one strategic goal. The team consulted the findings of external organizations such as the Better Business

Bureau and Charity Navigator, since those organizations publish standards and monitor the performance of nonprofits in the areas of stewardship and giving.

The team needed to create a system of reporting that was easy to manage. Some chapters have only a few employees and volunteers, and the organization does not want them to spend undue time or effort creating reports. The team committed to utilizing data drawn from existing sources and existing reporting requirements wherever possible.

Automation

The organization had a Web portal in existence before the implementation of the performance management system that allows employees to feed information to headquarters electronically. Headquarters staff use the numbers generated through these electronic avenues to measure against the standards. Performance against the chapter performance standards is measured annually (rather than on the five-year cycle previously employed). More frequent reporting helps chapters make midcourse corrections and understand the requirements of higher-level performance. The scorecard is reported to the chapters on a single page, front and back. The page provides the chapter boards and management with a score and a level of performance on all standards. The page also documents the chapter's performance in the previous year and the performance of its peers. The system allows scores to be rolled up so that the various service areas can know how they are performing and the American Red Cross as a whole can examine its performance.

Performance Standards

Two types of chapter performance standards were created: (1) 17 core requirements and (2) 30 critical performance standards.

The *core requirements* represent the basic, fundamental standards that chapters must meet at all times. They set threshold levels for governance, operations, and service delivery capabilities. They are uniform and consistent for all chapters; all core requirements must be met by all chapters at all times. Failing to meet a core requirement does not necessarily mean the chapter will be dechartered, but it does mean immediate intervention by the service area will take place. Performance against core requirements is a basic expectation and, as such, does not provide a good differentiator between chapters.

Critical performance standards are the higher-level standards that differentiate chapters and identify superior performance. Fifteen of the 30 standards have mandatory minimum requirements, and targets for these measures vary based on the chapter's peer groupings. Performance improvement (the ability to meet and exceed targets) is evaluated using two comparisons: (1) how well the chapter does against its own previous year's performance and (2) how well it does against the performance of its peers. The organization assigns weights to reflect the standards' priority. Performance on these standards is a differentiator; failure to perform does not elicit immediate and drastic intervention from the service area, but consistent underachievement can elicit additional support and management attention.

Process and Outcome Focused

The team worked to balance outcome and input (process) measures. The compliance nature of the core requirements means that those 17 standards mainly measure process. The overall system is outcome-oriented since most of the peer-based critical performance standards are outcome measures.

Performance Levels

Chapters can fall into four categories of performance:

1. *Highly Performing Chapter (Level 4).* For chapters that meet all 17 core requirements and also meet or exceed most of their peer-based targets and show improvement over the prior year on critical performance standards. These chapters are singled out for reward and recognition. When the design team first discussed rewarding highly performing chapters, it considered financial awards but eventually moved away from that idea. The chapters most deserving of financial awards tend to be ones with greater economic resources to begin with, and the organization wants to grow the amount of resources that each chapter has rather than aggravate the differences. Therefore, awards currently involve "recognition" rather than a financial incentive. Headquarters not only recognizes the highly performing chapters but also holds them up to the rest of the organization as examples of best practice and involves them more prominently in nationwide initiatives. Highly performing chapters can also promote their exceptional status when interacting with their local donors, partners, and communities.

2. *Successful Chapter (Level 3).* For chapters that meet all 17 core requirements and also meet or exceed some peer-based targets and show improvement over the prior year on some critical performance standards. Approximately 80% of the chapters are "successful."

3. *Provisional Chapter (Level 2).* For chapters that meet all 17 core requirements but lag behind peers in most areas or fail to show improvement on most standards. They also may be chapters that fail to meet one or more of the critical performance standard minimums. Service areas

and chapters are responsible for crafting action plans to move the chapters from "provisional" to "successful." If chapters can quickly remove the blocks preventing successful performance, they are permitted to move up within the year; in most cases, however, implementing the action plan takes more than a year.

4. *Charter Review Required (Level 1).* For chapters that fail one or more of the 17 core requirements. These chapters require significant intervention and organizational headquarters becomes involved.

Scoring Methodology

Exhibit 6.21 shows a sample scorecard. The first data column, "Actual Performance," lists the score itself. The second column notes whether the standard is required. The chapter's overall score is calculated by multiplying each item's score times a weight and summing for all items.

Benchmarking

The concept of "peer groups" is an important part of the performance management system because of the wide differences in environmental variables impacting chapters. Measuring a chapter against one that faces extremely different challenges does not help the chapter improve. The design team utilized extensive research to identify the key variables that most affect service delivery and fundraising.

A key design element was that, because not every community is alike, performance expectations should reflect community differences. Communities and peer grouping vary based on population size, population density, median

Chapter Standards	Actual Performance	Core Requirement	Critical Performance Standards					
			Minimum Performance Level (1)	Performance Target	Prior Year Performance	Score	Weight	Weighted Score
Service Delivery								
22 Provision of disaster services for both recurrent and non-recurrent disasters within jurisdiction (per ARC 3030)	Yes	Yes		Yes	Yes			
23 Chapter assures reliable, 24-hour public access to Red Cross emergency services (2)	Yes	Yes		Yes				
24 Provision of AFES emergency communication services (per ARC 1295)	Yes	Yes		Yes				
25 Provision of International Tracing services as required (per ARC 1295; chapter 7)	Yes	Yes		Yes				
26 Disaster Readiness Level (based upon community vulnerability)	2		TBD	2	2	3.0	3	9
27 Percent of population reached with Preparedness / Community Disaster Education (CDE) materials (4)	2.25%		>0	0.26%	1.50%	6.0	3	18
28 Percent of population trained in life-saving skills (First Aid, CPR and/or Aquatics) (4)	4.55%		>0	3.33%	4.50%	3.0	3	9

EXHIBIT 6.21   **Chapter Standards Actual Performance Critical Performance Standards**

household income, and population demographics. (The "demographics" variable is a proxy intended to help account for language and cultural differences among households served by the various chapters.)

The team identified 55 peer groupings. The number of chapters in each group ranges from 4 to 65, with an average size of 16 chapters.

Target Setting

Targets are not set from the top down but are derived from the bottom up. Targets for most critical performance standards are based on the median performance of the chapter's peer group. Because all chapters are continually directed to improve performance over their own prior-year levels, there is continual pressure to improve system-wide performance. As individual chapters work to raise their scores, they are raising the targets for everyone.

Accountability Structure

Chapters

Of the three groups that make up the American Red Cross (headquarters, service areas, and chapters), the chapters benefit most from the performance management system. The public also benefits because it is assured that the chapter that operates in its area meets minimum qualifications and works to improve.

The primary responsibilities of chapters include:

- Ensuring that all core requirements are met
- Submitting the required data elements
- Reviewing performance results
- Designing performance improvement plans
- Identifying best practices
- Acting to continuously improve overall performance

Service Areas

The eight offices that govern the service areas use performance reporting to identify chapters that exhibit excellence or require additional attention, such as corrective action or capacity building. Specific service area responsibilities include:

- Evaluating chapters' performances
- Reviewing required documentation
- Assisting with data collection
- Designing performance improvement plans
- Recommending charter actions

- Identifying, promoting, and leveraging highly performing chapters

Twenty-two of the 47 performance standards are evaluated by service area staff members who make recommendations to headquarters regarding rechartering. They also facilitate the sharing of best practices by highly performing chapters.

National Headquarters

National headquarters units manage and support the overall performance evaluation system by:

- Compiling overall performance data
- Conducting organization-wide analyses of performance
- Developing and refining the policies, procedures, tools, training, and communications
- Providing guidance on the development of performance plans
- Ensuring strategic alignment
- Ensuring annual evaluation of the system

The national headquarters is institutionalizing the belief that the 47 standards can be replaced or eliminated if they are no longer relevant to the strategy or if the chapters are doing so well in the area that the standard no longer needs to be measured.

Exhibit 6.22 displays how the three levels of the organization work together to manage the system.

The implementation effort was led by the national headquarters, which developed training and communication tools. The eight service areas provided feedback and input. Service areas were then responsible for providing the chapter education, capacity-building, and technical support needed to rollout the system.

The alignment of standards with strategic goals is deliberate. In fact, the same personnel that developed the strategic plan were involved in developing the standards. Particular attention was paid to the relationship between chapter performance standards and the American Red Cross strategic plan. A detailed plan outlined the strategic directions, related strategic goals, and the chapter performance standards that support each. Some standards support more than one goal; most of the goals are supported by multiple standards. Information is collected in a variety of ways depending on the standard. Some standards are measured electronically through numbers submitted by the chapters; these are the most objective. Twenty-two of the 47 standards are evaluative; they are collected by assessors located at the service area level.

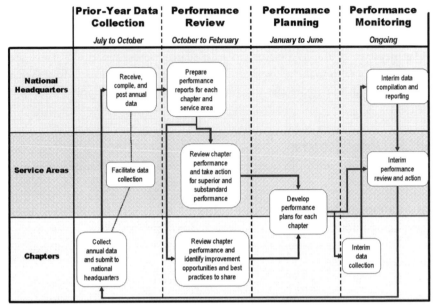

	Prior-Year Data Collection	Performance Review	Performance Planning	Performance Monitoring
	July to October	*October to February*	*January to June*	*Ongoing*
National Headquarters	Receive, compile, and post annual data	Prepare performance reports for each chapter and service area		Interim data compilation and reporting
Service Areas	Facilitate data collection	Review chapter performance and take action for superior and substandard performance	Develop performance plans for each chapter	Interim performance review and action
Chapters	Collect annual data and submit to national headquarters	Review chapter performance and identify improvement opportunities and best practices to share		Interim data collection

EXHIBIT 6.22   Roles and Responsibilities

BEST PRACTICE HIGHLIGHTS

Principle 3: Cascade and Manage Strategy

- *Partner with Business Owners.* Partnered with business owners including line and staff leadership team members to gain support and influence as partners to help them achieve results.
- *Develop Level 1 Balanced Scorecard.* Developed an executive-level BSC, the highest level in the organization.
- *Leverage Proven BSC or Comparable Methods.* Leveraged proven BSC methods.
- *Cascade BSC to Lower Levels.* Cascaded the BSC to the lowest levels of the organization, within chapters.
- *Align Teams and Individual Employees, and Support Services.* Defined team BSCs that align with higher-level and support services Balanced Scorecards.
- *Manage Using Measures.* Effectively managed the business using BSC meeting management techniques focused on exception-based management.
- Managed Balanced Scorecard meetings to address the appropriate mix of strategic and operational issues; link these issues with Principle 4, Business Improvement.
- *Automate Measurement.* Automated the BSC for broader distribution and usage.

If you are not measuring, you are just practicing.
                    —VINCE LOMBARDI

BRONSON METHODIST HOSPITAL: BEST PRACTICE CASE*

The strategic oversight teams (SOTs) oversee development of detailed tactics and action plans that include timelines, responsibility, and measurements, beginning in the fall phase of the strategic management model (SMM) (described in Chapter 5). Financial resources are allocated through the resource allocation process. During the planning process, the resources required to implement the strategic plan tactics (staffing, operating, and capital dollars) are identified by all leaders and consolidated by the finance department. The executive team reviews all requests, prioritizing items with the strategic objectives as well as the 10-year financial plan. The result is the annual operating budget that supports all operations, staffing, and education needs. Capital allocation begins with a day-long capital planning retreat in the summer phase of the SMM. At the retreat, all requests for facility, technology, and information technology (IT) capital are reviewed, prioritized using weighted criteria, and factored into the long-range capital financial plan. The executive team, key operational and service line directors, and the chief and vice chief of staff participate. The final operating and capital budgets are approved by the board along with the strategic plan in the late fall. The facility, capital, and IT committees meet monthly to review project

- Malcolm Baldrige National Quality Award
- Michigan Quality Leadership Award (2001, 2005)
- 100 Top Hospitals Award
- Governor's Award of Excellence for Improving Care in the Hospital Setting (2004, 2005).
- Governor's Award of Excellence for Improving Preventive Care in the Ambulatory Care Setting
- *Fortune* magazine's "100 Best Companies to Work For" (2004, 2005, 2006)
- *Working Mother*'s "100 Best Companies for Working Mothers" (2003, 2004, 2005)
- VHA Leadership Award for Operational Excellence (2005, 2006)

* The Bronson Medical Hospital case team adapted portions of this case from Baldrige Application 2005 and internal documents.

return on investment and approve specific projects. This provides tremendous flexibility in redirecting resources as priorities change. Each SOT also meets monthly to determine shifting priorities in terms of operational and staff resources. SOT chairs bring these changes to the weekly executive team meeting for approval and support by other executives. Once the executive team and board approve the annual strategic plan and budget, deployment of action plans begins in the fall. Effective deployment is essential to achievement of the strategic objectives.

Cascading Scorecard Objectives and Measures

In 2004, the executive team developed an enhanced strategic plan cascade (Exhibit 6.23) in an effort to strengthen alignment across the organization. The annual strategic plan, with specific tactics and action plans aligned by the three Cs, is deployed to the organization through this robust cascade.

The executive team and SOTs ensure that the Bronson scorecard measures are supported by the organizational performance indicators (OPIs) and aligned with the secondary scorecards. This alignment ensures that department, service line, and key process measures support the strategic objectives. Through careful monitoring of scorecard performance (at all levels), the executive team ensures that key process changes that support achievement of action plans are sustained. The staff performance management system (SPMS) described later

EXHIBIT 6.23   **Strategic Plan Cascade**

in this chapter aligns individual performance with organizational objectives and action plans. Seventy percent of individual leader performance is based on achievement of the strategic objectives as measured by the organizational scorecard. The remaining 30% is based on individual goals that must also support the strategic plan. The 90-day action planning process defines the necessary steps for execution of plans. This process allows for agility and rapid change or development of new plans, if required. Exhibit 6.24 is an example of measures cascaded through the cardiologists.

Linking Short- and Long-Term Action Plans

Exhibit 6.25 documents key organizational short- and long-term action plans to support strategic objectives. Key changes in services, programs, operations, customers, and markets are also listed. Action plans are aligned with strategic objectives through prioritized department, leader and individual employee goals that cascade through the organization. Bronson carefully plans new services to ensure they are implemented timely, address patient needs, and are current with the healthcare industry and local market. The annual strategic plan tactical grid, including specific action plans, is reviewed at least monthly by the SOTs, and quarterly by the executive team, to monitor progress toward achieving the organization's objectives. The quarterly plan progress and organizational scorecard results are communicated to the board, leaders, medical staff leadership, and staff.

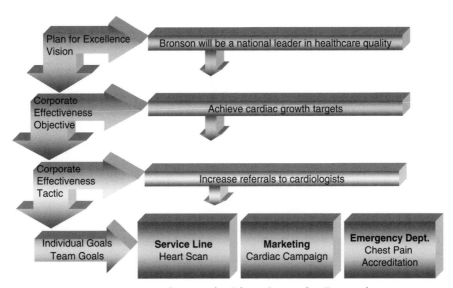

EXHIBIT 6.24   Strategic Plan Cascade Example

EXHIBIT 6.25   Short- and Long-Term Plan Linkages

Strategies and Strategic Challenges	ST Objectives	LT Goals	Key Tactics and Action Plans
CE: Achieve excellent patient outcomes SC1 SC2	Medicare mortality at CS top 15%, Recognized by Leapfrog as safe environment, Exceed national standards for core indicators	Top 100 hospital, 5 stars for targeted areas, Third-party recognition for patient safety	Decrease Vap, Optimize Medicare mortality and morbidity, Optimize core indicator performance, Build CPOE, Optimize communication among providers
CASE: Enhance service excellence, staff competency, and leadership SC3 SC4 SC5	Magnet status, Leader in MD satisfaction Overall turnover and vacancy better than national best practice, EOS diversity scores improve, Patient satisfaction scores improve from benchmark	Best practice customer and MD satisfaction, 100 Best Employer, Maintain magnet status	Implement respiratory care development program, Implement mentor program, Operationalize Diversity Council, Implement EOS and LPMS, Physical surroundings and discharge process recommendations
CORE: Achieve efficiency, growth, financial, and community benefit targets SC6 SC7	Meet growth targets for targeted service lines, profit margin	X market share in targeted services, profit margin, Baldrige recipient	Implement long-term campus expansion plan, Implement short-term technology/facility plan, Recruit key physician specialists

Legend: SC1-Application of evidence-based medicine, SC2-Meet needs of growing number of SC6-Capacity, SC7-Profitability, BP-best practice

Changes	HR and Education Plans	Key Performance Measures	Past Perf. 2004 Results	Performance Projections 2005	2010	Proj. Comp.
Hospitalists admitting ortho patients	SBAR education Fill CPOE team positions	Medicare mortality				+
		VAP				+
		Patient falls				+
		Skin ulcers				+
Medical management for adult patients w/chronic diabetes and HF		SIP				+
		Core measures				+
		(AMI, HF,				+
		pneumonia)				+
		Hand washing				+
Gallup survey with national benchmarks	Respiratory care development candidates, Mentor program education,	Vacancy				+
		EOS diversity score				+
		MD satisfaction				+
Campus expansion project moves some support services off campus	Diversity education plan	Patient satisfaction				+
		Patient satisfaction w/physical surroundings				+
		Patient satisfaction w/discharge				+
		Overall turnover				+
		RN turnover				+
MD ambulatory surgery and outpatient diagnostics centers	Realign campus project leadership, "Change management" training for move	SL market share				+
		SL market share				+
		SL market share				+
		SL market share				+
		Profit margin				+
Expansion of adult medical unit capacity,	Hire staff for new capacity, Train on new technology					

patients with complex conditions, SC3-Workforce shortage, SC4-Diversity, SC5-Customer service,

Performance Projections/Targets

Due to competitive reasons, Exhibit 6.25 does not include all the data. The format is provided for illustration purposes. The exhibit illustrates a summary of performance projections for key short- and long-term measures. Included is 2004 past performance, 2005 short-term projections, 2010 long-term projections, and long-term projected performance compared to competitors. These comparisons demonstrate that by 2010, Bronson will be the regional market leader in all key services and will also fulfill the vision of being a national leader in healthcare quality. Targets are set based on national best practice. In some cases, this may create a gap in performance between local competitors or organizations of similar size nationally. When a gap is identified,

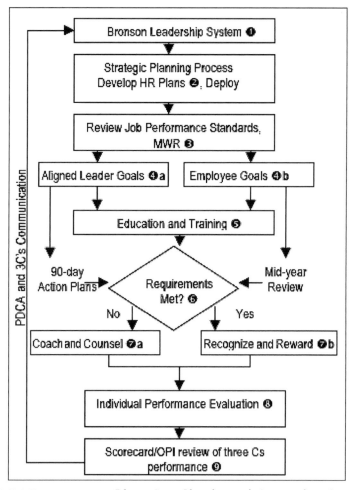

EXHIBIT 6.26   Plan, Do, Check, and Act and 3 Cs of Communication

the executive team assigns appropriate accountability to an SOT, which develops and deploys action plans and related measurement to address the gap.

Staff Performance Management System, Alignment to Strategic Objectives

The staff performance management system (SPMS) is designed to support organization-wide expectations of high performance work by all staff. It is the primary mechanism for the achievement of action plans. (See Exhibit 6.26 for SPMS)

During the deployment phase of the SMM, strategic plans are translated into performance requirements and deployed in step 2 throughout the entire workforce through the SPMS. In step 3, the annual review of job performance standards, as well as minimum working requirements, is completed so that job standards are derived from the planning process. In step 4a, leader goals are aligned with the strategic objectives and scorecard/organizational performance indicators (OPI) measures. At the individual staff level, in step 4b employees develop three personal goals that support the three Cs. These goals are created based on the appropriate organizational, department- or service line–specific action plans that relate to the individual job duties of the employee. Personal goals, educational needs, and career progression plans are discussed with employees during a midyear review and informally at staff meetings or on the job. In step 5, education and training provides staff with the skills and competencies necessary to accomplish their goals and achieve high performance. Through the annual performance review process and regular coaching sessions, employees are encouraged to use educational opportunities to improve their current skills as well as develop new skills for advancement within the organization. In step 6, leaders evaluate individual performance to determine if the job requirements are met. If requirements are not met, coaching, counseling, additional training, and corrective action planning are put into place to improve performance as shown in step 7a. In step 7b, reward and recognition mechanisms are tied to organizational strategy; they recognize employees who achieve high levels of performance and also motivate staff to contribute to overall organizational excellence. The gainshare program involves quarterly bonus payouts based on achievement of organizational and department-specific performance indicators, tied directly to the three Cs. Annual performance evaluations, step 8, provide a two-way feedback mechanism for staff to receive critical feedback on their performance as it relates to the expectations set by the executive team through the Bronson Leadership System. In addition, staff can provide valuable feedback to their leader regarding job satisfaction, personal development needs, career aspirations, and the refinement of job performance standards for the coming year.

Results of staff competency and performance evaluations are reviewed by the executive team and reported to the board annually. In step 9, the overall effectiveness of the SPMS is evaluated through performance in the scorecard measures/OPI. Results are communicated throughout the organization using the three Cs communication format. The Plan, Do, Check, and Act PDCA model provides a formal mechanism for continuous improvement of the SPMS.

Stoplight Color Coding

During the strategic planning process, the executive team determines the scorecard indicators that will measure the success of the organizational strategies (three Cs) and achievement of the specific strategic objectives. These measures, aligned by the three Cs, are displayed on an organizational scorecard using a stoplight approach: red (risk), yellow (moderate), and green (meets) format. This enables all levels of the organization to evaluate performance related to the strategic plan. In addition to the organizational scorecard, which includes measures of strategic importance, the executive team annually determines the OPIs necessary to track daily operations. The executive team uses a systematic process to select and develop OPIs that includes assignment of ownership within the executive team, validation of the data collection process, identification of best practice benchmark comparisons, and determination of appropriate reporting format and schedule. Once the organizational scorecard is finalized by the executive team, during the fall time frame of the strategic planning process, a series of secondary scorecards are created by the appropriate department, service line or process leader for the coming year. The SOTs approve the service line scorecards to ensure alignment of key healthcare services with the three Cs and the strategic objectives. Department and key process scorecards are developed by the appropriate leader and reviewed by the responsible executive team member. The division of nursing, for example, shares common scorecard indicators for all nursing units. The nursing scorecard is developed and monitored by the Divisional Level Nursing Council with support from the chief nurse executive and the nursing leadership team. This builds scorecard ownership with nursing staff through the shared governance structure. All scorecard indicators must align and support achievement of the three Cs, strategic objectives, and action plans.

Data and Systems Integrity and Management

Bronson uses the robust information management strategy (IMS) to ensure information is effectively collected, aggregated, and analyzed to track daily operations and overall organizational performance. The first step in the IMS is to digitize data from key healthcare and support processes. The clinical charting systems, PACS, and document imaging are examples of data digitization. In the second step, the data are aggregated into information and deployed in order to improve processes. For example, automated queues route digitized work documents from one process step to the next, allowing real-time measurement and management of work flows. The next steps in the IMS are to protect, support, and provide access to information. Mission-critical transactions are simultaneously written to disk arrays in two geographically separated data centers to provide a high degree of disaster recover protection. Similar efforts are used to protect data against intentional harm, to avoid breaches of confidentiality, and to ensure data integrity. Information users are supported by the first healthcare IT support center and only one of 17 support centers across all industries to earn the Help Desk Institute's (HDI) site certification for IT customer service. This reflects years of effort to improve the quality of IT help desk service provided to key internal customers—employees and physician partners. Secure access to data is granted through any Internet-enabled computer. Physicians, for example, can securely access patient records and diagnostic images, avoiding process delays and rework when the physician is not onsite at Bronson. Deployment of free wireless Internet access across the campus allows physicians, staff, patients, families, and visitors to remain productive and connected while they are on campus. Last and most important, Bronson uses the IMS to leverage information to achieve effective decision making related to patient care. After two years of due diligence and planning, Bronson is implementing computerized provider order entry (CPOE). This new technology will help to avoid errors and reduce practice variation by applying the data we already collect to best practice standards of care. CPOE will provide physicians with a powerful clinical tool.

Industry and Cross-Industry Benchmarking

During the strategic planning process, as scorecard indicators/OPIs are determined by the executive team, a key step is the selection and use of comparative information. Once the need for comparative data is identified, the executive team selects comparisons based on reliability, reproducibility, availability, and resources required to collect the information. Comparisons are collected from many local, state, and national sources for clinical excellence (e.g., CareScience), as well as for Customer and Service Excellence (e.g., Gallup) and corporate effectiveness (e.g., Moody's). When available, Bronson uses national databases for comparative sources due to the highly reliable nature of this type of information. However, literature from within and outside the healthcare industry is also used for comparison purposes when necessary. Availability of both average and best practice levels provides the organization with an understanding of our position on a relative basis and the knowledge of what it takes to be a national leader. Key comparative data is reviewed at least annually during the development of the scorecard/OPI measures. Bronson ensures the effective use of key comparative data by performing gap analyses with the scorecard/OPI measures. Once the gap analysis is complete, implementation of the PDCA process occurs to close the gap and improve performance. Benchmarking, evidence-based research, and best practice comparisons are all utilized in the Plan phase of the PDCA model. This is a key tool used to not only improve performance, but to develop innovative processes and services at Bronson.

Measurement Relevancy and Currency

Bronson keeps its performance measurement system current with healthcare needs and directions through the continuous improvement process inherent in the PDCA model. The IMS, as well as the specific scorecard/OPI measures, are reviewed, evaluated, and updated annually through the SMM. This validates alignment with organizational strategy, customer requirements, and industry trends. Performance measures are developed or changed through continuous monitoring of market and industry trends, regular updates from the Advisory Board, and professional conferences. Through the SMM, the executive team evaluates performance measures on a weekly basis. If immediate action is required to develop a new service or improve a current process, the process calls for a revision to the measurement system first so that preset targets can be deployed to leaders through the 90-day action planning process. Systematic review of the IMS and performance measurement system and executive team presence in professional organizations assist the organization in recognizing and responding to rapid or unexpected organizational and external changes.

CPM Review Meetings: Performance Analysis and Review

Systematic review of organizational performance and capabilities enables Bronson to maintain both stability and agility in the constantly changing healthcare environment. Exhibit 6.27 illustrates the organizational performance reviews used by the board, executive team and Quantity Strategic Planning (QSP) participate to assess and evaluate organizational success, competitive performance, and progress relative to short-term strategic objectives and long-term goals.

The executive team uses the scorecard/OPI to review organizational performance, capabilities and progress relative to the strategic objectives and action plans. The executive team meets weekly and reviews the OPI and scorecard information. Each executive is assigned to an SOT, and some indicators are delegated to the appropriate SOT for review according to schedule. Individual

EXHIBIT 6.27   Organization Performance Reviews

Review Type	Conducted By				
	BOD	ET	QSP	SOT	Individual Excellence
CE	Q	M	Q	B	O
CASE	Q	M	Q	M	O
CORE	Q	M	Q	B	O
Operational	M	W	Q	B/M	O
Governance	Y				
Leadership	A	Q	Q	Q	O

O-ongoing, Y-annual, Q-quarterly, M-monthly, B-biweekly, W-weekly

executives are responsible for review of performance indicators, reporting to the entire executive team when performance is not meeting targets. Through the strategic plan cascade, as well as the 90-day action planning process, Bronson ensures agility to rapidly respond to changing organizational needs and challenges in the healthcare environment. Analyses performed to support review of organizational performance include: gap, trend, financial-ratio, root cause, cause and effect, and failure mode and effects analyses. Conclusions are validated after a system of data integrity, logic, and reasonability checks are completed. The SOTs are responsible for monthly review of the annual strategic plan tactical grid, which includes specific action plans, with assigned accountability and timelines. Through review of the measures and tactical grid status, Bronson regularly assesses progress relative to the strategic objectives and action plans.

Translating CPM Results into Improvement Priorities

The executive team translates organizational review findings into priorities for continuous improvement and opportunities for innovation, the focus of Chapter 7. Through weekly monitoring of the scorecard/OPI, negative variations compared to best practice, historical or budgeted targets are identified. Indicators that are red or yellow trigger action plans as necessary to improve performance. Priorities for improvement are deployed by the SOTs, through multidisciplinary teams using the PDCA model for organization-wide initiatives. Individual executives deploy department-specific teams for more specific issues. The leadership communication process supports deployment, communication, and knowledge sharing relative to organizational priorities. During monthly management meetings as well as the day-long leadership development meetings, the executive team provides a systematic review and discussion

BEST PRACTICE HIGHLIGHTS

Principle 3: Cascade and Manage Strategy

- *Partner with Business Owners.* Partnered with business owners including line and staff leadership team members to gain support and influence as partners to help them achieve results.
- *Develop Level 1 Balanced Scorecard.* Developed an executive-level BSC, the highest level in the organization.
- *Leverage Proven BSC or Comparable Methods.* Leveraged proven BSC methods including use of the four perspectives and appropriate number of measures.
- *Cascade BSC to Lower Levels.* Cascaded the BSC to the lowest levels of the organization including to the individual employee level.
- *Align Teams and Individual Employees.* Defined personal BSCs for teams and/or individuals that align with higher-level and support services BSCs.
- *Align Support Services.* Aligned support services to the corporate BSC objectives and measures.
- *Link Compensation.* Aligned rewards, recognition, and compensation programs to the Balanced Scorecard.
- *Manage Using Measured.* Effectively managed the business using BSC meeting management techniques focused on exception based management.
- Managed BSC meetings to address the appropriate mix of strategic and operational issues; link these issues with Principle 4, Business Improvement.

of the scorecard and the strategic plan. All leaders are accountable to communicate this important information to their staff through staff meetings utilizing the prepared knowledge-sharing documents that provide consistency of the key messages. Bronson priorities are deployed to physician partners through the formal medical structure of multidisciplinary committees. First, the executive team shares the strategic priorities with the chief and vice chief of staff during weekly meetings. Next, information is shared with the medical board each month. Here the clinical practice group representatives receive information they share with other physicians through the section meetings and related communication mechanisms. Supplier scorecards have been developed with key suppliers as a formal mechanism to better align their performance with organizational objectives. This provides a formal mechanism to deploy priorities to suppliers. In addition, Bronson utilizes the leadership communication process, targeting specific communication mechanisms with suppliers, to communicate priorities and opportunities to ensure organizational alignment.

RICOH: BEST PRACTICES CASE

Few organizations experience immediate support and success when starting a project of this magnitude. Ricoh was no different. Despite all of the training, coaching, and successes in completing the first Strategy Map, there were still key managers skeptical of the project. Some felt that the existing business practices were too firmly established and that no amount of effort could wrestle them free. Others did not buy into the CPM approach—determining a strategic direction, establishing the infrastructure, and then making the improvements necessary to drive performance over time. What happened behind the scenes to win over these managers was a full-fledged campaign of internal partnership led again in large part by Marilyn Michaels.

For months she spent hours on the phone and in regional meetings with some of the most senior leaders persuading—and ultimately convincing them—of the potential of the CPM improvement approach. She worked behind the scenes shaping many of the existing management practices to mesh more completely with the efforts of her performance excellence office. She would even travel to host countries' meetings to carry the message herself regarding the virtues of continual improvement. After watching her for a period of two years, outside strategy expert Ed Barrows summed up his opinion of her efforts to partner with key executives. "She was singularly committed to the success of the project. If ever there was one key evangelist that carried the effort even during the most trying times, it was Marilyn." Her efforts continue today (which is, of course, the very point of continuous improvement!), and it is clear in the results that all of her activities did indeed make a difference.

One of those key activities that was, at times, exceptionally difficult was the development of the corporate-level BSC. Following closely on the heels of the completion of the 14th Mid Term Plan (MTP) Strategy Map, the senior-level project team began developing the performance measurement framework required to determine whether each of the objectives outlined in the Strategy Map was actually being achieved. This was challenging for two main reasons. First, Ricoh had firmly established practices that called for the use of

- Recipient of Balanced Scorecard Hall of Fame Award
- Recipient of Deming Quality Award

numerous and detailed performance measures. While this practice is effective in managing operations, it can be ineffective in managing strategy. The Strategy Map at Ricoh looked to have only one or two key performance measures for each objective. But given the operational focus of the company, it was clear there would be multiple measures for each objective. Second, the 14th MTP was focused on driving performance in several "Key Results Areas." These areas each had their own measures associated with them, and some differed from what was depicted on the initial Ricoh BSC. So the process of BSC creation for the corporation overall had to delicately manage both the numerous operational measures the company was collecting, mesh it with the prescribed measures from the 14th MTP, and ensure it captured the appropriate strategic measures needed to evaluate performance. The initial version of the BSC had scores of measures. But over time, through refinement and iteration, the team winnowed the listing down to a manageable, collectable set of performance indicators.

As had been laid out in the project plan at the end of 2001, Ricoh began cascading the strategy into its four operating regions during early 2002. Subsequent to business unit training where each of the cascaded business unit project teams was educated regarding the specifics of cascading, teams began creating their own regional Strategy Maps and BSCs that aligned with the enterprise level map and scorecard. The process, like the creation of the corporate map, required a significant investment of time and needed ongoing refinement to both understand the translation of the corporate strategy to the local regions as well as match the local strategies to that of corporate. Over the course of several months, each of the business units—Canada, Latin America, Ricoh U.S., and Lanier Worldwide—aligned its own strategies with that of Ricoh Corporate. The process was not without its challenges. Some regions posed greater challenges than others. "Latin America differs from the U.S. and Canada. We're dealing with different infrastructures, languages and politics." explained Julio Urrutia, Performance Excellence Manager, Ricoh Latin America. Eventually the first generation of cascaded business unit maps was created. Today, the process has been ironed out and strategy deployment is much more smoothly executed in part due to the comprehension of managers but also due to coordination by the Strategy and Planning Office SPO.

With the business units cascade completed, Michaels and Kuni Minakawa began the process of aligning key support activities. Kuni, in his capacity as chief financial officer, was responsible for not only the financial but for the administrative services that kept Ricoh running. Human resources (HR), information technology (IT), marketing, and environmental services, along with finance all fell within the purview of the senior finance officer. Their support played an instrumental role in successful execution of the strategy. The corporate-level Strategy Map was used in conjunction with input from the business units to ensure that priorities were established with the services areas that would best support the business units' key needs. In the case of the IT area, their direct business case development for each of the projects was requested by their internal partners. While IT provides the cost detail, the business unit partners constructed the benefits projections. Both parties then agreed on the information and then jointly establish measures of success. Business cases are then prioritized and finally approved to the extent to which there are resources available. This process plays out annually now at Ricoh and has proven to be a particularly effective way to ensure support activities do, in fact, *support* the business.

One of the key alignment activities that Ricoh committed to accomplishing early on was cascading of the strategy from the corporate level, through organizational units, departments, and, ultimately, to individual employees. Executives believed that a key success factor underlying strategy execution would be drawing the clear link from the corporate-level strategy to the individual. Otherwise individuals would not understand where and how they made a contribution. Like most other aspects of the project, this was a significant undertaking, requiring a major revamping of the performance management process.

Thus began the redesign of the Ricoh performance management system. The goal at the outset of redesign was "to support the achievement of the business plan through linkage and alignment of goals at all levels of the organization."[7] Annually each department head develops individual objectives aligned with the strategy. The manager then through a shared goal-setting process works with individual employees to align their goals with the department's and the organization's overall strategy. This process is supported by a performance management tool known as the Ricoh On-Line Performance Management System (see Exhibit 6.28). The Web-based system has screens that have been set up so that employees can click on drop down boxes that have the BSC perspectives listed, target dates for achievement, performance status (red, yellow, green) as well as which objective on the Strategy Map it relates to. Specific goals are entered as are specific performance measures. Development plan are entered too. As the year progresses, employees update the system and managers provide feedback regarding goal achievement. Individual performance can be rated by the managers as well.

In conjunction with the performance management system redesign, Ricoh HR leaders also realigned the performance incentive program to support the strategy. A majority of the employees are covered by the performance incentive plan (PIP), which consists of three primary evaluation factors upon which incentive compensation is determined:

A Performance Management System
Links the Strategy to Individuals

Performance Planning

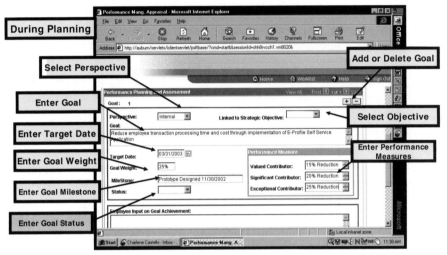

EXHIBIT 6.28   **Ricoh On-Line Performance Management System**

1. Business unit revenue achievement (40% weighted)
2. Business unit pretax profit (40%)
3. Balanced scorecard objectives (20%)

Senior-level employees' incentive compensation is linked to measures taken from the Mid-Term Plan and BSC at the corporate level. The Ricoh Long-Term Incentive Plan (LTIP) provides incentive compensation depending on how well the company performs relative to key strategic themes, corporate objectives, and objectives within the individual manager's area of responsibility.

With the underlying Strategy Maps and BSC created and the support systems developed, energies internally turned toward active monitoring of progress toward the strategy. The schedule for the review strategy meetings incorporates both monthly and quarterly review at both the business unit and the Ricoh corporate level. The purpose of the meeting is to monitor progress toward achievement of targets set for each of the measures and to determine where performance is stuck. Early on, the review meetings were challenging and not entirely productive. In many instances measure data were not available for review. In other cases data were presented but analysis had not been performed to uncover the true drivers of performance. Here is where the principles of performance improvement started to manifest themselves in the overall strategic management process.

Michaels's experience in quality management helped her recognize that certain parts of the organization had only basic skills in analyzing data, identifying root cause problems, and recommending what are commonly referred to as countermeasures. So over the course of several months, Ricoh executed a training program designed to help managers improve the depth of their analysis when performance was not meeting targets. The training and coaching—even from the most senior levels within the organization—mirrors the quality improvement approach of Plan, Do, Check, Act (PDCA). Originally developed in the 1930s with subsequent adoption by W. Edwards Deming, the PDCA cycle is a common performance improvement approach where the change to be made is planned. Then, the improvement approach is carried out.

BEST PRACTICE HIGHLIGHTS

Principle 3: Cascade and Manage Strategy

- *Partner with Business Owners.* Partner with line and staff leadership team members to gain support and influence as partners to help them achieve results.
- *Develop Level 1 Balanced Scorecard.* Translate strategy into level 1 BSC measures and measure targets at the highest organizational level.
- *Leverage Proven BSC or Comparable Methods.* Observe BSC or comparable design parameters, assigning one to two measures to each Strategy Map objective.
- *Cascade BSC to Lower Levels.* Cascade and align level 1 BSC to levels 2, 3, 4, and so on below depending on organizational and accountability structures.
- *Align Support Services.* Identify and define measures for all support services that align with levels 1 and below.
- *Align Teams and Individual Employees.* Define personal BSCs for teams and/or individuals that align with higher-level and support services BSCs.
- *Link Compensation.* Align rewards, recognition, and compensation programs to the BSC.
- *Manage Using Measures.* Manage BSC meetings to address the appropriate mix of strategic and operational issues; link these issues with Principle 4, Business Improvement.

The results are evaluated and then adopted whole scale, updated, changed, or abandoned,

Now when review meetings are held, managers are able to come to the table not only with performance data, but with robust analysis based on the principles of quality improvement. Due to the dramatic improvement in analysis quality, much more time is devoted to discussing issues and making decisions versus simply trying to understand why the results are what they are. The meetings are facilitated by the SPO—the architect of the BSC as well as the quality improvement approach.

Ricoh has made all of these improvements without the aid of an automated system. This is not because the company is not cognizant of such a system's value—it is. Ricoh is waiting until the technology selected to shift systems to a common platform is fully installed. Then Ricoh will select an appropriate application.

> *Facts are stubborn things, but statistics are more pliable.*
> —MARK TWAIN

KEYCORP: BEST PRACTICE CASE

The BSC supports the corporate Strategy Map with financial and nonfinancial metrics. Key continually evaluates the relevance of the metrics, particularly the nonfinancial ones, to ensure focus on the most critical drivers. (See Exhibit 6.29.) Much of Key's improved performance has been driven by its use of the BSC.

In May 2002, Key completed its first round of corporate and business group strategy reviews. To date, Strategy Maps and BSCs have been completed for Key's support areas (marketing, client services group, Key technology services, human resources, public affairs, and risk management), totaling 23 scorecards. The rationale for developing the support area cards after the business group and sub-business group scorecards were completed was to ensure alignment with their strategic priorities.

During the implementation phase, Key was faced with data integrity issues along with consensus around targets, goals, and the collection of measurement data. The process of implementing the BSC across Key forced its leadership to address those issues and to focus more directly on the drivers of performance.

It has been three years since Key's initial BSC reviews, and the BSC remains

• Recipient of the Global Balanced Scorecard Hall of Fame Award

EXHIBIT 6.29   1Key Corporate Balanced Scorecard: Sample Metrics

	Shareholder			Internal Process
S1	EPS Growth Relative to Peers		l1	Market Share
S1	Return on Equity		l1	Deposit Growth
S1	Dividend Payout		l1	Loan to Deposit Ratio
S1	Debt Rating		l2	Accounts/Customer
S2	Revenue Growth Relative to Peers		l2	Product Mix
S2	Net Interest Margin		l2	Consumer Acquisition/Attrition
S2	Non Interest Income/Total Revenue		l4	Regulatory Risk Review
S3	Criticized Ratio		l4	Coordinated Risk Review
S3	Nonperforming Assets			
S3	Loan Loss Ratio			
S4	Revenue Growth Less Expense Growth			
S4	Efficiency Ratio			
S5	Economic Profit Added			
S5	Capital—Tangible and Tier 1			

	Client			Employee
C1	External Client Advocacy		E1	Turnover
C2	External Client Satisfaction Survey		E1	Turner by Demographics
C2	Internal Client Satisfaction		E1	Employee Opinion Survey
			E1	Leadership Metrics

at the heart of Key's strategic management program. It has become institutionalized across Key and has helped Key to become better focused on the true drivers of performance.

The effectiveness of the BSC at Key is evidenced by Key's strategic improvement of shareholder value. Key Commercial & Investment Bank (KCIB), the largest contributor of Key's earnings in 2004 and an early adopter of the BSC, has experienced the most improvement since the BSC was adopted at Key as a strategic management tool. It is Key's largest line of business and contributes over 50% of net income.

All of Key's scorecards are aligned with the corporate BSC. The support area cards were developed to reinforce the corporate and business group strategic priorities. Exhibit 6.30 illustrates this alignment.

Every business group, support area, and employee scorecard aligns with the framework of the corporate BSC. They share the same perspectives and strategic themes:

- Enhance shareholder value.
- Be our clients' trusted advisor.

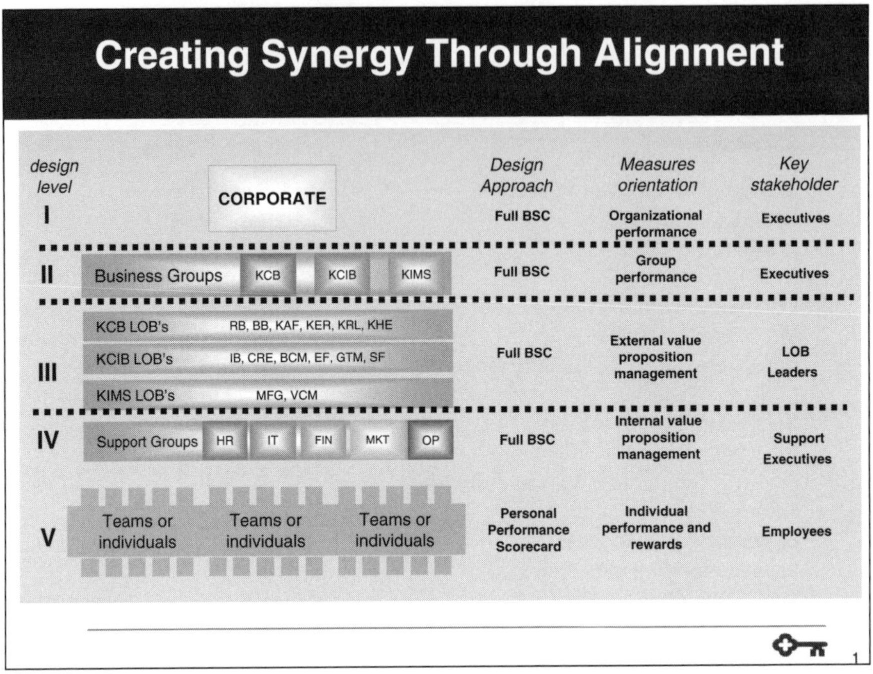

EXHIBIT 6.30   Key Balanced Scorecard Cascade and
Alignment

- Execute 1Key.
- Proud to be at Key.
- Live the Key Values.

Metrics are aligned to each of these strategic themes.

Cascading the BSC to Public Affairs, Breaking New Ground

Each of Key's support areas has BSCs aligned to the corporate scorecard. Public Affairs (PA) exemplifies a "best practice" in the support areas. The BSC team began to create the PA scorecard and asked the Balanced Scorecard Collaborative, the Corporate Executive Council's Communications Council Board, and public relations firms to identify best practices from other organizations. There were no examples. Key's PA group forged on to create a comprehensive Strategy Map with appropriate metrics and scorecard. The PA scorecard allows this function to demonstrate the value it brings to its clients and foster a more disciplined way to create a winning culture. Key has yet to find another organization that has gone to such lengths to create a PA scorecard.

Target Setting and Forecasting

All financial metrics have targets established for the next three years. For non-financial metrics, performance has been judged based on comparison to peer performance and improving trends. Key implements a rolling forecast process, and it is used to guide strategic decisions and strategy revisions. Key's CFO, Jeff Weeden, conducts monthly business review meetings to review financial performance as well as regularly scheduled meetings with the CFOs who report to him to specifically focus on forecast changes.

The quarterly strategic business review sessions include a three-year forecast for each line of business (LOB) based on historic financial trends, economic drivers, and competitive, and customer trends. Leaders are held accountable to these forecasts through a six-month update process.

Management Reviews Using the Scorecard

The BSC is the tool that Key's CEO has selected as the strategic management tool that he uses to manage the company's performance

Additionally, Key uses the BSC to manage execution of its strategy across the enterprise. It is reviewed and discussed quarterly at meetings attended by the Chief Executive Officer (CEO), Chief Financial Officer (CFO), Chief Administrative Officer (CAO), and senior LOB and support area leaders. It is also used as a reporting tool to the compensation committee of KeyCorp's board of directors. It has kept Key focused on the most critical drivers of performance. The focus on the strategy and use of the BSC has resulted in several critical process and cultural shifts in the enterprise. Major changes to its management processes are shown in Exhibit 6.31.

EXHIBIT 6.31 Critical Process and Cultural Shifts

	from . . .	to . . .
Outcomes	Performance awareness	Strategic performance— discussions and defined actions
Accountability	LOB/support group level— Financial performance	Total 1Key Balanced Scorecard
Mind-set	Silo approach	Collaborative KeyCorp
Focus	Financial measures	Financial/Nonfinancial measures
Frequency	Monthly	Monthly Specific Focus –Financial –LOB/support scorecards –Corporate scorecard
Attendance	CEO, CFO, EVP Finance	CEO and direct reports
Tool	Various financial reports	Balanced scorecard

This discipline has forever changed the approach executives use to strategically manage the enterprise. BSC meetings were focused to identify and resolve execution issues and build fact-base for strategic decision-making and profit planning. The four new executive meeting tracks (shown in Exhibit 6.32) are described more fully next.

1. CFO, group LOB executive, and LOB CFO conducted monthly review meetings that included leading indicator reviews, performance against strategic and financial goals, significant events, and short-term actions.

2. CEO, CFO, group LOB executive, and LOB CFO conducted quarterly BSC reviews to monitor strategy execution and focus on human capital issues and other nonfinancial metrics.

3. CEO, executive management team, and LOB executive conducted quarterly LOB meetings to complete a comprehensive strategy review; industry and performance outlook; competitive assessment; strengths, weaknesses, opportunities, and threats (SWOT) analysis; and long-term strategic and financial plans.

4. CEO and executive management team conducted annual reviews of corporate performance versus long-term financial goals, peer benchmarks, industry outlook, and strategic issues, Key's relative position and strategic options, and employee development review.

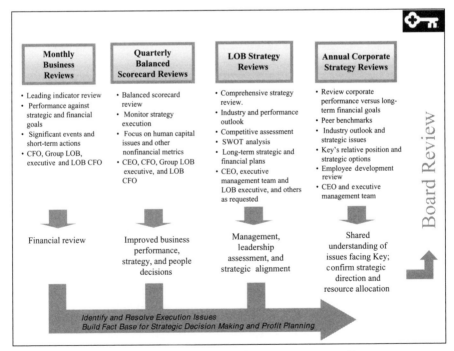

EXHIBIT   6.32   **Key Strategic Management Process**

With the recent announcement of Key's new Community Banking Model, it will be critically important to build and maintain this level of discipline in order for Key to deliver the kinds of results that its shareholders deserve and that KCIB has been able to experience. Key will continue to focus on data quality and on automating Key's BSC.

The executive team (Key's senior leaders) meets weekly to discuss strategic issues. Many of the topics covered at these sessions have been identified as areas for improvement on the corporate and LOB BSCs. These discussions also set the agenda for quarterly LOB strategy review meetings and two semiannual corporate strategy review meetings with expanded senior leadership representation.

This process allows Key's leaders to make decisions as a team more quickly. The required information for decision making is available in a consolidated format, and the meetings are scheduled on a regular basis, enabling the executive team to discern and react quickly.

Links to Personal Scorecards

The BSC has helped drive a level of accountability allowing the CEO to methodically remove low performers and reorganize the executive management team to drive for results as shown in Exhibit 6.33.

DHP Scorecard — **Differentiating High Performance**

Employee Name:	Employee Social Security #:
Manager Name:	Company #/Cost Center:
Department/LOB:	Date Completed: 12/13/2005

Balanced Scorecard Elements	Performance Goals			Employee Results*								Employee Rating**			
				Q1		Q2		Q3		Q4					
		FY Goal	FP Range	Actual	Goal	Actual	Goal	Actual	Goal	Actual	Goal	Q1	Q2	Q3	Q4
Enhance Shareholder Value															
Be the trusted advisor															
Execute 1Key															
Proud to be at Key															
Live the Key Values															
											Summary Rating:				
												Annual Performance Rating:			

Average each Balanced Scorecard element's Quarterly Ratings to determine Summary Rating
Average each Balanced Scorecard element's Summary Ratings to determine Annual Performance Rating
*Quarterly trend is cumulative
**Based on YTD Performance to Goal

Performance Ratings
1- Low Performance
2- Vital Core Performance
3- High Performance

EXHIBIT 6.33 **Employee Self-Assessment**

At the heart of Key's Differentiating for High Performance assessment is its link to Key's corporate Strategy Map.

Alignment Best Practice

While Key is "good" at aligning personal development plans to the achievement of its strategic results, its line of business, KCIB exemplifies a "best practice" in this area. KCIB overcame a particular alignment challenge involving the integration of its traditional corporate banking business with a recently acquired investment banking business. That is, the cultures of the corporate bankers and investment bankers were quite different, yet individuals from both groups had to learn to work together to sell seamlessly to corporate clients.

Key National Banking (KNB) (formerly KCIB) president partnered with his HR director to lead a project team focused on the human capital aspects of the KCIB strategy. This was accomplished through identifying and defining each critical job position and the associated skills and competencies necessary for that position. Also developed were the learning needs and ultimately, training courses, for each job to close the gaps in the areas of foundational sales,

---

BEST PRACTICE HIGHLIGHTS

Principle 3: Cascade and Manage Strategy
- *Partner with Business Owners.* Translate strategy into level 1 BSC measures and measure targets at the highest organizational level.
- *Develop Level 1 Balanced Scorecard.* Observe BSC or comparable design parameters assigning one to two measures to each Strategy Map objective.
- *Cascade BSC to Lower Levels.* Cascade and align level 1 BSC to lower levels to establish accountability structures.
- *Align Support Services.* Identify and define measures for all support services that align with levels 1 and below.
- *Align Teams and Individual Employees.* Define personal BSCs for teams and/or individuals that align with higher-level and support services BSCs.
- *Link Compensation.* Align rewards, recognition, and compensation programs to the BSC.
- *Manage Using Measures.* Manage BSC meetings to address the appropriate mix of strategic and operational issues.
- *Automate Measurement.* Implement CPM software to manage BSC program with links to other principles.

client management, functional, product, and technology skills. The goal was to identify the right people, train them to close any competency/skill gaps, and make an immediate impact with the new business model combining corporate and investment banking functions. The impact of this initiative is evidenced by KCIB's results. Revenues were up nearly 36% in 2004.

Key has been making significant improvements across the enterprise. In 2004, a new chief information officer was recruited to the organization, and significant progress has been made in aligning the strategic needs of Key's LOBs with the priorities of the IT team. Key identified strategic jobs across KCIB, the competencies and skills required for each of the positions, and the training programs to support those roles. The individual who led the process for KCIB has recently been promoted to oversee this process for the entire corporation. The creation of Key's Differentiating for High Performance process came as a direct result of the implementation of its BSC.

Balanced Scorecard and Lessons Learned

As cultural, process, and people changes became apparent, Michele Seyranian, Executive Vice President and Senior Planning Manager, Strategic Planning Group, was able to focus on lessons learned to continuously improve the BSC program. In so doing, she has set Key's BSC program apart from those of many leading organizations. The lessons learned included:

- Do not assume anything.
- Identify causal relationships.
- Teamwork is critical to success.
- "Warts" become visible.
- It is an iterative process.
- Cannot over communicate.
- Becomes more relevant as used.
- Analysts love it.

Balanced Scorecard Automation

Currently Key's BSCs are produced using Excel or PowerPoint. However, they will also be displayed on Key's financial system, called INEA, an online report delivery application. This application allows users in any Key location to access content from a variety of sources and formats through a single, browser-based desktop.

> *For myself I am an optimist—it does not seem to be much use being anything else.*
> —WINSTON CHURCHILL

SPRINT NEXTEL: BEST PRACTICE CASE

Once the strategy was defined, the next step was to mobilize the change necessary to successfully execute the strategy in the new company. This involved cascading the strategy within the SmartCard framework and partnering with the business to gain support for the strategy to influence successful strategic execution.

The goal of the newly merged company was to start using the SmartCard framework as soon as possible not only to effectively monitor the company performance on an ongoing basis but also to align the 80,000 employees around the strategy. However, before an effective corporate-level SmartCard could be designed, the company first had to have the key elements of its strategy detailed. "Strategy formulation is an exercise of fact-base analysis that requires access to key data which was not readily available before the merger was closed," says Corporate Strategy Organization (CSO) director Tolga Yaveroglu. "Although the new company had its vision defined right after the merger announcement, it was only after the official close of the merger that the two organizations could share key data and information and start formulating the details of its three-year strategic direction."

A successful BSC has to start with the strategy first. In the absence of this direction within the first couple of months of the combined operations, the CSO utilized a Balanced Scorecard based on the "stub year" objectives that were identified during the merger integration process in order to execute the immediate-term goals. As the corporate performance was being evaluated based on the stub-year scorecard, a tight window existed between defining the corporate strategy and the CSO goal of implementing a new Corporate SmartCard (Level I) by January 2006.

Toward this end, the functional scorecards (Level II) were developed simultaneously with the corporate card. To ensure the alignment of the corporate and functional scorecards in this unusual cascading process, the CSO worked very closely with the planning council (planning directors from each of the major functions). As strategic objectives and measures were defined at the functional levels, alignment with the six-pillar strategy was evaluated. In some cases, as the functions defined the critical operational success factors to realize the six-pillar strategy, this pointed to strategic objectives that were then incorporated into the internal perspective of the corporate Strategy

- *Forbes* America's Best Managed Company in the Telecommunications Services category

Map. According to CSO senior manager Jenevieve Creary, "It is fair to say that while the corporate strategy was cascaded down, the development of the specific strategic objectives in the internal perspective of the corporate Strategy Map was as much of a bottoms-up validation process as it was a typical cascade from the top down. This collaborative approach made sense in a postmerger scenario where timing was of the essence." An example of one of the corporate strategic objectives that was identified is represented in Exhibit 6.34.

The measures that were identified to gauge the performance against this objective scale, spending to drive leading Operating Income Before Depreciation and Amortization OIBDA margins, were controllable expenses by category (e.g., sales, marketing, care) and margin (by business unit) and Cash Cost Per Unit (subscriber) CCPU by functional organization. This objective is highly relevant and important to all organizations across the company. The finance organization in particular represented this on their card as an objective called "Manage Spending." Similarly, this was represented on the scorecard for a department cascade to the enterprise financial services department (EFSD). While the objective wording was the same for the departmental cascade, measures were very specific to the cost components of the function and the cost components of the department. Finance in turn has cascaded the

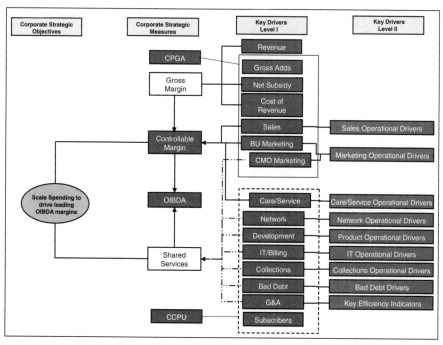

EXHIBIT 6.34   Sprint Nextel Corporate Key Drivers

SmartCard three to five additional levels below corporate depending on size, complexity, and team sizes.

While very few cascades have occurred at the department level (Level III) and the alignment of the support organizations is not scheduled to occur until second and third quarter 2006, the successful communication plan helped to rally the troops behind the strategy until that level of cascades could begin. In addition to the communication efforts at the corporate level, the functions also reinforced the corporate message using other tools tailored to meet their specific needs. For example, in the EFSD in the finance organization, the scorecard development process emerged out of a "grassroots" request for clearer departmental alignment to the functional and corporate strategy. According to department head William G. Arendt, Senior Vice President and Controller, "People would rather think about the future than the past. Adopting the SmartCard helped change the focus of my management team to one that is more forward-looking. We now give our group the option of using the functional Strategy Map as either a screen saver or wallpaper for their PC. As a result, throughout the day the organization is constantly reminded of the functional strategy. It is more effective than reminding them through e-mails, newsletters, or Web casts—all of which have a limited shelf life."

Strategy Reviews

Another key activity in enabling successful strategic execution is to align the strategic reviews with best practice guidelines. Both premerger organizations had established enterprise operations reviews. However, a new strategic review forum was necessary to effectively monitor the new company's progress in achieving the strategic goals in the critical post merger period. The CSO set about dissecting each component of the legacy meetings to assess their relevance and value and validated with the executive team to ensure that nothing was lost in the transition to a new meeting format. The CSO proposed the agenda in Exhibit 6.35 to the lead team, and this format was implemented for 2006 along with the new Strategy Map and scorecard.

The operational focus of the meeting was not eliminated. Rather, operational topics were reviewed within the context of the strategic objectives of the BSC. Focus topics, a key feature of the premerger Sprint meeting format, became deep dives into operation issues critical to the successful execution of the strategy, which often emerged as part of the prior month's action items. The meeting was reduced from eight hours to five and attendees were required for the full five hours to encourage cross-functional dialogue. Action items were well documented; ownership was assigned and target closure dates were identified, where applicable. These were well communicated to meeting participants and often became focus topics for the next meeting.

EXHIBIT 6.35   Enterprise Ops Reviews (EOR) Agenda Format

Purpose

The goal of the meeting is to establish a strategy-focused forum where the functional leaders review how the business is executing against key strategic objectives/plans and discuss action items, initiatives, remedy issues, and other forward-looking operational topics in a cross-functional environment

Agenda Format

Discussion Item	Required Attendees	Duration
Action item review	Lead team and other required attendees (please see next page for list of attendees)	10 minutes
Financials review		40 minutes
Competitive review		*[15 minutes—quarterly only]*
Break		10 minutes
Balanced scorecard discussion	Lead team and other required attendees	180 minutes
Focus topic discussion		90 minutes

An important factor in the effectiveness of these meetings is the premeeting activities. Prep meetings occur a few days before hand, with the meeting leader—the chief operating officer. The goal of these prep meetings is to set the agenda for the strategic review meeting. The SmartCard report is reviewed and those objectives that are in "red" and "yellow" status are typically selected for inclusion on the agenda. "Green" items, though included in the report, are not usually discussed in the review meeting. However, the meeting leader could select an objective in "green" status for review if it was an item that was of particular interest to the lead team. Objective owners are also encouraged to prep for the meetings so that they could actively participate in cross-functional dialogue on the objective status and the future plans for bringing the objective back on target.

The CSO continues to work with the functional teams to encourage greater alignment of their review meetings with the strategy and on making those meetings more effective.

Automation of the Balanced Scorecard Report

A vital tool in the successful cascading of the strategy via the BSC is the automation of the scorecards and the production of the monthly reports. A custom solution was implemented in premerger Nextel. It was built in-house using various off-the-shelf applications to support the backend functionality and various charting capabilities. The tool was adopted for implementation in the new company and so required further development to make it more scalable for implementation across the new, significantly larger organization.

The application allows users to design their own BSC in the application wizard using predefined company standards. Once design is complete, the scorecard is approved and released into the production environment for report production. While data loading is currently a manual activity, once the data are loaded, charts are automatically populated and e-mail notifications can be sent to various objective owners to enter the centrally located tool to write

---

BEST PRACTICE HIGHLIGHTS

Principle 3: Cascade and Manage Strategy
- *Partner with Business Owners.* Partner with line and staff leadership team members to gain support and influence as partners to help them achieve results.
- *Develop Level 1 Balanced Scorecard.* Translate strategy into level 1 BSC measures and measure targets at the highest organizational level.
- *Leverage Proven BSC or Comparable Methods.* Observe BSC or comparable design parameters assigning one to two measures to each Strategy Map objective.
- *Cascade BSC to Lower Levels.* The corporate strategy has been cascaded to the functions via the BSC (SmartCard framework).
- *Align Support Services.* Identify and define measures for support services that align with levels 1 and below. Departmental and support service cascades are under way. However, effective communication efforts have helped to link the corporate and functional objectives to individual goals.
- *Align Teams and Individual Employees.* Define personal BSC for teams and/or individuals that align with higher-level and support services BSCs.
- *Manage Using Measures.* Manage BSC meetings to address the appropriate mix of strategic and operational issues. Strategic reviews have been implemented at the corporate and functional levels. The CSO continues to work to achieve and maintain strategic focus in those meetings across the company.
- *Automate Measurement.* Implement CPM software to manage BSC program with links to other principles. Efforts to cascade the strategy have been and will continue to be supported by the continued use of the custom application designed to support the automation of the BSC report across all levels of the organization.

commentary and prepare for various reporting milestones. The use of the application is still very much in its initial stage. However, having this solution ready for implementation has the organization poised to make the production of the reports a more seamless effort and to further standardize the BSC as a tool for strategic execution management.

> *I too shall lie in the dust when I am dead, but now let me win noble renown.*
> —HOMER

NOTES

1. Adapted from Bob Paladino, "Strategic Balanced Scorecard-Based Budgeting and Performance Management," chapter 1A in Will Lalli, ed., *Handbook of Budgeting,* 4th ed. supplement (Hoboken, NJ: John Wiley & Sons, 2005).

2. Janice Koch, "The Challenges of Strategic Alignment: Crown Castle's CEO Shares His Perspectives," *Balanced Scorecard Report* (July-August 2004): 10.

3. Janice Koch, "Global Alignment: A Telecom's Tale," *Balanced Scorecard Report* (May-June 2004): 7.

4. "TVA Creating a Winning Performance" presentation, Cambridge, MA, June 1, 2004, p. 28.

5. Harvard Business School Press, Balanced Scorecard Hall of Fame Report 2004, p, 30.

6. *Journal of Public Health Management and Practice* 10, no. 5 (September/October 2004): 413–420.

7. Ricoh Balanced Scorecard Hall of Fame Application.

CHAPTER 7

Principle 4

IMPROVE PERFORMANCE

The game isn't over till it's over.
—YOGI BERRA

Exhibit 7.1 summarizes Principle 4 Best Practices, and the case studies provide rich content to support them. The Crown case study provides both

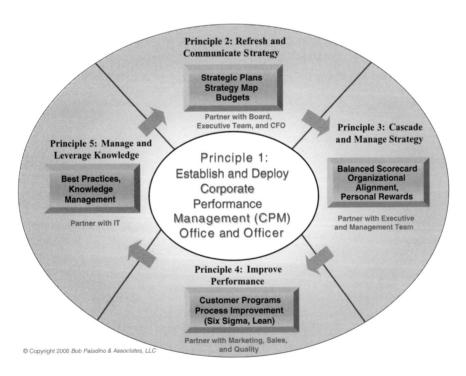

© Copyright 2006 *Bob Paladino & Associates, LLC*

EXHIBIT 7.1	Principle 4 Best Practice Summary

Best Practice	Description
Prioritize improvement projects	Identify and prioritize strategic and operational initiatives to improve organization's performance along financial, customer or constituent, process, and people dimensions.
Leverage customer facing processes	Develop and exercise customer and constituent processes to understand and recalibrate processes around changing customer needs. Gather customer and competitor intelligence using regular customer surveys, focus groups, call centers, quality function deployment, and related methods and approaches.
Leverage process improvement methods	Design and maintain an ongoing process improvement and problem-solving program based on Six Sigma black belt or green belt, or Lean methods and tools to identify and eliminate root causes of issues.
Realize value from benchmarking processes	Leverage benchmarking and comparative methods to identify and regularly improve core and support processes. APQC has developed a process classification framework with standard process definitions and benchmarking (www.apqc.org).
Create a performance improvement culture	Create a virtual community of practitioners to coordinate and optimize improvement efforts enterprise-wide.

the Crown-specific best practices and expands discussion on the normative Principle 4 best practices learned from the collective companies researched.

> *Major failures in business come not so much from unmet goals, as from lack of response to unforeseen changes.*
> —O. L. DUFF

Case study companies in this chapter also include recipients of these awards:

- U.S. President's National Malcolm Baldrige Quality Award
- Governor's Sterling Award for Excellence (based on Baldrige Criteria)
- Deming Quality Award
- American Quality and Productivity Center (APQC) Best Practice Partner Award
- Kaplan and Norton Global Balanced Scorecard Hall of Fame Award
- *Wall Street Journal* Ranked "Top 20 Most Improved Company in Shareholder Value Creation"
- *Fortune* "100 Best Companies to Work For"
- *Forbes* Best Managed Companies

INTRODUCTION TO SIX SIGMA

This section provides foundational understanding of six sigma to enable better appreciation for the cutomer focused, Six Sigma and quality-based case studies in this chapter. If you are grounded in six sigma, feel free to advance to the first case. I have been fortunate to have collaborated with Motorola and to have trained and led GE Six Sigma teams during their launch in the 90's. These experiences will be covered more fully in the Crown case study.

Motorola's Bill Smith pioneered Six Sigma and initially applied it to manufacturing; Motorola has reported over $17 billion savings from Six Sigma since 1986. Since the mid-1990s General Electric (GE) has successfully evolved this methodology, applied it to both its manufacturing and services businesses, and transformed its global operations.

Motorola Sig Sigma Methodology: An Overview of DMAIC

This section provides a road map to the DMAIC (define, measure, analyze, improve, and control) Six Sigma methodology including for each step key objectives, main activities, and key deliverables.

Define Opportunities: Step 1

To identify and/or validate the improvement opportunity, develop the business processes, define critical customer requirements, and prepare themselves to be an effective project team.

Main Activities	Key Deliverables
• Validate/identify business opportunity	• Team charter
• Validate/develop team charter	• Action plan
• Identify and map processes	• Process maps
• Identify quick win and refine process	• Quick win opportunities
• Translate voice of customer (VOC) into critical customer requirements (CCRs)	• Critical customer requirements
• Develop team guidelines and ground rules	• Prepared team

Measure Performance: Step 2

To identify critical measures that are necessary to evaluate the success, meeting critical customer requirements, and begin developing a methodology to effectively collect data to measure process performance. To understand the elements of the six sigma calculation and establish baseline sigma for the processes the team is analyzing.

Main Activities	Key Deliverables
• Identify input, process, and output indicators	• Input, process, and output indicators
• Develop operational definition and measurement plan	• Operational definitions
• Plot and analyze data	• Data collection formats and plans
• Determine if special cause exists	• Baseline performance
• Determine sigma performance	• Productive team atmosphere
• Collect other baseline performance data	

Analyze Opportunity: Step 3

To stratify and analyze the opportunity to identify a specific problem and define an easily understood problem statement. To identify and validate the root causes that assure the elimination of "real" root causes and thus the problem the team is focused on. To determine true sources of variation and potential failure modes that lead to customer dissatisfaction.

Main Activities	Key Deliverables
• Stratify process	• Data analysis
• Stratify data, and identify specific problem	• Validated root causes
• Develop problem statement	• Sources of variation
• Identify root causes	• FMEA (failure mode and effects analysis)
• Design root cause verification analysis	• Problem statement
• Validate root causes	• Potential solutions
• Comparative methods	
• Sources of variation studies	
• FMEA	
• Regression analysis	
• Process control and capability	
• Design of experiments	

Improve Performance: Step 4

To identify, evaluate, and select the right improvement solutions. To develop a change management approach to assist the organization in adapting to the changes introduced through solution implementation.

Main Activities	Key Deliverables
• Response surface methods	• Solutions
• Generate solution ideas	• Process maps and documentation
• Determine solution impacts: benefits	• Implementation milestones
• Evaluate and select solutions	• Improvement impacts and benefits
• Develop process maps and high level plan	• Storyboard
• Develop and present storyboard	• Change maps
• Communicate solutions to all stakeholders	

Control Performance: *Step 5*

To understand the importance of planning and executing against the plan and determine the approach taken to assure achievement of the targeted results. To understand how to disseminate lessons learned, identify replication and standardization opportunities/processes, and develop related plans.

Main Activities	Key Deliverables
• Develop pilot plan and pilot solution • Verify reduction in root cause sigma improvement resulted from solution • Identify if additional solutions are necessary to achieve goal • Identify and develop replication and standardization opportunities • Integrate and manage solutions in daily work processes • Integrate lessons learned • Identify teams next steps and plans for remaining opportunities	• Process Control Systems • Standards and procedures • Training • Team evaluation • Change implementation plans • Potential problem analysis • Pilot and solution results • Success stories • Trained associates • Replication opportunities • Standardization opportunities[2]

General Electric: An Overview of Six Sigma

What is Six Sigma? First, what it is not. It is not a secret society, a slogan, or a cliché. Six Sigma is a highly disciplined process that helps us focus on developing and delivering near-perfect products and services. Why "Sigma"? The word is a statistical term that measures how far a given process deviates from perfection. The central idea behind Six Sigma is that if you can measure how many "defects" you have in a process, you can systematically figure out how to eliminate them and get as close to "zero defects" as possible. To achieve Six Sigma quality, a process must produce no more than 3.4 defects per million opportunities. An "opportunity" is defined as a chance for nonconformance, or not meeting the required specifications. This means we need to be nearly flawless in executing our key processes.

Six Sigma is utilized to drive process improvement and consistency. It is a quality tool transformed into the management philosophy that strives for customer satisfaction through consistently meeting or exceeding their commitments.

At its core, Six Sigma revolves around some key concepts:

1. *Critical to quality.* Attributes most important to the customer
2. *Defect.* Failing to deliver what the customer wants
3. *Process capability.* What your process can deliver
4. *Variation.* What the customer sees and feels

5. *Stable operations.* Ensuring consistent, predictable processes to improve what the customer sees and feels
6. *Design for Six Sigma.* Designing to meet customer needs and process capability

What are the benefits of Six Sigma?

- Increase in customer satisfaction
- Improvement in productivity
- Building a quality mind-set within the company[1]

The foregoing materials are introductory. A deeper understanding and use of the DMAIC methodology would require more in-depth training and materials.

CROWN CASTLE: BEST PRACTICE CASE

I had the good fortune of being engaged to participate as a trainer to GE Capital Corporation, where we helped to launch their now well-known and highly regarded black belt program. I participated as a black belt trainer and facilitated instruction and team deployment to drive improvements using the DMAIC methodology. The DMAIC training model deployed involved a two-week hands on training course solving real business issues in addition to instructive case studies. The GE teams fully embraced this approach, and many teams attained significant results. However, not every company is ready for this approach, or has the culture for it. At Crown we had to evolve into using the DMAIC approach.

> *Habit is habit and not to be flung out of the window by any man, but coaxed downstairs a step at a time.*
> —MARK TWAIN

Initiative Prioritization

Crown's corporate performance management (CPM) Office was under a lot of pressure in a fast-clock-speed business to demonstrate rapid results. The

- Recipient of Balanced Scorecard Hall of Fame Award
- Recipient of APQC Best Practice Partner Award
- Ranked "Top 20 Most Improved Company in Shareholder Value Creation" by *Wall Street Journal* (out of 1,000 listed companies)

company faced many issues harmonizing and standardizing dissimilar port-folios of acquired towers, resulting in numerous improvement initiatives. However, at one point Crown had to rationalize and really focus improve-ment efforts. This is illustrated in the exchange that follows. The Crown chief executive officer (CEO) was asked, "Crown Castle had some 180 ini-tiatives before implementing the scorecard. How did you pare that down to 12?" The CEO responded, "When individuals are not certain about the specific objectives and goal of a particular area of the enterprise, they end up interpreting their own initiatives based on what they are hearing or see-ing on any given day or week. That is human nature. Typically, many things will occur in a given week that may cause part of an operation to believe that X is important. A while later, someone comes to talk to them and something else gets added to the list of what is important. If there is not an overall operating context, it becomes difficult for leaders of individual areas to know what is important or not. To ensure they are not missing some-thing, the list grows. Actually, it was pretty easy to cut the list down from 180 to 12 because people had a clear understanding of what our strategic priorities were. We racked and stacked all initiatives, and looked at which ones were most important relative to the four elements of our strategy [mentioned earlier in Chapter 5]. The Balanced Scorecard helped us give people context."[3]

The clarity in understanding and linking strategic objectives and mea-sures provided focus for our improvement efforts. In reality, we scored the 180 initiatives noted against the Balanced Scorecard (BSC) to arrive at the top 12 that would move measure dials to the right. Going forward in a steady state environment, the CPM Office provided monthly bench-marks of BSC results across 40 district offices, allowing for identification of underperforming districts that might warrant a performance improvement project.

In short, the CPM Office team facilitated BSC results, survey results, and performance improvement teams with country leaders on high-priority proj-ects that would generate rapid cash flow. The problem-solving approach used for these teams is the topic of the next section.

Ten-Step Problem-Solving Approach (GE Black Belt Light)

The CPM Office collaborated with Crown leadership teams and helped to facilitate performance improvement projects. Since employees had little appetite for the GE two-week, Six Sigma course, a distilled version of DMAIC was adopted called the "10-Step Problem-Solving Process" hand-book. We designed and delivered training on this approach. For instance, the

EXHIBIT 7.2   **Problem-Solving Pitfalls to Avoid**

Lessons from the Field

- Failure to clearly define the problem statement
  - Heavy focus on fighting fires; why has this problem been around for so long?
- Skipping validation of actual current performance
  - Can we risk relying on anecdotal evidence?
- Failure to set measurable improvement targets
  - How do we know if we have made progress?
- Lack of discipline to complete a proper root cause analysis
  - How can we be sure we are solving the real problem?
- Leaping prematurely to solutions
  - How do we know if the problem has been solved?
- Lack of understanding of customer requirements leads to poor solutions
  - Our clients lack confidence in our ability to deliver

excerpted example in Exhibit 7.2 builds awareness for the top reasons for project failure. Once understood by improvement teams, many requested a more disciplined approach.

The 10-step handbook simplified the road map and tool set to enable real-time learning and team results in a high-pressure environment. The 10 steps are shown in Exhibit 7.3 a more detailed version was shared with the project teams.

To provide you with a better perspective, step 2 consists of a goal statement and team charter (constraints, assumptions, team guidelines, resources,

EXHIBIT 7.3   **10-Step Problem-Solving Method: Short Version**

AS-IS Current State	1. Have we identified the right areas of focus? 2. What is the initial goal statement? Team charter? 3. What are 3 to 5 customer requirements/complaints? 4. What is the current process (map) and issues? 5. What are the prioritized choke points/issues and root causes?
TO-BE Future State	6. What are future state or desired process attributes? 7. What improvement level is expected—final goal statement? 8. What should the future process be (new map)?
GAP	9. What are the barriers to improvement? Countermeasures?
Implementation	10. What do we pilot? Results? What is the full implementation plan?

and project plan). We will explore the goal statement consisting of these elements:

- List specific improvement.
- Identify the process or scope of process you want to improve.
- Identifies the time frame for completion.
- Identify output (product/service).
- Identify customer and expected outcome to the customer (from their perspective).

A goal statement template and hypothetical project goal statement follow.

Goal Statement Template:
   Reduce the [cycle time/costs/number of defects] in the [process you want to improve] process [where] [by when], which provides [product/service] to [customers] and results in [expected outcome] for the customer.

Goal Statement Case Study:
   Reduce the employee report preparation time 50% and process cycle time by 66% in the time and expense process in the northeast regions in three months, which provide increased employee selling time and customer face time.

The 12 initiate teams adopted the 10 steps. The results were amazing, delivering millions in free cash flow in just 12 weeks.

DMAIC Green Belts at Crown: Moving beyond the 10 Steps

Once the 12 projects were completed using the 10-step approach, many managers and leaders were ready and more interested in a more robust problem-solving approach. A Six Sigma example at Crown illustrates how this method integrated with BSCs and knowledge management efforts.[4]

Crown collaborated with Motorola University and enrolled employees in the one-week, intensive Six Sigma green belt program to learn the DMAIC problem-solving method. The Crown vice president of Six Sigma said: "Motorola's DMAIC method has helped Crown Castle International move away from the anecdotal approach. Using this framework forces project teams to identify the underlying drivers of performance, measure and analyze their impact, and quantify the benefits of potential solutions. It has taken a lot of the guess work out of the process." The hands-on course linked Six Sigma to company strategy and the BSC and also leveraged experiential learning techniques and live case studies.

"At Motorola University, we enjoy working with green belt candidates from Crown Castle because they arrive for training with strategically important projects in hand," said Tom McCarty of Motorola University. "And they execute on those projects on a timely basis. That makes the learning relevant and immediately impact for everyone involved." The vice president of Six Sigma facilitated biweekly green belt program meetings, a virtual community of practitioners, to review common project issues, allocate resources, and establish a center of excellence.

> *I've always made a total effort, even when the odds seemed entirely against me. I never quit trying; I never felt that I didn't have a chance to win.*
> —ARNOLD PALMER

Six Sigma Case: Spotlight on Real Improvements

The Crown USA southern area president sponsored the Six Sigma (6S) "job close" project that forms this case study. She reported: "The job close project was selected from a list of ground up initiatives formulated at Crown's annual southern area kick-off meeting in January attended by all staff. For much of the prior year the southern area team was in the red on this BSC metric, and they wanted to improve their performance to that of green. Empowering the front line to self-select their desired project insured that we would have immediate buy-in to participate in the 6S project and more important allowed them to observe the direct linkage between BSC and 6S. Applying the 6S methodology resulted in a powerful quick win, which has since been converted into a best practice reflected company wide in the KM [knowledge management] system. The immediate relief on the work effort and boost to morale allowed the team to focus their efforts positively toward exceeding their financial and operational BSC metrics." If the job close process could be streamlined, then it would reduce both the amount of effort and reduce the number of rejections, thereby eliminating redundant effort. This Six Sigma job close project linked to Crown Castle International's BSC objective "Manage Projects Timely, Accurately, and Profitably," which in turn is supported by three scorecard measures:

1. Number of jobs open 90 days post-recognition
2. Amount of dollars spent on unrecognized jobs open more than 270 days
3. Number of unrecognized jobs open more than 270 days

The southern area president assembled a team for the project that included the area president and executive sponsor, district mangers and team leads, field managers, project coordinators, the area vice president of finance, the regional finance analyst, and a global performance six sigma leader and team member.

To reduce rejections, the team sought to understand why requests were being rejected by corporate accounting. The team captured defects over a one-month period for all five district offices and analyzed the root causes using the fishbone diagram in Exhibit 7.4, sometimes referred to in quality circles as the "five whys." As detailed in Exhibit 7.5, the defects could be grouped into the Xs (input indicators) and Ys (output indicators) that link back to the scorecard measure(in this case, the number of jobs open 90 days postrecognition.

From the analysis, the southern team identified two specific solutions:

1. *Streamline the job close process.* The current job closing process was streamlined to remove the steps that were not required to complete the job close form.
2. *Automate the job close form.* The job close form was automated so that the potential for normal errors was eliminated.

EXHIBIT 7.4   Fishbone Diagram

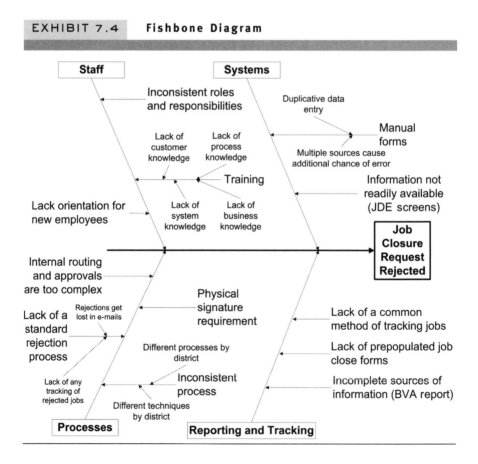

EXHIBIT 7.5 Xs (Input Indicators) and Ys (Output Indicators)

X's (Input Indicators)		Y's (Output Indicators)	
Input Indicators	Process Indictors	Y's Output Indictors	Y's (BSC) Output Indictors
Number of job closure requests	P1—Elapsed time from completion of application to submission to corporate	Average total elapsed time from completion to closure for all applications	BSC Measure: O12.1—# Jobs open 90 Days Postrecognition
	P2—Elapsed time from the receipt of job close request to the time it gets closed (non rejected requests only)		
	P4—Elapsed time from the receipt of rejection until the time it gets submitted to corporate		
	P5—Elapsed time from the receipt of a corrected job close request to the time it gets closed (non rejected requests only)		
	P3—Number of first-time job request rejections	Total number of job closure request rejections	
	P6—Number of corrected job request form rejections		

263

The team realized significant benefits from their new solutions:

- Reduced the average elapsed time spent preparing and approving job close from five days to one day of elapsed time
- Reduced the percentage of job close requests that are rejected from 13% to 2%
- Reduced the overall area effort for job rejections from 22 hours monthly to 2 hours monthly
- Annualized time savings equates to 1,719 hours for southern area personnel
- Annualized conservative base labor cost savings equates to more than $35,000 for the southern area personnel. (The potential of the benefit in one area, extended across five more areas or over 30 offices, could be more than $150,000).

The immediate relief on the work effort and boost to morale allowed the team to focus their efforts positively toward exceeding their financial and operational BSC metrics.

Given the southern area results, opportunities existed to share the "gems" or best practices with the other five U.S. areas comprised of approximately 40 district offices. Applying the Six Sigma method resulted in a powerful quick

---

BEST PRACTICE HIGHLIGHTS

Principle 4: Improve Performance
- *Prioritize Improvement Projects.* Identify and prioritize strategic and operational initiatives to improve the organization's performance along financial, customer or constituent, process, and people dimensions.
- *Leverage Customer Facing Processes.* Develop and exercise customer and constituent processes to understand and recalibrate processes around changing customer needs.
- *Leverage Process Improvement Methods.* Design and maintain an ongoing process improvement and problem-solving program based on Six Sigma green and to a lesser extent black belt methods and tools to identify and eliminate root causes of issues.
- *Realize Value from Benchmarking Processes.* Leverage benchmarking and comparative methods to identify and regularly improve core and support processes.
- *Create a Performance Improvement Culture.* Create a virtual community of practice of practitioners to coordinate and optimize improvement efforts enterprise-wide.

win that has since been converted into a best practice implemented company-wide through the KM system for gem capture and reuse, CCI-Link, knowledge management system. The Six Sigma team project team work papers and gems are housed in a dedicated, searchable repository for all internal users through a voluntary replication approach.

In summary, this project case focuses on developing a quality competency at the appropriate rate for the corporate culture and understanding the integration of its BSC, Six Sigma, and KM efforts at Crown. The job close project provides an example of the information flows and reinforcing links among these three proven methods.

> *Strong reasons make strong actions.*
> —WILLIAM SHAKESPEARE

CITY OF CORAL SPRINGS: BEST PRACTICE CASE*

Because the strategy development and deployment systems are so interrelated, the process improvement cycles for each coincide and are addressed at the same time. Deployment-related incremental improvements are made in departmental packages (forms and instructions), scheduling, training, and document design each year over the life of the system. Departmental performance measures, elements of the composite index, early warning system indicators, and some financial trend monitoring system are used to evaluate performance and are all included in the annual budget or in quarterly performance reports. In general, most measures have had positive trends and are projected to continue to meet stretch goals set each year. In fact, many of the key intended outcomes (KIOs) are already performing at such high levels that sustaining such a high level of performance in these challenging economic times is the goal. For the recent Sterling Award application, sustaining an overall quality rating of 96% is extremely challenging, particularly when you take into

- Recipient of Florida Governor Sterling Award for Organizational Excellence (based on Baldrige Criteria)
- Recipient of APQC Best Practice Partner Award

---

* The City of Coral Springs case team adapted portions of this case from "Performance Measurement in the Public Sector," *APQC* (November 2005), Governors Sterling Application 2003, and internal documents.

account the confidence interval of the survey instruments (±5%). Other monitoring tools include monthly financial statements and performance agreements with vendors.

Customer Segmentation

The city defines customers in three groups: indirect, direct, and internal.

- Indirect customers are residents who rely on the city to provide services to meet their needs as they arise. These customers may go long periods of time without directly using city services but rely on the city to provide vital services such as police protection, fire and emergency medical services, as well as recreational and other services. These customers' opinions of city services are based on what they hear, observe, and read about the city.
- Direct customers are those residents and nonresidents who are using city services to meet a specific need. These customers may have been rescued by emergency medical services paramedics, become a member of the city's tennis facility, or have called the city for information. These customers' opinions of city services are based on their direct experiences, or "moments of truth" when they are dealing with city staff.
- The last customer group is internal customers. These city employees and volunteers receive services from city departments such as human resources, financial services, and information services.

The city recognizes the need to segment customers and service programs to ensure that customers' needs are identified and that service programs meet or exceed their needs. Based on information from listening and learning mechanisms, customers are segmented by:

- Homeowners and renters
- Location within areas of the city
- Residents with children and no children
- Minorities and Caucasians

Customer segmentation is used to identify gaps in service programming and customer satisfaction. This information is used to design service programs, improve existing programs, fund new programs and services, and is targeted to specific segmented groups as identified.

Customer Intelligence: Listening

A variety of methods are used to listen and learn from customers to determine their key requirements (see Exhibit 7.6).

EXHIBIT 7.6   Customer Intelligence, Listening Methods

Method	Listen and Learn	Building Relationships	Complaint Management
Public Hearings	✔	✔	✔
Advisory Committees	✔	✔	✔
Customer Surveys	✔	✔	✔
Focus Groups	✔	✔	✔
"Slice of the Springs"	✔	✔	✔
City Hall in the Mall	✔	✔	✔
Complaint Tracking	✔	✔	✔
Web Site and "eFlash" System	✔	✔	✔
Citizen magazine		✔	
City INFO Line		✔	
PEG Television Channels		✔	
Welcome Packages	✔	✔	
Community Forums	✔	✔	✔
Police Substations	✔	✔	✔
Community-Oriented Policing	✔	✔	✔

Summary of methods used to listen and learn, build relationships, and manage complaints with our customers.

- The annual citizen survey is conducted by an independent research company, Profile Marketing Research. In-depth telephone interviews are conducted with approximately 800 residents and provide valuable, actionable feedback to the city on what is important to its customers. The questions focus on assessment of performance in relation to the city's KIOs, the indicators of quality. This information is used to provide direction for future planning and action. An annual survey has been conducted since the mid-1990s but was significantly improved in 1999.
- The city uses *focus groups* to frame questions, reviewing questions by experts to eliminate any bias, and adding key driver analysis to determine what factors strongly influence ratings. The key driver analysis has proven to be a major advance in the city's ability to determine customer requirements through regression analysis to determine what responses on single issue questions have a high correlation with the rating given on "overall satisfaction" with other functions. This kind of analysis of results creates meaningful information that can be acted on.
- Individual operating departments also *survey customers* to get actionable feedback on requirements. Some departments use phone surveys

immediately following a transaction. Others use written surveys, opinion cards, and online surveys at various sites.

- *"Slice of the Springs" neighborhood meetings* are another valuable way to learn about resident requirements. The Development Services Department conducts six neighborhood meetings yearly. Customers are invited for two-way communication with city staff on issues that are important to them in their neighborhoods. Residents are asked for realistic solutions to their concerns and are invited to improve their community through the Neighborhood Partnership Program. Over the past six years and 36 "Slice of the Springs" neighborhood meetings, approximately 165 partnerships have been formed and almost $470,000 has been spent on neighborhood improvements, $101,450 of which has been spent by the city. City staff answers questions on the spot during these meetings. Answers to all questions not addressed at the meetings are included in a meeting summary mailed to all meeting participants.

- The *Neighborhood Partnership Program* continues to expand in response to residents' suggestions and neighborhood needs. Through partnerships and partnership program initiatives, the staff hopes to continue maintaining and enhancing property values and customer satisfaction by addressing the concerns of neighborhoods through progressive, collaborative planning.

- The city's *communications and marketing department* has also been extremely helpful in gathering information from residents through the city's Web site. Besides being able to learn about the city, residents can access the Web site to request or comment on city services, request updates on city topics, and complete the "Slice of the Springs" meeting survey. Due to the highly visible nature of communications and marketing output, feedback is usually very immediate and specific.

- *E-mails, phone calls, and media reports* serve as early-warning indicators of topics or issues that might need additional attention. The flexibility of the Internet allows staff members to respond immediately, and since the city runs its own TV station, it can broadcast news and messages within just a few hours. Communications and marketing also conducts a communications survey. Advisory committees are organized to support the city's six strategic priorities.

- A city staff member acts as liaison to a *board* filled with residents for each priority. The boards develop mission statements, goals and objectives, and actions plans. For instance, the Multi-Cultural Advisory Committee supports the Respect for Ethnic and Religious Diversity priority. This committee coordinated a two-day "Diversity Dialogue" hosted by a city commissioner and invited over 100 residents with varying ethnic backgrounds from different sectors of the city. The committee distributed a survey to residents to prioritize issues prior to the dialogue. Eight issues were identified. At the dialogue participants selected an issue they wanted to work on, action plans were developed, and follow-up sessions are conducted to review the status, offer assistance, and make improvements as needed.

Customer Improvement Process

Improvement cycles are accomplished through the review and analysis of various factors including Web-based feedback, surveys, operational performance measures, and direct customer comments. As a result, cross-functional process improvement teams and focus groups are organized to research particular issues.

For example, the city's charter school began analyzing new feedback mechanisms from parents and teachers and made quick course corrections accomplished through a strategic planning process that included all stakeholders. Input was solicited through surveys, exit interviews, parent committees, and advisory boards. Many improvements were implemented including accountability for performance measures, a new principal, wider selection of curriculum choices, new clubs and sports teams, hours of operation, benefits for teachers, schools-within-a-school philosophy, and a better selection process for hiring new teachers. As a result, the school achieved an "A" rating in just three years after opening.

City Hall in the Mall, which provides weekend and evening access to city services at the local regional mall, has also been through many improvement cycles in its approach to listening and learning. Staff members at the mall are trained to actively listen to its customers and bring forth ideas to improve services. One such improvement was offering passports to customers. It not only was convenient for customers, but it also turned out to be a great revenue source for the city and has increased every year since its inception.

Customer Relationships and Satisfaction

Employees at all levels are dedicated to building relationships with residents. The city implemented a state-of-the-art "premier" customer service program, which includes training, accountability, recognition, reinforcement, measurement, and improvements. A focus group designed this program, which is based on five value dimensions:

1. *Presentation.* Creating a highly professional and caring environment
2. *Responsiveness.* Anticipating and fulfilling needs of customers
3. *Reliability.* Consistently delivering superior quality products and services
4. *Reassurance.* Increasing customer confidence through knowledge, competency, and integrity

5. *Empathy.* Creating and building relationships to exceed customers' expectations

The focus group also developed contact standards for each of the dimensions. All employees are trained on the value dimensions and standards that are linked to employee performance reviews. An "Applause Card" recognition program was developed to recognize and reward employees for modeling these behaviors. In addition, the city has an annual excellence award for customer service, for which the employee wins a trophy and a trip to the Sterling Conference. Message boards, e-mail messages, and payroll stuffers are used to reinforce standards and quality tips. "Quick Strikes," mystery shoppers, and follow-up transaction-based surveys have been used to measure compliance and to communicate results. After some time, results became so uniformly positive that we are now seeking other methods of measuring customer contact quality while continuing to use follow-up transaction-based surveys. Focus groups are periodically convened to review the premier customer service program and make improvements. For example, standards have been updated to include e-mail response time and using a new A to Z guide to assist customers. Transaction-based phone surveys were also added to get immediate and actionable feedback. The Police Department builds relationships with new homeowners by sending them a letter introducing the district captain and individual officers assigned to their neighborhood.

The city's complaint management process consists of a number of methods to collect and analyze complaints to make improvements. The city's complaint tracking system logs complaints into the city's work order system by designated front-line staff. It is used primarily by the City Public Works and Code Enforcement staff because resolving requests or complaints in their area often requires a work order. All activity on the complaint, including status reports to the complainants, is entered in the work order until completed.

A monthly "Letterman Report" (the top 10 complaints) is compiled and analyzed. When a trend is determined, an improvement team is assigned to the complaint to identify the root cause of the problem, generate a solution, and measure improvement. The newest means of tracking is through the Web-based "Request for Service" system. This allows customers to register complaints, questions, or concerns online and provides for a tracking system to ensure that the issue is handled in a prompt and satisfactory manner. The Webmaster sends the complaints to a predetermined staff member to handle. Every day, an automatic reminder is sent to the staff member who, in turn, updates the system with progress on the complaint until it has been satisfactorily resolved. This provides an online, real-time history of each complaint and specific individuals (e.g., city commissioners) can be given proxy rights to review the data at any time.

Trends are reported to the communications and marketing department for analysis and presentation to the senior management team. The partners are also held accountable for customer satisfaction and must effectively deal with customer complaints. Partner contracts include performance measures and customer service standards that must be adhered to. Such partners include Charter Schools USA, the charter school operator, Advanced Cable Communications, and Professional Facilities Management, Inc. at the city's cultural arts center.

Timelines are established as well as persons responsible for follow-through. Complaint tracking is an important means of determining customer dissatisfaction.

Cross-functional process improvement teams often assemble customer focus groups to pinpoint which features of the process are satisfiers and which features are dissatisfiers. Insight into satisfaction and dissatisfaction is also gleaned through commission meetings, advisory boards, and other public forums. It is critical, however, for a government to supplement this input with the results of a survey conducted with methodology that assures the sample is representative and provides data on trends in complaints or comments. A few vocal customers can overly influence the organization's perception of satisfaction or dissatisfaction, if data on the community at large is not available. Comments at public meetings do generate questions that can be explored through further, more structured research.

Customer Survey Benchmarking

The city compares its satisfaction ratings to data developed by the International City/County Management Association (ICMA) to compare customer satisfaction ratings of departments with those of other local governments. The data are not available for all cities and counties that are part of ICMA, but rather of the 100-plus that choose to participate in the work of the Center for Performance Measurement, the vanguard of cities using data to improve performance.

A new source of data on customer satisfaction in other cities is the National Research Center (NRC). It uses a methodology developed by its research staff to "normalize" the rating scales used by different city surveys to permit comparisons. The NRC database includes 23 Florida local governments, 6 of which are in Southeast Florida. Internet searches are also conducted to compare to organizations that have national reputations for excellence. At times focus groups provide information on customer satisfaction of neighboring cities.

Process Improvement Process

Exhibit 7.7 describes the city's design process for products and services and the related production and delivery processes.

EXHIBIT 7.7   **Design Process for Products and Services**

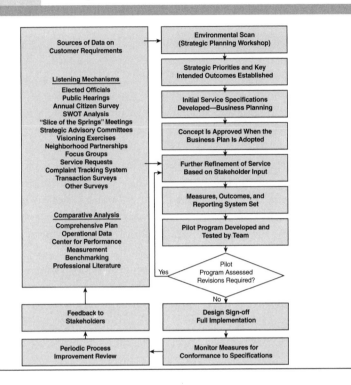

The left side of the exhibit shows the many sources of information on customer needs and preferences as well as the comparative analytics to identify and assess potential new services and delivery systems. This data gathering is ongoing during the year. As information becomes available, it is input to any active design process. In addition, all this information is incorporated into the annual environmental scan, which is the basis for the development of the strategic plan and the business plan. Significant new services and service enhancements are initially developed in the business planning process and are approved for further development when the business plan is approved.

A cross-functional process improvement team is appointed to refine the product specifications and develop a delivery system. The teams also develop performance measures and an approach to receiving ongoing stakeholder input. They test; they revise; they test again, as appropriate; and finally they implement an action plan. They monitor progress using the measures they chose. Each team's experience is shared with the stakeholders and other teams, to help prime further continuous improvement.

Changing customer and market requirements are incorporated into product and service designs and production and delivery systems by monitoring change through several mechanisms and then including the information in the environmental scan done for strategic planning purposes and in the analysis of ongoing design teams. Exhibit 7.8 presents the process improvement measurement process. Summaries and reports on significant changes are shared with design teams. The stakeholder input the teams receive during the design process may alert them to a change that they report to the senior management team. Information on changing requirements is reviewed by the team to determine if a change in service or delivery system specifications may be appropriate. An example of a change in a work in progress is the water playground at the Cypress Park Pool. Market research (focus group) information on what features should be included in the park was reflected in the initial park design. During the phase-in of the new equipment, it became clear that the clientele of the pool would become younger, and the requirement for more shade for parents and infants emerged. The team modified the design.

BEST PRACTICE HIGHLIGHTS

Principle 4: Improve Performance

- *Prioritize Improvement Projects.* Identify and prioritize strategic and operational initiatives to improve the organization's performance.
- *Leverage Customer Facing Processes.* Develop and exercise customer and constituent processes to understand and recalibrate processes around changing customer needs. Gather customer and competitor intelligence through the use of regular customer survey, focus groups, call centers, quality function deployment, and related methods and approaches.
- *Leverage Process Improvement Methods.* Design and maintain an ongoing process improvement and problem-solving program based on the six-step problem-solving approach to identify and eliminate root causes of issues.
- *Realize Value from Benchmarking Processes.* Leverage benchmarking and comparative methods to identify and regularly improve core and support processes.
- *Create a Performance Improvement Culture.* Create a virtual community of practice of practitioners to coordinate and optimize improvement efforts enterprise-wide.

EXHIBIT 7.8   Process Improvement Measurement Process

Key Process	Performance Requirements	Performance Measure for Control and Improvement	In-Process Measures*	Means of Supplier and Partner Input	Process Used to Prevent Errors
Development	Reliability and Responsiveness	Customer Service Rating	Surveys of Customers and Boards	Committees and Boards	Pre-Design Review of Projects, Cross-Training, and Collaboration
		Cycle Time for Small Permits	Daily Review of Status	Weekly Staff Meetings	Zoning Information Available on Internet
		Design Review Committee Cycle Time	Action Plan and Tracking	Development Review Committee	Pre-Design Review of Projects and Zoning Data
		Building Inspections Cycle Time*	Daily Update	Development Review Committee	Training for Contractors on Code
		Building Plans Review Cycle Time	Aging Report	Development Forum	Checklists
		Percent of Code Cases Cleared on First Reinspection	Aging Report	Code Board	Daily Updates
	Reassurance	Construction Projects on Time and in Budget*	Project Management Reports	Construction Review Committee	Weekly Meetings with Stakeholders

EXHIBIT 7.8 Process Improvement Measurement Process

		Department Quality Rating	Transaction Surveys	Comment Cards	Industry Standards
Public Works (PW)	Produced and Maintained to Specifications	Road Condition*	Conformance to Resurfacing Schedule	Florida Department of Transportation Standards	Maintenance Schedule from Computer Model
		Water Quality in Compliance*	Chemical Measures Required	Standards Established at Federal Level	Standard Operating Procedures for Testing, Manuals
Fire Rescue (FR)	Reliability and Responsiveness	Department Quality Rating	Service Standards	Fire Chiefs Meeting	Case Review Standards
		Number of Volunteers*	Monthly Quotas	Recruitment Staff	Extensive Screening of Potential Volunteers
		Response Time for Fire and EMS	Daily Reports by Shift and Station	"Slice of the Springs" Meetings and Mutual Aid	Every Call Tracked in Detail and All Outliers Reviewed
		Cycle Time for Fire Inspections	Daily Reports	Daily Contact with Customers	Review Committee
	Reassurance	Call Volume*	Monthly Data	Fire Chiefs Meeting	Monthly Review of Trends in Mix of Calls
		Percent of Customers That Feel Safe	Complaint and Comment Tracking	"Slice of the Springs" Meetings	Extensive Analysis on Patterns in Types and Locations of Calls

Employee Training on Problem Solving

Employees are trained in the six-step problem-solving model in Exhibit 7.9. During new employee orientation all employees receive training in a six-step approach to problem solving.

This general approach can be used at varying levels of rigor, depending on the problems being addressed:

Step 1. "Identify or Select the Problem" may occur as part of the business plan development or in reaction to data in unit operating reports, but at the team level will include the development of problem statement that is quantified.

Step 2. "Analyze the Problem" typically involves documentation of current practices and review of baseline data on performance. Based on brainstorming, the data are put in subsets to test ideas about the nature of the problem (e.g., response time is slowest during the second shift in the south part of town).

EXHIBIT 7.9   Six-Step Problem-Solving Model

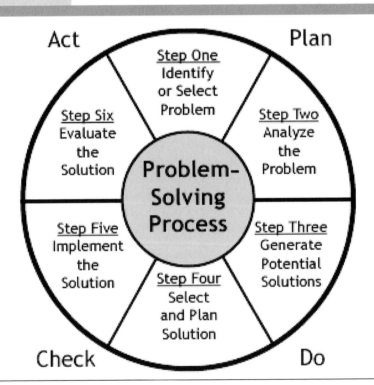

Step 3. "Generate Potential Solutions" looks at the practices of other organizations.

Step 4. "Select and Plan Solution" requires a test before a solution is selected.

Step 5. "Implement the Solution" includes the development of an action plan and measures and reports to monitor how well the solution is working.

Step 6. "Evaluate the Solution" is the basis for further improvements.

> *Always bear in mind that your own resolution to succeed is more important than any one thing.*
> —ABRAHAM LINCOLN

TENNESSEE VALLEY AUTHORITY: BEST PRACTICE CASE*

The Tennessee Valley Authority (TVA) has recently established a centralized benchmarking staff under Steve Saunders, General Manager, Benchmarking and Industry Analysis, to define an effective process and governance structure with TVA to focus on:

- Benchmark and best practice identification
- Data collection and dissemination
- Education
- Benchmarking consulting services

Due to the emphasis exerted by the new president and chief operating officer, there is a lot of momentum right now around employee skill set, best practice, and intellectual property retention. The objective is to create subject matter experts (communities of practitioners) within each organization. Both the benchmarking and knowledge retention foci are recent developments that have occurred in 2005; the knowledge retention dimension to these efforts will be discussed in Chapter 8.

> *Excellence is the gradual result of always striving to do better.*
> —PAT RILEY

- Recipient of APQC Best Practice Partner Award
- Recipient of the Balanced Scorecard Hall of Fame Award

* The TVA case team adapted portions of this case from "Performance Measurement in the Public Sector," *APQC* (November 2005) and internal company documents.

MEDRAD: BEST PRACTICE CASE*

Medrad began its performance excellence quest in 1988. It adopted a quality policy at its annual employee meeting in 1990. The quality policy clarifies how Medrad values customers, suppliers, and employees by clearly understanding their requirements and meeting those requirements on time, every time.

Medrad's Quality Policy

Medrad is dedicated to continually improving the quality of all its products and services such that its customers' satisfaction, loyalty, and respect are unsurpassed. It is its policy to clearly understand and agree on the valid requirements of the work it performs for its customers, both internal and external, and to pursue 100% conformance to those requirements, on time, every time. Medrad will:

- Empower, involve, and train each and every employee.
- Establish partnerships with its customers and suppliers.
- Foster quality improvement teams.
- Eliminate defects through prevention.
- Ensure that employees are recognized for achievements.

Medrad's performance improvement efforts began with the formation of the President's Quality Council (now known as the Performance Excellence Team [PET]), comprised of senior staff. In 1997 the senior leadership team began using a Balanced Scorecard featuring five corporate scorecard goals. The specific targets are reviewed each year at the beginning of portfolio planning. Medrad maintains an organizational focus on performance improvement by aligning the activities of functions, teams, and individuals with these corporate goals and the top 12 objectives.

Medrad's performance management system involves all employees in creating individual objectives and development plans that support corporate goals and individual growth.

At the corporate level, the annual strategic planning process identifies, selects, and allocates resources to critical projects to improve Medrad's ability to

- Recipient of Malcolm Baldrige National Quality Award
- Recipient of the APQC Best Practice Award

* Portions of this case are adapted from MEDRAD Malcolm Baldrige National Quality Award Application, internal company documents, and employee input.

achieve the corporate goals and objectives and to implement the portfolio plan. As needed, employees and work groups form teams to implement improvements and address process problems. Teams identify sponsors for their projects, usually higher-level managers, who procure resources for the group and provide feedback and direction. A charter between the team and the sponsor is developed for projects that are typically cross-functional and large in scope.

A corporate Performance Excellence Center and productivity centers in selected departments provide resources for improvement initiatives and also look for opportunities to share best practices with other parts of the company. At the organizational level, Medrad has been using the Baldrige Criteria to assess and improve its management system since 1994 and has received three site visits. Medrad's senior management uses the Baldrige Criteria feedback report in the PET meetings where improvement initiatives are reviewed and selected. Medrad fosters organizational learning most notably the quarterly quality forum (best practices sharing and introduction of performance excellence tools), the annual Performance Excellence conference (team best practice sharing and training in team skills), and learning and development.

Improve Performance: Customer Listening Posts

Marketing product line and marketing managers define market and customer segments through the portfolio planning process. The managers and other members of the platform teams determine customers and their needs according to three factors: (1) end user clinical modality, (2) geography, and (3) distribution channel. In the product line planning (PLP) phase of the portfolio planning process, PLP teams, using product line planning assessment guidelines analyze information that is gathered through the listening posts. PLP teams focus on Medrad's product platforms: Computed Tomography (CT) and Magnetic Resonance (MR) and Cardiovascular, Vascular products, with an incubator team dedicated to new products and markets.

Medrad listens to and learns from current, former, and potential customers, as well as customers of competitors, through the listening posts (see Exhibit 7.10).

The listening posts apply to both of Medrad's basic customer groups: end users and distribution channel customers. Field teams comprised of representatives from the sales and service organizations and technical applications specialists interact with customers worldwide. Team members enter information about these contacts into the field force automation (FFA) system. Field or corporate sales and services as well as marketing personnel, access FFA to find current information on equipment performance, customer requirements and satisfaction, sales opportunities, shipments, product orders, customer profile information, and other customer information. The sales, marketing, field management, reliability, and customer satisfaction departments use reports

EXHIBIT 7.10   **Voice of the Customer Listening Posts**

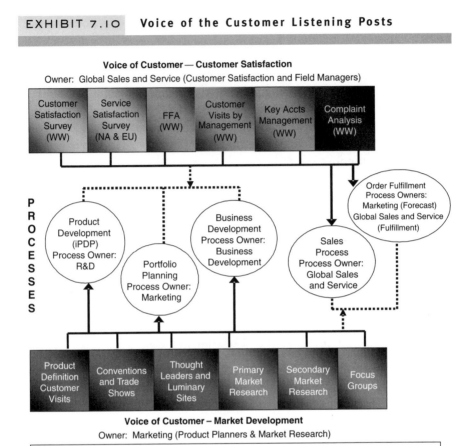

Voice of Customer — Customer Satisfaction
Owner: Global Sales and Service (Customer Satisfaction and Field Managers)

generated from FFA data and customer satisfaction surveys to determine key customer requirements and expectations and to analyze and improve customer satisfaction, product performance, and sales. As needed, managers generate tracking reports on equipment performance, customer satisfaction, and opportunities won or lost. In addition, reports using FFA data are created for all regional meetings of functional groups: sales, service, and applications.

The reasons for losing any customer are entered into FFA where they are available for analysis by marketing and sales managers. The customer satisfaction advisory board (CSAB) communicates progress on resolving top customer issues. This year CSAB is piloting a program to create a three-in-one opportunity map that identifies what will be done to win the lost customers back and address issues as they relate to all customers. Sales representatives and managers rely on listening post information to evaluate sales process efficiency and track customer retention. Sales use the "sales funnel" to quantify the efficiency and effectiveness of the sales process

Funnels are also used as forecasting tools to predict likely revenues from customers at different stages in the pipeline. In addition, sales use the funnels and FFA data on lost customers to identify the reasons they were lost. Marketing managers are responsible for analyzing listening post information to assess product and service requirements and to improve forecast efficiency. Product planners determine product and service features using the listening posts. Each of the product lines has a product planner assigned to determine customer and product requirements and set a five-year product road map. The requirements and road maps feed the strategic planning process and are used to define the direction for each modality and for the company. Those requirements or opportunities that extend beyond Medrad's current capabilities go to business development (BD). BD managers determine which organizations have the resources to capture the opportunity and then, with the approval of the BD advisory board, contact them about acquisition, joint venture, alliance, or a distribution agreement. Product development teams (PDTs) use extensive customer input from several listening posts to design and validate new product feature sets that respond to customer needs. In Stage 1 of the integrated product development process, the product planner and PDT use listening posts to define the product and check product development. Clinical partnering with end users is used to initiate market development, confirm product features, and perform beta site testing. As part of Medrad's ongoing customer relationship enhancement initiative, a project team assessed customer relationships along multiple dimensions that included product attributes, service, applications support, interactions, intimacy, information provider, and innovation. The assessments included all major customer groups across several geographic regions.

Listening and Learning Methods for Improvement

Medrad keeps its listening and learning methods current with the company's needs and directions primarily through zone manager meetings, European and Asian managers meetings, the CSAB, the market research department, and the global customer satisfaction department. Zone managers in North America meet formally every quarter, after which they meet with sales, service, and applications representatives in their respective zones to share information. Cross-functional team members attend the zone meetings and participate in discussions about customer preferences and requirements and the methods of determining and meeting them. Field team members use the customer information to develop and refine individual and team support strategies that enhance customer value and satisfaction. Sales managers in Europe and Asia meet quarterly to discuss sales progress versus objectives and to exchange information on the market dynamics. Twice yearly, corporate executives and marketing managers join these meetings. The CSAB leads improvement of the customer satisfaction process. Representatives of information technology, field, customer support, engineering, operations, marketing, and international subsidiaries participate on the CSAB, bringing diverse information about business needs and trends to the group. Improvements include refinement of listening posts, such as improvements in customer survey questions. The global customer satisfaction department manages and improves Medrad's customer surveys to keep them current with the company's directions.

Customer Relationship and Seven-Step Selling Process

Medrad builds and maintains customer relationships primarily through the sales process. With the help of Xerox Learning Systems, the North American sales and service departments adopted the process in 1993, which has since been improved and deployed to the European and Japanese direct field organizations. The customer selling process represents the complete integration of the sales, service, and support processes, providing a single company perspective for customers while allowing Medrad to know where it stands with a customer at any point in time. The sales process has seven phases, each of which is the umbrella for many activities that may or may not be used with a customer depending on the customer's needs and situation. The seven phases are:

Phase 1. *Earn the right.* Medrad sales, service, and applications representatives establish contact with a customer or potential customer and generate interest in doing business with Medrad. When a field representative "earns the right" with a customer, credibility has been established. The customer trusts the Medrad employee based on perceived knowledge of the business, products, and applications, and trusts in Medrad's commitment to deliver. All front-line employees are trained in communications and customer handling skills.

Phase 2. *Qualify the opportunity.* During this phase Medrad determines whether there is a qualified opportunity with the customer by asking questions about timeline, funds availability, impending event, decision maker identification, buying criteria, need, and competition or substitutes. Once at least four of these questions are answered positively, the opportunity is considered to be qualified. Continuous training of Medrad's customer contact employees ensures steady improvement in the company's ability to understand the customer's business situation and needs. Medrad refined this phase in 1999 with the conceptual selling process, a tool to help sales and service representatives effectively assess customer needs and requirements.

Phase 3. *Establish buying influences and criteria*. Medrad clarifies the decision makers and influencers and establishes the criteria (i.e., required information, support documentation, functionality proof) that each of them will use to determine their choice of product. Medrad representatives then create an action plan with the customer to satisfy their criteria.

Phase 4. *Satisfy buying criteria*. The action plan is executed. Medrad offers its customers proof sources, reference lists, site visits, and product demonstrations or evaluations as a means to satisfy their criteria. Customer contact employees receive product, service, applications, business, market, and customer training as needed to continuously improve their ability to offer the best solutions to the customer's problems and needs.

Phase 5. *Gain commitment*. Medrad obtains verbal commitment, negotiates a deal, provides a written quote, and obtains a purchase order.

Phase 6. *Implement*. Upon agreement, Medrad field teams deliver, install, service, and provide training on the products to ensure defect-free implementation and to continue building customer relations and satisfaction.

Phase 7. *Customer enhancement*. With a large percentage of sales from existing customers, maintaining customer satisfaction and loyalty is critical to Medrad. This phase of the sales process focuses on continuous follow-up and support. Medrad maintains routine contact through direct customer contact and follow-up satisfaction surveys. Medrad improved this phase in 1999 by implementing the large account management process for building relationships with original equipment manufacturers (OEMs) and national account customers.

Medrad's opportunity management process maps to the customer or process. The process monitors opportunities with a customer as they progress from casual interest to a "won" or "lost" resolution. A probability of winning is assigned based on customer interest, satisfaction of buying criteria, and the competitive situation. Opportunity maps and sales "funnels" provide input to sales projections and help guide the sales cycle. Key process performance measures are on-time deliveries, acceptance rates, and customer satisfaction surveys. Field team members use timely, comprehensive customer information to implement the customer process. The information is available through the FFA system, which Medrad deployed in North America in 1996, in Europe in 2000, and in Latin America, Australia, and Japan in 2001. With FFA, field team members use laptop computers to document and track customer contacts, check the status of orders and shipments, check account receivable status, review customer satisfaction results, track the status of complaint and inquiry responses, get current product information, review customer equipment service history, get leads, schedule installations or training, send and receive e-mail, and get product promotions and training materials from the corporate office.

Sales Customer Contact Management

Field team members enter contact information, installation status, maintenance actions, competitive information, and notes on customer preferences,
requirements, and expectations. A built-in report writer capability allows field
teams and management to use individual and territorial customer data in customized reports to identify territorial/zone opportunities. Medrad has several
customer access mechanisms (see Exhibit 7.11). After Medrad "earns the right"
to "implement" product solutions, it ensures that customer requests, needs,
expectations, questions, and comments are handled accurately and rapidly.
Customer contact employees understand that Medrad can "lose the right" to
serve its customers at any time. Customer contact employees include corporate
accounts, field sales, service, and applications representatives, and internal team
members in customer support, telemarketing, and marketing. Medrad provides
all customer satisfaction support personnel with formal and on-the-job training
in product knowledge, customer satisfaction, customer needs assessment, and

EXHIBIT 7.11   Customer Access Mechanisms

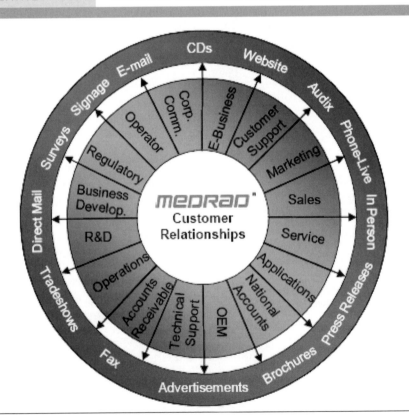

complaint handling. Service standards are set and reviewed to align with current customer expectations. Medrad ensures that contact requirements are fully deployed through training, instruction and observation by field and corporate management, and key performance measures such as the customer surveys. Customer contact processes and subprocesses are measured for response timeliness and the nature of the outcome. End-of-process measures include late shipments, installations, warranty calls, and customer credits. Medrad is also using Web-based technology to enhance customer access. Permission marketing efforts provide direct e-mail updates on products. A sales support locator on Medrad's Web site gives customers worldwide access to their sales representatives. Frequently asked questions and the ability to download brochures and other product and clinical information make access easy for customers.

Customer Complaints Management

All customer complaints are entered into a home office complaint tracking system to ensure timely follow-up and resolution and to support future analysis of the causes of problems and opportunities for improvement. Field team members, sales and service managers, the manager of global customer satisfaction, and regulatory personnel systematically investigate these complaints to resolve them in a timely and satisfactory manner and to identify and address root causes. Field team members and/or field managers follow up with customers to address dissatisfaction and resolve issues. During the follow-up, these field representatives draw on whatever resources are necessary to return the customer to satisfied status. Additional follow-ups will be conducted until the customer's needs have been met. During monthly Medrad management reviews (MMRs), issues raised by customer complaints and their recommended product and process improvements are tracked for closure. The vice president of operations also leads a weekly operations customer satisfaction meeting that involves the department heads for all operations including quality assurance, manufacturing, shipping, supply chain, and customer support/customer satisfaction to discuss and respond to shipping issues and customer complaints. Repetitive product customer complaints are escalated to the CSAB for tracking and resolution. A failure analysis team (FAT) meets routinely to determine the precise technical cause of a problem/complaint and ensure that the proper organizations are involved in resolving it. Both the MMR and FAT teams assign life cycle engineering, comprised of engineers and quality assurance representatives, to investigate issues and recommend improvement actions. Actions are prioritized and assigned to the appropriate department or team for implementation. Problems and complaints related to patient safety are documented and acted upon according to Federal Drug Administration (FDA) medical device reporting guidelines. When Medrad receives such a complaint, a field service representative is immediately dispatched to the customer's location. The representative fully inspects and tests the equipment and replaces any defective components. The representative then provides written and verbal feedback to the customer through the field service report (FSR). The representative returns any defective items to Pittsburgh for analysis by the quality assurance department, which reports the results of its testing to the FAT. The FAT identifies, prioritizes, and implements appropriate field procedure modifications and product improvements. Medrad regulatory compliance follows up with all parties including technologists, physicians, biomeds, and dealer contacts, to verify satisfactory resolution of the issue.

Medrad sales, service, and marketing own the processes for building relationships and providing access to customers. Cross-functional and functional improvement teams form to work on specific improvement activities. Inputs include the listening posts described earlier, Medrad's business results, management and employee ideas, and comparison and benchmark information. FFA and the conceptual selling process are two examples of improvements in building relationships, as is the addition of strategic selling to the sales process in 2001, expansion of FFA and strategic selling to European and Japanese sales teams in 2001, and refinement of the customer process in 2002.

Customer Satisfaction Survey and Improvements

The CSAB monitors current trends in customer satisfaction and develops strategies and approaches to improve them. Improving customer satisfaction, one of five corporate scorecard goals, is a major focus for the CSAB. The CSAB determines customer satisfaction and dissatisfaction through information from listening posts and through surveys. The global customer satisfaction department designs and improves third-party customer satisfaction surveys based on listening post information. Key listening post information from field representatives, focus groups, customer visits, and complaints helps shape and interpret Medrad's customer satisfaction surveys. In addition, the global customer satisfaction survey process owner visited customers and field managers in North America, Europe, and Japan to refine the surveys so that they ask about what is important to customers. All customer surveys are reviewed annually to make sure they are addressing the customer and market requirements revealed through listening post information. Marketing, sales, product planners, and field teams access survey results through a shared database. All surveys are conducted by third parties and are administered monthly or bimonthly. The surveys have been continuously improved since being introduced in 1992. Questions were added in 1999 to determine repurchase intent and to allow comparisons with the competition. In 2001 Medrad began setting performance objectives and measurements based solely on the company's ability to receive a "5" or "Top Box" rating from the customer. When customers assign a score less than "5," the surveys ask what Medrad could do differently to receive a "5" on future surveys. The CSAB and the global customer satisfaction department use survey feedback to identify and address areas to improve.

The global customer satisfaction department collects, aggregates, and analyzes data from the third-party surveys. It forwards key information to all field, marketing, and operations management personnel and to members of the CSAB. It also identifies negative comments or low ratings for follow-up and resolution by field management using the customer satisfaction follow-up process.

Color-Coded Results

For North America, Europe, and Australia, customer comments are color coded. *Yellow* highlighted comments indicate a high level of negative customer perception and require management follow-up, resolution, and documentation in the FFA database within 10 business days of receipt. Follow-up performance is reviewed quarterly by the CSAB. *Blue* comments indicate an unmet need or some level of negative customer perception and should be followed up by a field representative or manager. *Orange* comments indicate a high level of customer satisfaction and provide recognition for the field representative. The department publishes positive comments to recognize employee performance and reinforce customer expectations and requirements. Survey results are maintained within the FFA database for use by field teams in future customer interactions. The CSAB reviews customer satisfaction trends monthly and initiates improvements as needed. All customer satisfaction exceptional care surveys ask if customers would be willing to recommend Medrad to others. Recognizing that customers unwilling to recommend Medrad may be at risk, field managers contact them to better understand the source of their dissatisfaction. The goal is to address the customer's perception and to clarify future expectations and requirements. The monthly field service customer satisfaction surveys, which are conducted by an independent firm, asks customers who received emergency service in the previous 30 days to rate their on-site service. All calls are made within two weeks of the service interaction and customer contacts are provided weekly. The survey also asks what Medrad could do differently to receive a "5" overall on future surveys to help field service management identify and correct problems. The recently implemented monthly application in service survey administered by a third party asks up to half of customers who received product in-service training in the previous 30 days to rate the training they received. As with the other surveys, the application in-service survey asks what it will take to receive a "5" overall in order to help application management improve the team's performance.

Special project surveys are conducted as needed to determine satisfaction of specific customer groups and markets or with specific products or services. Medrad's field team members have primary responsibility for following up with customers on products, services, and transactions. The FFA database provides them with information about these events, and they report the results of their follow-up, including issues, problems, and/or action items, through the database to engineering, operations, marketing, and other departments. In addition, the field service customer satisfaction survey follows up with customers who have received recent emergency service

Competitor Intelligence

Medrad compares its customer satisfaction to that of competitors through competitive account surveys, a syndicated market research study, and a customer satisfaction study conducted by the industry magazine *Medical Imaging*. Field team members identify candidates for competitive account surveys and report their findings in the FFA database. The field uses the information to assess a competitor's strengths and weaknesses and to better understand the capabilities of Medrad and its competitors. Medrad purchases the results of a quarterly syndicated market research study of market size and share in selected markets. A third-party administrator validates the objectivity of the survey data. *Medical Imaging* conducts an annual North American customer satisfaction survey of 57 medical imaging companies. Magazine readers evaluate the companies on 10 categories including product quality and service and support. Medrad finished third overall in 2002 after finishing fifth in 2000 and 2001. Medrad is the smallest company in the top 10 with far fewer resources than the large companies that populate it.

The CSAB leads the evaluation and improvement of the surveys and other approaches described in this section. Senior managers and field, marketing, and operations personnel also participate in the evaluation and improvement process. The CSAB and global customer satisfaction department review and update all surveys annually to make sure they are addressing appropriate customer and market segments, asking about relevant customer and market requirements, collecting the right data, incorporating effective analytical methods and measurement scales, and recording and communicating results. Internal customers of the surveys help determine the appropriateness of the questions, which are added, deleted, or revised as part of this process.

Improving Processes

Medrad gathers, integrates, and delivers data and information from all sources through its extensive information technology network, which includes core information systems, desktop systems with e-mail, and the Medrad intranet. Examples include converting the financial tracker from paper to Web pages on the intranet; adding reporting via VAFA (value added financial analysis project); and business intelligence based reporting. Medrad intentionally gives extra attention to sharing data critical to achieving the five corporate scorecard goals. For example, data on revenues and margins critical to growth and profitability have been made available in real time capability released in 2003. The information stored in this "data warehouse" can be sorted and totaled in numerous ways, thereby enabling finance, marketing, and sales to track and analyze performance and plan and initiate effective field actions. Daily reports are published from 3D to the intranet, updating revenue and margin data globally for analysis of the very latest results. Departments such as operations, sales and service, marketing, and new product development deploy and maintain work-group–level systems and applications as well as support major systems such as FFA, product data management (product center), project management (TOPS), and computer aided design tools. The focus is on data that help achieve scorecard goals, such as daily production and on-time shipments, or those critical to ensuring prompt response to out-of-bounds conditions, such as quality levels. In-process measures are used to effectively manage a wide variety of functions. Field service uses statistics on preventive maintenance services due and average on-site labor per repair to assure proper customer service. Quality assurance monitors trends in warranty repair. Human resources uses data to manage filling of open positions including the number of day's jobs have been open, number of resumes and interviews, and more. The selection of overall organizational performance measures begins with the 5 corporate goals and the top 12 corporate objectives identified and updated during the strategic planning process.

In its PET meetings, the senior staff annually confirms and prioritizes the top 12 objectives and sets targets and measures. Since these objectives support corporate scorecard goals, Medrad approves only those proposals that project substantive improvement and innovation. The top 12 objectives are reviewed regularly by the objective sponsors, in depth on a rolling three-month basis by senior staff, and more frequently by exception. Executives responsible for each objective waterfall objectives and progress measures throughout the organization, working with relevant subfunctions and teams. At both the corporate and subfunction/team level, measures are selected based on their ability to predict performance or measure results, with collection and reporting established to enable course correction at appropriate time intervals. Exhibit 5.9, Strategic Planning Process shows how measures align with Medrad's philosophy, mission, and strategies. Functions and subfunctions also identify challenging continuous improvement objectives and measures that align with the corporate goals through the waterfall objective process. Support of the top 12 objectives demands improvement and innovation in these functional level goals.

Principle 4: Improve Performance
- *Prioritize Improvement Projects.* Identify and prioritize strategic and operational initiatives to improve organization's performance along financial, customer or constituent, process, and people dimensions.
- *Leverage Customer Facing Processes.* Develop and exercise customer and constituent processes to understand and recalibrate processes around changing customer needs. Gather customer and competitor intelligence through the use of regular customer survey, focus groups, call centers, quality function deployment, and related methods and approaches.
- *Leverage Process Improvement Methods.* Design and maintain an ongoing process improvement and problem-solving program based on either Six Sigma black belt or green belt methods and tools to identify and eliminate root causes of issues.
- *Realize Value from Benchmarking Processes.* Leverage benchmarking and comparative methods to identify and regularly improve core and support processes.
- *Create a Performance Improvement Culture.* Create a virtual community of practice of practitioners to coordinate and optimize improvement efforts enterprise-wide.

I will prepare and some day my chance will come.
—ABRAHAM LINCOLN

LB FOSTER: BEST PRACTICE CASE

During the course of establishing the CPM office with Jeff Poholsky as the leader and developing its first scorecards, integration with other functions was necessary to improve the business performance. The two principle linkages were for Senior Vice President Operations and Manufacturing John Kasel to improve business performance, most notably using Lean manufacturing techniques and understanding cost of quality (COQ), and the marketing manager to deploy electronic customer surveys and establish key account management programs—both objectives are on the recently developed Strategy Map and new Balanced Scorecard.

This section will primarily focus on these two competencies.

Lean Improvement Overview

Kasel, a veteran from Toyota's school of Lean manufacturing, brought substantial knowledge and practical implementation experience to LB Foster and its 10 operating plants. Lean manufacturing focuses on eliminating all waste in manufacturing processes. The Production System Design Laboratory (PSD) of the Massachusetts Institute of Technology (MIT) states that "Lean production is aimed at the elimination of waste in every area of production including customer relations, product design, supplier networks and factory management. Its goal is to incorporate less human effort, less inventory, less time to develop products, and less space to become highly responsive to customer demand while producing top quality products in the most efficient and economical manner possible."[5] Principles of a Lean enterprise are:

- Zero waiting time
- Zero inventory
- Scheduling—internal customer pull instead of push system
- Batch to flow—cut batch sizes
- Line balancing
- Cut actual process time

Lean Case in Georgetown Precise Plant

As a fabricator of structural steel for bridges, Precise Plant is engaged in the custom manufacture of large, high-labor, nonstandard products. As a first test of the application of Lean techniques, the team selected a category of product called stringer beams. These are the main members of the substructure of a steel bridge and are typically based on a rolled wide flange beam. Due to the uniqueness of the products, combined with intrinsic delays associated with portions of the manufacture (most notably painting and certain elements involving the introduction of heat), stringer beams seemed like an ideal area of first attack.

Georgetown general manager Jack Klimp said, "Put simply, we started by pulling together a team of shop and office personnel representing all elements of the skill sets required. We combined this team with an experienced Lean facilitator and broke down the production process to a level of detail that broadened the understanding of all, and exposed areas of waste in a completely new way."

With a variety of wastes exposed and trackable by way of the scorecard, the team went about attacking those wastes in a systematic way and tracking the impact of waste reduction on the speed of the part. Klimp stated, "In the course of a few short months we found that we were able to increase our production rate by a factor of four while at the same time significantly reducing our per unit costs. The most striking thing to all of us was the realization that by reducing batch size and having fewer products on the floor we could produce more. We did not plan on that result, but as the products picked up speed and floor area opened it was just amazing and in many ways contrary to much of what conventional wisdom would have led us to expect."

New Cost of Quality Process

LB Foster in connection with the Lean program recognizes the value in tracking and understanding the costs associated with poor quality. LB Foster studied COQ and developed the work paper in Exhibit 7.12 to communicate to employees.

Quality costs related to any Foster operation can be determined. Most costs are a portion of an object code, since operational costs include all quality assurance and quality control functions. After reviewing the cost centers, the most difficult activity is to calculate internal and external failure costs. Most of the operations report in a "scrap variance" account. It is difficult to say how much of this is nonconforming product generated at the plants. There have been only a few postings in the "defective work" object code.

Most of what is described can be determined by calculating all or part of the cost center object code. However, many hidden costs also occur as the result of these costs. These include, for example, the administrative time lost to post an entry as the result of a nonconformance, or the added time and cost to initiate a replacement purchase order for defective material or determine what the bottom-line effect is as the result of the loss of future business.

The most effective way to use COQ is to compare the quality costs to sales dollars or to the cost of goods sold by the company. Either way, the comparison can be an effective way to create a type of "quality index" that can be used on the Balanced Scorecard. Foster can start to analyze operations with the same yardstick and identify the best balance of prevention and appraisal costs for each of its operations

The COQ categories where Foster experiences quality-related costs are shown in exhibit 7.12. When the company finally identifies and understands quality costs, it can manage the cost of quality to determine the best way to improve profits.

New Customer Electronic Survey Process

Development of the Strategy Map and BSC underscored the need for LB Foster to gather, review, and act on "voice of the customer" inputs. The most expeditious and cost-effective manner of facilitating the new customer survey process was to leverage a third-party application service provider (ASP) and deploy a Web-based survey. Executive Management Team EMT, with input from the marketing manager devised a short, two- to three-minute Web-based survey to deploy (see Exhibit 7.13). The survey scoring methodology is based on the Likert scale, a type of survey question where respondents are asked to rate the level at which they agree or disagree with a given statement. For example:

I find this software easy to use.
Strongly disagree 1 2 3 4 5 6 7 strongly agree

EXHIBIT 7.12   Cost of Quality

- Prevention
    - Inspection Technology
        - Computer software
    - Assessments
        - Quality manual development and maintenance
        - Data collection and analysis
        - Failure analysis
        - Internal auditing
        - Corrective and preventive actions
        - Calibration
        - Maintenance of inspection and test equipment
        - New inspection and test equipment
    - Training
        - In-house training expenses
        - New hire orientation (for QC/QA personnel)
        - External training expenses
- Appraisal
    - Inspection
        - Inspector and test personnel labor and overhead
    - Support
        - Quality management salary and overhead
        - Relevant office supplies
        - Material assessments and source inspection costs
    - Data Package Preparation
        - Control of records; preparation for customer acceptance
- Failure
    - Internal Failure Costs
        - Nonconforming Material
            - Rework and repair costs
            - Scrap costs
            - Other nonconformance costs
            - Disposition costs of material for customer concurrence
        - Production Losses and Administrative Expenses
            - Material Shortages
            - Overtime
            - Rescheduling costs
            - Handling and transportation costs
    - External Failure Costs
        - Warranty Costs
            - Material
            - Material shortages
            - Added labor to remake
            - Rescheduling costs
            - Potential subcontracting costs
        - Administrative Expenses
            - Added transportation costs
            - Preparation of NCR

EXHIBIT 7.13 Web-Based Customer Survey

1. Please rate LB Foster on each of the following criteria:

Criteria	Very Satisfied	Somewhat Satisfied	Neutral	Somewhat Dissatisfied	Very Dissatisfied	Does Not Apply
Q1. Delivers on time, as promised, according to delivery terms						
Q2. Accurate and timely responses to questions or problems						
Q3. Products meet specified requirements						
Q4. Incorporates new advancements into product offerings						
Q5. Meets customer quality assurance requirements						
Q6. Sales support during quotation, order placement, and delivery process						
Q7. Works to find solutions to customer needs						
Q8. Price paid relative to value received						

Q9. Project management					
Q10. Timeliness, clarity, and accuracy of paperwork and billings					
Q11. Reasonable lead times					
Q12. Provides a range of products necessary to meet our requirements					
Q13. Ease of doing business					
Q14. Ability to contact with a question or a problem					
Q15. Works as a partner to improve operating efficiencies					
Q16. Product information (technical specifications, etc.)					

(**NOTE:** IN THIS SECTION WE WOULD LIKE A LOGIC BRANCH TO THE FOLLOWING QUESTION IF THE RESPONSE TO ANY CRITERIA ABOVE IS VERY DISSATISFIED.)

Please provide us with any specific reason you may wish to help us better understand why you are very dissatisfied:

2. Please pick the three (3) most important attributes to you when selecting a supplier:

Attribute   **Selection**

Technical Support
Product Development
Delivery
Quality
Product Value and Price
Sales Support/Customer Service
Product Performance

295

EXHIBIT 7.13 *(Continued)*

3. Do you intend to continue to purchase LB Foster products in the future?

YES   **NO**

4. Overall, how satisfied are you with LB Foster:

Very Satisfied   **Somewhat Satisfied**   **Neutral**   **Somewhat Dissatisfied**   **Very Dissatisfied**

5. Please rate LB Foster on each of the following attributes, *relative to our best competitor.*
Please provide the name of our best competitor used for the rankings_____

Attribute	**Better**	**Same**	**Worse**	**Does Not Apply**
Technical Support				
Product Development				
Delivery				
Quality				
Product Value and Price				
Sales Support/Customer Service				
Product Performance				

6. Would you be willing to recommend LB Foster to others?

YES   **NO**

7. I believe that the best thing that LB Foster does is:

8. My biggest complaint about LB Foster is:

9. The best thing that LB Foster could do to improve itself would be to:

10. What other products or services would you be interested in purchasing from LB Foster:

11. Please identify your job function:

Function	Selection
Executive Management	☐
Purchasing and Supply Chain Management	☐
Engineering/Project Management	☐
Maintenance	☐
Sales/Marketing	☐
Product Development/R&D	☐
Operations	☐
Other	☐

(**Note:** IF OTHER, PLEASE PROVIDE A LOGIC BRANCH TO THE FOLLOWING QUESTION.)

Please provide your job function_____

As our way of saying thanks for completing this survey, we would like to send you a small token of our appreciation. Please provide your current company address below.

Company Name_____
Street Address_____
City_____
State_____
Zip Code_____

A Likert scale is used to measure attitudes, preferences, and subjective reactions. In software evaluation, we can often objectively measure efficiency and effectiveness with performance metrics such as time taken or errors made. Likert scales and other attitudinal scales help get at the emotional and preferential responses people have to the design.

The first survey was viewed a success from both a process and content perspective. From a process perspective, the customer response rate was very high in comparison to paper-based surveys and the electronic survey will be deployed on a semiannual basis.

From a content perspective, the ongoing survey process enabled LB Foster to understand customer trends with consideration to:

- Customer satisfaction is a point-in-time measurement
- Measuring opinion, which may not reliably predict future behavior.
- Customer's perception of needs will change over time.
- Need to understand the trend of change over time.
- Do not be misled: Customers may be satisfied with our performance but more satisfied with performance of our competitors.
- Awareness of possible bias in response.

LB Foster leveraged survey response data to complete six analytics:

1. Overall analysis of responses
2. Correlation of key criteria to overall satisfaction
3. Importance versus performance
4. Competitive positioning
5. Breakdowns by demographics
6. Patterns in anecdotal information (open-ended questions)

For instance, for item 3, Foster was able to understand customer priorities and how well the company performed against this prioritized list. The two-by-two matrix (performance by importance) outlines results to determine corrective action.

	Low Importance	High Importance
High-Performance Scores	1. Nice to do	2. Strengths
Low-Performance Scores	3. No action needed	4. Vulnerable

- *Quadrant 1,* high performance in a low-importance customer satisfier, indicates the client does not place a high value on this attribute of service delivery (e.g., quality, speed to market) so the company could be overdelivering. This may represent resources that could be reallocated to address quadrant 4, vulnerability.

- *Quadrant 2,* high performance in a highly important customer satisfier, indicates company strength and is likely a competitive advantage.
- *Quadrant 3,* low performance on a low-importance customer satisfier, indicates there is no real need for action.
- *Quadrant 4,* low performance on a highly valued customer satisfier, is a potential service vulnerability that requires action plans to raise these scores.

New Customer Key Account Management Process

The survey provides intelligence to support the company's key account management (KAM) program. In an effort to improve relationships and to better understand customer requirements, the company designed, developed, and deployed a KAM program focused on the top company accounts by sales volume. The marketing manager developed the outline in exhibit 7.14 to organize KAM customer information. The sales team meets

---

BEST PRACTICE HIGHLIGHTS

Principle 4: Improve Performance

- *Prioritize Improvement Projects.* Use the strategic planning, Strategy Mapping, and BSC reporting processes to identify and prioritize strategic and operational initiatives to improve organization's performance along financial, customer or constituent, process and people dimensions.
- *Leverage Customer-Facing Processes.* Develop and exercise customer and constituent processes to understand and recalibrate processes around changing customer needs.
- *Leverage Customer-Facing Processes.* Gather customer and competitor intelligence through regular customer surveys and the use of a robust key account management program consisting of three key sets of data elements.
- *Leverage Process Improvement Methods.* Design and maintain an ongoing process improvement and problem-solving program based on Lean methods and tools to identify and eliminate root causes of issues.
- *Realize Value from Benchmarking Processes.* Leverage benchmarking and comparative methods to identify and regularly improve plant location processes. This is happening within but not across plants.
- *Create a Performance Improvement Culture.* Create a virtual community of Lean practitioners to coordinate and optimize improvement efforts enterprise-wide.

EXHIBIT 7.14 Key Account Customer Profile

Customer Name: _____

Parent Company Name: _____

Location(s)

Headquarters   Plant(s):

Key Management Personnel															
Executive			Purchasing			Project Mgmt./Engineering			Other		
Name	Telephone	E-mail	Name	Telephone	E-mail	Name	Telephone	E-mail	Name	Telephone	E-mail

Key Customer Information

Key Customer Information	
Estimated/Actual Annual Sales Revenue	
Estimated/Actual Annual Net Income	
Estimated/Actual Accounts Payable DSO	
Publicly Traded/Privately Held	
Union/Nonunion	
Estimated Number of Employees	
Key Regional/National/International Markets	
Unique Equipment/Crane Limitation/Other	

Overall Sales History

2004 Actual			2005 Actual			2006 Budget		
Tonnage	Dollars	GP%	Tonnage	Dollars	GP%	Tonnage	Dollars	GP%

Key Competitors/Estimated Share of Business

EXHIBIT 7.15   Product and Competitor Intelligence Data

Key Product Purchases/Requirements

Product	Total		LB Foster		Competitor 1		Competitor 2	
	Tonnage	Dollars	Tonnage	Dollars	Tonnage	Dollars	Tonnage	Dollars

How are product purchasing decisions made?

LB Foster product/company advantage(s)

Competitor's product/company advantage(s)

How can LB Foster increase gross profit %?

Comments regarding logistics

What cross-selling opportunities exist within LB Foster?

What are new product/service selling opportunities?

Other key factors or information (including recent events such as new awards, complaints, approvals, etc.)

Other comments

EXHIBIT 7.16   Value-Driven Customer Strategy

Overall Customer Goal(s)

| | Customer Value Strategy | | |
Customer Value Needs	Value Offering(s)	Value Strategy	Action Items (who/what/when)

Target Sales

Product	Application	Competitor	Start Date	Volume Potential		Dollar Potential		GP% Potential		Probability of Success
				Year 1	Annualized	Year 1	Annualized	year 1	Annualized	

Prepared by: _____   Date: _____   Approved by: _____   Date: _____

quarterly to discuss customer survey results and to devise new strategies for exceeding customer expectations. The program is organized into three primary bodies of knowledge:

1. Key customer information containing the data sets shown in Exhibit 7.14
2. Product and competitor intelligence data sets as shown in Exhibit 7.15
3. Value-driven strategy to expand the account with a focus on the key account elements shown in Exhibit 7.16

In summary, LB Foster improved performance by deploying Lean process improvement methods across its diverse manufacturing plants. The company also deployed its first electronic surveys and a KAM program to proactively manage customers and drive revenue and value.

> *Far and away the best prize that life offers is the chance to work hard at work worth doing.*
> —THEODORE ROOSEVELT

FLORIDA DEPARTMENT OF HEALTH: BEST PRACTICE CASE*

Exhibit 7.17 shows an integrated model of the performance management system used by the Florida Department of Health (FDOH) to track data, make necessary improvements, and ensure decisions are data driven. This model is based on the Turning Point Performance Management National Excellence Collaborative.

No system can improve without support from its employees. FDOH has helped people work together through its use of technology to gather feedback from the field. The FDOH considers itself a catalyst or a facilitator for work that involves the entire community. Local health departments depend on their communities to meet health goals. They create multiple partnerships to ensure

- Miami-Dade County Health Department Recipient of Governors Sterling (Baldrige) Award (2002 and 2006)
- Department of Health Recipient of APQC Best Practice Partner Award

---

* The Florida Department of Health case team adapted portions of this case from "Performance Measurement in the Public Sector," *APQC* (November 2005), Governors Sterling Applications 2002 and 2006, and internal documents.

EXHIBIT 7.17   Performance Management System

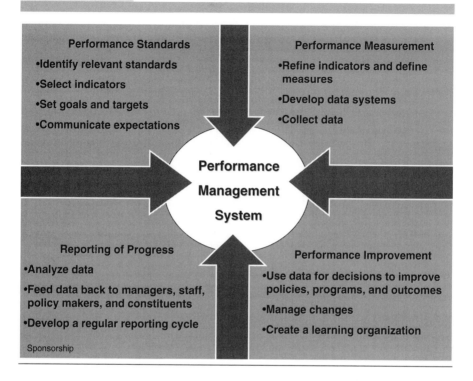

Performance Standards
•Identify relevant standards
•Select indicators
•Set goals and targets
•Communicate expectations

Performance Measurement
•Refine indicators and define measures
•Develop data systems
•Collect data

Performance
Management
System

Reporting of Progress
•Analyze data
•Feed data back to managers, staff, policy makers, and constituents
•Develop a regular reporting cycle
Sponsorship

Performance Improvement
•Use data for decisions to improve policies, programs, and outcomes
•Manage changes
•Create a learning organization

public health, organize the community to promote the community's active role in public health, and rely on community members for feedback. FDOH leaders realize that involving community stakeholders in public health is a never-ending and critical challenge.

Performance management systems have to be more manageable and better understood by employees, and employees must know their roles in making improvements. Success comes only when ownership of the improvement efforts extends to the lowest of the hierarchy of those affected.

Quality Improvement Process Integration with Measurement

In 1992 FDOH implemented the Florida quality improvement process to replace its quality assessment process. A central focus of this new process was an emphasis on health outcome indicators and associated health problem analysis methodologies. The FDOH created key work groups and services councils to guide the development of the new quality management process.

For each health problem domain, the organization created a fishbone model that helped in problem analysis. The model helps work groups begin with outcomes and then identifies the direct, indirect, and contributing factors influencing the outcomes. For example, if infant mortality is the outcome measure, the team identifies low birth weight, access to care, behaviors during pregnancy, smoking, and substance abuse as factors that have an impact on infant health. The quality improvement process enabled the organization to select measures that were driving a change in the outcomes.

Strong impetus to further integrate other types of service, client, and process indicators into the public health performance measurement system was provided by the statutory requirement for implementing a system of performance-based program budgeting. In the spring of 1996, the department began a process of examining all key health objectives with the purpose of selecting additional impact measures that affect the major health goal areas, with health status indicators used as the outcomes. The process had two major products:

1. Development of a comprehensive quarterly performance indicator reporting system for county health departments
2. Development of a performance-based program budgeting system of measures to be used for reporting agency performance to the governor and the legislature.

The quarterly county health department performance report was developed to integrate the performance measures contained in the quality improvement process, agency strategic planning objectives, performance-based program budgeting, the long-range program plan, and local contracts with county commissions. Key measures of system inputs, outputs, processes, and outcomes are incorporated into a quarterly performance report for each program within a county health department. The reporting system brings together data from all primary data collection systems into a single page for each of 17 program areas. The report shows the agency strategic plan/long-range program plan; quality improvement indicators and other outcome indicators; performance/service effectiveness measures; and data on amount of services provided, clients served, full-time equivalent (FTEs) positions, and expenditures. The report allows managers at local and state levels to review progress in each program area and make adjustments during the year, aligning measures used at the state level for quality improvement, agency strategic plan objectives, and performance-based program budgeting with the local performance management/quality improvement (QI) processes.

Continuous Performance Improvement

The FDOH has been redesigning the quality improvement process during 2005–6. The new process is being designed to increase use of data, to optimize resources, and encourage local performance management systems. The focus of the redesign is on the county health department (CHD) performance improvement process. Redesigning the process included bringing together stakeholders to develop a process and a BSC tool the county health departments could utilize to measure and improve performance. Beginning in July 2005, the department piloted the redesigned performance improvement process for the county health departments. Some highlights of this pilot process are:

- Twenty counties completed a performance report card designed to identify organizational strengths and opportunities for improvement.
- Each county in the pilot utilized the report card results and other data to plan and implement improvement activities.
- All counties in the pilot received technical assistance tailored to the needs identified by the county health department. The technical assistance was provided in two distinct venues. The first was on-site technical assistance, which included putting together a team to visit the CHD and address their needs on-site. The teams often included a peer reviewer (a CHD employee from another CHD who has expertise in the area of need). The peer reviewer shares ideas that have been implanted at his or her health department as a way of assisting the CHD in need of identifying a solution. The second venue was off-site technical assistance. This consisted of sending the CHD information via e-mail or assisting them via conference call.
- A sample statewide performance report card was created utilizing the results from the counties that participated in the pilot.
- The FDOH is currently developing an action plan to address two of the statewide opportunities for improvement. The department will be implementing the action plan in June 2006.

The pilot process is based on the plan-do-check-act cycle. Currently the pilot process is being evaluated. Modification to the process and report card will be made during the summer 2006. Implementation of the new CHD performance improvement process to all 67 CHDs is targeted for fall 2006 or early spring 2007. After the implementation of the CHD process in all 67 CHDs, a similar process will be developed for the central office programs.

The vision of the performance management team in the office of performance improvement is to facilitate a process through which the entire department can measure, improve, and compare performance to achieve excellence and promote healthy communities. This process will be continuous and will strive to identify and share best practices and lessons learned.

Drive thy business or it will drive thee.
—BENJAMIN FRANKLIN

BEST PRACTICE HIGHLIGHTS

Principle 4: Improve Performance
- *Prioritize Improvement Projects.* Identify and prioritize strategic and operational initiatives to improve the organization's performance along financial, customer or constituent, process and people dimensions.
- *Leverage Customer-Facing Processes.* Develop and exercise customer and constituent processes to understand and recalibrate processes around changing customer needs.
- *Leverage Process Improvement Methods.* Design and maintain an ongoing process improvement and problem-solving program based on plan-do-check-act to identify and eliminate root causes of issues.
- *Realize Value from Benchmarking Processes.* Leverage benchmarking and comparative methods to identify and regularly improve core and support processes.

AMERICAN RED CROSS: BEST PRACTICE CASE*

Performance improvement among American Red Cross chapters is encouraged by systematic target setting designed to create continuous improvement pressure. Because all chapters are continually directed to improve performance over their own prior-year levels, there is continual pressure to improve system-wide performance. As individual chapters work to raise their scores, they are raising medians and thus raising the targets for everyone.

Additionally, a chapter evaluation guide is available to assist service areas in their performance improvement work with individual chapters. This guide enables the development of the required chapter performance development plan for chapters with a chapter performance rating of 1 or 2. The guide also serves as a blueprint for capacity building and troubleshooting specific issues at chapters. Training is provided for service area personnel to utilize tools available to further assess individual chapter situations and customize plans to meet

- Recipient of APQC Best Practice Partner Award

---

* The American Red Cross case team adapted portions of this case from "Performance Measurement in the Public Sector," *APQC* (November 2005), and internal documents.

> ## BEST PRACTICE HIGHLIGHTS
>
> ### Principle 4: Improve Performance
> - *Prioritize Improvement Projects.* Identify and prioritize strategic and operational initiatives to improve the organization's performance.
> - *Leverage Customer Facing Processes.* Develop and exercise customer and constituent processes to understand and recalibrate processes around changing customer needs.
> - *Realize Value from Benchmarking Processes.* Leverage benchmarking and comparative methods to identify and regularly improve core and support processes.

special needs. Implementation of chapter development plans is also linked to chapter executive work performance reviews and personal development needs.

Furthermore, data are analyzed to determine if performance issues are organization-wide and require a systemic solution, such as chapter training and education; or if issues are based in individual chapters, requiring a consultative approach. Along with service area specialists, volunteers or staff from chapters that excel in particular areas may be recruited to consult with chapters on such areas as fundraising, service delivery, or financial management.

> *An investment in knowledge always pays the best interest.*
> —BENJAMIN FRANKLIN

BRONSON METHODIST HOSPITAL: BEST PRACTICE CASE

This section explores Bronson's approach to improving performance using continuous improvement and problem-solving methods focused on customer and core processes. Recall using the Information Management Strategy (IMS) in conjunction with the scorecard/organizational performance indicators (OPI) (see Exhibit 7.18), the executive team, strategic oversight teams (SOTs), leaders and departments use the timely performance data to support decision making. Bronson focuses on those measures that do not meet selected targets and uses the plan, do, check, act (PDCA) model to create specific action plans to bring performance into compliance with preset benchmarks.

To support innovation as a healthcare provider, all Bronson leaders received focused training through the leadership development initiative related to innovation and how it must be coupled with improvement efforts. In order to be a national leader in healthcare quality, Bronson is focused on being both better and different. Innovation, doing what others have not done, is viewed as a

- Malcolm Baldrige National Quality Award
- Michigan Quality Leadership Award (2001, 2005)
- 100 Top Hospitals Award
- Governor's Award of Excellence for Improving Care in the Hospital Setting (2004, 2005).
- Governor's Award of Excellence for Improving Preventive Care in the Ambulatory Care Setting
- *Fortune* magazine's "100 Best Companies to Work For" (2004, 2005, 2006).
- *Working Mother*'s "100 Best Companies for Working Mothers" (2003, 2004, 2005)
- VHA Leadership Award for Operational Excellence (2005, 2006)

key element of Bronson's culture and the PDCA model. Through daily use of the PDCA model, Bronson achieves improvement, learning, and innovation. The focus PDCA model for improvement (see Exhibit 7.19) creates the mechanism for improvement of key processes and continuous organizational learning.

EXHIBIT 7.18   Bronson Organization Scorecard

Three Cs	BMH Organizational Scorecard
Clinical Excellence	Medicare mortality Leapfrog patient safety measures Ventilator acquired pneumonia rate Patient falls Hospital acquired pressure ulcers Hand washing compliance Core indicator performance
Customer and Service Excellence	Magnet status achievement Overall turnover, RN turnover, vacancy rates Physician satisfaction EOS diversity scores Patient satisfaction (overall Top Box, discharge process, physical surroundings)
Corporate Effectiveness	Growth (neuro, cardiac, surgery) Profit margin Inappropriate ER utilization

EXHIBIT 7.19 **Bronson Plan, Do, Check, Act Improvement Model**

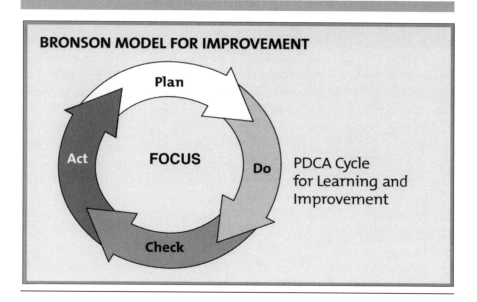

Improving Customer Focus: Patients and Market Segments

Bronson has identified its key customer group as patients but also recognizes the important role that family members play in the delivery of healthcare services to patients. Therefore, family members are considered in conjunction with patients as the same key customer group. The two primary patient segments are inpatients and outpatients. Patients are further segmented by geographic location (primary, secondary, tertiary market service areas), service lines, and age demographics. Patient requirements drive all leadership actions in alignment with the mission, values, and vision. A critical success factor for Bronson is to be recognized for a culture of service excellence, differentiating the hospital from the competition, and serving as a foundation for achieving the vision.

The quarterly strategic planning (QSP) retreats include the executive team and key directors. These organizational leaders actively participate in the process to determine/target current and potential customers, customers of competitors, and healthcare markets. During the input step of the strategic planning process held each spring, the QSP participants review and analyze the strategic input document (SID) and the Quarterly System Indicator Report QSIR. These documents contain an extensive compilation of industry trends and specific market data including population demographics, market share by product line, utilization rates, discharges by geographic area, profitability, technology updates, customer satisfaction and preference data, physician referral and admission trends, and key competitor information. At the retreat, the attendees review the final section of the SID, a strengths, weaknesses, opportunities, and threats (SWOT) analysis of the organization, to identify key strengths and opportunities for Bronson, to determine changing customer requirements and to define/redefine customer groups and market segments. Guided by the mission, values, and vision, the planning attendees consider and discuss market growth, needs or opportunities, competition, profitability, strategy, adjustments, and segmentation determinations.

When a new market segment is identified at the retreat, the appropriate service line administrator is charged with developing a formal business plan. This plan comes back to the executive team for review and approval on or before the next phase of the SMM held in the summer. The formal business plan step ensures that all relevant data is researched and analyzed. The Business Development Division is responsible for continuous review of healthcare markets in order to take advantage of market opportunities and may develop a business plan for review by the executive team at anytime during the year. In addition, the QSIR, which is presented at each QSP retreat, provides a quarterly systematic review of the relevant market information needed to determine/target customers and healthcare markets. This continuous planning cycle is a key characteristic of the Strategic Management Model SMM, creating agility and the capability to meet ever-changing market needs at any time during the process.

Improving the Customer Experience: Listening and Learning Methods

Understanding customers and their requirements is essential to achieving success. Bronson utilizes both qualitative and quantitative listening and learning methods (see Exhibit 7.20) for annual strategic planning as well as monthly reviews by the Customer and Service Excellence (CASE) SOT and the executive team, to determine customer requirements.

The primary source of customer information is the formal patient satisfaction survey, administered by the Gallup Organization. Some listening and learning methods are different for current patients versus identified potential patients. Current patients provide feedback regarding their direct patient experience with Bronson, while potential patients have not actually used Bronson services but may have experience with other healthcare organizations. Potential patient information is related strongly to preferences and desired requirements. As part of the SMM input, Bronson uses feedback from

EXHIBIT 7.20   Customer Listening and Learning Methods

Listening and Learning	Current Patients	Potential Patients
Patient satisfaction survey	W	
Post-discharge telephone calls	D	
Point-of-service satisfaction surveys	D	
Focus groups	B, N	N
Leader rounds	D	
Patient relations rounding	D	
Patient complaint management process	D	
Community attitude survey	A	A
Event/program evaluations	M	M
Newsletter surveys	N	N
Direct marketing	N	N
Web site/e-mail	D	D
Health Fair	A	A
Open houses	N	N
Physician satisfaction survey	A	A
Community organization involvement	D	D

D-daily, W-weekly, M-monthly, B-bimonthly Q-quarterly, A-annual, N-as needed

current patients, potential customers, customers of competitors, and the community. This valuable feedback is gathered through a variety of means. Bronson contracts with independent survey organizations, including Arbor Associates, Inc. (Arbor) and Gallup to collect survey data. Other feedback mechanisms include focus groups (with current patients and also "ghosted" where the sponsoring institution is not identified), networking with the community, formal participation by leaders and staff in local business and community groups, and from Bronson medical staff members who also have admitting to competing hospitals.

The customer research program (CRP) and its listening and learning methods are kept current through the PDCA model used by the CASE SOT. This includes ongoing review and evaluation by the CASE SOT to determine whether a particular method yields actionable information to assist in performance improvement. Survey tools, techniques, and questions are added or modified to ensure utility, based on market changes and customer needs. The frequency pattern of each method is reevaluated to ensure customer information is available in a timely manner. An annual, formal evaluation of the effectiveness of the CRP and particularly the listening and learning methods is completed by the CASE SOT during the spring component of the SMM to ensure that listening methods capture new and changing customer requirements.

Improving Performance: Building Customer Loyalty

In pursuit of excellence, Bronson has moved beyond monitoring patient satisfaction to measuring patient loyalty. Since loyalty is a predictor of future behavior, it is central to achieving the Bronson mission and vision. Bronson believes that loyalty is fostered by providing high-quality patient outcomes in a safe, consistent manner, while delighting patients with superior customer service, state-of-the art facilities and technology, and innovative amenities. Building patient loyalty begins with staff being recruited and selected based on their commitment to providing superior customer service. All employees are trained and held accountable to follow the customer service standards and expectations, which outline the personal accountability that every staff member has every day, with every interaction, with every customer. The standards, along with service recovery, the interaction process, and scripting, give staff members the tools they need to meet patient requirements and build customer loyalty. Positive patient relationship building is practiced by all employees as part of their daily work activities. Early identification of issues through leader and patient relations most often neutralizes dissatisfaction and promotes loyalty. Customer requirements and expectations are formally included in the PDCA model, ensuring that customer needs are considered.

Improving Customer Relationships

Managing and Resolving Complaints

The customer service standards and expectations is a key tool for employees to provide excellent customer service and minimize dissatisfaction. All employees are empowered and expected to resolve patient complaints 24/7. Employees are oriented, trained, and coached to proactively handle complaints using the service recovery process. The process includes specific steps to acknowledge, apologize, and amend. This approach is used to mitigate dissatisfaction and resolve issues at the bedside. In the event an employee is unable to resolve a patient concern, the concern is forwarded to department leadership, patient relations representatives, the house manager, or the administrator on call via face-to-face communication, telephone, e-mail, or pager. The individual who receives the complaint assumes responsibility for investigation, follow-up, and resolution, according to the detailed steps in the patient complaint management process (see Exhibit 7.21).

Complaints are responded to promptly and according to defined timelines depending on how the complaint is received. Any delays in resolution are communicated to the patient along with a specific timeline identified for resolution completion. All complaints are recorded in the patient complaint management database. The director of customer service monitors the database on a weekly basis to determine specific root causes and trends and to

EXHIBIT 7.21   Complaint Management Process

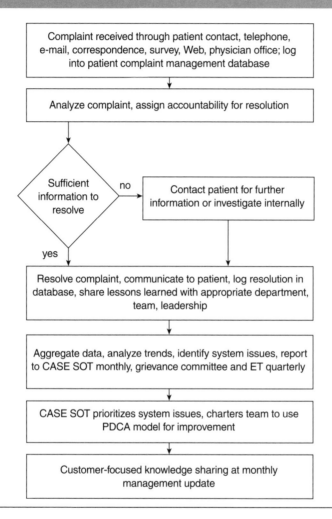

monitor department-specific process improvements. On a monthly basis, a detailed report is provided to the CASE SOT for review and analysis. The CASE SOT prioritizes system issues and charters teams to improve system-wide processes using the PDCA model for improvement. The grievance committee and the executive team review analyzed and aggregated quarterly patient complaint management reports and improvement team status reports. The executive team uses this information to plan future services, customer requirements, and establish department and individual performance goals. The patient complaint management process is a formal input in the listening and learning methods. These data become part of the CRP that is used during the strategic planning process.

Keeping Approaches Current

The relationship-building approaches and customer access methods are kept current through the PDCA model used by the CASE SOT. During PDCA improvement, information is gathered from customer feedback, market and industry trends, feedback loops of organizational processes, conferences, and literature reviews as well as best practice benchmarking with Baldrige recipients. The CASE SOT is responsible for ongoing review and evaluation to determine whether the approach or access method meets customer requirement and yields actionable information to assist in performance improvement. Much like the CRP, an annual formal evaluation of the effectiveness of the relationship-building approaches and customer access methods is completed by the CASE SOT, during the spring component of the SMM, to ensure approaches and methods meet new and changing customer requirements.

Focus on Surveys and Survey Feedback

The process used to determine customer satisfaction/dissatisfaction is led by the CASE SOT, beginning with the CRP data, which includes analysis of the findings from the qualitative and quantitative listening and learning methods. The primary source of information is patient satisfaction surveys. Gallup measures patient satisfaction and loyalty utilizing a telephone methodology on randomly selected patients for both inpatient and outpatient services. The Gallup survey measures 4 major attributes (loyalty, overall evaluation, people, and processes) for 11 service areas. Weekly patient satisfaction reports are available to all leaders via the *Inside* Bronson intranet each Friday. These cumulative reports provide timely access to patient satisfaction information segmented by inpatient, outpatient, and unit-specific data. The reports contain Gallup database and best practice comparisons as well as percentile rankings. The CASE SOT monitors patient satisfaction according to Gallup on a monthly basis. Cumulative quarterly reports provide customer service performance data that are part of the employee gainshare program.

Direct customer contact is another mechanism to solicit actionable feedback. Leaders and patient relations representatives also make rounds to collect timely and actionable feedback on services. The CASE SOT is responsible for the monthly systematic review of the CRP, identification and prioritization of improvement opportunities, and appointment of leaders, departments, process owners, or teams to use the PDCA model to improve healthcare service delivery. The CASE SOT ensures performance indicators are in place to track results and evaluates the impact of the improvement.

To ensure appropriate follow-up with patients to receive prompt and actionable feedback, Bronson has created systematic processes at various levels throughout the organization. The first occurs at the staff level during each interaction with patients at the time of care delivery. Staff is scripted to ask, "Is there anything else I can do for you?" This enables caregivers to respond immediately to a patient's needs. The second level occurs during rounds, where leaders and patient relations representatives make contact with patients to ask questions to address areas that need immediate resolution. The third approach is the prompt follow-up that occurs with every patient complaint. Finally, post-discharge calls provide actionable feedback as well as the ability to assess the general well-being of the patient.

Gathering Competitor Intelligence

Satisfaction data relative to competitors in the local market is obtained in the CRP. Listening and learning methods related to competitive information include focus groups, consumer perception surveys, and benchmark data. Three consumer perception surveys are performed in their community by third-party administrators that focus on consumers' perceptions of Bronson's services as compared to those of competitors. These include the Adams Outdoor Survey, National Research Corporation Quality and Image Profile Survey, and a community attitude survey. The three surveys compare healthcare providers in the community relative to reputation, image, preference, and quality. Quarterly focus groups conducted by Bronson include questions for discussion regarding the performance of Bronson as compared to other hospitals and healthcare services in the community. Gallup provides comparative information and benchmarks from over 380 hospitals across the nation on weekly and quarterly reports. The comparative information is service- as well as attribute-specific. The CASE SOT uses the information to stay focused on the critical success factors that differentiate Bronson from its competitors. In addition, the SOT identifies improvement opportunities as well as organizational strategic objectives, action plans, and targets during the strategic planning process.

The CASE SOT is responsible for keeping approaches to determining satisfaction current with healthcare service needs and directions. This is accomplished monthly by the CASE SOT through use of PDCA cycles of improvement as well as annually through the strategic planning process, which includes formal evaluation of all customer processes and approaches. By contracting with industry leaders like Gallup to administer the patient satisfaction survey, Bronson is effectively gathering the information needed to support its journey to become a national healthcare leader. Through Quest for Excellence and Baldrige benchmarking, Bronson receives best practices and information relative to changing standards.

Improving Key Healthcare Process Performance

Bronson determines its key healthcare services and service delivery processes by identifying services and processes that support its mission, values and vision, and strategic objectives, and meet the healthcare market segment and customer needs. This determination is accomplished through the SMM. During the spring planning retreat, the executive team begins with a comprehensive analysis utilizing data from the SID. After the executive team finalizes the healthcare market segments and growth strategies, the key healthcare services and service delivery processes are determined. Should new opportunities be identified at other times of the year, the continuous planning cycle of the SMM allows for healthcare services and processes to be added or modified at any time deemed necessary. Key services and service delivery processes are defined as meeting one or more of these criteria:

- Affects a large majority of our patients
- Identified as high-risk and/or problem prone
- Improves patient care quality through evidence-based practice
- Provides an opportunity for growth
- Essential to the community
- Enhances the ability to attract and retain top talent
- Balances profitable versus unprofitable services to maintain a positive bottom line

Key service delivery processes (see Exhibit 7.22) create value and contribute to improved healthcare service outcomes for patients by delivering high-quality, efficient services that meet defined patient requirements and expectations. Key healthcare process requirements are determined by using input from the customer listening and learning methods as well as physician partner and supplier inputs, in the plan phase of the PDCA model. This approach incorporates input received from patients, physicians, and suppliers early in the plan phase through direct contact, surveys, focus groups, and participation on teams and committees. Accreditation and regulatory requirements are identified through industry and professional association listening posts. All requirements are aggregated and analyzed during the input step of the SMM to ensure key process requirements are met and used to continually drive organizational process performance and improvements.

Improving Key Healthcare Process Performance: PDCA in Action

Bronson uses the PDCA model for process design and improvement. This improvement model is used to design, implement, and measure the effective-

EXHIBIT 7.22 **Key Healthcare Service Delivery Processes and Measures**

Key Process	Key Requirements	Key Measures
Admission: Patient Throughput, Scheduling, Precertification, Registration		Occupancy, Wait Time, Diversion, ER Door to MD, Registration Accuracy and Productivity, Preregistration Percentage, Average Wait Before Answered, Denials Due to No Authorization, Physician Satisfaction
Plan of Care: Assessment, Provision of Care, Implementing and Evaluating Care	Quality Outcomes Communication Responsiveness Efficiency Empathy Cycle Time Productivity	Patient Satisfaction, Patient Loyalty, Adequately Informed, Mortality, Hospital-Acquired Skin Ulcers, Falls, CORE—SIP, Handwashing, Verbal Order Read-Back, Device Days, VAP Rate, Chronic Lung Disease, Pain Management, % of Babies Discharged Home on 02, RN Assessment, Plan of Care, Evaluation of Care, Responsiveness, Concern Shown by Staff
Discharge: Plan, Education, Billing, Coding		Willingness to Refer, CHF Discharge Instructions, Appropriate Education, Length of Stay, Readmissions, Discharges, Days in HIM, Gross Days in AR, Bad Debt/Charity Care, Monthly Denials, Discharged but Not Final Billed

ness of new or modified key processes and services. The next example illustrates usage of the PDCA method to improve key processes:

Step 1. *Focus.* During the spring QSP retreat, the executive team analyzes the SID and determines the key healthcare services and service delivery processes. Using a comprehensive business planning process, the executive team carefully considers market research, competitive data, customer input, testing, analysis, and planned implementation, before a new process or service is introduced. The executive team fulfills the focus step of the PDCA model by determining the need for a new service or delivery process and assigning oversight for design to the appropriate SOT. The SOT organizes the team, clarifies the scope of the work and the timeline requirements. The team is composed of key stakeholders of the service or process including staff, physicians, leaders, suppliers, and patients, as appropriate. Physician partners play a key role in the development of new services and processes. For example, through active physician involvement in cardiac service line development, Bronson was the first hospital in the region to introduce pulmonary vein isolation for the treatment of atrial fibrillation, the most common heart rhythm problem in the United States, affecting more than 2.2 million people.

Step 2. *Plan.* In this step, the team builds on the current business plan and designs the action plans. Because Bronson strives to achieve exceptional healthcare outcomes for patients, evidence-based research, benchmarking, and best practice comparisons are utilized in the plan phase. Action plans are developed that are compliant with regulatory, accreditation bodies, payors, patient, and operational requirements. Operational requirements include in-process indicators to evaluate service delivery as well as outcome measures to measure effectiveness and sustainability. Evaluation of technology as a means to decrease costs, promote efficiency, reduce cycle time, and enhance accuracy in the delivery of service is considered in this phase.

Step 3. *Do.* In this step, Bronson deploys and measures the plan against the identified and agreed-on targets developed in the planning stage. Communication and knowledge sharing are important elements of deployment; therefore, information regarding the plan and expected outcomes is shared with physicians, staff, and patients, and Bronson gains acceptance from the process participants. Pilots are conducted to test the plan prior to full deployment.

Step 4. *Check.* During this phase, Bronson learns and innovates by evaluating results of the initial implementation and modifying the plans as needed to achieve sustained results. Bronson assesses whether the design requirements were met during the process implementation. Corrective action plans are put into place during this phase if process variations from the original design are identified. Alternative solutions are determined and implemented.

Step 5. *Act.* This is a critical phase for the organization in sustaining results over time. During this phase, lessons learned are reviewed and shared with the organization and other stakeholders. Based on the outcomes of the plan/do/check steps, implementation on a wider scale throughout the organization is initiated, and the PDCA cycle continues.

Improving Key Healthcare Processes

Linking Measurement and PDCA

In process and outcome indicators are used for the control and improvement of healthcare processes. These performance measures are defined during the plan phase of the PDCA model whenever new healthcare processes are developed. Methods of data collection, frequency, and accountability are assigned during the plan phase, and results are reported to the appropriate group. Key performance measures are formatted in the scorecard format and systematically reported to the appropriate SOT assigned oversight for the process design. Examples of measures for Bronson's key healthcare processes are listed in Exhibit 7.22. During the plan phase of the PDCA model, action plans are developed that are compliant with regulatory, accreditation bodies, payors, patient, and operational requirements. These action plans are then piloted, deployed, assessed, and monitored through the various steps in the PDCA model to ensure that requirements are met in the daily operation of the process. Processes are maintained and monitored by department leaders. If a leader determines that a process is not working effectively, corrective action is taken using the PDCA model. If the problem is within the scope of the individual leader's responsibility, he or she can immediately initiate steps to correct the problem. If the process is determined to be a system problem, the leader requests assistance from the appropriate SOT who will provide the necessary focus and initiate the PDCA process. Patients, suppliers, and physician partners give input about process performance through direct interviews with the process owner or staff, focus groups, participation in satisfaction surveys, and patient rounds. These inputs are used by process owners to manage and improve processes using the PDCA cycle.

Bronson minimizes overall costs associated with errors and rework through effective process design, focused on standardization and proactive identification of potential failures during the plan phase of the PDCA model. New services and products are piloted to identify and evaluate potential issues and to prevent errors and rework. Ongoing quality inspections and audits are reported to, and analyzed by, the accreditation and regulatory oversight committee and the patient safety committee. Through these committees, Bronson reviews evidence-based research and conducts root cause analysis and failure mode effects analysis on key processes to determine further opportunities to reduce errors. Bronson is committed to providing a safe environment for patients. Investments in technology and standardized processes are important to Bronson's patient safety program.

Linking Listening and Learning Methods and Process Redesign

Patient expectations, identified through listening and learning methods (LLMs), are addressed and considered in the design, delivery, and improvement of healthcare service delivery processes. Bronson analyzes information obtained from the customer LLMs to identity patient needs and expectations. Healthcare services and processes are designed to address patient expectations in the plan phase of the PDCA model. Patient expectations are addressed in the delivery of key healthcare services by staff use of the customer service standards and expectations and evaluated based on patient feedback. This feedback drives efforts to meet patient expectations using the PDCA model to improve current processes and services. When patients enter the system, it creates an opportunity to assess and incorporate patient expectations into an individualized plan of care. Prior to delivery of healthcare services, patients are given a full explanation of the risks, benefits, and alternatives related to their individual needs. The individualized plan of care is initiated during the admission process. During this time, there is an exchange of information between members of the healthcare team and the patient. Information is gathered from the patient regarding previous and current health status, discharge needs, and financial information. Patient needs are identified, and the plan of care is designed to meet these needs. The plan of care includes a pathway with mutually-agreed-on expected clinical outcomes and anticipated discharge planning needs. Care pathways include evidence-based research that promotes patient progression through the care delivery process. The pathways are regularly evaluated and modified, if warranted, to reduce variation in care and outcomes and to promote patient safety.

Keeping Current

Annually, during the spring planning retreat, Bronson reviews key healthcare processes to determine if they are current, continue to meet customer requirements, and add value to the organization. During the year, methods to keep healthcare processes current include medical staff input, participation in professional organizations, attendance at conferences and seminars, site visits and sharing with Baldrige recipients, formal research, and subscriptions to professional journals. Through SOT review of the key process performance measures on the scorecards, the SOTs challenge process leaders to achieve better performance and best practice standards. Comparative database sources (e.g., CareScience and Solucient) are used to benchmark best-in-class performance. Bronson uses the PDCA model to improve key healthcare services and processes, reduce variability, and keep current with healthcare service needs and directions. Significant improvement opportunities identified through the SMM are prioritized and managed with SOT oversight and direction. Resources from the clinical operations improvement department are allocated to assist teams as they work with the PDCA model and other appropriate improvement tools to address system-wide process issues. Upon hire, and annually as a minimum working requirement, all employees receive training on the use of PDCA as the model for improvement. PDCA is a key element of the Plan for Excellence, and continuous improvement is part of the organizational culture. Bronson reduces process variability by determining standards of practice, operating guidelines, and protocols deployed through hospital policies. Process automation as well as documentation, training, and procedure standardization further reduce variability. A key element of every new hospital policy is the necessary training and competency check for employees so they have the knowledge and skills to administer the new process. Improvements and lessons learned are communicated and implemented throughout Bronson using the three Cs format and leadership communication process. Sharing "lessons learned" presentations at leadership development, monthly management, nursing division, and department-level meetings, the employee *Healthlines* newsletter, the *Inside* Bronson intranet, skills fairs, and, an annual quality fair are mechanisms for organizational learning.

Improving Support Process Performance

Key business and other support processes are defined as those processes that are most vital to Bronson's business growth and success. Like key healthcare processes, Bronson determines its key business and support processes by identifying those services that support the mission, values, and vision, and strategic objectives, and enable staff to deliver high-quality, efficient healthcare services. This determination is also accomplished annually through the SMM during the spring planning retreat with review of the SID. With direction from an SOT, business and support process owners charter a team to design and improve key support processes. During the plan step of the PDCA model, the team incorporates key requirements, new technology, organizational knowledge, the need for agility, and efficiency and effectiveness factors into action plans for designing the process. During the check step of the PDCA model, the team learns and innovates by evaluating results of the initial implementation and modifying the plans as needed to achieve sustained results. The team assesses whether the design requirements were met during the process implementation. Corrective action plans are put into place during this phase if process variations from the original design are identified. Alternative solutions are determined and implemented. Measures for Bronson's key business and other support processes are listed in Exhibit 7.23.

In-process and outcomes indicators are developed during the plan phase of the PDCA model and used for the management and improvement of business and support processes. Methods of data collection, frequency, and accountability are assigned during the plan phase, and results are reported to the appropriate group. Like healthcare processes, key performance measures are formatted in the scorecard format and are reported systematically to the appropriate SOT assigned oversight for the business or support process design. During the plan phase, action plans are developed that are compliant with regulatory, accreditation bodies, payors, patient, and operational requirements. These are then piloted, deployed, assessed, and monitored through the various steps in the PDCA model to ensure that the requirements are met in the daily operation of the process. Patients, suppliers, physician partners, and staff give input about process performance through direct interviews with the process owner or staff, focus groups, participation in satisfaction or customer service surveys, patient rounds, and leadership rounds on staff.

Improving Overall SMM Process

A key improvement in the SMM was the integration of the strategic and financial planning processes. Using Baldrige feedback, these two processes have been integrated to ensure adequate financial resources are available to support operations and to determine the resources needed to meet financial obligations for both the short- and long-term planning horizons. Bronson uses a 10-year financial plan that tracks debt outstanding and planned debt issuance (principal and interest payments), financial ratios, cash flows, major capital projects, consolidated balance sheet, and targeted net income for long-term planning. The 10-year plan is updated at least annually in conjunction with the SMM but can be updated at any time should changes or new financial obligations arise as part of the continuous planning process. The annual budget is designed to meet short-term or current financial obligations, and the targeted annual bottom line flows from the 10-year plan. Through the SMM planning process, the board and executive team balance priorities and plans to ensure that adequate financial resources are available to support major new business investments and to reach the targeted bottom line. Bronson assesses financial risks with current operations and new investments using a comprehensive business planning process that contains very detailed financial performance analysis including a payor mix review, contribution margin and profit (loss) comparisons and projections, physician contribution margin and profit (loss) trend, return on

Key Process	Key Requirements	Key Measures
Materials Management	Quality, low cost, timely, productivity, cycle time, efficiency	Cost savings Total materials/total hospital expense Internal fill rate Linen fill rate
Environmental and Safety Management	Environmental responsibility, efficient, clean, safe, prepared, productivity, cycle time	Energy conservation Recycled waste Satisfaction with security Cleanliness satisfaction Employee perception of safety OSHA injuries Sprains and strains Annual employee MWR Safety drill completion Infant abduction drills Dept. health and safety review Bed turnaround
Financial Management	Accurate, timely, efficient, profitable, productivity, cycle time	Gross days in AR Audit findings Return on assets Profit margin Current ratio Profit Profit margin by delivery mechanism Donations Community benefit
Human Resource Management	Competitive, low cost, timely, competent, work/life balance, productivity, cycle time, efficiency	Turnover Vacancy Internal referral Job growth Timely performance appraisals Training hours per FTE Development investment Tuition assistance Satisfaction Job mobility TB test compliance BAC reimbursement
Information Management	Timely, accurate, efficient, available, effective, productivity, cycle time	IT first-call resolution Document delivery Document delivery cycle time Medical record delinquency H&P transcription TAT
Guest Services Management	Timely, responsive, quality, productivity, cycle time, efficiency	Security satisfaction Concierge requests Food service quality Meal delivery time

Principle 4: Improve Performance
- *Prioritize Improvement Projects.* Identify and prioritize strategic and operational initiatives to improve organization's performance along financial, customer or constituent, process and people dimensions.
- *Leverage Customer-Facing Processes.* Develop and exercise customer/patient processes to understand and recalibrate processes around changing customer needs. Gather customer and competitor intelligence through the use of regular customer surveys, focus groups, call centers, quality function deployment, and related methods and approaches.
- *Leverage Process Improvement Methods.* Design and maintain an ongoing process improvement and problem-solving program based on PDCA, root case, and failure modes effects analysis methods and tools to identify and eliminate root causes of issues.
- *Realize Value from Benchmarking Processes.* Leverage benchmarking and comparative methods to identify and regularly improve core and support processes.
- *Create a Performance Improvement Culture.* Create a virtual community of practice of practitioners to coordinate and optimize improvement efforts enterprise-wide.

investment, and payback period (if capital required). For new business opportunities that are not budgeted during the SMM, there are contingent funds available for new capital investments. This allows for agility and rapid implementation of new plans as part of the continuous planning process.

> *Energy and persistence conquer all things.*
> —BENJAMIN FRANKLIN

RICOH: BEST PRACTICES CASE

Shortly after development of the corporate BSC, the project team met to discuss management of key improvement projects. The team initially thought this would be a straightforward process. This was anything but the case. The

- Recipient of Balanced Scorecard Hall of Fame Award
- Recipient of Deming Quality Award

challenge came not because Ricoh managers did not know how to manage initiatives—on the contrary, they were very effective in managing initiatives. The problem was they simply had too many of them. The initial data call to identify corporate-wide projects yielded 75 initiatives the company was managing that they felt were critical to the future success of the company. Over the course of several meetings, the project team mapped each of the initiatives to the objectives on the Strategy Map. The discussion occurring during the process was fascinating. "I remember the project team wondering why I kept saying it was going to take so long to align the initiatives. The fact was while people had heard of many of them, they really weren't sure what they were designed to accomplish and how they were being managed," said strategic management expert Ed Barrows. "It was an eye-opening process for everyone involved."

After the mapping was completed, each initiative was assigned a specific owner and then coordinated through the Strategy and Planning Office SPO. Further, the office began the discipline of requiring that business cases be completed for any future, corporate-level initiatives and that funding be approved through the strategic investment fund.

Customer-Focused Initiatives

Much of the actual Ricoh strategy hinged on establishing consultative relationships with customers. That challenge was that for years, Ricoh had largely a product-based sales relationship. While some might argue that a good salesperson is a consultative seller, Ricoh was looking to develop capabilities beyond satisfying the customer with the basic product. Ricoh wanted to create an entire sales organization dedicated to enhancing customer productivity. But what did that mean? "Initially it meant capturing a whole host of customer data that we did not have." said Marilyn Michaels, Director, Quality and Performance, Ricoh U.S. Recognizing this was the case, Michaels, in partnership with the marketing organization, began the process of collecting and analyzing additional customer information. This effort was directly linked to one Strategy Map objective, "Capture and Analyze the Customer Voice." In addition to gathering the typical survey and focus group information that every company collects, Ricoh created a powerful new way not only to discuss customer needs but to demonstrate potential solutions: the Ricoh Technology Portal.

The Technology Portal is an interactive experience located in Ricoh Business Systems and Lanier Worldwide offices in New York, San Francisco, and Chicago. The portal enables customers the opportunity to witness a fully integrated office environment that demonstrates how Ricoh solutions can be constructed to meet the document and print management needs. While only a few years ago the idea seemed like a far-flung concept, in 2004 the initiative drove over $40 million in additional business. Through a clear comprehension of what the strategy was trying to accomplish with customers, Ricoh was able to develop a completely out-of-the-box solution that bridged the gap between customer needs and their desired consultative sales approach.

Adopting a Six Sigma Improvement Method

In early 2004, Ricoh started an internal program called "IMPROVE." This improvement approach contained five steps and was patterned after Six Sigma. The process quickly gained interest and support, but it was evident that a more robust, full-scale Six Sigma effort would be needed. Thus, in the latter part of 2004, the Performance Excellence Group (PEG) began the process of implementing Six Sigma full scale. Ricoh's implementation of Six Sigma is fundamentally different from other companies because it is being performed concurrently with several other critical initiatives, such as the One Company/One System project. This project—a company-wide enterprise resource planning (ERP) installation designed to integrate the previously disparate business units into one company—is massive in terms of time and resources required. Thus Six Sigma is literally being performed around the project. The PEG has trained a cadre of approximately 200 employees in the principles of Six Sigma and has customized the deployment within each of the business units. The initial push represents a focus on key customer value creation processes that are linked to the strategy in the BSC. While too early to predict the final tally, so far the company has saved over $2 million. This process will continue indefinitely and will be the primary way employees think about and analyze the business in the future.

BEST PRACTICE HIGHLIGHTS

Principle 4: Improve Performance
- *Prioritize Improvement Projects.* Identify and prioritize strategic and operational initiatives to improve organization's performance along financial, customer or constituent, process and people dimensions.
- *Leverage Customer-Facing Processes.* Develop and exercise customer and constituent processes to understand and recalibrate processes around changing customer needs. Gather customer and competitor intelligence.
- *Leverage Process Improvement Methods.* Design and maintain an ongoing process improvement and problem-solving program based on six sigma to identify and eliminate root causes of issues.
- *Create a Performance Improvement Culture.* Create a virtual community of practitioners to coordinate and optimize improvement efforts.

Hide not your talents, they for use were made.
What's a sun-dial in the shade?
—BENJAMIN FRANKLIN

HOUSTON CHRONICLE:
BEST PRACTICES CASE*

In June 2003, the *Houston Chronicle* recognized the need to improve productivity and began to look at process improvement methods and their application within the organization. The first step was introducing management to process mapping, which soon led to exploring the advantages of six sigma.

With the help of Motorola University, Six Sigma was introduced at the *Houston Chronicle* and was based in the human resource division. Mary Ann Wendt, the director of organizational development, led the initiative. An internal systems programmer applied for and was hired to fill the newly formed position of process improvement specialist, whose sole role was to lead Six Sigma projects. Staff training consisted of the director and the specialist both becoming black belts through Motorola University and 24 managers throughout the organization trained as green belts.

Although the first projects were centered in the advertising division, within two years, the *Chronicle* completed 14 projects involving all 8 divisions and saving in excess of $12 million. There was a problem, however. The 14 project teams were made up of between 6 to 12 team members. Out of an organization of 1,600 people, that left many people unaware of the Six Sigma program and why it was worthwhile. The team needed to leverage the knowledge to move the organization toward becoming a process-oriented company.

Adopting the Balanced Scorecard and Human Resources Strategy

The BSC was the next logical step. It was evident that the scorecard would provide a link to strategy that could guide the *Chronicle*'s Six Sigma efforts in a direction that would benefit the organization strategically and secure support at all levels.

The biggest obstacles the teams had encountered to date were with technology. Six Sigma put a spotlight on just how out of date systems were. The scorecard only enhanced that picture.

The plan to introduce the BSC was to begin with a pilot scorecard for human resources (HR). The HR scorecard had three themes on its Strategy Map, defining the path for HR to become a strong strategic partner:

* We kindly acknowledge *Houston Chronicle* director Mary Ann Wendt (former director, organizational development), Director Human Resources, and Anna Singletary (former Six Sigma organizational leader), Director of Productivity, for their assistance with this case study.

Securing the Base, Building and Strengthening Relationships, and Growing the Business (see Exhibit 7.24). It was clear, before HR could move forward, that automation of its internal HR processes was crucial.

In order to do this successfully, the directors of the HR division met and outlined specifically what the processes were, who were responsible for them, and what had to happen to move to the point where the majority of employee time and effort was spent as consultants to colleagues rather than paper pushers neck deep in minutiae. This would be the point where HR could partner with the *Chronicle's* clients, using Six Sigma methodology and the BSCS to help the organization meet its strategic goals.

The implementation of Six Sigma first and then the BSC may seem backward to many. However, states Wendt, "I think it is proof that there is no one right way to initiate process improvement. It is important to measure the readiness of the organization and take the path most indicated for success. Had we not started with Six Sigma and met with success that continued to grow, I'm not sure the Balanced Scorecard would have gained ground."

Focus on Two Key Six Sigma Projects

Direct Marketing

The direct marketing department is responsible for selling advertising pieces for direct mail and insertion in the daily newspaper. The director of this department was aware that her sales force seemed to be spending a lot of time in the office rather than out with clients. It was evident they were spending too much time processing paperwork.

The goal of this team was to streamline the direct marketing work flow to increase sales and planning time to 75%, improve profitability and efficiency by increasing the accuracy of paperwork to 100%, and increasing profit margin to a 35% average. (See Exhibit 7.25.)

It is important to note that, when the project team began, there was no valid data to measure how much time direct marketing sales reps were spending out of the office actually selling. The director only had a hunch that it was not enough time. Amazingly, after conducting a time study to measure time spent on different activities throughout the department, it was determined that the sales reps were only spending 27.5% on selling and the remainder on internal administrative tasks. These data pointed the team in a direction for action.

During the 60 days following the time study, customer service reps were trained to take over the administrative tasks of the sales reps. Sales reps were given handheld personal digital assistants (PDAs) with updated market information for quick access to customers, database marketing support was moved into this department, and forms were customized and automated to increase accuracy and efficiency.

EXHIBIT 7.24 Houston Chronicle Strategy Map

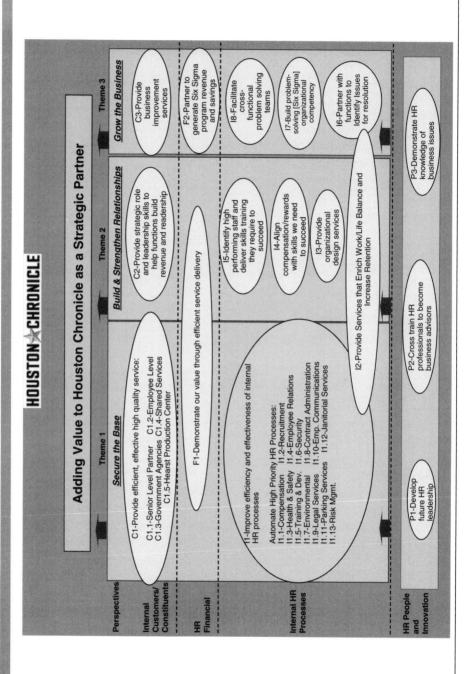

333

EXHIBIT 7.25   Direct Marketing Team Charter

Team Charter

Project : Direct Marketing

Business Case	Opportunity Statement
Streamlining the Direct Marketing job workflow will increase sales and planning time, improve profitability and efficiency, increase revenue.	Standardizing processes for the Direct Marketing jobs gives the opportunity to increase internal and external customer satisfaction, accuracy, productivity and revenue generated by the direct marketing sales team.

Goal Statement	Project Scope
– Increase sales and planning time to 75%. – Increase accuracy of paperwork to 100%. – Increase profit margin to a 35% average .	Process : Direct Marketing job Start Point : Customer inquiry End Point : Customer sent bill

Project Plan

Task/Phase	Start Date	End Date
Evaluate current process flow	10/21/03	11/20/03
Quick Wins	11/20/03	12/8/03
Roles and Responsibilities	11/18/03	12/16/03
Form Consolidation and Re-Design	11/25/03	3/31/04
Data Collection	11/12/03	3/11/04
Pilot CSR	11/13/03	5/3/04
Data Analysis	1/5/2004	4/19/04
Final Recommendations/Controls in place	5/1/04	5/1/04

Team Members

Sponsor : Todd Neal
Black Belt : Anna Singletary
Team Leader : Katherine English
Member : Kim Holland   Member : Deborah Sambrano
Member : Kyle Reynolds   Member : Thuy Cong Tang
Member : Shannon Chapin   Member : Sam Hafez
Member : Christine Stevens
Member : Heinrich Meermann
Member : Fran Lindsay

One year after the team began, sales time had increased 53%, revenue increased 12.65% ($1,950,787), and the profit margin hit 40%. At the end of the second year, sales times had increased 126% and continue to improve. Revenue is up 55% ($8,184,525), and the average profit margin is at 45%.

Ad Services

Ad services are responsible for accepting advertising orders and copy from sales reps and processing it through graphics and art to the final print product. The goals of this team were to analyze the current work flow in the ad services area (including the quality control and service desks) in order to identify work flow inefficiencies and recommend appropriate staffing levels. This area was staffed by 1 *Houston Chronicle* employee and 20 employees from an on-site subcontractor for the *Chronicle*. The team charter is shown in Exhibit 7.26.

This project was finished within 60 days with recommendations that resulted in a decrease of three staff members for a savings of $120,000. The findings of this team also led to the formation of a second Six Sigma team to look at the electronic file delivery process. As a result, the negotiation of the *Chronicle*'s contract with its subcontractor was significantly reduced for 2006 ($2.7 million).

EXHIBIT 7.26   Ad Services Team Charter

Team Charter

Project : Ad Services

Business Case	Opportunity Statement
Identify work flow inefficiencies and appropriate staffing levels in Ad Services.	Reduce costs associated with the current Ad Services work flow through automated and efficient processes. The Ad Services area includes the QC and Service desks and is comprised of 20 American Color employees.

Goal Statement	Project Scope
- Maximize efficiencies in the Ad Services through automation - Reduce labor cost by 15% - Minimize job processing touch points to 1	Process: Ad Services work flow Start Point : Ticket arrives in service End Point : Job processed and jacketed

Project Plan

Task/Phase	Start Date	End Date	Actual End
Form Team	17-Jan-05	21-Jan-05	21-Jan-05
Finalize Charter	17-Jan-05	24-Jan-05	24-Jan-05
Define Current Process	20-Jan-05	27-Jan-05	27-Jan-05
Gather Data	1-Feb-05	28-Mar-05	28-Mar-05
Analyze Data	1-Mar-05	28-Mar-05	28-Mar-05
Select Solution	17-Mar-05	28-Mar-05	28-Mar-05
DevPlan to Implement	17-Mar-05	28-Mar-05	31-Mar-05
Closure and Recognition	28-Mar-05	31-Mar-05	4-Apr-05

Team Members

Sponsors : John Paradysz
                   Wayne Matthews
Team Leader: Don Grant
Black Belt : Anna Singletary
Members : Mike Daniel   George Chaffin
                 Mick Berryman
                 Leo Poche
                 David Courtney
                 Cliff Nunley

One of the most amazing examples of "low-hanging fruit" uncovered by Six Sigma methodology is reflected in the work of the ad services team. The *Houston Chronicle* has always offered a lamination service to customers for obituaries. The ad services desk handled this task. The rate charged for these laminations amounted to less than $5,000 collected annually. This team's data revealed that one employee was spending 22 hours a week doing laminations, spending almost five times what was brought in. Changes were made to automate and streamline this function.

Summary

These are only two examples of the *Chronicle*'s Six Sigma team successes and the value of the BSC. One huge advantage not highlighted is the value that these initiatives bring to the organization in staff development.

Wendt states, "As director of organizational development shouldering the responsibility for staff development, this was accomplished in part by bringing training initiatives onsite, delivering leadership models, communication workshops, etc. Six Sigma and the Balanced Scorecard are tools that build and develop staff in ways that are not easily recognized before using them.

BEST PRACTICE HIGHLIGHTS

Principle 4: Improve Performance
- *Prioritize Improvement Projects.* Identify and prioritize strategic and operational initiatives to improve organization's performance along financial, customer or constituent, process and people dimensions.
- *Leverage Customer-Facing Processes.* Develop and exercise customer and constituent processes to understand and recalibrate processes around changing customer needs.
- *Leverage Process Improvement Methods.* Design and maintain an ongoing process improvement and problem-solving program based on six sigma black and green belt competencies.
- *Create a Performance Improvement Culture.* Create a virtual community of practice of practitioners to coordinate and optimize improvement efforts enterprise-wide.

Communication and listening skills, conflict management, team building, problem solving, leadership, speaking and writing skills, and presentation preparation are only a few of the skills that are honed.

"These initiatives also empower employees to use their knowledge to make their environment a better place to work. They grow more confident, feel more valued, and become more productive. Needless to say, the organization benefits greatly as a result."

> *Nothing astonishes men so much as common sense and plain dealing.*
> —RALPH WALDO EMERSON

■ **NOTES**

1. http://www.ge.com/en/company/companyinfo/quality/whatis.htm.
2. Adapted from Motorola University Six Sigma Green Belt training manual, 2004.
3. Janice Koch, "The Challenges of Strategic Alignment: Crown Castle's CEO Shares His Perspectives," *Balanced Scorecard Report* (July–August 2004): 10.
4. Adapted from Bob Paladino, "Integrating Balanced Scorecard, Six Sigma and Knowledge Management to Drive Value at Crown Castle," APQC (2004).
5. http://lean2.mit.edu/.

CHAPTER 8

Principle 5

MANAGE AND LEVERAGE KNOWLEDGE

Each Warrior wants to leave the mark of his will, his signature, on important acts he touches. This is not the voice of ego but of the human spirit rising up and declaring that it has something to contribute to the solution of the hardest problems, no matter how vesting!

—PAT RILEY

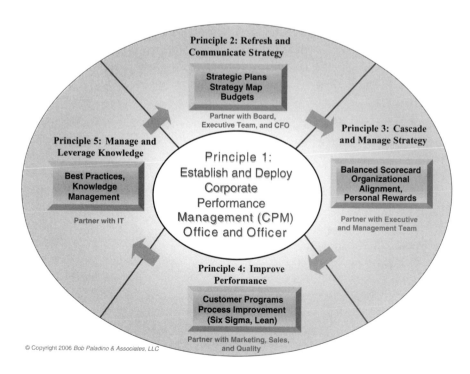

© Copyright 2006 *Bob Paladino & Associates, LLC*

EXHIBIT 8.1   **Principle 5 Best Practice Summary**

Best Practice	Description
Develop knowledge management (KM) processes	Establish and leverage best practice identification, gathering and sharing processes and technology solutions. (APQC has compiled an impressive list of KM best practice case studies; go to www.apqc.org).
Leverage technology	Partner with the information technology (IT) function to launch and maintain KM systems.
Develop expert locater systems	Design and use expert locater systems to capture employee skills inventory within the enterprise to accelerate problem solving in Principle 4 and to optimize human capital.
Link KM with improve performance process	Link best practice or knowledge management processes with Principle 4 processes to capture solutions and innovations.
Share best practices with strategic planning	Share best practices with strategic planning processes to better understand core competencies and possible strategic advantages.
Maintain a virtual KM network	Establish and maintain virtual network of KM experts throughout the enterprise to optimize knowledge and to keep processes evergreen.

Exhibit 8.1 summarizes Principle 5 best practices. The case studies in this chapter provide rich content to support them. The Crown case study provides both the Crown-specific best practices and expands discussion on the normative Principle 5 best practices learned from the collective companies researched.

> *Although the last, not least.*
> —WILLIAM SHAKESPEARE

Case study companies in this chapter also include recipients of these awards:

- U.S. President's National Malcolm Baldrige Quality Award
- Governor's Sterling Award for Excellence (based on Baldrige Criteria)
- Deming Quality Award
- American Quality and Productivity Center (APQC) Best Practice Partner Award
- Kaplan and Norton Global Balanced Scorecard Hall of Fame Award
- *Wall Street Journal* Ranked "Top 20 Most Improved Company in Shareholder Value Creation"

- *Fortune* "100 Best Companies to Work For"
- *Forbes* Best Managed Companies

CROWN CASTLE: BEST PRACTICE CASE*

The Crown knowledge management (KM) capability and portal evolved significantly over several years. Janice Koch notes, "Perhaps Crown's most potent strategy management tool, one that advances alignment and governance, is CCI-Link, a knowledge management (KM) portal launched by the Crown CPM office (called Global Performance) in 2003."[1]

The development of Crown Castle's KM portal started humbly with stand-alone best practices resulting from specific performance improvement projects posted on a shared corporate drive. This passive approach evolved and matured through valued employee suggestions and inputs into a leading intranet site enabling daily access to a globally distributed workforce. In the interest of delivering practical, actionable best practices in this book, I describe key steps in the evolution but focus on best practice KM design principles you can readily leverage in your enterprise. The company has set two specific KM goals:

1. Capture Crown's intellectual property to help a workforce that is spread throughout the United States, United Kingdom, and Australia to share ideas and best practice.
2. Continually improve performance in a challenging business environment.

From Good to Great

Crown's portal started with a collection of searchable best practices, plus a section for field guides, project reports, and presentations. It was linked to all information technology (IT) applications and measured using the balanced scorecard (BSC). While these features contributed to CCI-Link's early success, Web usage statistics indicated a relatively small number of heavy users. In some respects the CCI-Link CPM office design team in (my Global Performance department) fell victim to the "field of dreams" approach. They built it, and some people came, but what about the rest of Crown's employees? The team realized it had to make a midcourse correction to take CCI-Link to the next level.

* Portions of this case were adapted from a KM review article on Crown's knowledge management system.

- Recipient of Balanced Scorecard Hall of Fame Award
- Recipient of APQC Best Practice Partner Award
- Ranked "Top 20 Most Improved Company in Shareholder Value Creation" by *Wall Street Journal* (out of 1,000 listed companies)

How Much Productivity Is Lost?

Rather than continuing to rely on omniscience, the CPM team conducted an employee Web survey to better understand their needs and to provide a guide for corresponding changes to CCI-Link. To design our questionnaire, we customized an existing employee survey from the American Productivity and Quality Center (APQC). We initially targeted staff in the United States because they produce two-thirds of company revenues. Employees could reach the survey by clicking on a link that was sent to their e-mail in boxes.

First the survey asked respondents for job information, which provided data about position level (management, technical, or support), geographic location (corporate or the field), categories for possible communities of practice (e.g., sales or finance), and insight into how each community might like to communicate (group channel, chat room, etc.).

Then the e-survey asked questions designed to measure how much productivity was being lost because of the inefficient use of intellectual property. Questions included:

- "How frequently do you look for information, have difficulty finding/retrieving it, and just move on to the next task at hand?"
- "How many extra hours per week do you estimate you spend looking for information or finding the right person for an answer that you feel should be readily available?"
- "How long do you wait beyond what you feel is reasonable to acquire the information or get a response?"

Finally, the survey solicited written input from employees on their information problems. In general, the survey asked, "What is the biggest problem you have when looking for information?" Written responses were grouped into primary, secondary, and tertiary themes so action could be prioritized.

I wish I had an answer to that because I'm tired of answering that question.
—YOGI BERRA

Overwhelming Response

The CPM team had doubts about how many employees would take the time to finish the survey. The telecommunications business has recently expanded, but Crown is reluctant to hire in a newly growing market, so our employees were very busy. There had been another recent employee survey, so survey burnout was also a concern. As a result, the CPM team estimated that only about a third of the 600 employees in the United States would finish the multiple-choice part of the survey and still less, about a quarter, would provide written comments. We turned out to be very wrong. Within two hours of sending the link, half the employees in the United States had responded, and they provided more than 600 written comments. Within five days we had an 83% response rate, and received more than 1,200 written comments with meaningful suggestions and input. It is difficult to know for sure why there was such an overwhelming response, but after holding town meetings with a cross-section of employees to discuss the results, it became clear that information inefficiency and KM was a pressing concern. The survey had obviously tapped into a huge unmet need. The CPM team also thought the survey would return more homogenous responses and show that a large majority favored the same technology and process solutions across the company. But because our data cuts could give us specific responses by function and geography, we saw that needs widely varied in some areas and were homogenous in others. Some of the most striking examples included:

- *Intellectual property needs varied by position.* The survey defined different methods of interacting virtually, including "channels," a central Web site to broadcast news and information to a select group, and chat rooms, where staff could discuss relevant issues. In one function there was a real split between managers who strongly favored using channels and front-line employees who preferred chat rooms. The front-line employees liked the informality and real-time nature of the chat rooms, as opposed to the more prescriptive channels Web site, which seemed static by comparison. The Web site was also exclusive, requiring special permission in order to post.
- *Intellectual property needs varied by function.* Some functions were more ready to implement communities of practice than others. One function, for example, was already meeting regularly by conference call and could immediately see the benefits of rapidly sharing information across geographies. Others were not so far along.
- *Expertise location.* All functions wanted an expert locator system (ELS) based on job skills. For instance, if a manager needed an engineer with

radio frequency planning experience, he or she usually made numerous phone calls to the internal network, and wanted a more convenient way to find talent. What the data and follow-up interviews told us was that we could have spent the time and money to give all of the teams five different ways to communicate, but they would have migrated to the one or two that they use the most.

Forming Tiger Teams

Crown Staff often complained that surveys are not followed up with corrective action. The Corporate Performance Management (CPM) team was determined not to let this happen with the KM survey—it was too important. So "tiger teams" were created to make sure that the survey was followed up. This section spotlights one team, the Livelink Power User Team, which has rapidly evolved into a Community of Practice (CoP). Recall the earlier question about the ease of locating intellectual property within Crown: "How frequently do you look for information, have difficulty finding/retrieving, and just move on to the next task at hand?" Although 61.3% of respondents readily found information, 38.7% aborted searches 11% or more of the time, which is a productivity figure the GP (CPM) team thought could be improved. Written comments provided further action points to improve our Livelink document management system, and these were grouped into primary, secondary, and tertiary themes.

- *Primary.* Many employees stated that forms and templates were simply too hard to find. There were several reasons, but three stood out in particular. Employees felt the Livelink search engine was not operating effectively. They also felt documents were scattered throughout Livelink and that the locations were not intuitive.
- *Secondary.* Forms are not current, or the posting date is so old that users cannot be sure. Because of this, once people find a form they download it to avoid having to search again. If the form is revised on the portal, they will not realize it until they submit the version held on their hard drive, which is very frustrating.
- *Tertiary.* Several users said there are multiple versions of a form or template in different places on Livelink, "so even if you find a form you don't know if it's the right one." The company knew Livelink had not been maintained well. When permission holders moved departments, their permissions often were not updated. In addition, Crown does not have a taxonomy, and search terms have not been regularly attached when posting content. That means the search engine was not working as well as it could. In addition, the Livelink Power User team completed an analysis of the current Livelink folder structure across the U.S. operation. The team identified that 56% of the folders required five or more

mouse clicks. We needed to clean out the old content, change the folder structure to a more logical layout, adjust posting permissions, and develop taxonomy to increase the effectiveness of the search engine. We also needed to develop an easily maintained version control, so that updates are readily visible and accessible. The Livelink Power User Team set a goal to develop a new folder architecture that would:

○ Enable users to reach documentation in three mouse clicks.
○ Provide alternative search avenues for users to reach documents (accepting that people think differently).
○ Do so with minimal disruption to business and content owners (who know and may want to keep their current folder structure).
○ Establish version control procedures and assist with training business owners and Livelink users. Suppose an employee wanted to find a dental form. In the old system forms were located in several different functional folders. The Livelink Power User team identified multiple paths "by topic" to this one document, all within three clicks to the user. The form was tagged with three topics: department, category, and alphabetical title. This new design flattened the file structure and provided faster access to information to the end user where they will have at least three different ways to access information—by topic. But how did the team deal with the cultural "change" issue that functional owners maintained functionally based folders? They had a creative answer: Allow the two worlds, topics and functions, to coexist.
○ Documents in the new "topic-based" subfolders will have an alias (or hyperlink) that will take the user directly to the functional folder containing the document, no matter how many levels down in the department folder structure it has been posted.
○ When new documents are posted to departmental folders, alias names will be added to all applicable "topic" folders.

The Journey Continues: Benefits

When it came to managing the tiger teams, an executive steering committee was established consisting of the CPM director responsible for CCI-Link and country leaders to provide governance and direction to resolve intercountry and intracountry issues. The most pressing issue was to design CCI-Link to meet local market needs yet maintain a consistent look and feel globally. The steering committee entertained several concept designs and reached consensus for a fixed format but flexible content. The committee also provided top-down support and communications to the broader employee base. The benefits of this approach have been:

- Rapid posting and re-use of strategic and operational gems or best practices deriving from Balanced Scorecard results.
- Higher utilization of existing organization capacity
- Shorter cycle time in document retrieval for faster issue resolution
- Greater employee participation and buy-in
- Higher employee awareness of common issues and creative employee-driven solutions
- Clarity of intellectual property (IP) ownership and maintenance
- Increases in standardization of document filing and retrieval
- Minimal disruption to the organization—the stealth topic and functional approaches

CCI-Link was migrated from Livelink to Microsoft SharePoint Services (SPS) software to continue upgrading functionality and to more seamlessly link into MS Office documents for automatic updates and to more closely control versions. At the time of my departure, the new owner was continuing to recalibrate CCI-Link around changing company and employee needs. Crown has realized success from CCI-Link by making the necessary midcourse correction, moving from the "field of dreams" approach to the employee requirements

BEST PRACTICE HIGHLIGHTS

Principle 5: Manage and Leverage Knowledge

- *Develop Knowledge Management (KM) Processes.* Establish and leverage best practice identification, gathering and sharing processes, and technology solutions.
- *Leverage Technology.* Partner with the IT function to launch and maintain KM systems.
- *Develop Expert Locater Systems.* Design and use expert locater systems to capture employee skills inventory within the enterprise to accelerate problem solving in Principle 4 and to optimize human capital.
- *Link KM with Improve Performance Process.* Link best practice or KM processes with Principle 4, Improve Performance, processes to capture solutions and innovations.
- *Share Best Practices with Strategic Planning.* Share best practices with strategy management processes using the Balanced Scorecard to better understand core competencies and possible strategic advantages.
- *Maintain a Virtual KM Network.* Establish and maintain virtual network of KM experts throughout the enterprise to optimize knowledge and to keep processes evergreen.

driven approach. The KM e-survey provided insights into employee IP issues and provided the business case for tiger teams to achieve quick wins. The executive steering committee provided necessary direction. These factors accelerated KM portal development and usage and value creation

> *Whenever you find that you are on the side of the majority, it is time to reform.*
> —MARK TWAIN

CITY OF CORAL SPRINGS: BEST PRACTICE CASE*

Results and learning are shared through staff meetings at all levels. Quarterly communications meetings and the supervisory forum (a quarterly meeting of supervisors) are used to transfer learning. Cross-functional process improvement teams report results and what they have learned at senior management team meetings. Several team projects have been presented as storyboards and stage presentations at the Sterling regional team showcase. Cross-functional process improvement teams produce a cross-fertilization of ideas by their structure. Staff of information systems, human resources, and financial services collaborate with departmental staff on major process improvement initiatives and bring the knowledge they acquire to the rest of the city.

> *Every great and commanding moment in the annals of the world is the triumph of some enthusiasm.*
> —RALPH WALDO EMERSON

BEST PRACTICE HIGHLIGHTS

Principle 5: Manage and Leverage Knowledge
- ***Link KM with Improve Performance Process.*** Link best practice or KM processes with Principle 4, Improve Performance, processes to capture solutions and innovations.
- ***Share Best Practices with Strategic Planning.*** Share best practices with strategic planning processes to better understand core competencies and possible strategic advantages.

---

* The City of Coral Springs case team adapted portions of this case from "Performance Measurement in the Public Sector," *APQC* (November 2005), Governors Sterling Application 2003, and internal documents.

- Recipient of Florida Governor Sterling Award for Organizational Excellence (based on Baldrige Criteria)
- Recipient of APQC Best Practice Partner Award

TENNESSEE VALLEY AUTHORITY: BEST PRACTICE CASE*

Tennessee Valley Authority (TVA) Nuclear faces the challenge of replacing a large part of its workforce over the next few years. This is due to the demographics of the so-called baby boom generation and past downsizing efforts. Attrition, primarily in the form of retirements, may cost TVA Nuclear 30 to 40 % of its workforce over the next five years. These experienced employees possess much unique, undocumented knowledge. Many of these employees *literally* built the plants and facilities that they now operate and maintain.

Process Summary

To address this challenge, TVA Nuclear has developed, piloted, and deployed a three-step process to capture the undocumented knowledge of employees nearing retirement. This process and associated tools and support enable line managers to:

- Identify critical "at-risk" knowledge and skills, especially that associated with impending attrition.
- Assess the risk associated with losing this critical knowledge and skills.
- Develop, implement, and monitor action plans (documentation, mentoring, training, reengineering, sharing expertise, etc.) for managing this risk.

This "knowledge retention" process provides a systematic approach to ensuring that the critical knowledge of its veteran workforce is transferred to the workforce of the future.

- Recipient of APQC Best Practice Partner Award
- Recipient of the Balanced Scorecard Hall of Fame Award

* The TVA case team adapted portions of this case from "Performance Measurement in the Public Sector," *APQC* (November 2005), and internal company documents.

The first step in the process is designed to identify positions and/or people where the potential knowledge loss is greatest and most imminent. It includes ratings of two factors:

1. Retirement factor (time until retirement)
2. Position risk factor (criticality of position)

TVA captures potential retirement data by asking each employee to voluntarily provide a projected date. Employees increasingly understand that this information is driving planning and the labor "pipeline," and is not being used to make individual personnel decisions. About 80% complete the voluntary questionnaire. Coupled with an overall estimate of the position's criticality (provided by the employees' manager), this retirement estimate drives a "total attrition risk factor." Scores between 20 and 25 are considered high priority, with immediate action required. Guidelines for conducting this Knowledge Loss Risk Assessment appear in the next section.

Knowledge Loss Risk Assessment: Guidelines for Assessing Attrition Risks

All new supervisors must attend the first-line supervisor training to obtain the knowledge and skills necessary to perform supervisory duties in a manner that promotes safe and reliable plant operations. As part of the attrition planning process, managers will perform a Knowledge Loss Risk Assessment for each person/position in their organization. This assessment is based on two factors:

1. Retirement factor
2. Position risk factor

Retirement Factor

The projected retirement dates in the workforce planning system (whether based on employee estimates or calculated based on age and tenure data) will be assigned a retirement factor in this way:

5 – Projected retirement date within 1 year
4 – Projected retirement date within 1 to 2 years
3 – Projected retirement date within 2 to 3 years
2 – Projected retirement date within 3 to 5 years
1 – Projected retirement date is > 5 years

Position Risk Factor

An estimate of the difficulty or level of effort required to replace the position incumbent. Managers/supervisors are responsible for making these ratings based on these criteria:

5 - *Critical and unique knowledge and skills.* Mission-critical knowledge/skills with the potential for significant reliability or safety impacts. TVA- or site-specific knowledge. Knowledge undocumented. Requires three to five years of training and experience. No ready replacements available.

4 - *Critical knowledge and skills.* Mission-critical knowledge/skills. Some limited duplication exists at other plans/sites and/or some documentation exists. Requires two to four years of focused training and experience.

3 - *Important, systematized knowledge and skills.* Documentation exists and/or other personnel on-site possess the knowledge/skills. Recruits generally available and can be trained in one to two years.

2 - *Procedural based or nonmission-critical knowledge and skills.* Clear, up-to-date procedures exist. Training programs are current and effective and can be completed in less than one year.

1 - *Common knowledge and skills.* External hires possessing the knowledge/skill are readily available and require little additional training.

The workforce planning system will calculate the total attrition factor by multiplying the position risk factor by the retirement factor. For example:

Projected retirement date—within 1 yr	Retirement factor:	5
Critical/unique skills/Industry training	Position risk factor:	$\times$ 5
	Total attrition factor	25

Total Attrition Factor

This methodology has been used to estimate the effort and urgency necessary to manage attrition effectively.

- *High priority.* Immediate action needed. Specific replacement action plans with due dates will be developed to include: method of replacement, knowledge management assessment, specific training required, on-the-job training/shadowing with incumbent.
- *Priority.* Staffing plans should be established to address method and timing of replacement, recruitment efforts, training, shadowing with current incumbent.
- *High importance.* Look ahead on how the position will be filled/work will be accomplished. College recruiting, training programs, process improvements, reinvestment.
- *Important.* Recognize the functions of the position and determine the replacement need.

The next step is to interview the incumbents and their supervisors to learn the job's "knowledge content." Since it is important to identify both explicit and tacit knowledge, the interviews include four kinds of questions:

BEST PRACTICE HIGHLIGHTS

Principle 5: Manage and Leverage Knowledge
- *Develop Expert Locater Systems.* Design and use expert locater systems to capture employee skills inventory within the enterprise to optimize human capital.
- *Maintain a Virtual KM Network.* Establish and maintain virtual network of experts throughout the enterprise to optimize knowledge and to keep processes evergreen.

1. *General questions,* such as "What knowledge will the TVA miss most when you leave?"
2. *Task questions,* such as how to conduct specific tests or operate certain pieces of equipment.
3. *Fact or information questions* focus on what the employee knows and generate lists of contacts, maps, manuals, and other recorded information.
4. *Pattern recognition questions* ask about lessons learned and insights about what is likely to go wrong and how to fix it.

Based on these interviews, TVA compiles a list of potential "knowledge loss items" for the job. These items are analyzed to determine their importance and decide on the appropriate course of action.

Summary

As a result of this analysis, TVA knows which issues to ignore, which it can correct with minor effort, and which require immediate action, either because that knowledge can be lost rapidly or the organizational consequences would be significant if someone with that specific knowledge suddenly left the organization. Once the focus is on the knowledge and skills that are truly critical, specific plans are established to retain the knowledge/skill or to lessen the impact of losing it.

All you need in this life is ignorance and confidence; then success is sure.
—MARK TWAIN

MEDRAD: BEST PRACTICE CASE*

Medrad fosters organizational learning most notably the quarterly quality forum (best practices sharing and introduction of performance excellence

---

* Portions of this case are adapted from MEDRAD Malcolm Baldrige National Quality Award Application, internal company documents, and employee input.

- Recipient of Malcolm Baldrige National Quality Award
- Recipient of the APQC Best Practice Award

tools), the annual Performance Excellence conference (team best practice sharing and training in team skills), and learning and development.

The cross-functional learning and development leadership team identifies critical learning needs for the organization and designs and implements programs to meet them. Departments also have knowledge-sharing forums, such as Q-First in corporate services and the OPS quality council in operations.

Medrad uses existing systems to share knowledge assets, including the information center, which puts knowledge capital such as standards, journals, and other business information, on the corporate intranet. The intranet is used to share policies and procedures, business results, new product information, and "darn good examples" of useful tools and approaches. Field sales and service representatives share customer information through a system called Avenue. Medrad launched a competitive database to formalize the collection and communication of competitive information.

Concentration comes out of a combination of confidence and hunger.
—ARNOLD PALMER

BEST PRACTICE HIGHLIGHTS

Principle 5: Manage and Leverage Knowledge
- *Leverage Technology.* Partner with the information technology function to launch and maintain KM systems.
- *Link KM with Improve Performance Process.* Link best practice or knowledge management processes with Principle 4, Improve Performance, processes to capture solutions and innovations.
- *Share Best Practices with Strategic Planning.* Share best practices with strategic planning processes to better understand core competencies and possible strategic advantages.
- *Maintain a Virtual KM Network.* Establish and maintain virtual network of KM experts throughout the enterprise to optimize knowledge and to keep processes evergreen.

FLORIDA DEPARTMENT OF HEALTH: BEST PRACTICE CASE*

The Florida Department of Health (FDOH) supports a data and information-sharing culture that is key to knowledge management. The department has a wealth of data available to its 16,000+ employees. The data are provided in easily accessible formats utilizing advancements in technology. The FDOH utilizes both an intranet and the Internet to share information. By organizing data and increasing accessibility, staff members are able to utilize the information in many aspects of their jobs, such as community health improvement planning, analyzing and developing solutions to improve performance, and decision making.

As the department's performance measurement system has evolved so has the use of technology to provide a venue for data collection and retrieval to manage performance. Some examples of internal systems developed to assist the performance measurement system follow.

The CHD Contract Management System (CHD–CMS) was developed in 1985 and served as the first tangible example of an integrated approach to performance measurement. This system provided monthly levels of program costs, staffing, clients, and services to compare with targeted levels. As the focus on health improvement increased, there was a need for county-specific health data. This caused the department to embark on the development of a comprehensive Public Health Indicator Data System (PHIDS). PHIDS was designed to be an indicator warehouse of annual statistical data used in performance measurement. While PHIDS was an internal data warehouse, the system has continued to grow over the years and is now known as Florida CHARTS (www.floridacharts.com). The FDOH has continued to develop various reports that utilize the data and information available to assist senior leaders throughout the department in decision-making and performance management efforts. In addition, the department has a number of other ini-

- Miami-Dade County Health Department Recipient of Governors Sterling (Baldrige) Award 2002 and 2006
- Department of Health Recipient of APQC Best Practice Partner Award

---

* The Florida Department of Health case team adapted portions of this case from "Performance Measurement in the Public Sector," *APQC* (November 2005), Governors Sterling Applications 2002 and 2006, and internal documents.

tiatives that promote the identification and sharing of best practices as well as knowledge sharing. Some examples are:

- *Development of a Web-based submission process to highlight best practices and most promising practices.* This process encourages anyone in the FDOH to submit initiatives, resources, innovative ideas, tools, administrative practices, and internal processes that demonstrate exemplary and replicable actions. The process was developed utilizing a model used by the National Association of City and County Officials (NACCHO). FDOH is currently looking to expand this initiative to include an online searchable database of the best practices and promising practices.
- *Development of a peer reviewer network as part of the performance improvement process.* Peer reviewers from health departments assist neighboring health departments in analyzing performance gaps and providing guidance and/or resources to help improve performance. Peer reviewers have given accolades to this system and indicate that they are able to gain new insights while they are providing insights to their peers.
- *Hosting an annual quality showcase to share best practices and recognize those who have improved.* When the showcase began in 2001, it attracted a small crowd of 100 people; by 2004, attendance had increased to 350.
- *Utilizing a team approach.* Quality improvement and other process management teams establish cross-functional meetings to foster cooperation, communication, and knowledge/skill sharing among work units to identify and resolve problem areas and improve processes, policies, procedures, and services.

BEST PRACTICE HIGHLIGHTS

Principle 5: Manage and Leverage Knowledge
- *Develop Knowledge Management (KM) Processes.* Establish and leverage best practice identification, gathering and sharing processes and technology solutions.
- *Link KM with Improve Performance Process.* Link best practice or KM processes with Principle 4, Improve Performance, processes to capture solutions and innovations.
- *Leverage Technology.* Partner with the IT function to launch and maintain KM systems.
- *Maintain a Virtual KM Network.* Establish and maintain virtual network of KM experts throughout the enterprise to optimize knowledge and to keep processes evergreen.

- *Utilizing electronic communication.* E-mail, Internet, and intranet availability is provided to employees to ensure online access to policies, procedures, staff directories, meeting minutes, interactive training programs, department plans, meeting announcements, training, awards ceremonies, and other events. The FDOH has established satellite sites in each county and holds frequent interactive teleconferences that, in addition to promoting communication throughout the department, provide employees with flexible training, convenient statewide meetings, and access to senior level management staff.
- *Development of a virtual toolbox available to employees on the FDOH intranet that assists staff in finding the best resources to improve individual and organizational performance.* The tools included are low-cost and no-cost performance improvement resources. The "toolbox" looks like a toolbox, and each "drawer" represents one of the Florida Sterling categories with related resources including online information, training programs, books, and videotapes. (Florida Sterling is modeled after the Malcolm Baldrige criteria.)

Knowledge management is critical to every organization. The department strives to make data and information available to its employees and for the employees to share knowledge among themselves to better improve individual and organizational performance on a daily basis.

> *The thing always happens that you really believe in; and the belief in a thing makes it happen.*
> —FRANK LLOYD WRIGHT

AMERICAN RED CROSS: BEST PRACTICE CASE

The American Red Cross has a multifaceted approach to knowledge management. The interaction between service area staff and chapter staff is a key component in the knowledge transfer process. The knowledge transfer work of the service areas has been augmented by the creation of service area communities of practice. At the American Red Cross these communities of practice are referred to as "neighborhoods." An additional resource for chapters is the best practice system, which is a Web-based repository of successful business

- Recipient of APQC Best Practice Partner Award

Principle 5: Manage and Leverage Knowledge
- *Develop Knowledge Management (KM) Processes.* Establish and leverage best practice identification, gathering and sharing processes and technology solutions.
- *Leverage Technology.* Partner with the IT function to launch and maintain KM systems.
- *Link KM with Improve Performance Process.* Link best practice or KM processes with Principle 4, Improve Performance, processes to capture solutions and innovations

practices. Highly performing chapter experiences are documented via surveys with the findings distributed to the service areas and incorporated into the best practices system.

> *Believe one who has proved it. Believe an expert.*
> —Virgil

BRONSON METHODIST HOSPITAL: BEST PRACTICE CASE

Bronson makes needed data and information both available and accessible to staff, suppliers, partners, and patients through the state-of-the-art Information Management Strategy (IMS). Validation of data availability and accessibility are key elements of the processes that support the IMS. Bronson maintains a computer network of digitally available data for all stakeholders. Access to the network is obtained through locally attached workstations, wireless-enabled devices, and the public Internet. Wireless-enabled laptops and other devices are available for checkout to patients, family members, or physicians so they can remain productive and connected while on our campus. Interactive kiosks, integrated with the public Bronson Web site, assist patients and visitors with facility maps, service directories, and other information useful while in our facilities. E-mail is provided to all staff, and is accessible from hospital PCs (including general-purpose "surf stations" for staff members who do not use PCs as part of their day-to-day jobs) and is also available via the Bronson wireless network and the Internet. Nondigital information is made available through paper-based media (and, increasingly, by converting nondigital information into digital format via PDF files, document scanning, and other approaches). The HealthSciences library, found in a central and highly visible location of the hospital, provides easy access to both nondigital and digital health information.

- Malcolm Baldrige National Quality Award
- Michigan Quality Leadership Award (2001, 2005)
- 100 Top Hospitals Award
- Governor's Award of Excellence for Improving Care in the Hospital Setting (2004, 2005)
- Governor's Award of Excellence for Improving Preventive Care in the Ambulatory Care Setting
- *Fortune* magazine's "100 Best Companies to Work For" (2004, 2005, 2006)
- Working Mother's "100 Best Companies for Working Mothers" (2003, 2004, 2005)
- VHA Leadership Award for Operational Excellence (2005, 2006)

Organizational Knowledge Management

Organizational knowledge is a critical asset as Bronson pursues excellence as a healthcare provider. A two-step approach is used to manage organizational knowledge. First, the *Inside* Bronson intranet is set up to be a repository for all knowledge sharing, best practices, improvement tools, education, and communication with employees and physician partners throughout the organization. Second, the Staff Performance Management System (SPMS) and the annual education plan with a wide range of skill and knowledge sharing mechanisms provide a systematic approach to manage organizational knowledge. This supports deployment to all areas of the organization as well as alignment and accomplishment of strategic objectives. The leadership communication process ensures that information is communicated with the appropriate audiences and its effectiveness is evaluated. Knowledge transfer from patients, physicians, and suppliers is accomplished through the effective communication methods in the leadership communication process. Web-enabled technologies (public kiosks, Web portals to access electronic medical records information, e-mail, etc.) provide a 24/7 process to transfer knowledge between Bronson and its patients and physician partners. Weekly value engineering meetings with key suppliers provide a forum for ongoing needs assessment and performance feedback. In-room patient/family education is used to transfer important self-care knowledge to help patients as they prepare for discharge. Follow-up contact with the patient after discharge provides a feedback loop to reinforce the prior knowledge transfer and to solicit feedback on Bronson's performance during the patient's care episode. Active participation in a wide variety of comparative databases gives Bronson early insight into emerging best practices. These insights are identified and evaluated by the executive team or the appropriate strategic oversight teams (SOT). If an SOT determines the identified best practice should be pursued by Bronson, the SOT communicates with appropriate stakeholders to generate organizational buy-in and charges the appropriate group(s) to implement the necessary process changes using the PDCA model. The leadership communication process, with scheduled sessions (leadership development retreats, "lunch and learns," monthly management update meetings, skills fairs, continuing medical education, and grand rounds programs for physicians, etc.) provides forums to share best practice information across large segments of Bronson stakeholders. In addition, the *Inside* Bronson intranet provides resources (online articles, printable forms, chat rooms, etc.) for ongoing communication throughout the adoption of best practices.

Effective Skill Sharing and Communications

Communication and skill sharing are recognized as being critical to organizational success. A systematic process to facilitate and ensure effective communication, skill sharing, and knowledge transfer has been developed, incorporating formal and informal mechanisms (see Exhibit 8.2). The prehire and selection process, new hire orientation, and nursing core orientation are formal mechanisms to set the tone for promoting communication, skill sharing, and knowledge transfer with the newest members of the Bronson team. Systematic use of the leadership communication process by all leaders makes planning, targeting, delivering, and evaluating communication part of the culture. Leaders are accountable to cascade information from all leadership communication forums (monthly management meeting, leadership development retreats, etc.) to the department level.

Leader communication tools, in the three Cs format, are provided through knowledge sharing documents, handouts, and PowerPoint presentations to ensure that consistent communication messages are deployed. At the department level, various forms of communication occur depending on the nature of the information and the needs of the staff. Department-specific communication mechanisms include meetings, bulletin boards, communication books, e-mail, instant messaging, department-specific newsletters, and daily huddles. The leadership development initiative, a key element of the workforce development plan, is a mechanism for growth, communication, and sharing. Other mechanisms include the safety champions, preceptors, and externships/internships. Through teams, work groups, councils, and committees, communication and skill sharing occur on a daily basis. The Diversity Council, Divisional Level Nursing Council, and department-specific councils are examples.

For example, a key element of every new hospital policy is the necessary training and competency check for employees so they have the knowledge and skills to administer the new process. Improvements and lessons learned are

EXHIBIT 8.2   Mechanisms for Communication

Mechanisms for Communication, Skill Sharing, and Knowledge Transfer	Type
• Prehire and selection process	C, SK, ↔
• New hire orientation	C, SK, ↔
• Nursing care orientation	C, SK, ↔
• Leadership Communication Process (LCP)	C
• Leadership communication forums	C
• Knowledge-sharing documents	C, SK
• Department meetings	C, SK, ↔
• Bulletin boards	C
• Communication books	C
• E-mail for all employees	C, ↔
• Instant messaging	C, ↔
• *Inside* Bronson intranet	C, SK, ↔
• Department-specific newsletters	C
• Shared directories	C
• Daily huddles	C, SK, ↔
• *Healthlines* newsletter	C
• CEO/CNE open office hours	C, ↔
• LEADERship	C, SK, ↔
• Competency assessments	C, SK, ↔
• Workshop and educational courses	C, SK, ↔
• Employee forums and focus groups	C, ↔
• Employee neighborhood meetings	C, ↔
• Computer-based learning modules (CBL)	C, SK
• Leader rounds	C, SK, ↔
• Self-study modules	C, SK
• Skills fairs and learning labs	C, SK, ↔
• Safety champions	C, SK, ↔
• Preceptors	C, SK, ↔
• Externships/internships	C, SK, ↔
• Management mentor program	C, SK, ↔
• Shared governance (DLNC)	C, SK, ↔
• Teams, work groups, councils, and committees	C, SK, ↔
• Staff Performance Management System	C, SK, ↔
C-communication, **SK**-skill sharing and knowledge transfer, ↔-two-way	

communicated and implemented throughout Bronson using the three Cs format and leadership communication process. Sharing "lessons learned" presentations at leadership development, monthly management, nursing division, and department-level meetings, the employee *Healthlines* newsletter, the *Inside Bronson* intranet, skills fairs, and an annual quality fair are mechanisms for organizational learning.

Reinforcing Use of Knowledge and Skills

Leaders, preceptors, and educational instructors are formally charged with reinforcing the use of knowledge and skills on the job. This is accomplished through direct observation, immediate reinforcement of specific skills, annual competency assessment, and performance appraisal. A key role of the preceptor is to mentor and reinforce skills of new employees on a daily basis. Educational instructors complete the competency audits and assessments. Leader rounds are effective mechanisms to see staff in action and provide verbal reinforcement. Handwritten thank-you notes are also sent to acknowledge accomplishments. The process for transferring knowledge from departing employees depends on the level of the position. For executive-level positions, there is an expectation of at least 90 days' notice before departure. This allows for recruitment of a replacement, as well as preparation of a formal written transition plan. For salaried professional positions, four weeks' notice is sufficient to allow time for knowledge transfer and transitioning of duties. Two weeks' notice is standard for staff-level positions. Bronson promotes cross-training and team education as part of the culture. This fosters ongoing knowledge sharing to ensure vital information and skills are not lost when any employee departs the organization.

BEST PRACTICE HIGHLIGHTS

Principle 5: Manage and Leverage Knowledge
- *Develop Knowledge Management (KM) Processes.* Establish and leverage best practice identification, gathering, and sharing processes and technology solutions.
- *Leverage Technology.* Partner with the IT function to launch and maintain KM systems.
- *Link KM with Improve Performance Process.* Link best practice or knowledge management processes with Principle 4, Improve Performance, processes to capture solutions and innovations.
- *Share Best Practices with Strategic Planning.* Share best practices with strategic planning processes to better understand core competencies and possible strategic advantages.

Courage and perseverance have a magical talisman, before which difficulties disappear and obstacles vanish into air.
—JOHN QUINCY ADAMS

RICOH: BEST PRACTICE CASE

Like many organizations, early on in its CPM improvement efforts Ricoh did not pay particular attention to best practices sharing, given most of the company's energy was spent working to get the Strategy Map, Balanced Scorecard, and process improvement programs up and running. However, as the company gained momentum, it realized there were significant efficiencies to be gained across the company by improving the way information was shared. Today Ricoh identifies, codifies, and communicates best practice information in a host of ways.

Clearly customer relationships and solutions have become an integral part of Ricoh's success. One way the company works to develop this area is through a global sales event held each year. The event starts locally when each major geographic region identifies case studies that exemplify the relationship that it wants to have with customers as well as identifying solutions that have uniquely solved a customer's problem. Local, national, and international events are held that serve as vehicles for sharing this information. Ultimately each of the cases goes into a database to facilitate sharing globally. This process culminates with an evaluation performed by senior leaders to identify the very best case study.

In addition to the sales-specific events, Ricoh has formalized a general best practice sharing event where again, starting on a local level, any best practice in any part of the business is identified. Local sharing rallies are held to promote the exchange of this information. Ultimately, each region can submit three best practices for the global competition. Regardless of which cases ends up being the winning one, there is extensive worldwide information sharing. All case information resides in the Tokyo-based database. This process is also replicated for manufacturing specifically through a Kaizen rally. In 2005 some of the very first Ricoh U.S. Six Sigma cases were submitted to the Kaizen rally. All of the Six Sigma information is held locally by the Performance Excellence Group in a Lotus Notes database for almost everyone internally. To facilitate ease of sharing, virtually all of the cases—manufacturing, general, and sales—are maintained in English.

- Recipient of Balanced Scorecard Hall of Fame Award
- Recipient of Deming Quality Award

BEST PRACTICE HIGHLIGHTS

Principle 5: Manage and Leverage Knowledge

- *Develop Knowledge Management (KM) Processes.* Establish and leverage best practice identification, gathering and sharing processes and technology solutions.
- *Leverage Technology.* Partner with the IT function to launch and maintain KM systems.
- *Link KM with Improve Performance Process.* Link best practice or knowledge management processes with Principle 4, Improve Performance, processes to capture solutions and innovations.
- *Share Best Practices with Strategic Planning.* Share best practices with strategic planning processes to better understand core competencies and possible strategic advantages.
- *Maintain a Virtual KM Network.* Establish and maintain virtual network of KM experts throughout the enterprise to optimize knowledge and to keep processes evergreen.

Along with the formal structures that exist, the executives themselves serve as carriers of best practice information. Throughout the year executives conduct visits to each other's offices during BSC reviews. During the sessions they share ideas regarding how they use the balanced scorecard to drive performance in their own organizations. This in turn enables the host organization to learn from those who are visiting.

> *A hero is no braver than an ordinary man, but he is braver five minutes longer.*
> —RALPH WALDO EMERSON

RAYTHEON COMPANY: BEST PRACTICE CASE*

Given Raytheon's tight integration of KM content with IT Six Sigma improvement methods, I elected to share them in a considerable manner in this chapter.

Raytheon Co. is one of the top four defense contractors in the United States, along with Lockheed Martin Corp., Northrop Grumman Corporation, and the Boeing Co. The company's defense offerings include missile systems (i.e., Patriot, Hawk, and Tomahawk); radars; and reconnaissance, targeting, and navigation systems. Raytheon also makes radios, air traffic control systems and radars, and satellite communications systems. Raytheon offers commercial electronics products and services, with the U.S. government (including foreign military sales) accounting for more than 70% of sales.

* This case study was contributed by APQC (2004).

The information shared in this case study focuses on Raytheon's Six Sigma (R6s) integrated business strategy, which has three components: customers, tools, and enabling environment (i.e., culture). Knowledge sharing and reuse are embedded into the R6s process. The operational definition of R6s is that it is a "knowledge-based process we will use to transform our culture in order to maximize customer value and grow our business." Additionally, one of the R6s principles is to continuously improve the organization's knowledge in pursuit of perfection.

R6s uses a six-step methodology based on the popular Define, Measure, Analyze, Improve and Control (DMAIC) Six Sigma methodology:

1. Visualize.
2. Commit (i.e., gain management commitment).
3. Prioritize (i.e., identify the appropriate priorities).
4. Characterize (i.e., detail the steps).
5. Improve (i.e., implement changes).
6. Achieve (i.e., celebrate and share knowledge).

R6s also includes Lean methodology and proven change management techniques. R6s is a philosophy of continuous improvement, including throughput improvement and defect/cycle time reduction in all business processes and products by focusing on the customer value stream. The combination of all four elements (i.e., Six Sigma, KM, Lean, and change management) will sustain the process changes and will involve the whole Raytheon organization in R6s.

Each step of the R6s process has three components: inputs, processes, and outputs (IPO). All R6s experts and specialists are change agents (roughly equivalent to black belts and green belts but with more training) and are trained in this process and components. Each step has certain tools available for use, and it is up to the R6s change agent to select those tools. The last step, achieve, is where the emphasis on knowledge capture really comes into play. The team should capture and transfer any knowledge gained through the process and link it back to other projects and people.

Since 1999, R6s has achieved $1.8 billion in gross benefits and $500 million in net benefits (by the end of 2002). More than 1% of Raytheon's population of approximately 76,000 people is trained as experts, or "Black Belts+," and more than 18% of the organization's population is trained as specialists ("Green Belts+").

Connecting People to People and People to Information

The success of Raytheon's R6s depends on many people at various levels and functions across the organization working together to capture and leverage knowledge to improve core business processes. The R6s community includes roles such as master experts, experts, specialists, and team members, as well as knowledge management champions and brokers. Definitions for these roles follow:

- *KM champions* lead KM in support of business improvements throughout the company by practicing and promoting the research and sharing of solutions to shorten the cycles of learning and achieve new process breakthroughs. KM champions are also responsible for KM training of leadership teams and R6s communities in their businesses.
    KM champions also promote:
    ○ Capturing and sharing R6s project best practices and lessons learned
    ○ The abstraction of collected information from projects so that it can be easily shared
    ○ The deployment of a KM process across business units
    ○ Discovering, researching, and understanding emerging and effective methods of improvement
    ○ Broadly disseminating R6s best practices and lessons learned through business unit communities and information networks
    ○ Connecting individuals and subject matter experts with one another and with the knowledge and tools they need to improve
- *KM brokers* predictably broker KM activities for a business or process. They are proficient with KM tools and processes and coordinate networking and collaboration for knowledge sharing and reuse. Brokers also mentor communities of practice to help them get started, encourage the use of knowledge repositories, and explore the knowledge needs of the business. They help others outside of their business unit by sharing and recognize key contributors for knowledge sharing and reuse.
- *Champions* are senior leaders who plan and execute the deployment of R6s in their organizations.
- *Master experts* are fully trained, highly experienced, and full-time leaders responsible for planning, training, mentoring, and results related to R6s projects. Master experts understand all the Six Sigma/Lean tools but can also sit at the business table.
- *Lead experts* are not quite validated master experts but perform many of the same jobs and are the leaders of their organization's R6s efforts.
- *Experts* are fully trained, full-time change agents who lead improvement teams, work complex projects across the business, and mentor specialists.
- *Specialists* are trained to apply R6s skills to projects in their job areas on a part-time basis. One goal for the R6s program is to train all exempt/salaried employees as specialists.
- *Team members* are people with expertise or experience in particular business process areas who are brought in to participate, usually part time,

on an R6s project in their business. Many members are also qualified R6s specialists.

Not only does Raytheon embed KM within its R6s process, but it also integrates KM people into the business by enabling them to respond in real time to the organization's knowledge needs.

Tools Supporting Raytheon's Six Sigma Projects and People

Raytheon connects people to people and people to information from previous projects through several Web-based tools. These tools include an intranet site (URKM), the R6s home page, the Raytheon missile system portal, its specialist training system, and its project library. By using these tools, members of the R6s community can communicate and gain access to project details and results along with many other knowledge resources. Most often, this information is exchanged among middle managers and peers.

- *URKM.* Raytheon's internal KM Web site provides a search capability with links to various databases. It also has external search capabilities. The site also lists the various Raytheon communities. Other resources include book reviews, best practices searches and submissions, benchmarking library searches, and success stories.
- *R6s home page.* The R6s community celebrates certifications and success stories on its home page. This page connects the supply chain, the business units, and the project library. It lists the R6s master experts and experts. It also has tabs for different business units with their own R6s home pages.
- *Specialist training system.* This site lists candidate registration with schedules, profiles and qualifications, management reports, and links to other resources.
- *KM tool set on Raytheon missile systems (RMS) portal.* This tool allows users to have a personal home page. One current project is to list all communities in this portal so it can serve as a community locator. It has links to other knowledge sources (e.g., URKM, external search, and six sigma sites) as well. Its "power search" function allows searching multiple databases with one click. It has e-mail capability and uses Docushare™ and templates to drive content capture and organization.
- *Project library.* The library has links to internal and external resources. It can be personalized and can show an R6s team's work items. It uses a Web form to upload documents or project information (e.g., name, control plan, problem statement, cultural assessment, and supplier/customer involvement). It serves as the focal point for expert projects.

These various resources house project summaries that contain detailed methodologies and results. They can be found within the business unit sites as well as on the organization-wide sites. This information is shared not only via the tools just mentioned, but also in appropriate communities and in regional meetings and internal conferences.

Building Steps and Behaviors into Improvement Methodologies and Training

As described, Raytheon chose to embed KM into its R6s process in order to become more competitive. Perhaps the most prominent evidence of this is in the DMAIC process itself, where modifications were made to the IPO process and tools. These modifications include questions, such as the ones listed here, that must be addressed as part of the project methodology:

- Have you searched for Six Sigma projects relating to your process for improvements that can be reused?
- Have the project, solutions, and lessons learned been documented to encourage sharing and reuse by others?
- Can your team reuse any available knowledge to achieve commitment to change?

Raytheon also embedded various knowledge capture and transfer approaches into its R6s methodology. These approaches include dedicated KM roles, communities of practice, project tools, internal conferences, and training.

Raytheon's leadership recognizes that a formal KM strategy is a key enabler to improving the benefits from the R6s process. To that end, the leadership group established a KM champion at the enterprise level and sponsored a R6s KM champions' network to deploy a repeatable process across the company. KM champions are chartered to ensure that knowledge creation, capture, sharing, and reuse occurs within the business processes. KM brokers support the champions. Brokers are responsible for KM activities in a business unit or process.

Raytheon also created a knowledge capture and transfer infrastructure to capture and transfer knowledge across the enterprise. The explicit knowledge infrastructure involves:

- R6s champions, masters, experts, and specialists (required to capture explicit knowledge within their projects in the project library)
- An R6s KM champion (at the enterprise level) and the KM champions' network (at the business level)
- A KM brokers network (at the business unit level)
- The Raytheon market intelligence team

- The knowledge transfer and benchmarking core team (focused on external benchmarking to capture best practices and bring them back to the organization)
- The R6s suppliers network
- A leadership development program

The tacit knowledge infrastructure includes:

- Communities of practice
- Process councils (that meet regularly and share tacit knowledge)
- A business leadership program network
- A strategic leadership program network
- Technology networks
- Collaboration councils

Training and Learning

In addition to embedding its KM strategy into its R6s process, the organization provides training on knowledge capture and transfer to its R6s community. Integrating KM training into its R6s training allows Raytheon to further solidify the integration of the two improvement approaches. Comprehensive knowledge capture and transfer training materials have been integrated into the R6s curriculum. Anyone going through the training now receives the enhanced training with the KM component embedded. This ensures that they are leveraging these resources and tools. Additionally, master experts, experts, and specialists are required to share knowledge as part of their certification or qualification process.

Cultural and Behavioral Issues

As with any major cultural change, executive leadership commitment is crucial. Raytheon recognized the need for executive commitment early during its KM journey and took steps to address it by educating its leadership teams on how KM could support their R6s program and push it to the next level of success. In addition to the KM video and briefings, the leadership development program and business development program help to train leaders and show them the benefits of KM and tacit knowledge sharing via social networking. Additionally, the company's chairman uses words like "knowledge," "best practices," and "sharing" in speeches, which shows his support for this change.

R6s is an integrated business strategy that defines Raytheon's culture by guiding how employees work. To ensure R6s success, Raytheon carefully aligns R6s and the business through strategic plans and reviews, operating plans and reviews, and HR reviews. The one thing missing from this picture was how to leverage knowledge sharing and reuse across the R6s community in order to improve the benefits from the R6s process.

Raytheon's current KM organization is a hybrid of a centralized and decentralized model. The actual execution of activities occurs at the business and program levels of the organization, and the enterprise-level KM champion and business leaders ensure alignment and support of these activities. Raytheon's KM strategy is to:

- Promote and expand KM as a core competency at Raytheon.
- Apply the right knowledge to the right person at the right time to enable customer success.
- Integrate KM into the R6s process and embed knowledge sharing into the company's culture.
- Enable the value chain (e.g., suppliers and customers) to improve profitability through reduced cycles of learning.
- Connect people to knowledge.

As a result, "Raytheon will become more competitive by embedding knowledge management practices and principles into existing work processes utilized under the umbrella of R6s."

Communication

Raytheon developed a comprehensive communication strategy to increase awareness, obtain buy-in, and ensure success of the R6s program. Some of the tools include:

- R6s KM brochures
- A KM video (used for leadership briefings, team briefings, and R6s forums)
- A KM passport (designed to promote knowledge sharing, it is used at R6s forums or conferences. It looks like a real passport and has questions a person has to complete by sharing knowledge. The person receives a stamp when the passport is complete, and there are drawings for awards.)
- KM briefing presentations
- KM newsletters
- KM "thank-you" e-mails to employees for knowledge sharing

Finally, a communication community was established, and its members have been enlisted to help spread the word and promote knowledge-sharing principles.

Communication tools are deployed across multiple venues to ensure a broad communication reach. Communication venues include R6s forums and R6s celebrations, R6s expert and specialist trainings, R6s master expert meetings, R6s council meetings, business leadership meetings, and customer/supplier conferences. There may be anywhere from 150 to 600 people at any of these events.

Reward and Recognition

To recognize and reward its people for sharing and reusing knowledge, Raytheon embedded celebrations into the "achieve" step of its R6s process. It did not create a new infrastructure for reward and recognition but instead leveraged the organizational infrastructure already in place. These celebrations are one way to acknowledge employees for the value of sharing knowledge and achieving project success. Except for the occasional spot award, none of these is a cash award. R6s celebration processes and venues include:

- R6s specialist recognition
- R6s expert and master recognition (embedded as part of the process)
- R6s forums and celebrations (which highlight particular projects based on innovation and other criteria)
- R6s KM airline ticket and travel award
- A KM thank-you e-mail (in return for submitting a best practice or lesson learned, a person receives a "thank you" via e-mail with copies to his or her boss and KM champions, etc.).

Measures and Indicators of Success

As of September 2003, Raytheon's leadership is not asking for many measures. The existing measures focus on the outputs of the process, including the number of people trained and project financials. However, Raytheon no longer tracks the number of completed projects.

Raytheon's R6s uses a KM scorecard with four quadrants: people, process, tools, and enabling environment. These four quadrants are aligned with the four key results areas. For 2003, the people metrics include the number of trained existing experts, the number of trained others (i.e., business leaders), the number of identified subject matter experts, and the number of identified communities of practice. The process metrics include the number of success stories collected and the number of best practices captured in the best practices knowledge base. The tool metrics include the number of hits to the URKM Web site, the number of hits to the benchmarking Web site, and suggestions and improvements.

Additionally, Raytheon collects metrics on the URKM site, such as the number of registered communities and how many times the KM video has been viewed. It also collects metrics concerning the benchmarking Web site, such as the number of best practices submitted and the number of searches.

Raytheon does not set replication goals, nor are there minimum requirements for replication that must be met. Raytheon instead measures success of its replication process by gauging culture change. Additionally, it captures success stories and looks at increased awareness within the organization.

Principle 5: Manage and Leverage Knowledge
- *Develop Knowledge Management (KM) Processes.* Establish and leverage best practice identification, gathering and sharing processes and technology solutions.
- *Leverage Technology.* Partner with the IT function to launch and maintain KM systems.
- *Develop Expert Locater Systems.* Design and use expert locater systems to capture employee skills inventory within the enterprise to accelerate problem solving in Principle 4 and to optimize human capital.
- *Link KM with Improve Performance Process.* Link best practice or knowledge management processes with Principle 4, Improve Performance, processes to capture solutions and innovations.
- *Share Best Practices with Strategic Planning.* Share best practices with strategic planning processes to better understand core competencies and possible strategic advantages.
- *Maintain a Virtual KM Network.* Establish and maintain virtual network of KM experts throughout the enterprise to optimize knowledge and to keep processes evergreen.

Recommendations for Success

Raytheon recommends that organizations focus on their people as they seek to improve their internal processes through six sigma, Lean, or other improvement strategies. According to members of the Raytheon KM community, getting people involved in networks and communities (formal or otherwise) is crucial to creating and sustaining a knowledge-sharing environment. Organizations should also decide if they are going to take a technology-driven approach or focus more on the cultural side. Raytheon made a conscious decision to blend the two. Whichever approach an organization takes, the key is to use the process consistently throughout the organization.[2]

NOTES

1. Janice Koch, "Global Alignment: A Telecom's Tale," *Balanced Scorecard Report* (May-June 2004): 8.

2. Replicating the gains of Six Sigma and Lean, case generously provided by APQC, 2004

CHAPTER 9

Five Key Principles Self-Diagnostic and CPM Research Resources

Accept the challenges so that you can feel the exhilaration of victory.
—GEORGE S. PATTON

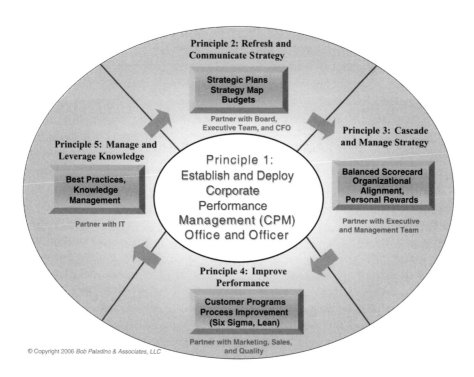

© Copyright 2006 *Bob Paladino & Associates, LLC*

Case study companies in this book have included recipients of these awards:

- U.S. President's National Malcolm Baldrige Quality Award
- Governor's Sterling Award for Excellence (based on Baldrige Criteria)
- Deming Quality Award
- American Quality and Productivity Center (APQC) Best Practice Partner Award
- Kaplan and Norton Global Balanced Scorecard Hall of Fame Award
- *Wall Street Journal* Ranked "Top 20 Most Improved Company in Shareholder Value Creation"
- *Fortune* "100 Best Companies to Work For"

This chapter provides you with a diagnostic tool to conduct a self-assessment and baseline where you are in your corporate performance management (CPM) best practice journey and a value-added, very selective CPM resource reference list for continuous learning.

> *Pleasure in the job puts perfection in the work.*
> —ARISTOTLE

CPM DIAGNOSTIC: THREE EASY STEPS

The three-step CPM diagnostic will enable you to conduct a self-assessment of your CPM program.

Step 1. Score your CPM program against best practices in this book.
Step 2. Create a gap analysis to identify your highest-impact improvement opportunities.
Step 3. Develop and deploy your action plan to close the gaps.

Step 1: Score Your CPM Program against Best Practices

Exhibit 9.1 presents the best practices for Principle 1, Establish a CPM Office and Officer Role. In column 1 note the self-assessment scores on a five-point scale with 1 being a low rating and 5 a best practice rating.

For example, focus on Principle 1, Best Practice 1.1, Executive Sponsorship, and score your achievement of this best practice. Since your CPM Officer reports five levels below the chief executive officer (CEO), would score low or a 1 on this best practice.

Step 2: Create a Gap Analysis

Column 2 in Exhibit 9.1 shows the opportunities for improvement. For example, executive sponsorship was rated a low at 1 as your CPM program

EXHIBIT 9.1   **CPM Diagnostic: Principle 1: Establish a CPM Office and Officer**

Best Practice	Description	Column 1 Self Scoring	Column 2 Gap Analysis Points below 5
1.1 Executive Sponsorship	CEO or direct report actively sponsors CPM Office and CPM projects for sustained period and with the right visibility to enable maturity to processes state	1	4
1.2 Organizational Level and Reporting Relationship	CPM Office executive reports to the CEO or a CEO direct report	4	1
CPM Office staff	Small senior team (3–8 people) experienced in change programs, full-time role in CPM Office	3	2
1.3 Leadership, influence factors	Able to organize large-scale virtual teams to drive results in one of more CPM methods	5	0
1.4 Ownership of CPM processes and methods (Principles 2–5)	Office owns or substantially influences portfolio of CPM processes enterprise-wide, with each office CPM practitioner possessing deep expertise in at least one methodology	2	3
1.5 CPM, industry and company knowledge	One or more team members with deep industry and company-specific knowledge to help guide resolution of project issues	4	1
1.6 Collaborative maturity	Experienced in working horizontally and vertically through the organization	4	1
1.7 Ability to learn	Open to new ideas, methods, and approaches; ability to streamline, integrate, and adapt methods; think concurrently	3	2

lacks high-level CEO or CEO direct report sponsorship. Since best practice organizations achieved a 5 on this best practice, there is a gap of 4 points. This becomes an opportunity to upgrade your CPM program to improve its effectiveness. Using this logic, you would proceed to score your program against the 20+ best practices.

Step 3: Develop and Deploy Your Action Plan to Close the Gaps

Once you have scored all 20+ best practices, you are in a position to prioritize the highest-order opportunities or gaps as described in the prior step. Bear in mind that Hall of Fame, Baldridge, and APQC award winners did not achieve their stunning results overnight. Rather I encourage appropriate thoughtfulness, and a prudent time-phased plan for closing your gaps. At Crown, the CPM program bore early fruit; however, it was the concerted and cumulative effects of these efforts over time that created sustainable achievement. My CPM firm studies successful enterprises and provides diagnostic and implementation planning services to aid your efforts.

> *We make a living by what we get, we make a life by what we give.*
> —SIR WINSTON CHURCHILL

CPM RESEARCH RESOURCES

The balance of this chapter builds on the best practices from case study organizations by providing links to leading edge and globally recognized resource centers to assist you with your CPM journey of excellence. Several of these organizations also conferred the awards to case study organizations profiled in this book. For example, APQC provided awards to several case study companies.

Bob Paladino & Associates, LLC

Bob Paladino & Associates, LLC is a professional service firm in the CPM field. Clients have won the coveted APQC Best Practice Award and Balanced Scorecard Hall of Fame award. The firm offers CPM services for implementing and integrating the Balanced Scorecard (BSC), Six Sigma, activity-based management (ABM), and customer survey programs to drive breakthrough results. While many firms offer methodologies, Bob Paladino & Associates, LLC focuses on "Implementing for Results." For more information visit www.paladinoassociates.com.

American Institute of Certified Public Accountants

The American Institute of Certified Public Accountants (AICPA) is the national professional organization for all certified public accountants. Its mission is to provide members with the resources, information, and leadership that enable them to provide valuable services in the highest professional manner to benefit the public as well as employers and clients. In fulfilling its mission, the AICPA works with state CPA organizations and gives priority to those areas where public reliance on CPA skills is most significant. For more information, visit www.aicpa.org.

APQC

An internationally recognized resource for process and performance improvement, APQC helps organizations adapt to rapidly changing environments and build new and better ways to work and succeed in a competitive marketplace. With a focus on productivity, knowledge management, benchmarking, and quality improvement initiatives, APQC works with organizations to identify best practices, discover effective methods of improvement, broadly disseminate findings, and connect individuals with one another and the knowledge, training, and tools they need to succeed. Learn more about APQC at www.apqc.org.

American Strategic Management Institute

The American Strategic Management Institute (ASMI) is the nation's leading authority on measurement and management methodologies for improving individual and organizational performance. ASMI's mission is to identify, study, and disseminate the leading strategic management and performance measurement practices pioneered by best-in-class organizations. Through national conferences, in-house training programs, consulting services, and ongoing research, ASMI helps organizations access cutting-edge expertise in planning, implementing, and evaluating business strategies to address their management challenges and improve organizational results. To learn more go to www.managementweb.org.

Balanced Scorecard Collaborative

Balanced Scorecard Collaborative (BSCol) is a Palladium company and dedicated to the worldwide awareness, use, enhancement, and integrity of the BSC as a value-added management process. It helps organizations successfully execute strategy to create breakthrough results. As long-term partners in their success, BSCol builds the capability to execute strategy and accelerate time to results. BSCol offers a wide variety of services for organizations at any stage of developing and using the BSC. Its advisory, educational, online, and training services can be extensively customized to develop solutions for organizations small and large throughout the world.

For more information on Palladium, go to www.palladiumES.com.

Organizations chosen for the Balanced Scorecard Hall of Fame are best-practice exemplars of the *Five Key Principles* of a strategy-focused organization as defined by Robert S. Kaplan and David P. Norton, creators of the BSC and strategy-focused organization concepts. Hall of Fame members are personally selected by Kaplan and Norton.

CAM-I

CAM-I is an international consortium of management and service companies, government organizations, consultancies, and academic and professional bodies that have elected to work cooperatively in a precompetitive environment to solve management problems and critical business issues that are common to the group. CAM-I's Collaborative Model produces value for members through:

- *Participative research*. By working together the participants understand the journey—the best practice path.
- *Targeted intellectual efforts*. Each program targets results and produces implementable deliverables by our members.
- *Human networks*. Develop and continue to share, challenge ideas, and learn long beyond the end date of the specific result.

For more information go to www.cam-i.org.

Deming Award

The Deming Cooperative aims to provide information about programs, conferences, seminars, discussion groups, consultants, literature, videos, and materials that focus on the understanding, application, and extension of the work of W. Edwards Deming, renowned consultant to management on quality and statistical methods. For more information go to www.deming.edu.

The Conference Board

Founded in 1916, The Conference Board is a world-leading business membership and research organization with a dual mission to *help businesses strengthen their performance and better serve society*. The Conference Board creates and disseminates knowledge about management and the marketplace by informing business leaders about important social and economic forces that will affect them and by connecting business and policy decision makers over important issues to further discussion and improve decision making. As a global independent membership organization in the public interest, The Conference Board conducts conferences, makes forecasts and assesses trends, publishes information and analysis, and brings executives together to learn from one another. Its core competencies include human capital management, economic forecasting, workforce and productivity research, leadership, corporate governance, and corporate citizenship. It produces major economic and management reports that have an impact on financial markets and executive decision-making worldwide. As a nonadvocacy, not-for-profit research and membership organization, The Conference Board is uniquely positioned to create awareness, educate, and affect change in the business community. Press coverage of Conference Board research routinely appears in the *Wall Street Journal,* the *Financial Times, Business Week,* the newswires, and executive magazines. Some 2,000 companies in 60 nations are members of The Conference Board's global network. To learn more go to www.conferenceboard.org.

Institute of Management Accountants

The Institute of Management Accountants (IMA) is the world's leading organization dedicated to empowering management accounting and finance professionals to drive business performance. With a network of nearly 65,000 professionals, IMA is the voice for a community of professionals who work inside organizations worldwide, providing decision support, planning and control. IMA provides a dynamic forum for management accounting and financial professionals to develop and advance their careers through its Certified Management Accountant (CMA) program, cutting-edge professional research, education, networking, and the advocacy of the highest ethical and professional practices.

IMA recognizes that the majority of accounting and finance professionals in the United States work in-house at companies, rather than in public accounting. The roles of these professionals (which include chief financial officers [CFOs] and controllers) are different from the functions of auditing and financial reporting. Through advocacy and education, IMA works to "rebalance" the profession by returning focus to the roles and responsibilities performed by management accountants, who build quality financial and governance practices and build business value where they work.

Through advocacy of the highest ethical business standards, IMA is committed to protecting business and society by assuring that accounting and finance professionals are ethically sound and appropriately qualified to exercise effective decision support, planning, and control over the organization's value-creating operations. For more information go to www.imanet.org.

International Productivity and Quality Center

The International Productivity and Quality Center (IQPC) provides business executives around the world with tailored practical conferences, large scale events, topical seminars, and in-house training programs, keeping them up-to-date with industry trends, technological developments, and the regulatory landscape. IQPC's large-scale conferences are market leading "must-attend" events for their respective industries. Founded in 1973, IQPC now has 14 offices across six continents with additional openings scheduled. To best address the changing needs of its diverse audience, each office is divided into core industry practices. These divisions leverage a global research base of best practices to produce an unrivalled series of conferences. For more information go to www.iqpc.com.

Malcolm Baldrige Award

The Baldrige Award is given by the President of the United States to businesses—manufacturing and service, small and large—and to education and healthcare organizations that apply and are judged to be outstanding in seven areas: leadership; strategic planning; customer and market focus; measurement, analysis, and knowledge management; human resource focus; process management; and results.

Congress established the award program in 1987 to recognize U.S. organizations for their achievements in quality and performance and to raise awareness about the importance of quality and performance excellence as a competitive edge. The award is not given for specific products or services. Three awards may be given annually in each of these categories: manufacturing, service, small business, education, and health care. In October 2004, President Bush signed into law legislation that authorizes National Institute of Standards and Technology (NIST) to expand the Malcolm Baldrige National Quality Award Program to include nonprofit and government organizations. The program may begin to solicit applications from nonprofit organizations in 2006 for a pilot program, with awards commencing in 2007. While the Baldrige Award and the Baldrige recipients are the very visible centerpiece of the U.S. quality movement, a broader national quality program has evolved around the award and its criteria. A report, *Building on Baldrige: American Quality for the 21st Century*, by the private Council on Competitiveness, said, "More than any other program, the Baldrige Quality Award is responsible for making quality a national priority and disseminating best practices across the

United States." The U.S. Commerce Department's NIST manages the Baldrige National Quality Program in close cooperation with the private sector. To learn more go to www.nist.gov/.

Melcrum Publishing: Knowledge Management Review

Melcrum Publishing is the publisher *of Knowledge Management Review,* which provides the latest trends, techniques, and ideas in knowledge management. In every issue, you'll receive corporate case studies, practitioners' insights, and a wealth of practical ideas you can apply immediately to your work. What makes *KM Review* different is that it is written by practitioners for practitioners. No pitches, just practical independent advice to help you do your job. Melcrum is a research and information company. Through its publications, research, training materials, and events, it gathers best practices from businesses around the world to help practitioners make better business decisions. Melcrum has customers in over 90 countries and has an international reputation not only for editorial and research products of the highest standards, but also for tracking important trends in organizational communication, corporate communication, human resources, KM, and intranet management. For more information go to www.melcrum.com.

Motorola University Six Sigma Training

As the inventor of the Six Sigma methodology, Motorola can lay claim to the most long-standing and time-tested experience in the industry. Motorola has built on this experience and continue focusing our efforts on advancing the Six Sigma methodology to bring you the most powerful Six Sigma training available. Motorola has been implementing Six Sigma throughout the organization now for over 18 years, extending the practice beyond manufacturing into transactional, support, and service functions. As a result, we have documented over $17 billion in savings to our own organization!

Over the last few years, the company has been working its customers and suppliers to deliver the benefits of its Six Sigma methodology. Naturally, Motorola has helped customers in the manufacturing arena, and has solid experience in service sectors as well, including financial service companies and healthcare organizations.

With a presence in over 20 countries around the world, Motorola is proud to offer Six Sigma experience that is as broad and accessible as it is deep. Its global reach and in-depth experience as Six Sigma practitioners affords it an expansive inventory of best practices and lessons learned, as well as the ability to continuously refine and advance the methodology. When you take advantage of Motorola's combined history of innovation and experience applying Six Sigma in the real world, you can expect to achieve the quickest, most sustainable results possible, whatever the size of your organization, wherever it may be. For more information go to www.motorola.com/motorolauniversity .jsp.

John Wiley & Sons

John Wiley & Sons is a global publisher of print and electronic products, specializing in scientific, technical, and medical books and journals; professional and consumer books and subscription services; and textbooks and other educational materials for undergraduate and graduate students as well as lifelong learners. The company provides "must-have" content to targeted communities of interest. Wiley's deep reservoir of quality content, constantly replenished, offers a tremendous source of competitive advantage. Technology is making this content more accessible to customers worldwide and is adding value for them by delivering it in interactive and/or fully searchable formats. Approximately 25% of global revenue is currently Web-enabled. For more information go to www.wiley.com

The empires of the future are the empires of the mind.
—SIR WINSTON CHURCHILL

Index